西安交通大学 本科"十四五"规划教材

中华典籍英译选读

Anthology of Selected Chinese Classics in English Translation

田荣昌 编著

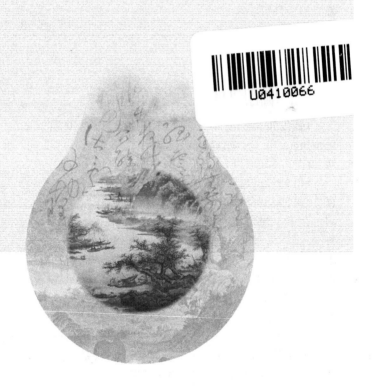

西安交通大学出版社
XI'AN JIAOTONG UNIVERSITY PRESS

图书在版编目(CIP)数据

中华典籍英译选读 / 田荣昌编著. — 西安：西安交通大学出版社，2023.3
ISBN 978-7-5693-3145-5

Ⅰ.①中… Ⅱ.①田… Ⅲ.①古籍-英语-翻译 Ⅳ.①H315.9

中国国家版本馆 CIP 数据核字(2023)第 048453 号

书　　名	中华典籍英译选读 ZHONGHUA DIANJI YINGYI XUANDU
编　　著	田荣昌
责任编辑	牛瑞鑫
责任校对	庞钧颖
装帧设计	伍　胜
出版发行	西安交通大学出版社 (西安市兴庆南路1号　邮政编码 710048)
网　　址	http://www.xjtupress.com
电　　话	(029)82668357　82667874(市场营销中心) (029)82668315(总编办)
传　　真	(029)82668280
印　　刷	西安五星印刷有限公司
开　　本	720mm×1000mm　1/16　印张 20.125　字数 351千字
版次印次	2023年3月第1版　2023年3月第1次印刷
书　　号	ISBN 978-7-5693-3145-5
定　　价	55.00元

如发现印装质量问题，请与本社市场营销中心联系。
订购热线：(029)82665248　(029)82667874
投稿热线：(029)82665371

版权所有　侵权必究

序

美国当代人类文化学家马文·哈里斯（Marvin Harris）曾说过，世上有个中国，幅员辽阔、文化发达。这并非溢美之词。众所周知，世界上有四大文明古国：非洲东北部尼罗河畔的古埃及、美索不达米亚平原上两河流域（底格里斯河和幼发拉底河）的古巴比伦、西南亚印度河河谷的古印度，以及亚洲东部由黄河和长江两大水系孕育的中国。这四大古老的文明体系，各以其独特的文化形态，对整个人类世界的文明进程产生了巨大而深远的影响。而前三个文明古国，其文化或者出现了断代，或者早已被其他文明形态取代。只有中华文明，在东亚这片神奇而古老的土地上，如同一条汤汤大河，赓续绵延，奔流不息。中华上下五千年的悠久历史，孕育了数不胜数辉煌灿烂的文化结晶，诞生了卷帙浩繁传承千载的文化典籍。四大文明古国中，中华文化的成果最为富庶，文化传承最为久远，文化内容最为丰富。

中华传统文化博大精深，数以万计的传世典籍文本，无疑是几千年来中国传统文化的"知识库"，是中华民族伟大思想和集体智慧的结晶，是一笔取之不竭、用之不尽的文化宝藏。中华民族，赓续绵延五千余年，从汉字出现至今，中华典籍的数量远高于世界上其他民族，内容亦比以其他语种书写的文本丰富得多。中华典籍形式多样、内容丰富，包括最早的甲骨文卜辞、青铜器铭文、金石文字，后来出现的竹简纪文、帛书绢字，以及纸质书写（印刷）的文本，或是刻写在石碑上的铭文、诗词、歌赋等。

中华传统文化典籍浓缩了中国人独特的人生观、价值观和世界观，是中国人对自身、对自然、对世界，乃至对宇宙千百年来的认识和思考，是历经时间检验和岁月萃取的智慧和情感、哲思和情怀、憧憬和愿望……

文化典籍是人类命运共同体得以生成并存在的精神来源和思想承载。虽然东西方文化表达和传承的途径和语言载体迥异有别，但东西方文化都有不可否认的价值共性，即文化是人类心灵的家园，是人类灵魂的归处，是人类生生不息的精神支柱；文化是无国界的，是超种族、超语言、超时空的。

2014年3月，教育部印发《完善中华优秀传统文化教育指导纲要》（教社科〔2014〕3号），明确指出："加强中华优秀传统文化教育，是深化中国特色社会主义教育和中国梦宣传教育的重要组成部分。"2020年5月，教育部印发《高等学校课程思政建设指导纲要》（教高〔2020〕3号），强调要在所有高校、所有学科专业中全面推进高校课程思政建设："系统进行中国特色社会主义和中国梦教育、社会主义核心价值观教育、法治教育、劳动教育、心理健康教育、中华优秀传统文化教育，"切实提升立德树人的成效。"……立德树人成效是检验高校一切工作的根本标准。落实立德树人根本任务，必须将价值塑造、知识传授和能力培养三者融为一体，不可割裂。"

由此可见，中华传统文化，对于今日之中国，对于中国当下大学教育之成败，甚至对于中华民族的伟大复兴，都有非同凡响的独特意义。中国，作为四大文明古国之一，其文明之所以能赓续至今从未中断，甚至历久弥新，是因为中华文明具有其他文明形态无法比拟的强大生命力、传播力和稳定性。中华优秀传统文化典籍是中华民族文化的积淀，是生活在中华大地上的无数先民集体智慧的结晶，熔铸着中华民族独特的语言习惯、思维模式、生活理念、哲学思想、文化传统和人文情怀，凝聚着中华民族广泛认同和普遍接受的道德观、人生观、价值观和世界观，因此具有极为丰富的思想内涵、道德价值和精神力量。

对于所有中国人，尤其是当代大学生而言，学习、传承并发扬中华民族的优秀文化，其实是在守护华夏儿女共同的精神家园，是在捍卫华夏族群的民族形象，是在凝铸中华儿女的家国情怀，其意义非同寻常，可谓遥承古人，今恤侪辈，后抚来者。

已故国学大师季羡林先生生前特别强调翻译的重要性,他说,"翻译是中华文明永葆青春的万应灵药"。毋庸置疑,传播汉语与中华文化的一个重要途径,就是加大传统文化典籍的英译力度,加强中国文化的对外传播。传统文化典籍英译是西方世界了解中国的一种有效途径,是提升中国全球文化影响力和塑造中国形象的一个至关重要的手段。

本教材以"重温经典,回归传统,放眼世界,关注国际"为编写宗旨,以"历史经典、文学经典、哲学经典、伦理经典"四分法作为每章汉语原始典籍文本选择的标准和依据,同时秉承"求同存异、开放包容、互学互鉴"的基本原则,精选对于学生而言较为熟知,但并不一定深入阅读过的中华传统典籍文本(精典篇章),筛选与之相对应的由西方著名汉学家或权威学者翻译完成的经典译本(附有中国译者的英译本方便学生对照研读),引导学生采用英汉对照方式,逐词逐句进行解读,并提供比较权威的专家鉴赏和解读范例,两相对照,既能帮助学生快速深入地理解汉语典籍的原始文本,又能帮助学生对照式地理解和掌握西方译本的文句表述方式、译者的翻译策略,以及文本的涵义、艺术魅力等。

入选本教材的中华典籍大致分类如下:

哲学经典(代表性作品为《道德经》《庄子》);

伦理经典(代表性作品为《论语》《大学》);

文史经典(代表性作品为《文选》《文心雕龙》);

文学经典(代表性作品为《诗经》《楚辞》及唐代诗文)。

本教材每一章根据不同时代代表性作品的题材特点和行文长短,从以上所列举的经典作品中精选出三至五篇(首)能够充分体现该类典籍属性和特质、难易适中、内涵丰富的章节或段落,每篇(首)后均附有详细的音、形、义的训诂注疏、白话译文(释义)、作品简介、重点语句解读。英译文本均不提供任何生字词的注释,目的在于为学生提供开放、独立、自学式的阅读文本。教师可根据课堂所需或依据学生的语言能力和个人兴趣,自由灵活地选择或布置英译文课前预习及课后自学任务。学生可于课前逐一查找不同英译文本中的生字词,详加注释,以便进行课堂讨论。学生可在对汉语经典文本的详细训诂与解读的基础上,对英译文本中的关键字词句的释义、文本内涵、翻译策略和技巧等问题进行深入思考和讨论。同时,编者建议,学生可根据各自兴趣,搜集整理与汉语术语或文化负载词相对应的英译词条,并建立个性化术语库,以便深度系统地掌握汉语典籍语辞、句式的权威英译方法和方案。每章课后附有易于学生操练和实践的适量而实用的备选习题,供学生课后个人实践或小组任务演练之用。

本教材的编写目的是为学生提供一种内容覆盖面广且易读易懂的中华典籍英译参考方案和文本借鉴,帮助学生树立起对中华民族优秀传统文化的自信心和自豪感,提升学生将中国文化向外传输的文化意识、自觉性和参与度。同时,我们希望借此创新教材,使传统以英语语言文化为核心和重点的单向化、单边化的语言培养模式和目标有所改变,寻找一种将英语教育与母语教育双向融合互为参照的融合式、浸透式的语言和文化习得的有效结合模式,积极培养"脚踏中西,肩挑英汉"的人才,即既熟知并掌握甚至精通中国语言和文化,又兼通英语语言且熟悉西方文化的"双语兼通"的复合型人才。中国需要了解世界各国,世界各国更需要了解中国,这也是提升中国文化全球影响力的一个至关重要的内容。

本教材在编写过程中参考了大量国内外文献资料(详见书后参考文献),在此对所有文献的作者和出版机构表示衷心的感谢!同时还要感谢西安交通大学对本教材的慷慨资助,感谢我的工作单位西安交通大学外国语学院诸位领导的支持和鼓励!感谢本教材编写组诸位同事在繁忙的教学之余,牺牲自己宝贵的休息时间为本教材献言献策,无私供稿!

中华文化典籍博大精深,浩如烟海,经典文本数量浩繁,要选出适合读者阅读趣味且最具时代特质的篇章并非易事,所选篇章也许有负重望。恐吾辈才疏学浅,多有舛误谬见之处,诚望各位业界专家和热心读者不吝赐教!

田荣昌

目 录

第一章 《道德经》经典篇章英译选读 ……………………………（ 1 ）
 《道德经》经典篇章英译选读之一 ………………………………（ 8 ）
 《道德经》经典篇章英译选读之二 ………………………………（ 12 ）
 《道德经》经典篇章英译选读之三 ………………………………（ 17 ）

第二章 《庄子》经典篇章英译选读 ………………………………（ 23 ）
 《庄子》经典篇章英译选读之一 …………………………………（ 41 ）
 《庄子》经典篇章英译选读之二 …………………………………（ 51 ）
 《庄子》经典篇章英译选读之三 …………………………………（ 57 ）

第三章 《论语》经典篇章英译选读 ………………………………（ 69 ）
 《论语》经典篇章英译选读之一 …………………………………（ 74 ）
 《论语》经典篇章英译选读之二 …………………………………（ 79 ）
 《论语》经典篇章英译选读之三 …………………………………（ 84 ）

第四章 《大学》经典篇章英译选读 ………………………………（ 94 ）
 《大学》经典篇章英译选读之一 …………………………………（ 97 ）
 《大学》经典篇章英译选读之二 …………………………………（103）
 《大学》经典篇章英译选读之三 …………………………………（110）
 《大学》经典篇章英译选读之四 …………………………………（114）
 《大学》经典篇章英译选读之五 …………………………………（118）

第五章 《诗经》经典篇章英译选读 ………………………………（124）
 《诗经》经典篇章英译选读之一 …………………………………（127）
 《诗经》经典篇章英译选读之二 …………………………………（135）

《诗经》经典篇章英译选读之三……………………………………（144）
第六章　《楚辞》经典篇章英译选读……………………………（154）
　　《楚辞》经典篇章英译选读之一……………………………………（160）
　　《楚辞》经典篇章英译选读之二……………………………………（169）
　　《楚辞》经典篇章英译选读之三……………………………………（176）
第七章　《文选》经典篇章英译选读……………………………（187）
　　《文选》经典篇章英译选读之一……………………………………（190）
　　《文选》经典篇章英译选读之二……………………………………（198）
　　《文选》经典篇章英译选读之三……………………………………（203）
　　《文选》经典篇章英译选读之四……………………………………（207）
　　《文选》经典篇章英译选读之五……………………………………（216）
第八章　《文心雕龙》经典篇章英译选读………………………（230）
　　《文心雕龙》经典篇章英译选读之一………………………………（237）
　　《文心雕龙》经典篇章英译选读之二………………………………（245）
　　《文心雕龙》经典篇章英译选读之三………………………………（252）
第九章　唐代诗文经典篇章英译选读……………………………（264）
　　唐代诗文经典篇章英译选读之一……………………………………（274）
　　唐代诗文经典篇章英译选读之二……………………………………（277）
　　唐代诗文经典篇章英译选读之三……………………………………（283）
　　唐代诗文经典篇章英译选读之四……………………………………（291）
参考文献……………………………………………………………（303）

第一章

《道德经》经典篇章英译选读

【导读】

　　《老子》,又名《道德经》,由春秋时期思想家李聃(老子)所著,是公认的最古老最有影响力的中国哲学典籍之一,也是中国道家哲学思想的核心著述,对中国人的思想意识产生了非常深远的影响,并广泛流传到世界各国。《道德经》被视为中国第一部最为完整的哲学著述,是中国古代哲学本体论学说的开创之作(任犀然,2016),是了解和研究道家思想的必读书目。《道德经》系统论述了"道""无为""虚静""天人合一"等道家所主张的哲学思想,对宇宙万物的起源、人的存在、人与人之间及人与自然和社会的关系、政府的功能、生老病死等方方面面的问题做出了非常独到的解释。可以说,它是全世界第一部从哲学角度来阐释与人类息息相关且需要共同面对和解决的"生存"与"发展","和平"与"战争","政治"与"人权"等诸种问题的肇始之作。针对以上问题,老子主张以"无为而为""不争之争""无为之用""致虚极,守静笃""持盈之道""道法自然"等方法化解,从而实现"天之道,利而不害;人之道,为而不争"这一治世为人的终极目标,这也是《道德经》全书一以贯之的最高宗旨。如此主张,时隔千载,却并不古旧过时,继续引领着世人,拨开人性之云雾,看清世界之本末,砥砺前行,探知未来。

　　关于老子的生平,史书载录者说法不一。据西汉史学家刘向《列仙传》(一说为六朝时期的伪作)载:"关令尹喜者,周大夫也。善内学星宿,服精华,隐德行仁,时人莫知。老子西游,喜先见其气,知真人当过,候物色而迹之,果得老子。老子亦知其奇，为著书。与老子俱之流沙之西，服具胜实，莫知其终。"意思是说，老子晚年归隐，途经函谷关，关令尹喜问道于老子，老子遂留下五千余言的《道德经》，尹喜因之感化，随老子向流沙之西而去，不知所踪。"流沙之西"所指何处？《山海经·大荒西经》有"流沙之西"语，大概是指中国西北部昆仑山以北的沙漠腹地。

西汉司马迁的《史记》对老子有如下简介：

"老子者，楚苦县厉乡曲仁里人也，姓李氏，名耳，字聃，周守藏室之史也。……或曰：老莱子亦楚人也，著书十五篇，言道家之用，与孔子同时云。……或曰儋即老子，或曰非也，世莫知其然否。老子，隐君子也……"

"（太史儋）居周久之，见周之衰，乃去。至关，关令尹喜曰：'子将隐矣，强为我著书。'于是老子乃著书上下篇，言道德之意五千余言而去。"

关于老子是谁、老子最后的归宿等等问题，莫衷一是。

司马迁至少给出了三种答案：一是周朝守藏史李聃；二是周太史儋老子；三是隐士李耳。由此，老子其人其书似乎成了中国学术史上悬而未决的重大问题，就连两千多年前"博古通今"且距离老子时代不远的太史公司马迁也未能妄下断言，后代学者就更如雾里看花了。值得庆幸的是，1993年湖北省荆门郭店村出土了战国楚简《道德经》，并公之于世。楚简《道德经》不但优于今本，而且是一个原始的、完整的传本，它出自春秋末期与孔子同时期的老聃；而今本（《道德经》），则出自战国中期与秦献公同时期的太史儋（郭沂，1998）。

另外，魏晋以来，《道德经》传本很多，比较流行的有三国时期曹魏经学家王弼的《王弼注本》、汉文帝时河上公的《河上公注本》。唐初学者傅奕（555—639）得到汉初古本，但他们要定的古本篇是根据几个旧本参校的，未能保留汉初古本的原貌。清代乾嘉以来，考据之学盛行，校订《老子》者有多家，如罗振玉、马叙伦、劳健、朱谦之等，但他们所根据的《道德经》文本，基本上是以唐碑和敦煌出土的唐写卷《道德经》为最古，没能见到唐代以前的写本，也没能留意到《老子想尔注》（东汉张道陵注本）中保留的《道德经》残篇。除了敦煌藏经洞的《道德经》各类写卷外，迄今考古发现的《道德经》文本有两种，时代上分属西汉早期和战国中期偏晚时期，即人们习称的长沙马王堆帛书《道德经》和湖北郭店楚墓竹简《道德经》。

据长沙马王堆汉墓出土的帛书《道德经》（甲、乙本），其中将"常道"做"恒道"表明该版本是汉文帝（公元前203—公元前157）以前的旧本，该版本的出土，解决了许多章节中历来争论不休的问题。如通行本38章"上德无为而无以为"句下有"下德为之而有以为"句，或作"下德为之而无以为"，与下文"上仁为

第一章 《道德经》经典篇章英译选读

之,而无以为"或"上德为之而有以为",语意重叠。帛书甲、乙本俱无"下德"句,证明"下德"句系衍文。又如通行本 61 章"故大国以下小国,择取小国;小国以下大国,则取大国",取"小国"句与取"大国"句无别,帛书甲本作"大邦(以)下小(邦),则取小邦;小邦以下大邦,则取于大邦",乙本作"故大国以下(小)国,则取小国;小国以下大国,则取于大国"。"取小邦与取于大邦:固然有别,证明通行本多一"于"字。类此之例尚多,表明帛书《道德经》确胜于通行本。

由此,《道德经》历史上的版本可以做一排序,依次是郭店楚简《道德经》、帛书《道德经》、"河上公注本""王弼注本""傅奕注本"等。

《道德经》全书分上下篇:《道经》(上篇)、《德经》(下篇),共 81 章,体例见表 1-1。

表 1-1 《道德经》体例

章节		体例说明
上篇:《道经》	体道第一:天地之始	道经集中体现了老子"道"的思想主张,是其对于天地万物运行规律的总的阐发,开篇"体道":言"道可道,非常道;名可名,非常名。无,名天地之始;有,名万物之母。"解释了"道"的本义和本源。"道"是主宰万物又超越万物的精神本体,是宇宙的起源和万物运行必须依凭的法则。它在时空上处于永恒的状态,不可名状,不可描述;它无处不在,无迹可寻,但它又是真实存在的一种"物质",宇宙中一切事物的运动和变化,万物的出现、发展、壮大、消亡的过程无不以"道"之轨迹在进行。 "道"先天地而生,至虚至无,却是万物之源,"道生一,一生二,二生三,三生万物"。世间所有事物都要遵循于道,天地万物在道的作用下生生不息,运动不止,垂示给人很多迹象,"人法地,地法天,天法道,道法自然"。……道是独立不改的客观规律,无所不包,周行不殆对任何事物而言,都是绝对的,不可能被超越的。
	养身第二:功成弗居	
	安民第三:圣人之治	
	无源第四:和光同尘	
	虚用第五:多言数穷	
	成象第六:谷神不死	
	韬光第七:天长地久	
	易性第八:不争无尤	
	运夷第九:持而盈之	
	能为第十:明白四达	
	无用第十一:无之为用	
	检欲第十二:去彼取此	
	厌耻第十三:宠辱不惊	
	赞玄第十四:执古之道	
	显德第十五:微妙玄通	
	归根第十六:致虚守静	
	淳风第十七:功成事遂	
	俗薄第十八:大仁大义	
	还淳第十九:少私寡欲	
	异俗第二十:独异于人	

续表

章节		体例说明
	虚心第二十一：孔德之容	
	益谦第二十二：圣人抱一	
	虚无第二十三：希言自然	
	苦恩第二十四：物或恶之	
	象元第二十五：道法自然	
	重德第二十六：宜戒轻躁	
	巧用第二十七：常善救人	
	反朴第二十八：常德乃足	
	无为第二十九：去奢去泰	
	俭武第三十：不以兵强	
	偃武第三十一：恬淡为上	
	圣德第三十二：知止不殆	
	辩德第三十三：自知者明	
	任成第三十四：不自为大	
	仁德第三十五：往而不害	
	微明第三十六：柔弱刚强	
	为政第三十七：道常无为	
下篇：《德经》	论德第三十八：处实去华	有一种观点认为《德经》要早出于《道经》，因此有些版本将《德经》置于《道经》之前。 《德经》的"德"并非狭义上的个人的"德行""品德"。当然，"德"包括对于人的言行思想的制约，但又不限于此。"道"为本，"德"为支，"德"是依存于"道"的另一种隐性的自然规律或法则，对具体的人、世间的万事万物，以及抽象的自然界、宇宙、天地等，都具有无形而有力的约束作用。"道"和"德"的关系相当于根和叶的关系，"德"是"道"发生作用的方式和结果，要通过"德"方能理解"道"。
	法本第三十九：贱为贵本	
	去用第四十：有生于无	
	同异第四十一：大器晚成	
	道化第四十二：或损或益	
	遍用第四十三：无为之益	
	立戒第四十四：知足不辱	
	洪德第四十五：大成若缺	
	俭欲第四十六：知足常足	
	鉴远第四十七：不为而成	
	忘知第四十八：为学日益	
	任德第四十九：圣无常心	
	贵生第五十：出生入死	

第一章 《道德经》经典篇章英译选读

续表

章节	体例说明
养德第五十一:尊道贵德	
归元第五十二:天下有始	
益证第五十三:行于大道	
修观第五十四:善抱大道	
玄符第五十五:物壮则老	
玄德第五十六:知者不言	
淳风第五十七:以正治国	
顺化第五十八:福祸相倚	
守道第五十九:长生久视	
居位第六十:治国烹鲜	
谦德第六十一:各得其所	
为道第六十二:万物之奥	
恩始第六十三:为大于细	
守微第六十四:慎终如始	
淳德第六十五:善为道者	
后己第六十六:不争之争	
三宝第六十七:持保三宝	
配天第六十八:不争之德	
玄用第六十九:哀者胜矣	
知难第七十:被褐怀玉	
知病第七十一:知不知矣	
爱己第七十二:自知自爱	
任为第七十三:天网恢恢	
制惑第七十四:民不畏死	
贪损第七十五:民之轻死	
戒强第七十六:柔弱处上	
天道第七十七:功成不处	
任信第七十八:柔之胜刚	
任契第七十九:报怨以德	
独立第八十:小国寡民	
显质第八十一:为而不争	

中华典籍英译选读

老子是中国历史上第一位哲学家,中国道家思想的开创者,对中国文化的影响长达两千多年。春秋战国时期的九流百家大都受过老子的影响,即使汉武帝独尊儒术之后,老子思想仍为历代思想家和各种对立的学派所重视。从横向看,老子及其学说对中国哲学、政治、军事、文化、伦理、道德,乃至对整个民族的生活方式、心理结构、思维模式都有着极重要的影响。

因此,在中国哲学史上,老子与后起的庄子一并被称为"道家"哲学的两大奠基者。华裔学者陈鼓应先生对老庄尤为推崇,他说:"从哲学史的观点看,老庄思想的重要性,一如苏格拉底和柏拉图在西方哲学史上的地位……老庄哲学自成一套独特的宇宙论、认识论、方法论、自然哲学及人生哲学……老子五千言,确是一部辞意锤炼的'哲学诗',其中充满了对人生体验富有启发性的观念"。

所以说,"作品的伟大与否不在于字数的多少,甚至也不在于其是否为读者指出了明确的生活方向,而在于它能让读者挖掘出多少宝藏。《道德经》为读者留下了一个巨大的思考空间,数千年来,人们不断从中得到新的体悟。无论是修身养性,还是写诗作文、为人处世,甚至是治国理政,个中智慧都包容在这本书中"。

正因道家思想光耀可鉴,所以迄今为止,《道德经》的外文译本已近1100多种,涉及多个语种,是目前世界上翻译最多、流传最广的经典著作之一。同时,由于版本繁多,所以《道德经》的翻译就存在一个版本选择的问题。从笔者搜集到的1982年以来国内外出版的《道德经》英译本看,自帛书《道德经》出版后,《道德经》译者在版本的选择上有三种做法:第一种做法是,不考虑帛书本,仍以世传本作为源本,如何光沪、冯家福和简·英格里希、史蒂芬·米切尔、吴光明、戴闻达、辜正坤、郭家湘、彭马田、齐拉姆、保罗·卡鲁斯、弗里克以及大卫·亨顿;第二种做法是,以世传本作为源本,参考帛书本,如米凯尔·拉法格、斯蒂芬·阿迪斯、斯坦利·伦巴多、伯顿·华兹生、王柯平、勒吉恩和西顿以及罗伯茨;第三种做法是,以帛书本作为源本,参考世传本,如刘殿爵、韩禄伯、梅维恒以及汪榕培和普芬伯格等。

根据姚达兑的研究,《道德经》最早的英译本是如今珍藏在耶鲁大学的耶鲁稿本。而在此之前,大家公认的最早译本是由来华的苏格兰传教士湛约翰牧师(John Chalmers,1825—1899)于1868年翻译并在伦敦出版的《老子,关于玄学、政体和道德律的思考的老家学说》(又名《老子玄学、政治与道德律之思辨》,*The Speculations on Metaphysics, Polity, and Morality of the Old Philosopher Lau-Tsze*)。丁巍在《老子典籍考:二千五百年来世界老学文献总目》中对《道德经》的外文版本做了具体的统计:英文(182种)、法文(109种)、德文(240种)、俄语(12种)、西班牙文(2种)、意大利文(11种)、捷克文(3种)等。

第一章 《道德经》经典篇章英译选读

虽然英译本很多,但早期的英译本主要转译自拉丁语、法语、德语、俄语等其他语种。

第一个翻译《道德经》的中国人是胡子霖先生,其译本《老子译注》(*Lao Tsu Tao Teh Ching*)于1936年出版。胡子霖先生做了一件开创性的工作,功不可没,特别是译本出现在民族危亡的艰难时刻和世界格局动荡不安的第二次世界大战前夕,更加可贵,表现了译者崇高的爱国主义精神和国际主义精神。译者在前言里谈及自己的翻译动机时说:"之前的很多译本均系欧洲人所为,没有咱中国人的份;老子强烈地反战,学习他的教诲,能给世界人民带来和平的希望。"

可以说,在所有的中华典籍文本中,被翻译的次数最多,翻译人数最多的除了《论语》之外,第二部应该非《道德经》莫属。其中影响力比较大的译本包括海星格、老沃尔特·高尔恩、翟林奈、亚瑟·韦利、吴经熊、宾纳、林语堂、泰戈尔、陈荣捷、辜正坤、许渊冲,等等。

【《道德经》英译简评】

西方最早翻译《道德经》始于17世纪欧洲的殖民主义扩张和基督教东传运动。据英国科学家李约瑟(Joseph Needham)考证,《道德经》最早的西方文字译本是17世纪末比利时传教士卫方济(Francois Noel)的拉丁文译本。此后,翻译、研究《道德经》的外语语种与文献数量逐渐增多,在西方社会的传播广度和深度也逐渐加大。但是这个时期西方学者、传教士等人翻译《道德经》的主要目的在很大程度上是服务于西方文化殖民的需求。

随着中西文化交流的日益频繁,西方学者逐渐认识到中国这一古典巨著所蕴含的丰富深远的哲学内涵,各个国家的汉学家陆续展开对《道德经》的深入研究和译介。进入二十世纪,随着马王堆汉墓和郭店考古发掘的最新成果被公之于众,《道德经》的翻译和研究呈现出新局面,更多的中国译者加入这支翻译和研究的队伍中,借此让全世界更多的人认识中国,了解中国文化。时至今日,随着我国综合国力的逐渐提升,以及多年来英语教育的大力发展,中国国内涌现出一批学贯中西的优秀学者,为《道德经》的译介提供了更加广阔深厚的人力资源和智识支撑。同时,随着中国文化"走出去"的大力推进,中国古籍翻译事业向更深推进,越来越多的西方学者对中国文化有了更深入的了解,他们也加入《道德经》的翻译队伍当中。因此,《道德经》英译出现了百花齐放、中西互通的繁荣景象。

总之,《道德经》的翻译之路,反映了处于不同历史发展阶段的译者,对于

《道德经》在宗教、政治、文化及哲学等各方面不同的认知特征,同时也体现了不同历史阶段世界政治经济格局的变化,最终阐释了《道德经》不仅是中国的文化财富,也是全世界人民的精神宝藏。《道德经》具有放之四海而皆准的道德准则,吸引着国内外的学者不断研学不断追求其中所蕴含的真知,这不仅有利于我们在新的历史时期和国际化的背景下理解、运用道家思想,也为中国文化走向世界提供了有益的借鉴(吴雪萌,2011)。

  本章共选取《道德经》中三个代表性章节的英译本供学生阅读鉴赏。第一篇节选自至今发现的最早的英译本耶鲁版本"道经"首章("体道第一");第二篇节选自"德经"中"同异第四十一"的英译本,第三篇节选自保罗·卡鲁斯博士(Dr. Paul Carus)翻译的"德经"的末章。

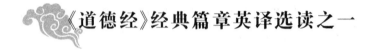《道德经》经典篇章英译选读之一

体道第一

道^①可道,非常^②道;
名可名,非常名^③。
无名,天地之始;有名,万物之母^④。
故常无欲,以观其妙^⑤;
常有欲,以观其徼^⑥。
此两者^⑦,同出而异名,同谓之玄^⑧。
玄之又玄,众妙之门。

【注释】

① 本篇起始句连用三个"道"字,但意义和词性差别很大,其中第一个和第三个"道"字,是老子哲学的专用名词,谓宇宙之本体。第二个"道"字,为动词,是言说、描述之意。在古代哲学家中,老子首先把"道"字作为哲学范畴,并从各个方面进行论证。《道德经》一书用"道"字74次,用作哲学概念的"道"含义有三:一为宇宙本体;二为万物本原;三为宇宙万物运动变化必循之规律。

第一章 《道德经》经典篇章英译选读

"道"是老子哲学思想的最高范畴,也是老子哲学思想论述的核心。关于道的原始形态,在中国古籍中由两部分组成,即"行"与"首",所谓"道从行从首"就指此而言。而且在这两部分的关系中,"首"字在"行"字中间,也就是说,"行"字又再分成两半,成为"首"字的左右。因此,古代的道字是"衜",道的原始意义就是用"首"去"行"。其延伸之意,也就包含了思想与实行,或者说,用理性去行动,用头脑去做事。辞海中解释"道"用"从行从首",而其中"行"的意思是"乍行乍止",其内部隐含的意义就是"知道行止"。这"行"和"止"意义的延伸与另外一个中国哲学概念"德"相应。"德"的原始意义也是包含在其文字的基本结构上。"德"字由两部分构成,先是"行",是积极行动之意,完全与中国古代的"主行"与"实践"的学说相符。"德"的第二部分是比较复杂的:先是"十目",然后是一个开放的"心"。"十"表示"十全十美",是完美的意思。"十目"也就是用最清晰的方法,来注意行为的对象和动向。"开放的心"表示做事首要的是"内心的真诚"。因此,"德"的真意也就是小心翼翼地去实行,而且用一颗开放的心去待人接物。所以,"诚"是德行的根本。谨慎行事,知道行止是人生活的理性基础,也就是中国古代社会中人的最高生活理想。

② 〔常〕马王堆汉墓帛书《道德经》中的"常"字写作"恒"字,因避西汉汉文帝刘恒讳,改为"常"。"常"与"恒"义同。

③ 第一、第三两个"名"字,为《道德经》中的特有术语,是称"道"之名,作名词用。第二个"名"意为"称谓",犹言"叫得出",作动词用。老子的"道",包含宇宙万物的发源、生长、变化、归宿种种道理,是非常玄妙且难以言说的,但又不能不说,只好立五千言。但老子虽立言,又怕后人过分执着于他的文字,故开宗明义指出这五千言所说并非"常道",只是通往"常道"的桥梁,所以闻道者不可过分执着文字。

④ 〔始〕原始。〔母〕根本。《说文·女部》:"母,牧也。从女,从女,象裹(怀)子形。一曰像乳子也。"今本作"无名,天地之始",但从王弼注中可知,原本应为"万物之始",马王堆帛书及北大汉简中也均作"无名,万物之始","天地"二字,或为后人所改。这两句在断句上有不同看法,宋代司马光、王安石、苏辙等以"有""无"两字后为断,作"无,名天地之始;有,名万物之母",似不合适。蒋锡昌云:"司马光、王安石、苏辙辈读此皆以'有''无'字为逗,不知'有名''无名'为老子特有名词,不容分析。三十二章'道常无名……始制有名',三十七章'吾将镇之以无名之朴',四十一章'道隐无名',是岂可以'无'与'有'读乎?《庄子·则阳》'万物殊理,道不私,故无名。无名,故无为,无为而无不为。'《文子·原道》'有名产于无名。'《史记·日者列传》'此老子之所谓无名

9

者,万物之始也。'古人皆以'有名''无名'为读也"(《老子校诂》)。张松如云:"今验之帛书,高(指高亨)读误,当从蒋。四十章'有''无',即'有名''无名'之义,老子所谓'有生于无',即前引《文子》所谓'有名产于无名',不足以证成以'无'字、'有'字为逗之说"(《老子说解》)。因此,《老子》书中"有名""无名"常连读,不宜断开。

⑤〔妙〕王弼注云:"妙者,微之极也。万物始于微而后成,始于无而后生。故常无欲,可以观其始物之妙。"

⑥〔徼(jiào)〕边际界。陆德明《老子音义》:"徼,边也。"吴澄《道德真经注》:"徼,犹言边际之处,孟子所谓端倪也。"另有张松如《老子说解》释:"'徼'通'邀''要',即追求、求索、循求之义,引申为'功用'"。今人多从此解。

⑦〔两者〕指"无"与"有"。王弼注云:"凡有,皆始于无。故'未形''无名'之时,则为万物之始,及其'有形''有名'之时,则长之育之,亭之毒之,为其母也。言道以无形无名始成万物,以始以成而不知其所以,玄之又玄也。"

⑧〔玄〕带赤的黑色,引申为幽远。沈一贯说:"凡物远不可见者的,其色黝然,玄也。大道之妙,非意象形称之可指,深矣、远矣,不可极矣,入名之曰玄。"苏辙《老子解》:"凡远而无所至极者,其色必玄,故老子常以玄寄极也。"

Chapter First (Yale Script)

The way that can be expressed by the word is not the eternal way.
The name that can be named is not the eternal name.
The being without a name is the origin of Heaven and Earth, with a name the origin of the all things.
For this name, they who are constantly exempt from passions see his spiritual essences; they who indulge in passions see the Tao under a limited form and imperfectly.
These two principals have the same original and receive different names.
They are called the two mysteries, double mysteries.
This is the door of all spiritual things, of all mysterious doctrine.

——Elijah Coleman Bridgman(裨治文)

第一章 《道德经》经典篇章英译选读

英译鉴赏简评

本章为全书之总纲,上述译文为美国来华传教士裨治文(Elijah Coleman Bridgman)翻译而成。

在先秦诸子百家中,道家之所以和其他诸家不同,正是因为它提出具有本体性和万物根源的形上观念之"道"。在这里,道是天地万物的本原,是宇宙的初始状态。宇宙、天地、万物均由"道"所化生。"道"深邃而奥妙,要认识它,应当经历从"无欲"到"有欲"的认识过程。老子在本章中开宗明义,提出一系列重要的哲学概念,道、名、有、无、玄、妙等,这对于下文的展开论述,无疑起到纲领性的作用。

历来许多学者都注意到《道德经》语言之美、音韵之和谐,其目的是明显的,老子要借助韵律和语言美来广泛宣传自己的主张,使之为人所接受。朱谦之在《老子校释》中说:"《道德经》著五千之文,于此首发其立言之旨趣。盖道者,变化之总名。与时迁移,应物变化,虽有变易,而有不易者在,此之谓常。自昔解《道德经》者流,以道为不可言。"朱谦之此说体会到《道德经》一书的核心思想,即万事万物均处于变化的状态中,"道""名"也不例外。这一观点是辩证法的核心思想,可谓得其本心。

首句"道可道,非常道",值得我们深入分析。在耶鲁译本里,第一、三个"道"字,是名词,被译为"way",有"道路、方法"之意,而第二个"道"字,是动词,被译为"express",即"表达"之意,故整句意为,"可以被言辞表达的'道',便不是永恒之道。"在这里我们知道,"道"的译法有三种,或作名词的"道路""方法"(way),或作动词的"表达""道出"(express),或直接音译为"Tau"("Tao")保留了不译、难译之义。对于"道"字这一哲学概念的翻译,现在都基本采取直接音译为"Tao"。"道"字的翻译嬗变,从最初的"tau"(reason)到"The Tao"再演绎到"Dao",现在汉语拼音的"Dao"已经逐步取代了威妥玛拼音直接进入到英文的表达中。鉴于社会文化等背景的变化,"道"字的英译也经历了多种变化和回归。这反映了西方汉学家对于老子之"道"内涵理解的升华,体现了中国文化从古至今在国外由不为人知到一知半解再到深知的传播过程。

《道德经》经典篇章英译选读之二

同异第四十一

上士①闻道,勤②而行之;

中士闻道,若存若亡③;

下士闻道,大笑之。不笑不足以为道④。

故建言⑤有之:

明道若昧⑥;进道若退;夷⑦道若类⑧;上德若谷⑨;广德若不足⑩;

建德若偷⑪;质真若渝⑫;大白若辱⑬;大方无隅;大器晚成;大音希声;

大象无形⑭;道隐无名⑮。

夫唯道,善贷且成⑯。

【注释】

①〔上士〕品行高尚的人。

②〔勤〕积极,勤奋。

③〔亡〕假借为"忘",或通"无"。高亨云:"若"犹"或"也。留于心之谓存,去于心之谓亡。〔若存若亡〕言似有似无,将信将疑。

④〔河上公注〕上士闻道,自勤苦竭力而行之。中士闻道,治身以长存,治国以太平,欣然而存之,退见财色荣誉,或于情欲而复亡之也。下士贪狠多欲,见道柔弱为之恐惧,见道质朴谓之鄙陋,故大笑之。不为下士所笑,不足以名为道。

⑤〔建言〕一说言是书名,老子引用其中的话;一说建言可能是古代现成的谚语、歌谣等;一说建言就是立言、设言,意思是通常有这样的说法。今多采用第二种说法。

⑥〔昧〕暗昧。〔明道若昧〕明显的"道"好像很暗昧而不容易看见。

⑦〔夷〕平坦。

⑧〔类〕广雅释言:类,节也。通俗文,多节曰类。故"类"引申为"凹凸不平"。

第一章 《道德经》经典篇章英译选读

⑨〔上德若谷〕谷亦作"俗"。谷者虚空卑下,为水所归,故老子以此比道。故"上德若谷"意思是"告上之德,反如流俗"。

⑩〔广德若不足〕成玄英疏义云:"广,大也,言怀大德之士,体道虚忘,故内至有余,而外若不足。"

⑪〔偷〕苟且,怠惰。〔建德若偷〕刚建之德,反若偷惰也。

⑫〔质真若渝〕质朴之德犹如羸弱输愚。〔真〕"直"之讹。〔渝〕变污,空虚,虚假。

⑬〔大白若辱〕洁白无瑕之物好像含污纳垢一般。〔辱〕黑垢,污垢。

⑭〔大〕加"大"字则表示意义相反。"方"为有隅,角落,"大方"则"无隅";"音"为有声,"大音"则为"无音";"象"为"有形","大象"则为"无形"。

⑮〔道隐无名〕"道"隐微而不可名状。

⑯〔夫唯道,善贷且成〕只有道善于施于万物,而且善于成就万物。〔夫〕发语词。〔贷〕施与,给予。〔成〕终也,成就。

41

one

Scholars of the highest class, when they hear about the Tao, earnestly carry it into practice. Scholars of the middle class, when they have heard about it, seem now to keep it and now to lose it. Scholars of the lowest class, when they have heard about it, laugh greatly at it. If it were not (thus) laughed at, it would not be fit to be the Tao.

two

Therefore the sentence-makers have thus expressed themselves:

'The Tao, when brightest seen, seems light to lack;

Who progress in it makes, seems drawing back; Its even way is like a rugged track.

Its highest virtue from the vale doth rise;

And he has most whose lot the least supplies.

Its firmest virtue seems but poor and low;

Its solid truth seems change to undergo;

Its greatest beauty seems to offend the eyes;
Its largest square doth yet no corner show;
A vessel great, it is the slowest made;
Loud is its sound, but never word it said;
A semblance great, the shadow of a shade.'

three

The Tao is hidden, and has no name; but it is the Tao which is skilful at imparting (to all things what they need) and making them complete.

——James Legge（詹姆斯·理雅各）

英译鉴赏简评

由于考古工作的推进,《道德经》先后出现了多个版本。译者所处的历史背景决定了译者所选择的中文版本,从而在内容理解上有所差异。本篇译者是詹姆斯·理雅各(James Legge),他明确指出他参考了六个注本。

根据严复先生所提出的"信(faithfulness)、达(expressiveness)、雅(elegance)"翻译理论,"信",即译文相对于原文的忠实性,保真性被放在首位。理雅各虽然是非常著名的汉学家,但中文毕竟不是他的母语,再加上《道德经》本身立意高远,言辞深奥,即使是中国学者,对于某些文辞的解读也是仁者见仁,智者见智。其次,影响译文保真性还包括中西文化层面的复杂因素。总之,非母语文化因素和《道德经》文本的多重解读也许决定了理雅各英译本的质量高下。

当然,我们应该褒奖理雅各对于《道德经》的翻译,因其对向西方介绍中国文化起到了非常重要的作用。他是最早一批将中国文化介绍给西方世界的代表性人物,这些译本对于西方世界理解中国、接纳中国和中西文化思想交流具有重大的奠基作用。然而他的身份首先是一名传教士,并且是一位具有很高语言天赋的传教士。他到中国来的首要目的不单是为了了解和传播中国文化,更多的是传播教义,宣扬西方思想,是服务于当时的大英帝国主义的,这属于一种文化殖民。

在理雅各的译文中,首先,在忠实性(信)方面,笔者认为有三处译文存在纰漏。第一处就是对"士"的翻译。理雅各作为著名的汉学家,被认为是英国第一位精通汉语言文化的大家,是第一位系统全面地翻译中华四书五经的权威译

第一章 《道德经》经典篇章英译选读

者。表面看来,他对于"士"的概念有一定深度的文化解读,明白"士"在中国文化里面的特指意义,即有一定社会地位,并且有学识的人。所以他把"士"翻译为"scholars",进而把"上士""中士""下士"分别翻译为"scholars of the highest class""scholars of the middle class""scholars of the lowest class"。春秋时期,"士人"一般分为三等,即"上士""中士""下士","上士"指出身高贵的贵族阶层,"中士"指平庸的贵族阶层,"下士"指浅薄的贵族阶层。然而仔细研读上下文,就会发现这里的"士"不一定是古代四民(士、农、工、商)之一中的"士",而是指宽泛意义上的对"道"的认知有高低之分,能识文断字的"学识之士",是对于有道之人的一种尊称或统称,根据得道之人悟道的程度,"士"可分为"上士"(悟道最高者)、"中士"(悟道一般或半信半疑者)、"下士"(未悟道者或对道抵触鄙视嘲讽者)。也许"上士"只是一介武夫,如"风萧萧易水寒,壮士一去不复还",大家都知道这一句里面的"壮士"指刺杀秦王的勇士——荆轲。因此,"scholars"一词似乎不足以表达此文本中的"士"的概念。如果翻译为"men of (highest/medium/lowest) wisdom"可能优于"scholars"。

第二处是"故建言有之"这一句中"建言"的翻译。理雅各把此处的"建言"翻译成了"sentence-makers",而实际上此处的"建言",大致同于上下文的转承关系"因此有以下……说法,由此",所以后来大多数译者把这句翻译成"therefore it is said"。

第三处就是对"道隐无名"中的"名"字的翻译。这里的"无名"的意思是"不可名状,不可描述",而不是常见的"姓名"中的"名字"的意思。所以"道隐无名",指的是"道隐微而不可名状",而不是译文"The Tao is hidden, and has no name"(道隐匿而没有名字)的意思。

显而易见,对西方人来说,他们在阅读这样的译文时是没有办法认识到这样的错误的,更无法真正理解老子深层次的智慧。

其次,根据以上三处译文纰漏分析,理雅各译文的"达"就受到了一定程度的影响,无法通过英语准确无误地再现《道德经》的隐含语意和深奥智慧。所以近年来,中医典籍翻译专家李照国先生在提及典籍翻译时,认为典籍翻译最好由中国人自己来做,只有这样才能确保译文信息传递的准确性和真实性。当然除了这三处因对原文理解错误而出现的误译,其他大部分内容的翻译基本保留和再现了原文的信息,此不赘述。

最后,我们来看看理雅各的英译文是否如同《道德经》原文一样优美雅致,是否达到了"雅"的标准。

本篇总共四句,长短不一:中长、短、超长、短。这样的布局显得此段落错落有致，犹如"道之隐"，不能一下子看明白。然而总体又都多为四字短语，浅显易懂，犹如"大道至简"。在内容排列方面，从第一句的具象描述，经过第二短句的嘲弄之谈，犹如人嗤之以鼻，发出"哼"声的感叹词一样，衬托"道"之谦卑姿态。欲扬先抑之后，第三句则通过十一个四字成语，一个五字成语对"道"进行阐释，极尽奢华，排比堆砌，语音顿挫，铿锵有力，大声朗读就会感受到文句有"大珠小珠落玉盘"的音效之妙。如果第三句是勾琴弦，那么最后一句则是用力一拨，终成佳音！第四句短句完成抽象之功能，总结出道的伟大之处在于善施万物、成就万物，故循道而行则事终成！

除了结构形式上的整饬紧凑，在语言韵律上也是竭尽所能，巧妙运用了对仗、头韵（如大）、脚韵（如昧、退、类；谷、辱、足；偷、渝、隅；成、声、形、名、成）等，使文章朗朗上口，易于传授背诵，达到"寓乐于教"的目的。所以《道德经》不但是为人处世的"道德"之经，更是具有极高语言表现力和艺术渲染力的"文学"杰作，是先秦诸子百家典籍中的上乘之作。

总之，《道德经》中文兼具形美、音美和精神意境之美。那么理雅各的英文翻译是否具有这些特点呢？让我们来看看英译本：

1. Scholars of the highest class, when they hear about the Tao, earnestly carry it into practice.

Scholars of the middle class, when they have heard about it, seem now to keep it and now to lose it.

Scholars of the lowest class, when they have heard about it, laugh greatly at it. If it were not (thus) laughed at, it would not be fit to be the Tao.

2. Therefore the sentence-makers have thus expressed themselves:
"The Tao, when brightest seen, seems light to **lack**;
Who progress in it makes, seems drawing **back**;

Its even way is like a rugged **track**.

Its highest virtue from the vale doth **rise**;
And he has most whose lot the least **supplies**.

Its firmest virtue seems but poor and **low**;

Its greatest beauty seems to offend the **eyes**;

Its solid truth seems change to **undergo**;

第一章 《道德经》经典篇章英译选读

<u>Its</u> largest square doth yet no corner **show**;
A vessel great, it is the slowest **made**;
Loud is its **sound**, but never word it **said**;
A semblance great, the shadow of a **shade**."

3. The Tao is hidden, and has no name; but it is the Tao which is skilful at imparting (to all things what they need) and making them complete.

首先,从形式上看,由于中文原句具有独特的形式,理雅各保留了其长短句的布局。同时每一个英文句子力求形式上贴近中文的对仗和押韵。所以说理雅各的语言天赋确实不低,贯通中西,能够把《道德经》的内容基本无误地翻译出来,而且又能富有技巧地采用英文的韵律之美、形式之美再现汉语文句的音形义。

然而这里补充一点,笔者认为"大方无隅"的中文意思有待商榷。大部分文献注解为很大的正方形,没有棱角。然而笔者认为此处的"方"应该是"方向"里"方"的意思,"大方"应该理解为很大的空间,"大方无隅"则是"空间太大而看不到棱角"(The space is too large to see the edges and corners)的意思。

总而言之,虽然理雅各的《道德经》译文有一定的纰漏,但瑕不掩瑜,在形之美、音之美,及精神意境之美方面还是非常成功的英译范例。

《道德经》经典篇章英译选读之三

显质第八十一

信言①不美,美言②不信。

善者不辩③,辩者不善。

知④者⑤不博,博⑥者不知。

圣人不积⑦,既以为人已愈有,既以与人已愈多。

天之道,利⑧而不害;

圣人之道⑨,为⑩而不争。

【注释】

①〔信言〕由衷之言，真诚之语。

②〔美言〕谓华美之言，虚泛之语。

③〔辩〕能说会道，会申辩。

④〔知〕"智"的本字，意为明智，有智慧。《说文》："智，知也。"《孟子》："是非之心，智之端也。"《周易·临卦》："知临，大君之宜。"用智慧君临天下，施行善政、仁政。《荀子修身篇》："是是非非，谓之知。"

⑤〔者〕具有某种特征的人或事物。《说文》："者，别事词也。"《增韵》："又即物之辞，如彼者，如此者。""智者"，明智的人，有智慧的人。

⑥〔博〕《说文》："博，大通也。"《玉篇》："广也，通也。"《增韵》："普也。"《荀子修身篇》："多闻曰博。"因此，这里的"博"，是指自己炫耀卖弄学识，以显示自己见识广博。

⑦〔积〕积，聚也。

⑧〔利〕《易》曰："利者，义之和也。"

⑨今本作"圣人之道"，帛书乙本作"人之道"。

⑩〔为〕做事情，有所作为。

81

Real words are not vain,

Vain words not real;

And since those who argue prove nothing

A sensible man does not argue.

A sensible man is wiser than he knows,

While a fool knows more than is wise.

Therefore a sensible man does not devise resources:

The greater his use to others

The greater their use to him,

The more he yields to others

The more they yield to him.

The way of life cleaves without cutting:

第一章 《道德经》经典篇章英译选读

Which, without need to say,
　　Should be man's way.

——Witter Bynner（威特·宾纳）

英译鉴赏简评

　　本篇是《道德经》的最后一章，为美国汉学家威特·宾纳（Witter Bynner）所译。前三句主要阐述信与美、善与辩、知与博这些同是正面、看似一致的品质之间往往存在反向、矛盾的关系。这些认识既是经验的升华，也是老子一以贯之的辩证思想的体现。后半部分着重表彰圣人"不积"与利他的美德。圣人不聚积财物，而且把"给予"看作一种收获，把"付出"看作一种回报（汤漳平等，2014）。

　　对于本篇，大部分译者都能够准确翻译出原文的意思。然而就西方译者来说，"知者不博，博者不知"这一句，因译者解读不同，译文也有所不同。比如保罗·卡鲁斯（Dr. Paul Carus）把这一句译为"The wise are not learned; the learned are not wise"，这样的语句会让西方读者心生疑惑："为什么有智慧的人不能博学呢？"而厄休拉·勒吉恩（Ursula K. Le Guin）则把这一句翻译为"People who know aren't learned, learned people don't know"，回译成中文就是"知道的人并不是很博学，而博学的人并不知道。"她在这里误认为"知"意为"知道"，而实际上这里的"知"同"智"，表示有智慧的意思。根据严复的翻译理论，翻译首要做的是忠实于原文（信），翻译这部中国古籍经典《道德经》更应是如此。比较几部英译文，很显然，宾纳的版本首先在意思上更忠实于原文，基本再现了原文的意思；从形式上看，他的译文注意保留回还、顶针、押韵等原文语句中所使用的修辞手法，以诗歌的形式再现了《道德经》原文的语言风格，可谓"信达雅"三者皆有。

本章课后练习

一、请尝试翻译以下句子。

1. 天下皆知美之为美，斯恶已；皆知善之为善，斯不善已。（《道德经》第二章）

　　白话释义：

　　英译：

2. 道冲,而用之或不盈。(《道德经》第四章)
   白话释义:
   英译:

3. 知人者智,自知者明。(《道德经》第三十三章)
   白话释义:
   英译:

4. 静胜躁,寒胜热。(《道德经》第四十五章)
   白话释义:
   英译:

5. 知者不言,言者不知。(《道德经》第五十六章)
   白话释义:
   英译:

二、请比较以下各句两种英译文本的异同。

1. 反者道之动;弱者道之用。(《道德经》第四十章)
   英译1:Reversal is the moving of the Way; Weakness is the using of the Way. (Edmund Ryden)
   英译2:The divine law may go opposite ways; even weakness is useful. (许渊冲)

2. 上士闻道,勤而行之;中士闻道,若存若亡;下士闻道,大笑之。(《道德经》第四十一章)
   英译1:Top officials hear the Way: they can (hardly) fare by her. Average officials hear the Way: parts they keep; parts they lose. Low officials hear the Way and greatly mock her. (Edmund Ryden)
   英译2:Having heard the divine law, a good scholar follows it; a common scholar half believes in it; a poor scholar laughs at it. (许渊冲)

第一章 《道德经》经典篇章英译选读

3. 不言之教,无为之益,天下希及之。(《道德经》第四十三章)

　　英译1:Wordless teaching, the benefit of not acting: There are few in the world who attain to it. (Edmund Ryden)

　　英译2:The teaching by saying nothing and the utility of doing nothing are seldom known to the world. (许渊冲)

4. 甚爱必大费;多藏必厚亡。(《道德经》第四十四章)

　　英译1:Extreme love leads to great waste; Much hoarding leads to much loss. (Edmund Ryden)

　　英译2:The more you love, the more you spend. The more you store up, the more you lose. (许渊冲)

5. 大直若屈,大巧若拙,大辩若讷。(《道德经》第四十五章)

　　英译1:Great straightness seems bent; Great skill seems clumsy; Great eloquence seems tongue-tied. (Edmund Ryden)

　　英译2:Do thou what's straight still crooked deem; Thy greatest art still stupid seem, And eloquence a stammering scream. (James Legge)

6. 祸莫大于不知足;咎莫大于欲得。(《道德经》第四十六章)

　　英译1:(There is no graver crime than wanting too much;) There is no bigger disaster than not knowing what is enough; There is no greater misfortune than wanting to get. (Edmund Ryden)

　　英译2:There is no guilt greater than to sanction ambition; no calamity greater than to be discontented with one's lot; no fault greater than the wish to be getting. (James Legge)

7. 治人事天,莫若啬。(《道德经》第五十九章)

　　英译1:In governing others and serving heaven, there is nothing like storing. (Edmund Ryden)

　　英译2:To rule people and serve heaven, nothing is better than frugality. (许渊冲)

8. 治大国,若烹小鲜。(《道德经》第六十章)

　　英译1:Governing a large country is like steaming small fish. (Edmund

Ryden)

英译2：A large state should be ruled as a small fish is cooked.（许渊冲）

9. 美言可以市尊，美行可以加人。(《道德经》第六十二章)

英译1：Eloquent speech can be used for bargaining; Fawning conduct can be used for bribing others. (Edmund Ryden)

英译2：Fair words can win respect and fair deeds can influence people.（许渊冲）

10. 图难于其易，为大于其细；天下难事，必作于易；天下大事，必作于细。(《道德经》第六十三章)

英译1：Plan what is difficult while it is yet easy; Undertake what is great while it is yet small. Tasks that are difficult in the world [are sure to] begin from what is easy; Tasks that are great in the world [are sure to] begin from what is small. (Edmund Ryden)

英译2：Big or small, more or less, any difficulty has an easy part, any great deed has a small detail.（许渊冲）

三、段落试译。

上善若水。水善利万物而不争，处众人之所恶，故几于道。居善地，心善渊，与善仁，言善信，正善治，事善能，动善时。夫唯不争，故无尤。

(《道德经》第八章)

上德不德，是以有德；下德不失德，是以无德。上德无为而无以为；下德无为而有以为。上仁为之而无以为；上义为之而有以为。上礼为之而莫之应，则攘臂而扔之。故失道而后德，失德而后仁，失仁而后义，失义而后礼。夫礼者，忠信之薄，而乱之首。前识者，道之华，而愚之始。是以大丈夫处其厚，不居其薄；处其实，不居其华。故去彼取此。

(《道德经》第三十八章)

第二章

《庄子》经典篇章英译选读

【导读】

　　享誉国内外的道家文化学者陈鼓应先生曾说:"中国哲学的主体部分为宇宙论和人生哲学,其建构者主要是道家……在人生哲学方面,庄子的成就是空前的,后代也是无人可及的。"

　　说起中国历史上的哲学大家,老子、孔子当仁不让地被归于最一流者,而庄子、孟子似乎次之。因此,陈先生对庄子的溢美之词也许会引起某些人的反驳,但不可否认的事实是,庄子在中国文化史上的地位与影响力不容小觑。《庄子》与《道德经》,堪称代表道家思想的两部巨著,《庄子》在中国古典文学、哲学、艺术、思想史上具有不可动摇的绝对经典的地位。

　　而庄子何人,所做何事?对这类问题,读者首先想到的可能是"北冥有鱼"和"庄周化蝶"的故事,而关于他的生平事迹等其他方面却知之甚少或语焉不详,根本原因在于有关庄子生平的记录文字鲜见于各类经籍史料。汉代司马迁的《史记》中有关庄子的生平事迹,可能是所有经籍史料中最为完整的记录。

　　　庄子者,蒙人也,名周。周尝为蒙漆园吏,与梁惠王、齐宣王同时。其学无所不窥,然其要本归于老子之言。故其著书十余万言,大抵率寓言也。作《渔父》《盗跖》《胠箧》,以诋訾孔子之徒,以明老子之术。《畏累虚》《亢桑子》之属,皆空语无事实。然善属书离辞,指事类情,用剽剥儒、墨,虽当世宿学不能自解免也。其言洸洋自恣以适己,故自王公大人不能器之。

楚威王闻庄周贤,使使厚币迎之,许以为相。庄周笑谓楚使者曰:"千金,重利;卿相,尊位也。子独不见郊祭之牺牛乎?养食之数岁,衣以文绣,以入大庙。当是之时,虽欲为孤豚,岂可得乎?子亟去,无污我。我宁游戏污渎之中自快,无为有国者所羁,终身不仕,以快吾志焉。"(《史记·老子韩非列传》)

此段文字大致呈现了庄子的基本履历:庄子姓庄名周,宋国蒙人(今河南商丘市东北),曾经做过漆园吏(一说为管理漆树园的小官;一说为漆园这个地方的小吏),大致与梁惠王、齐宣王同时代;学识渊博,一生著述丰赡,有十余万言,多为寓言;批判儒家、墨家;不事权贵,终身不仕云云。隋唐陆德明在《经典释文·序录》中说庄子"字子休",这种提法仅从唐代开始,且持此说者不在多数。关于庄子生卒年,有学者推断庄子出生于魏文侯、武侯之世,最晚在梁惠王初年。据闻一多先生考证,庄子大概生于魏武侯末叶,周烈王元年,一生穷困寂寞。

据学界说法,在中国古代历史上,庄周其人及作品《庄子》一书倍受公众瞩目的时期大致如下。

其一为魏晋时代。两汉偏重黄老之学,而藐轻老庄之学。西汉初中期,倍受汉武帝赏识的大儒董仲舒(公元前179年—前104年)提出"罢黜百家,独尊儒术",使孔孟儒学成为显学,老庄之学似乎无法与因官方垂青而独领风骚的儒家学说相提并论,但实际崇信者不在少数。至东汉时期,随着中央皇权的日渐衰颓,社会矛盾愈发凸显,儒学昔日的迅猛势头有所削弱,至魏晋时期,社会矛盾逐渐加剧,儒学式微,开始让位于"无为而治"的道家学说。老庄学说在魏晋时期摆脱了儒家经学桎梏,崇尚清谈无为的文化氛围,从不受重视的冷遇状态逐渐向主流文化过渡,随后占据流行文化的主位达百余年之久。但有些学者往往将老庄之学与逃离政治,隐居山野的魏晋玄学混为一谈。实际上,从本质而言,此两者有诸多分野,虽然在形式上有千丝万缕的关联性和相似度,这一点应引起重视。

闻一多先生说:"一到魏、晋……庄子忽然占据了那全时代的身心,他们的思想,生活,文艺——整个文明的核心是庄子。他们说'三日不读庄子,则舌本间强。'《庄子》,是清谈家灵感的泉源。从此以后,中国人的文化上永远留着庄子的烙印。他的书成了经典。他屡次荣膺帝王的尊封。"庄子成为魏晋显学的过程呈现波浪式渐进的特点,在时间跨度上,大致历经三百余年。

在这个历史时期,不仅对《庄子》一书而言,而且对中华后人而言,意义最为

第二章 《庄子》经典篇章英译选读

重大的事件是西晋玄学家郭象(252年—312年)对该书所做的编纂和注解。据《汉书》载，《庄子》原书共有52章，计十余万字，但经郭象系统化删减整理和逐词逐句注释后，留存至今的版本仅包括"内篇(7)""外篇(15)""杂篇(11)"三部分，共33章，八万余字。该版《庄子》被学界视为流传至今最受欢迎且最为权威的经典版本，甚至被称为"南华经(《庄子》)注本之宗"。不过，对于《庄子》33篇是否全部为庄子本人所作，目前学界仍存在一定的争议。传统认为，只有"内篇"7篇为庄子本人所作，而其他章节皆为庄子的追随者或门徒整理辑佚其言论思想而成。

其二为思想开放文化包容的唐代。这一时期，因受到不同社会群体的认可和接纳，儒释道各有数量广众的拥趸，可谓三分秋色，各领风骚。

唐代开国皇帝唐高祖及其继位者唐太宗，对道家持支持和肯定的态度。从高祖朝始，老子即被奉为李氏始祖。据《封氏闻见记》载：

> 国朝以李氏出自老君，故崇道教。高祖武德三年，晋州人吉善行于羊角山见白衣老父，呼善行谓："为吾语唐天子：吾是老君，即汝祖也。今年无贼，天下太平。"高祖即遣使致祭立庙于其地。遂改浮山县为神山县，拜善行为朝散大夫。高宗乾封元年，还自岱岳，过真源县，诣老君庙，追尊为玄元皇帝。玄宗开元二十一年，亲注老子《道德经》，令学者习之。二十九年，两京及诸州各置玄元皇帝庙，京师号玄元宫，诸州号紫极宫。寻改西京玄元宫为太清宫，东京玄元宫为太微宫，皆置学生。

开创唐代盛世的第九代皇帝唐玄宗(685年—762年)，对道家的支持远超于前代，达到痴迷忘我的程度。在位期间，他不仅亲注《道德经》，而且于开元二十九年(741年)开设崇玄学，设博士，掌教玄学生。天宝元年(742年)又追封庄子为"南华真人"，尊封《庄子》一书为《南华真经》。在唐代官办的道教学校崇玄馆中，《庄子》与《道德经》一并，一直都是生徒们的必修课业。《南华真经》在道教中的地位，也一直被视为仅次于老子的《道德经》。因此，在李唐王室崇尚道教的政治背景下，庄周与老子的地位不相上下。两宋以来，《庄子》之学逐渐降温，不如魏晋至唐代那般受人关注。

学界所谓的老庄之学(道家)在某种意义上指两者之间有学术传承关系，即庄子"然其要本归于老子之言……以名老子之术"。但实际上，无论是老子与庄子，还是孔子与孟子，他们之间并没有直接的嫡传关系。从时间跨度上看，老与孔子属于同时代人,庄子与孟子属于同时代人,前两者与后两者大概相隔一个世纪左右。在哲学思想上,老庄、孔孟亦无严格的高下尊次之分。之所以有此称谓,大概是因为老子与庄子在道家思想,孔子与孟子在儒家思想上的前后相承关系或相似相合之处甚多。

事实上,老子与庄子并称"道家",似乎有些大而化之。倘若细究深挖,就会发现老子与庄子对"道"的认知和诠释尚有迥异。至于何为老子的"道",何为庄子的"道",可谓仁者见仁,智者见智,答者莫衷一是。林语堂先生有言:"道"不是一个中国的思想流派,而是中国人的一种深邃而根本性的思维模式,是中国人对待生活、认识社会的一种态度。道以一种无形的方式不仅丰富了中国人的诗歌和想象力,而且给中国人的闲适、无羁、诗意和悠游的灵魂赋予了一种哲学上的界限。具体而言,老子的道之思想着眼于外物和人际,而庄子的思想着眼点在于自体和宇宙;前者像一位年长智高的老者,站在旁观者的位置上,眯缝着眼睛,看着世俗里的芸芸众生争名夺利、喧闹不休,然后说出"水善利万物而不争"这样居高临下的睿智之语;而后者像一位孑然于众人之外的青年独行侠,不在意凡夫俗子的任何言语或举动,而是以个体的形式在内省与自查中积极探寻着生命独行与个体独存的真谛:"不累于俗,不饰于物,不苟于人,不忮于众"(《庄子·杂篇·天下》),但最后失望至极,故而发出"天下为沈浊,不可与庄语(庄严之语)"(《庄子·杂篇·天下》)的喟叹。

《庄子》在西方世界的传播和被认识并接受较《论语》《孟子》《道德经》等其他诸子典籍要晚许多年。19世纪末期,《庄子》主要经由西方传教士之手传入欧美诸国。

第一部《庄子》英译本为1881年英国来华传教士弗莱德里克·亨利·巴尔弗(Frederic Henry Balfour)翻译的《南华真经:道家哲学家庄子的著作》(*The Divine Classic of Nan-Hua*; *Being the Works of Chuang Tsze, Taoist Philosopher*)。巴尔弗在该书附记(Excursus)部分对《庄子》有这样的评价:"在道家的后继者中,有一个人的名字无人可比,他就是庄子,在此,我们用英语第一次将他的作品送给全世界。……他的那些被长期封存于中国文学沉积之中的作品,是一座神秘而伟大的不朽丰碑。"据统计,从1881年巴尔弗《庄子》英译本发行至今,已有24种译本陆续发行,其中全译本11部,选译本13部。

1889年,英国汉学家赫伯特·翟理斯(Herbert Allen Giles)在巴尔弗《庄子》英译本的基础上,发行了全新译本《庄子:神秘主义者、伦理学家与社会改革家》(*ChuangTzu, Mystic, Moralist, and Social Reformer*)。该译本一经发行,便备受学界瞩目和读者的好评。翟理斯通过自己的传神妙笔,将庄子哲学

第二章 《庄子》经典篇章英译选读

之精华传递给英国读者,让他们感受到了中国哲学的魅力。评论者认为,在翟理斯的笔下,庄子的形象和智慧都充满了魅力,这对于"西方了解中国与中国人是很有帮助的"。

1891 年,英国著名汉学家詹姆斯·理雅各(James Legge)的《道德经》英译本 *The Tao Te Ching of Lao Tzǔ*,与《庄子》英译本 *The Writings of Chuang Tzǔ*,作为中国典籍英译系列读本《东方圣书》(*The Sacred Books of the East*)的第 39 卷、第 40 卷,一并由牛津大学出版社出版发行。理雅各 1839 年来华(香港)传教,居中国三十余年,对中国文化深谙于心,并穷其一生,孜孜不倦地将中华典籍陆续引介到欧美各国。他的译本在中西方学术领域的权威性不容置疑。因此,*The Writings of Chuang Tzǔ* 一书,成为之后其他研究中国文化的东西方学者及翻译家的必读书目之一。然而,有学者批评该译本文辞直拙佶屈,无法再现《庄子》一书的文学价值和魅力。但该译本受读者的欢迎程度并未消减,反而与日俱增。因深受读者的欢迎和喜爱,1959 年,英国牛津大学出版社重印理雅各《庄子》英译本。之后,美国多弗出版社对《东方圣书》系列进行再版,更名为《中国圣书》(*The Sacred Books of China*),于 1962 年在全美发行。

1939 年,亚瑟·韦利(Arthur David Waley)的《古代中国的三种思维方式》(*Three Ways of Thought in Ancient China*)由伦敦乔治·艾伦与昂温出版公司出版。该书是韦利精选《庄子》《孟子》《韩非子》三部中国哲学著作中他认为最为精华部分的英译杰作。在韦利看来,他选译的篇章最能代表庄子、孟子和韩非子三位哲人的核心主张和思想内容。由译本章节排列及文字占比来看,韦利对庄子尤为推崇,评价亦最高。韦利曾称赞:"《庄子》是世界上最有趣且最深刻的书籍之一。"他认为"庄子的魅力在于其瑰丽的想象力,一个人若能读懂诗歌,那么就能够读懂庄子。……庄子的技巧如同诗人的技巧。"

美国著名汉学家伯顿·华兹生(Burton Watson)对亚瑟·韦利的英译本评价颇高:"在我看来,迄今为止,《庄子》译本中最值得阅读、最为可靠的是亚瑟·韦利的译本,虽然令人遗憾的是,它们只展现了文本的一小部分。"

也许基于此遗憾,1964 年,伯顿·华兹生亲自执笔,翻译了《庄子》中的 11 章《庄子菁华》(*Chuang Tzu: Basic Writings*),由美国哥伦比亚大学出版社出版。在该译本前言中,华兹生称赞道:"《庄子》一书自问世到今天的两千余年间,因其表现的逍遥和自由的精神,在中西方读者中享有经久不衰的盛誉。……庄子所讲述的轶事及其背后蕴藏的无穷睿智和幽默,早已越过亚洲的边境。世界上几乎无人不晓庄周梦蝶的故事。"由于该译本深受读者的肯定和喜爱,之后华兹生倾注了四年的时间和心血完成了《庄子》"外篇"之外其他章节的翻译，合为《庄子全译本》(The Complete Works of Chuang Tzu)，由哥伦比亚大学出版社出版，以期向西方读者全方位再现这位享誉千载的中国哲人。汪榕培教授评价华兹生译本"是《庄子》英译本中的佼佼者"。

1965年，美国诗人托马斯·默顿(Thomas Merton)出版了《庄子》英译本《庄子的道》(The Way of Chuang Tzu)。默顿重新翻译《庄子》一书的主要动机在于他认为以前的译本"因译者汉语功底薄弱，或对庄子'道'的认知有限，都是建立在猜测的基础上。……任何对《庄子》的翻译都是一种个体化的诠释，并非严格意义上的翻译。"而他所要做的，无非是希望自己对这位精深、诙谐、引人深思而又无法靠近的中国哲人直觉式的解读能够让读者得到些许快乐。但伯顿·华兹生对默顿的译本推崇备至："对该文本的文学品味感兴趣的读者，应该阅读托马斯·默顿据现有的西语翻译文本在他所完成的《庄子之道》中对这些篇章的"模仿"。这些篇章体现出生动且充满诗意的庄子风格，而且实际上他的译文与《庄子》原文几乎完全贴近。"

1981年，英国伦敦大学东方及非洲研究院(School of Oriental and African Studies, London University)古汉语教授、汉学家葛瑞汉(Angus Charles Graham)先生选译了《庄子》的部分章节，结集为《庄子：内七篇和外篇选》(Chuang-tzǔ: the Seven Inner Chapters and Other Writings: from the Book Chuang-tzǔ)，由伦敦乔治·艾伦与昂温出版公司出版。葛瑞汉一生致力于汉语诗词、中国哲学及汉语语言文字的研究和推广，尤其钟情于庄子的哲学思想和文学气质，研究成果极其丰硕。

1991年，位于美国旧金山的哈珀出版社出版了由托马斯·克利里(Thomas Cleary)翻译的《道的要义》(The Essential Tao: An Initiation into the Heart of Taoism through the Authentic Tao Te Ching and the Inner Teachings of Chuang Tzu.)。他在这本书里翻译了《道德经》全文和《庄子》的内篇，译文通畅，但是并不完全忠实于原文。他在书后所附的"论道家、《道德经》和《庄子》的历史背景"一文对道家学派的形成过程和《老子》《庄子》的成书过程进行了介绍，他的注解也有一定的特色。

克利里对《庄子》有中肯的评价："中国有两本描述'道'的基本哲学和实践的经典书籍，如众所知，很久以前就成为通往'道'之路线图——《道德经》和《庄子》。这两部作品早已超越了文化界限，成为举世公认的世界文学经典作品。《道德经》和《庄子》创作于两千多年前，是世界上最古老、最实用的智慧书籍之一。……《庄子》既是中国最著名的文学作品之一，也是道家思想的重要文献来源。"

第二章 《庄子》经典篇章英译选读

1994年,美国汉学家、敦煌学家梅维恒(Victor H. Mair)的全译本《逍遥于道:庄子的早期道家寓言故事》(*Wandering on the Way: Early Taoist Tales and Parables of Chuang Tzu*, New York: Bantam Books, 1994.)出版。此前他曾编著《庄子》考证与诠释方面的论文集 *Chuang-tzu: Composition and Interpretation*。1998年,《逍遥于道:庄子的早期道家寓言故事》由夏威夷大学出版社出版。汪榕培教授认为梅维恒的译本特色之一是极力突出《庄子》一书的文学色彩,因此他把汉语的诗体部分全部用英语的诗体来翻译;书中带有意义的人名也采用了意译法,例如,在《庄子·养生主》中,"公文轩"译为"His Honor Decorated Chariot",连"老聃"也译为"Old Longears"。

1996年,英国汉学家彭马田(Martin Palmer)与伊丽莎白·布鲁伊里(Elizabeth Breuiliy),杰伊·拉姆齐(Jay Ramsay)等学者合作翻译出版了《庄子》全译本(*The Book of Chuang Tzu*)。彭马田毕业于英国剑桥大学,主攻神学宗教研究和中国古文典籍研究,曾出版《尚书》《易经》《道德经》等中国古籍经典英译,三十余年致力于中华典籍的翻译和推广工作。

2015年是中英文化交流年,中方记者专访汉学家彭马田,问他"如何对中国文化和这些中国古籍经典产生兴趣的?"彭马田解释说,因为他发现所有的英译本都翻译得不好,所以他要重新翻译这些中国的经典。"我需要指出的是,我并不认为我自己是在翻译,其实我是在解读。一种文化是不能被翻译成另一种文化的,我们能做的是将一种文化向另一种文化进行解读。不同文化也会因此加深彼此之间的了解。"他的译本深受西方读者的喜爱,彭马田说"关于《庄子》有很多有意思的点评。一个读者给我写信说:'我买了这本书想要读哲学,但是它不是哲学。书里面全都是笑话和故事。'我回信道:'这就是最好的哲学。'大多数人们喜欢这些译文是因为它们很容易理解。读者可以读懂它们。……我想《庄子》告诉了西方人中国是有趣的。在《庄子》里,有非常精彩的对于'道'的描述,还有对于道和天、道和地,以及道和人类关系的阐释。它里面蕴含了与西方哲学在根本上不同的对于自然和我们生活环境的理解。西方哲学基本上强调那是自然,这是我们人类。我们没法对自然做任何事。我们观察它、注视它、控制它,同时我很抱歉地说,我们摧毁了它。破坏环境可能是我们做得最大的一件事。道家,尤其是在《庄子》中,说花、你、我、这杯茶和这张桌子,在天之下,在地之上,所有事物都归一。我们人类有责任保持阴阳的平衡以及气的顺畅流动。所以说这是(和西方)在根本上不同的观点。所以我认为,在一定程度上,《庄子》为西方提供了一个迥然不同的角度来看世界,并和世界取得联系。同时,它还是非常有趣的。我认为道家具有普遍性,而《庄子》具有独特性。它以令人接受的方式对一些西方哲学和西方政治中的假设提出了挑战。所以说《庄子》对西方产生了很大的影响。"西方读者对《庄子》的欢迎程度也许部分得益于像彭马田一样热衷于中国典籍翻译的汉学家们的翻译之功。

1997年,美国诗人、翻译家大卫·亨顿(David Hinton)出版了选译本《庄子:内篇》(*Chuang Tzu*：*The Inner Chapters*)。大卫·亨顿是20世纪第一位将中国古代最著名的四部哲学典籍《论语》《孟子》《道德经》和《庄子》全部独自译成英语的西方翻译家。辛顿采用通俗自然的语言和清新简洁的风格,把博大玄妙的儒道思想展现给西方普通读者,为当代西方英语读者了解中国传统文化打开了方便之门。除儒家、道家典籍之外,辛顿还翻译了大量的中国古诗和现代诗,包括《杜甫诗选集》《陶潜诗选集》《孟效晚期诗歌》《李白诗选》《谢灵云山地诗》《中国古典诗歌:选集》《王安石晚年诗选》以及北岛的《距离的形式》《零度以上的风景》。

因《李白诗选》《零度以上的风景》及《孟郊晚期诗歌》三部译作的突出成就,辛顿获得了1997年度美国诗人学会(Academy of American Poets)颁发的"哈罗尔德·莫顿·兰登诗歌翻译奖"(Harold Morton Landon Translation Award)。辛顿近期获得的奖项有来自威特·宾纳基金会(Witter Bynner Foundation)、英格拉姆·梅里尔基金会(The Ingram Merrill Foundation)、美国国家艺术基金会(The National Endowment for the Arts)和国家人文基金会(The National Endowment for the Humanities)等的多项殊荣。2014年,美国艺术与文学学院授予其桑顿·怀尔德终身成就奖(Thornton Wilder Lifetime Achievement Award)。

总体而言,大卫·亨顿作为诗人,在翻译《庄子》的过程中,比较关注文本的文学性和艺术性,而对于庄子哲学思想的把握较为欠缺,但其语言简洁,用词通俗易懂,既能再现《庄子》的文学特质,又比较适合普通大众阅读。

1998年,美国著名汉学家、中西比较哲学研究的领军人物、夏威夷大学和美国东西方中心亚洲发展项目主任安乐哲(Roger T. Ames)编辑出版了《庄子》研究论文集——《逍遥于庄子》(*Wandering at Ease in the Zhuangzi*)。该书由美国纽约州立大学出版社出版。该论文集共收录11篇西方学者对《道德经》《庄子》《论语》等中国典籍的学术研究成果,既涉及中国哲学流派的内在关联,又探讨了《庄子》中的哲学概念和对哲学语汇的理解和翻译等,为中西方《庄子》研究提供了非常独特而深入的思路和素材,为了解庄子的历史、作品文本及其哲学思想提供了新视角。

第二章 《庄子》经典篇章英译选读

安乐哲教授的学术研究关注儒家哲学及中西比较哲学,其学术贡献主要包括中国哲学经典的翻译和中西比较哲学研究两大部分。他翻译的中国哲学经典主要包括《论语》《孙子兵法》《孙膑兵法》《淮南子》《道德经》《中庸》《老子今注今译及评介》等。安乐哲教授对中国哲学独特的理解和翻译方法改变了一代西方人对中国哲学的看法。他力求将中国哲学放置在汉语和中国文化自己的世界观中去理解和诠释,使中国经典的深刻含义越来越为西方人所理解。安乐哲关于中西比较哲学的系列大作包括《主术:中国古代政治思想研究》(1983)、《孔子哲学思微》(1987)、《期待中国:探求中国和西方的文化叙述》(1995)、《汉哲学思维的文化探源》(1998)、《先哲的民主:杜威、孔子和中国民主之希望》(1999)、《自我的圆成:中西互镜下的古典儒学与道家》(2006)、《儒学角色伦理学:一套特色伦理学语汇》(2011)等。这些著作在一定程度上纠正了西方人对中国哲学思想几百年的误会,清除了西方学界对"中国没有哲学"的偏见,开辟了中西哲学和文化深层对话的新路。

1999年,美国两位著名诗人兼翻译家山姆·汉米尔(Sam Hamill)与西顿(J. P. Seaton)合作翻译了《庄子》"内篇"的所有篇章,以及"外篇"和"杂篇"的部分章节,共计二十二篇,以《庄子经典》(*The Essential Chuang Tzu*)为名由美国香巴拉出版公司出版。该书前言开篇说:"如果所有曾经在世的中国诗人、画家和作家被问及自己最喜欢的一本书,那么答案肯定是《庄子》。"由此可见哈米尔和西顿对《庄子》的偏爱程度之深。

2019年,多伦多大学博士、香港中文大学哲学系副教授柴大卫(David Chai)出版了《庄子与虚无的形成》(*Zhuangzi and the Becoming of Nothingness*)。该书共包括六个章节,分别从六个维度对庄子提出的诸如"虚无""无为""无无""时间""自然""真人"等哲学概念展开深度剖析。书中根据每章内容的需要选译了《庄子》一书中的不同片段,译文浅显易懂,用词平实简洁,适合普通读者阅读欣赏。此书为近几年西方学者庄学研究的一部杰作,对西方世界进一步认识和理解庄子的哲学思想和"道"之精髓大有裨益。

以上所述的《庄子》英译本(或翻译研究论文集),均出于西方译者和学者之手,各译本之优劣短长,读者可翻阅评鉴,此不赘述。

迄今为止,由中国人完成的《庄子》英译和释译,共有五部杰作,简介如下。

第一部是被誉为中西贯通的哲学大师冯友兰先生的《庄子》选译本(内篇七章)(*Chuang-Tzu: A New Selected Translation with an Exposition of the Philosophy of Kuo Hsiang*),由商务印书馆于1931年出版;1989年、2016年北京外文出版社再版。冯先生的译本实现了中英文字转换过程中原始文本的语义保真,同时,深度再现了《庄子》一书的核心哲学思想,可谓《庄子》英译本中的上乘之作。冯先生解释了翻译《庄子》的必要性:第一,从文学或语言学角度看,已有的《庄子》英译本可圈可点,但均未能再现《庄子》内在的哲学思想;其次,清代以考据学著称,得益于大量的高水准的文本批评及考据著作,大多数古籍变得更具可读性,更易于读者理解。而早期庄子的英文译本似乎并没有利用清代学者的学术成果,因此,需要一个新译本来呈现当下的学术成果。冯友兰先生的译本重点关注的内容不仅是语言层面的对应或保真,而且深入到语言背后的哲学文化和思想层面。

第二部为 1942 年由美国纽约兰登书屋出版的林语堂先生的《中国印度之智慧》(*The Wisdom of China and India*)。该书收录了林先生翻译的《老子:道德经》(*Laotse, the Book of Tao*)和《庄子:神秘主义者和幽默家》(*Chuangtse, Mystic and Humorist*)(选译 11 篇)两部道家大作。之后,林语堂对内容进行了较大修改,以尽量忠实于原作。修改后的《庄子》(节选)英文版与《道德经》英文版(*The Wisdom of Laotse*)由兰登书屋于 1948 年出版发行。

林语堂先生在《庄子》英文版序言中说,总的来说,庄子应被视为周朝最伟大的散文家,正如屈原被视为最伟大的诗人一样。这样的地位,不仅源于他瑰丽的文采,也源于他深邃的思想。有人说,庄子的文采可以概括为八个字"汪洋恣肆,奇谲吊诡",的确恰如其分。

林语堂先生的英译本并非全书翻译,而是特意剔除了被视为"伪作"的章节,仅选取了 11 篇庄子的"真作",如下所示。

"A Happy Excursion"(《逍遥游》)

"Levelling All Things"(《齐物论》)

"Preservation of Life"(《养生主》)

"This Human World"(《人间世》)

"Deformities"(《德充符》)

"The Great Supreme"(《大宗师》)

"Joined Toes"(《骈拇》)

"Horses' Hooves"(《马蹄》)

"Opening Trunks"(《胠箧》)

"On Tolerance"(《在宥》)

"Autumn Floods"(《秋水》)

林语堂先生说他的英译本是在参考赫伯特·翟理斯(Herbert Allen Giles)英译本的基础上,"取其所长,补其所短"而成,主要原因在于他认为翟理斯的译文

第二章 《庄子》经典篇章英译选读

"欠缺考量,过于随意,且口语体太强",同时他对翟理斯的贡献赞不绝口。

第三部为1974年华裔汉学家冯家福(Gia-Fu Feng)与其夫人简·英格里希(Jane English)共同翻译的《庄子:内篇》(*Chuang Tsu Inner Chapters: A Companion Volume to Tao Te Ching*),由阿尔弗雷德·克诺夫公司出版社与年代图书出版社联合出版发行。该译本之后由多家出版社出版发行:1997年地球之心出版社(Earth Heart)出版第二版,2000年、2008年,琥珀莲花出版社出版第三版、第四版;2014年,海氏出版公司出版第五版。多次重版足以见得冯家福译本受欢迎程度之高。汉学家任博克(Brook A. Ziporyn)曾说,他与老子发生共鸣,就是因为读了冯家福先生的译本。冯家福与简·英格里希还曾共同翻译了《道德经》(*Lao Tsu: Tao Te Ching*),在当时深受西方读者的好评,"它提供了每一个词的真意,使老子的学说直观而生动(It offers the essence of each word and makes Lao Tsu's teaching immediate and alive)。"这主要是因为冯氏夫妇的译本语言比较简洁明了,版式精美,更适合普通读者的阅读习惯。

第四部为1990年美籍华裔学者吴光明(Wu Kuang-ming)教授出版的《以蝴蝶为伴:<庄子>前三篇沉思录》(*The Butterfly as Companion: Meditations on the First Three Chapters of the Chuang Tzu*),由美国纽约州立大学出版社出版。此书为《庄子》前三章的翻译兼释义,无论在形式还是内容上,均有别于其他《庄子》英译本。吴光明先生以西晋郭象《庄子注》为参考底本,汉字文本以传统汉语典籍竖排式编排,即"用中国古典的评注文体";英译文则以西方英诗体例的结构编排,每五行为一节,以期西方读者能够直观感受中国古典文本的排版体例,同时兼顾英文的阅读习惯。每篇正文之后均附有中国、日本及西方不同学者非常详赡缜密的注释和术语翻译方案,以帮助读者更加深入地阅读和理解原文。这种全新的译释法被吴光明称为"用英文书写中文、吟唱中文。……用中文的语法组织英文,使其诗化。"

从青年时代开始,吴光明先生内心深处便有了"庄子情结",与《庄子》的相遇使吴光明的人生发生了改变。他将自己称为"庄子的知心人",在生活中践行庄子哲学,"他(庄子)是我生命的维生素,是我的活力","我阅读庄子,是为了活出他的样子"。他对《庄子》的评价也极高:"全部的中国思潮结晶于庄书哲思,全部的中国哲学传统,皆不外乎庄子一连串的注解。"

实际上,1982年,吴光明先生历时五年完成的第一部作品《庄子:逍遥的世界哲学家》(*Chuang Tzu: World Philosopher at Play*)一书,就奠定了他日后在庄学研究领域的大师地位。此书专门就学术界对庄子的误读误解现象展开了深入浅出的分析和有理有据的驳斥,"以最直观的方式向英语世界呈现了《庄子》'说什么',并借助西方哲学传统中的意义(meaning)、反讽(irony)和游戏等观念分析《庄子》中的故事,指出《庄子》语篇的连贯性,反驳当时西方'中国哲学碎片化'的论断。"

虽然吴光明先生谦称此书为"中西文化互动的初步尝试",但事实上,此书一出版,便在由西方人多年掌握的庄学研究领域激起了不小的波澜。这是一部由中国人以中国人的视角来诠释庄学的嚆矢之作,为中西读者打开了一扇"中国式"解读《庄子》的哲学天窗,成为他所提出的"让中国人的思维成为中国人的,而不是西方人的(Let Chinese Thinking Be Chinese, not Western)"哲学主张的有力证明,更是一次英语世界中西学术话语权较量角逐的决胜明鉴。吴光明先生穷毕生之力来探求中国哲学的精髓,多年深耕于老庄之学,他对中国古代哲学的研究可谓登峰造极,对庄子的解读创设极多。他的这两部深有见地的大作,不但有力地反击了西方人秉持的"中国人无哲学"的学术偏见,而且成功重塑了庄子在西方学术界的哲学家形象,为20世纪90年代之后国内外的"庄学"研究开启了一条创新之路。

第五部为大陆已故学者汪榕培先生的《庄子》英译本。该译本1997年由湖南人民出版社出版,1999年录入《大中华文库》系列,由湖南人民出版社再版发行。此书前言有一段对庄子哲学造诣及影响力评价的文字:"西方要是有人认为中国是个哲学贫乏的国家,他在读完《庄子》以后,就会发现其博大精深的哲学体系足以跟任何一位古希腊哲学家的哲学体系相媲美。庄子的文学才华也远在任何一位古希腊哲学家之上,不仅在中国文化史上是绝无仅有的,在世界范围内也是无与伦比的。"

因此,有评论者说:"庄子继承并发扬了老子的'道'的学说,其著作《庄子》一书是继《老子》之后,体现道家思想的另一部重要之作,是中国古代精神自由史上的第一名著,在中国古典文学、哲学、艺术、思想史上均有不可动摇的绝对经典地位。……无论是治学修身、处世待人,还是经商置业、从政为民;无论是高官大吏、富商大贾,还是贩夫走卒、平民百姓,总能在《老子》和《庄子》中找到自己需要的智慧。"

时至今日,"老庄之学"与《道德经》《庄子》一并成为中西方学术研究的热点之一,也是西方世界认识中国,了解中国的"文化桥梁",更是西方读者研究中国哲学思想,阅读中国文学不可忽略的重要内容之一。闻一多先生说:"哲学的起点便是文学的核心。《庄子》会使你陶醉,正因为那里边充满了和煦的、郁蒸的、焚灼的各种温度的情绪。"美国学者爱莲心(Robert E. Allinson)甚至称庄子为"心灵的哲学家",并评价说:"像《庄子》这样的经典可以对来自另一种文化的人

第二章 《庄子》经典篇章英译选读

产生影响,……这表明,《庄子》拥有普遍的价值。"《庄子》在诙谐中释放着严谨和缜密,在睿智中透露着思考和冥想,在自问中渗透着思辨与探讨,在清丽中施展着哲理与放达——这就是被同一个"道"字所笼罩却与宽泛意义上的"道"并不趋同的独特的庄子。《庄子》全书结构及各章节内容见表2-1。

表2-1 《庄子》全书结构及各章节内容概略

总章	篇名	各篇主旨简介
内篇	(1)《逍遥游》	本篇庄子三度描写大鹏寓言,意在肯定人可以凭借修行而成其大。由此上承老子所说的"道大,天大,地大,人亦大"(《道德经》第二十五章)。人若成其大,则有望成为至人、神人、圣人,抵达无待之境而自在逍遥,也化解了世俗所在意的有用无用之争
	(2)《齐物论》	感官让人迷惑于现象,理性使人执着于自我。"形如槁木"与"心如死灰"是修行过程,由此可摆脱相对的知见与价值,回归"道通为一"的整体。此时的体验是"天地与我并生,而万物与我为一",进而可以领悟至高智慧未始有物。在道之中,万物平等,而人依然有所不同,有其悟道的可能性
	(3)《养生主》	养生的原理是什么?以"庖丁解牛"为例,人在世间行走,犹如以利刃解牛,要做到依乎"天理"(自然的条理)与因其"固然"(本来的结构),才可以游刃有余,令这把刀用了十九年而毫无损伤。因此,培养自己具备透视整体的眼光,再以"安时而处顺"的心态去面对挑战,就可以安其天年
	(4)《人间世》	人间多患难,而化解之道在于改变国君的心态。如何改变呢?任何方法都有不足,唯有靠学习者修养自己,抵达虚而待物的"心斋"之境。具体表现是"知其不可奈何而安之若命"。在人间,不能不分辨有用与无用,但结果却是:有用往往自陷困境,而无用却能长保平安
	(5)《德充符》	学习道家的关键,在于明辨"道"与"德"。道是万物的来源与归宿,德是万物得之于道者,亦即万物的"本性与禀赋"。人若保持本性与禀赋,就不会在意身体方面的缺陷(如老、残、弱)与世俗方面的不足(如贫、贱、无用)。能够顺其自然而保持和谐,即是"德充",而其"符",则是验证,可由本篇观之

续表

总章	篇名	各篇主旨简介
内篇	(6)《大宗师》	大宗师就是"道"。悟道者为真人,真人的表现无异于神人与至人,是庄子笔下的完美典型。本篇对"道"的描述,得自老子真传,尤其"自本自根"一词可谓画龙点睛。中间论及悟道七关,由"外天下"到"不死不生",值得省思。悟道者相忘乎道术,彼此为友,则相视而笑,莫逆于心
	(7)《应帝王》	人不能脱离世间而生活,那么应该采取什么态度呢?庄子的立场是无心而为与用心若镜。"无心而为"指顺其自然而无容私焉,任何作为都不必怀有刻意的目的。若非如此,连看相算命的人都可以眩惑我们。"用心若镜"则可以胜物而不伤。这是两不相伤,天人相洽。混沌之喻提醒人守住本性与禀赋,便可一切具足
外篇	(8)《骈(pián)拇》	天生万物,各有其性,也各有其命。人有理智与自由,因此可能自作聪明,为自己增加各种人间的价值,结果反而丧失了性命的真实状况。真正的善,不是仁义,而是善待自己所得的一切,亦即保存性命的原貌,不为任何外在的目的而有所牺牲,进而可以自适其适
	(9)《马蹄》	马是万物之一,有它自身的性与命,但是从人的角度来判断,就要设法让它变得有用。结果呢?善于驯马的伯乐会淘汰一半以上的劣马。儒家所谓的圣人,为了治理百姓而制作礼乐,倡言仁义。结果呢?人们脱离了道与德,苦不堪言。道是根源,德是本性,人实在不必刻意作为而自寻烦恼
	(10)《胠箧(qū qiè)》	本篇主旨与《马蹄》篇相同,但思想更深刻,言辞更犀利,大胆批判了儒家所谓的圣人,"圣人不死,大盗不止",可谓不遗余力。圣人以仁义礼乐来治理天下,大盗学会了这套方法,就会不择手段来取得天下,然后也以仁义礼乐作为号召。那么,不如回到"小国寡民"(《道德经》第八十章)的原始社会吧!古代的"至德之世"可供我们缅怀
	(11)《在宥(yòu)》	治理天下时,如果有所作为,那么不论为善为恶,结果都会带来灾难。何以如此?因为"人心"一旦受到挑拨,就会像捅开的蜂窝,后患无穷。万物皆生于土而反于土,依循自然规律,人为何不能因而忘记自己,不要刻意有所作为呢?本篇认为,有为将带来痛苦,但人类可能回复到原始社会吗

第二章 《庄子》经典篇章英译选读

续表

总章	篇名	各篇主旨简介
外篇	(12)《天地》	从"道"的角度看来,万物没有缺憾。人若悟道,万物成为一个整体,死生也不足为意。此时,人与天地同乐,有如复归于混沌,无机巧也无机心。但是,这不表示要否定人间价值,而是随物而化,对"寿、富、多男子"也能欣然接受。"上如标枝,民如野鹿",一片自在祥和。然而,使人"失性"的机会太多了,可不慎乎
	(13)《天道》	本篇谈天道,一并述及帝道与圣道,并且肯定黄帝、尧、舜等人的作为。其中描写的圣人是以道为师、得享"天乐"的,不但享受自然之乐,也能蓄养天下万民,抵达"太平"之境。唯独对于孔子之标举仁义,仍有未安。至于"桓公读书"之喻,则提醒我们要崇本抑末,以求亲自验证悟道之妙
	(14)《天运》	如果真有天籁,则本篇描写的黄帝演奏《咸池》可以作为代表。它使听者体验"惧、怠、惑"。惧使人难以安于现实,怠使人陷入心灵空虚,惑使人由愚可以悟道。接着,孔子面对道家老子时,受到什么教训与启发,在本篇说得既生动又深刻。在庄子笔下,儒家似乎只能甘拜下风。另外,有关"孝"的六境可谓神来之笔。《庄子·天运》这样写着:"用恭敬来行孝容易,用爱心来行孝较难;用爱心来行孝容易,行孝时忘记双亲较难;行孝时忘记双亲容易,行孝时使双亲忘记我较难;行孝时使双亲忘记我容易,我同时忘记天下人较难;我同时忘记天下人容易,使天下人同时忘记我较难"
	(15)《刻意》	"刻意"为立定心志要做成某些事。凡是设定目的的人都将有所期待。唯圣人可以做到"德全而形不亏",他的表现与真人无异,可以恬淡无为,守住精神
	(16)《缮性》	本篇谈到改善本性,由此而"复其初",但方法可能错了。自古及今,步步堕落,从"至一"到"顺而不一",又到"安而不顺",再到"不安而乱",无法回复原状。最后谈到"古之得志者",让人警惕。本篇"复其初"一语常被宋朝学者借用,但意思大不相同
	(17)《秋水》	本篇论述之精巧,可与《齐物论》篇并列佳构。七个问题层层深入,化解了争竞比较之心,也肯定了万物各有其价值,最后聚焦于分辨天与人。人的智慧可分高下,有人悟道,也有人像井底之蛙。庄子借几段寓言描述自己的境界,充分显示了自信与自得之乐。最后则是"鱼乐"之辩,但其真谛何在?值得仔细品味

续表

总章	篇名	各篇主旨简介
外篇	(18)《至乐》	人间有最大的快乐吗？像富贵、长寿、名声，都要人付出代价，并且享受这些快乐的后遗症也很大。"无心而为"才是至乐。这种觉悟使人看透生死。本篇有"庄子妻死"与"见空骷髅"等章，助人深思。至于鲁侯与海鸟之喻，以及列子的体悟之悟，皆各有理趣
	(19)《达生》	本篇寓言最多，亦广为人知，如"丈人承蜩(tiáo)""津人操舟""吕梁泳者""梓庆削木""醉者驾车""呆若木鸡"等，有的由技入艺，臻于化境；有的无心而为，顺其自然；契机皆在由忘而化、由化而游，以至"形全精复，与天为一"。至于"桓公见鬼"一章，则显示出庄子的知见之广
	(20)《山水》	处世秘籍在于判断"材与不材"何者安全。然后"虚已以游世"，不受万物拖累。本篇一再谈及孔子的受困，足以提醒世人如何自求多福。庄子自身亦有乱世求生的法则，如"见利思害"。篇中借孔子之口说"人与天一也"，是古代所谓"天人合一"的最早版本，而其所说的"天"是指自然界而言。从"道"看来，万物合成一个整体
	(21)《田子方》	本篇多为寓言与重言，其中有不少高明之士，如东郭顺子、温伯雪子、臧丈人、伯昏无人、孙叔敖、真儒士、真画师等。颜渊师法孔子，但觉"夫子奔逸绝尘"；孔子往见老子，才知"天地之大全"；真是人外有人，天外有天。这些作品的用意，依然是要勉人领悟大道，以成就老子所谓"人亦大"的理想
	(22)《知北游》	人之生死，有如气之聚散，因此人须觉悟，身体、生存、性命、子孙皆非自己所有。然而人生又非徒然与枉然，因此要修行以求悟道。"精神生于道"一语是重要契机。精神一展现，则可体验"道无所不在"，则可欣赏"天地有大美"。由此再转换为处世的上策，则是"外化而内不化"，外在和光同尘，内心自有天地，与道结伴而游
杂篇	(23)《庚桑楚》	本篇从学生请益的角度，让老聃发挥他的观点。若想在世间做到"知、仁、义"，则难以抉择对谁有利。老子为此畅谈"卫生之经"，提出九个问题要人自省。文中再度提及古之人的至高智慧是明白"未始有物"。然后行走于世间，则像圣人一般，全依"不得已"而定

第二章 《庄子》经典篇章英译选读

续表

总章	篇名	各篇主旨简介
杂篇	(24)《徐无鬼》	古代政治由上而下,只要说服统治者,天下就太平无事。但这正是艰难的挑战。今日情况不同,人人皆可自修自省,亦可以逍遥无待,但调节自己的观念并非易事。首先要去除外在包装,以真心与人相待,不必炫耀,不可偏执,不慕荣利。然后修养身心,体验"未始有物"而成为真人
	(25)《则阳》	失去本性,代价太高。人的本性有如旧国旧都,"望之畅然"。不必追求外物,不必迎合众人,若是入世从政,则须设法"得其环中以随成",与物同化但内心始终不化。本篇最后谈到"万物之所生",但悟道之人对此不会太过费心
	(26)《外物》	有关善恶的报应,实在没有一定标准;甚至连分辨善恶都不太可能。庄子才华卓越,但穷得向人借米;孔子有心救世,却总是受人教训;儒者口诵诗书,做的竟是盗墓;白龟可以托梦,难以避开噩运;我们要学习的是:顺人而不失己。一切以悟道为先,得鱼而忘荃(quán),得意而忘言
	(27)《寓言》	本篇谈庄子的写作方法,有"寓言、重言、卮(zhī)言",重要性自不待言,他所表达的是万物。"始卒若环,莫得其伦",因此言说有其限制,不可拘泥。难得的是庄子对孔子的肯定,他说:"吾且不得及彼乎!"在修行方法上,则有颜成子游说的九步骤,从"野"到"大妙",可供参考。最后,阳子居听从老聃教诲,放下身段,以平常心与人相处
	(28)《让王》	谁愿意把王位让给别人?问题更在于:让了别人还不要,不但不要,甚至认为自己受到侮辱。这是相当极端的观点,但是从道家"全身保真"与儒家"安贫乐道"的角度来看,却显得并不突兀。"日出而作,日落而息",亦可自得其乐。何必为了射一只麻雀而浪费"随侯之珠"?孔子与几位弟子在此受到表扬,并不使人意外
	(29)《盗跖(zhí)》	本篇是《庄子》全书最偏激者,对孔子所代表的儒家思想,提出了犀利的批判。重点有三:一是善恶并无适当报应;二是人生在世苦多乐少;三是人性本身大有问题。这三点虽有过激之处,但也能使人觉悟,要寻求一完整而根本的理解。任何学说皆有破有立,本篇所言未尝不可以抹杀

续表

总章	篇名	各篇主旨简介
杂篇	(30)《说剑》	本篇似一短篇小说,义理较浅。庄子在此装扮为武士,也可算是不计形象了。他分析了"天子剑、诸侯剑、庶人剑",其格局、气魄、眼光与口才,皆值得欣赏。赵文王或任何世间帝王皆应有所感悟。最后,一批剑士因为得不到大王赏识而自杀,亦可见某种对生命的态度,让人觉得遗憾
	(31)《渔父》	本篇也像是短篇小说,但渔父并非盗跖,他给孔子的建议显然较为正面。孔子不改其一贯的好学心态,乐于倾听智者的言论。渔父为孔子分析"八疵四患",劝他不必过度忧心,以免庸人自扰。文中论及"真者,精诚之至也",以及"圣人法天贵真",皆为庄子之意。在这段寓言中,孔子此时已六十九岁,依然好学至此,可见儒家亦有不凡之处
	(32)《列御寇》	世间价值观极为纷乱。儒墨相争可以使家人无法共存,渴求富贵则必须行卑贱之事、冒生命危险。人心难测,要如何判断及测试之?明智的做法是培养觉悟的智慧,化解自我的执着,向往那"泛若不系之舟,虚而遨游者也"。本篇有关"庄子将死"的一段,道尽其逍遥自得之生命情调
	(33)《天下》	本篇总结古代思想,分七派而论之,是研究哲学史的重要资料。首先,描述古人如何具有完备的智慧,亦即,"内圣外王之道"。接着介绍儒家的演变,可谓客观而有见地,再及于墨家等学派,皆得古人之一偏。至老聃、关尹方可称为"古之博大真人",而对庄子的评述,则可谓登峰造极,让人神往。最后,再以惠子为例,提醒人们不可惑于小智,往而不返

第二章 《庄子》经典篇章英译选读

《庄子》经典篇章英译选读之一

内篇·逍遥游(节选)

北冥①有鱼,其名为鲲②。鲲之大,不知其几千里也;化而为鸟,其名为鹏③。鹏之背,不知其几千里也;怒而飞,其翼若垂天之云④。是鸟也,海运则将徙于南冥。南冥者,天池也。《齐谐》⑤者,志怪者也。《谐》之言曰:"鹏之徙于南冥也,水击三千里,抟⑥扶摇而上者九万里,去以六月息者也⑦。"野马⑧也,尘埃也,生物之以息相吹也。天之苍苍,其正色邪?其远而无所至极邪?其视下也,亦若是则已矣。且夫水之积也不厚,则其负大舟也无力。覆杯水于坳堂⑨之上,则芥⑩为之舟,置杯焉则胶⑪,水浅而舟大也。风之积也不厚,则其负大翼也无力。故九万里,则风斯在下矣,而后乃今培风⑫;背负青天而莫之夭阏⑬者,而后乃今将图南⑭。蜩与学鸠⑮笑之曰:"我决起而飞,抢榆枋⑯而止,时则不至,而控于地而已矣,奚以之九万里而南为?"适莽苍⑰者,三飡⑱而反,腹犹果然;适百里者,宿舂粮⑲;适千里者,三月聚粮。之二虫又何知!

小知不及大知,小年不及大年⑳。奚以知其然也?朝菌不知晦朔㉑,蟪蛄不知春秋㉒,此小年也。楚之南有冥灵者,以五百岁为春,五百岁为秋;上古有大椿者,以八千岁为春,八千岁为秋,此大年也。而彭祖㉓乃今以久特闻,众人匹之,不亦悲乎!

汤之问棘㉔也是已。汤问棘曰:"上下四方有极乎?"棘曰:"无极之外,复无极也。穷发之北㉕有冥海者,天池也。有鱼焉,其广数千里,未有知其修者,其名为鲲。有鸟焉,其名为鹏,背若泰山,翼若垂天之云,抟扶摇羊角而上者九万里,绝云气,负青天,然后图南,且适南冥也。斥鷃㉖笑之曰:'彼且奚适㉗也?我腾跃而上,不过数仞而下,翱翔蓬蒿之间,此亦飞之至也。而彼且奚适也?"此小大之辩也。

　　故夫知效一官,行比一乡㉘,德合一君,而征一国者,其自视也,亦若此矣。而宋荣子犹然笑之㉙。且举世誉之而不加劝,举世非之而不加沮,定乎内外之分,辩乎荣辱之境,斯已矣。彼其于世,未数数㉚然也。虽然,犹有未树也。夫列子御风而行,泠然㉛善也,旬有五日而后反。彼于致福者,未数数然也。此虽免乎行,犹有所待者也。

　　若夫乘天地之正,而御六气之辩㉜,以游无穷者,彼且恶乎待哉?

　　故曰:至人无己㉝,神人无功㉞,圣人无名。

【注释】

① 〔北冥(míng)〕北海。〔冥〕通"溟",这里指"海"。《说文解字》:"溟,小雨溟溟也。《太玄经》:密雨溟沐。《玉篇》曰:溟蒙小雨。庄子南溟北溟,其字当是本作冥。""或倒景于重溟。"(孙绰《游天台山赋》)。

② 〔鲲(kūn)〕传说中的大鱼。《列子·汤问》:"终北之北有溟海者,天池也,有鱼焉,其广数千里,其长称焉,其名为鲲。"唐人陆德明《音义》载:"鲲当为鲸。"

③ 〔鹏〕中国神话传说中最大的一种鸟,据说由鲲变化而成。

④ 〔怒〕通"努",鼓起翅膀,振翅而飞。〔垂〕清人郭庆藩《庄子集释》引崔撰说:"'垂犹边也,其大如天一面云也。'则读垂为陲之古字。《说文·土部》:"垂,远边也。"即边陲。〔怒而飞,其翼若垂天之云〕当大鹏振翅高飞时,它的翅膀像天边的云。

⑤ 〔《齐谐》〕先秦时期记载逸事传闻的志怪神话集。另说为姓齐名谐的人。唐人陆德明《经典释文》:"齐谐,户皆反。司马及崔并云人姓名;简文云书。"唐人成玄英疏:"姓齐,名谐,人姓名也。亦言书名也,齐国有此俳谐书也。"

⑥ 〔抟(tuán)〕《说文解字注》:"抟,以手圜之也。"用手把东西揉成团。此指大鹏拍击翅膀高飞貌。

⑦ 〔去以六月息者也〕大鹏振翅飞往南海,是依凭六月的大风。〔息〕风。

⑧ 〔野马〕指天地之间的游气,犹如野马奔腾。

⑨ 〔坳(ào)〕地面凹凸不平。〔坳堂〕堂上地面低洼不平。

⑩ 〔芥〕喻微小之物,此指小草。

⑪ 〔胶〕黏住,黏合。

第二章 《庄子》经典篇章英译选读

⑫〔培〕凭借。清人王念孙《读书杂志馀编·庄子》:"培之言冯也,冯,乘也,风在鹏下,故言负;鹏在风上,故言冯……冯与培声相近,故义亦相通。"清人段玉裁《说文解字注》:"冯,或假为凭字。凡经传云冯依,其字皆当作凭。"

⑬〔夭〕夭折,夭亡。〔阏〕阻塞,遏制。〔夭阏(yāo è)〕阻碍,遮挡。

⑭〔图南〕计划飞往南方。〔图〕谋划。

⑮〔蜩(tiáo)〕蝉。《说文解字注》:"螽风传曰:蜩、螗(táng)也。大雅:如蜩如螗。"学鸠,学,通"鷽",即鷽鸠。小鸠。陆德明《释文》云:"学又本作'鷽',音同……学鸠,小鸠也。"又作斑鸠。

⑯〔榆枋〕榆树和枋树。另一种说法,榆枋喻指狭小的空间。

⑰〔莽苍(mǎng cāng)〕苍茫的郊野。成玄英疏:"莽苍,郊野之色,遥望之不甚分明也。"

⑱〔飡〕音义同"餐"。

⑲〔宿〕前一夜。〔舂(chōng)〕捣粟也,把东西放在石臼或钵里捣去皮壳或捣碎。〔宿舂粮〕前一夜备好向南海出发的食物。

⑳〔小知不及大知,小年不及大年〕小智慧不及大智慧,寿命短的不及寿命长的。〔知〕通"智"。〔年〕年寿,寿命。

㉑〔朝菌不知晦朔〕早晨的菌类不到晚上即死去,因而不知黑夜与黎明为何物。

㉒〔蟪蛄不知春秋〕蟪蛄(huì gū),俗称"知了",为体型较小的蝉类,一般春生夏死,无法感受四季的变化,故言"不知春秋"。

㉓〔彭祖〕道教传说中上古五帝中颛顼的玄孙,姓彭祖名铿。据说彭祖历尧、舜、夏、商诸朝,至商末纣王时,几七百六十七岁,是世上最懂养生之道、寿命最长之人。

㉔〔汤〕商朝开国之君商汤,即成汤,姓子名履,又名天乙(殷墟甲骨文称成、唐、大乙,宗周甲骨与西周金文称成唐),河南商丘人。统治商朝12年,在位期间,社会矛盾比较缓和,政权较为稳定,国力日益强盛。《诗经·商颂·殷武》称颂道:"昔有成汤,自彼氐羌,莫敢不来享,莫敢不来王"。〔棘〕"革""棘"古音相近,故为通用。此指夏革,夏末至商初的大贤人,商汤以之为师,常向其请教问题。

㉕〔穷〕荒蛮之地。〔发〕毛发,此指草被,草木。〔穷发之北〕意指不毛之地的北边。

㉖〔斥鴳(yàn)〕鴳雀,鹌的一种,又名冠雀,指小鸟。

㉗〔奚〕何,哪里。〔适〕之,往。〔彼且奚适〕它(大鹏)要飞往何处呢?

㉘〔知(zhì)〕通"智",智慧,才能。〔效〕效验,胜任。〔行〕品行,行为。〔比〕符

合,合乎。〔知效一官,行比一乡〕才智能力可以胜任一官之职,品行行为符合全乡民众的心愿。

㉙〔宋荣子〕一名宋钘(jiān),战国时期宋国思想家。〔犹然〕嗤笑貌。

㉚〔数数(shuò shuò)〕速,迫切。〔未数数然〕汲汲求名逐利貌。

㉛〔泠(líng)然〕冷散飘零,此指飘逸洒脱。

㉜〔御〕驾驭。〔六气〕阴阳风雨晦明六种气候。《左传·昭公元年》注云:"天有六气,谓阴阳风雨晦明也。"〔辩〕通"变",变化。

㉝〔至人〕意近于下文的"神人""圣人"。〔无己〕物我两忘之境。

㉞〔无功〕无功名禄业的束缚。

白话释义

　　北方的大海里有一条鱼,它的名字叫作鲲。鲲的体型巨大无比,不知道有几千里;它能变化为鸟,名字叫作鹏。鹏的脊背,也不清楚有几千里宽;当它振翅高飞时,翅膀就好比天边的云彩。这只大鸟,风吹浪涌时打算飞往南方的大海。南方的大海,被称为"天池"。《齐谐》是一本载录志怪神话的书,书里说:"大鹏往南海迁徙时,翅膀在水面上拍击,能激起三千里的海浪,大鹏旋击翅膀,扶摇而上,冲向九万里的高空,乘着六月的风离开北海。"犹如天地间野马般奔腾的游气,好像空气中飞腾的尘埃,大自然中的生物就是以各自的气息与他物相交互,无拘无束。高远天穹,苍茫一片,那是它原本的颜色吗? 它如此邈远,是不是达不到边际? 大鹏从天上往下看,大概就是这样的景象吧。如果积水很薄,就无法承载巨大的舟船。给厅堂上的低洼里倒入一杯水,放一棵小草,小草就成为一叶小舟,如果放置杯子,则杯子会粘在地上,这是水太浅而舟太大的缘故。如果风太小,就无法承载巨大的羽翼。因此,大鹏能够扶摇九万里,就因为有大风的托举,才能凭风翱翔;因其背负青天,无所阻挠,才可以筹划着飞往南海。知了和斑鸠嘲笑大鹏说:"我展翅而飞,飞到榆树和檀树就行了,有时飞不到树枝上,落到地上也无妨,何必要朝南海飞越九万里的高空呢?"到苍茫的郊野,只需备足三天的饭食,肚子照样吃得饱饱的;去百里之外的地方,却要准备三个月的食粮。知了和斑鸠又怎能明白这些道理啊!

　　小智慧比不上大智慧,寿命短的不懂寿命长的。这是什么道理呢? 早晨出生的菌类不到黑夜就会死去,因而不知黑夜与黎明;寒蝉春生夏死或夏生秋死,因而不知春天与秋天。楚地之南有一棵大树,名为冥灵,五百年为一个春季,五百年为一个秋季;上古有一棵大树,名为大椿,八百年为一个春季,八百年为一

第二章 《庄子》经典篇章英译选读

个秋季,这就是长寿。彭祖被称为长寿之人,人们要和他一较寿命短长,难道不觉得可悲吗?

商汤也曾向他的贤臣夏棘请教过同样的问题。商汤问夏棘:"上下四方有极限吗?"夏棘回答说"无极之外,还是无极。在那荒远的北方之北,有一片广袤无垠的大海,叫作天池。天池里有一条大鱼,身宽好几千里,无人知晓它究竟多长,它的名字叫作鲲。有一只鸟,名字叫鹏,脊背宽如泰山,展开的羽翼遮挡天幕,它飞升而上,展翅翱翔九万里,超越云气,背负青天,一路向南,飞往南海。鴳雀讥笑道:'它这是飞往哪儿呢?我扑腾翅膀,不过离地几尺,然后落下,在蓬蒿间飞来飞去,不也飞得很开心!它这是往哪儿飞呢?'"大与小的区别即在于此。

因此,有些人,才能胜任一官之职,品行合乎一乡之意,德行符合国君的意志,取得一国的信任,便自我膨胀,不正如此吗?宋国的宋荣子嗤笑他们。因为宋荣子不会因为他人的美誉而勤勉,也不会因为他人的非议而沮丧。他能分清自我与外物,荣誉与耻辱,原因正在于此。他对于世俗的荣誉,并未孜孜以求。不止于此,他还有许多未能列举的品性。列子凭风而行,飘逸洒脱,十五天后方才返回。他对幸福的追求,并未苛求。像他这样,虽然不费徒步之劳,但还是有所依凭。

如果人能遵循自然之道,顺应六气之法,游逸于无穷之境,那还需要有什么依凭呢?

所以说,高人超越于自我,神人不羁于功名,圣人不在乎声名。

◉ 主题鉴赏

闻一多先生说:"向来一切伟大的文学和伟大的哲学是不分彼此的……哲学的起点便是文学的核心。"而庄子无人能敌的文学气质和才华,从《庄子》一书的开篇之作《逍遥游》便可见一斑。

《逍遥游》可谓一幅大气磅礴、势可冲天的壮丽画卷:"北冥有鱼,其名为鲲。鲲之大,不知其几千里也;化而为鸟,其名为鹏。鹏之背,不知其几千里也;怒而飞,其翼若垂天之云。"在阅读这样的文字时,读者既能体会到如此奇崛的文辞所带来的视觉快意,而且还能从更深层次的想象世界,看到一幅绵亘千里的动态画面——一条北海的鲲鱼,渐化为一只展翼高飞的大鹏,飞越千山和万水,要抵达(庄子本人)意识深处的南海。而大鹏这一跨越千里搏击云天的南飞壮举,却遭到了蜩(知了)与学鸠(斑鸠)的讥笑。表面看来,《逍遥游》是在写两类不同的动物,而实际则是借类比手法来摹写人类社会:大鹏代表为精神自由而敢于尝试，勇于突破的革新派，而蜩与学鸠则代表拘囿于个人狭小的生存圈不敢做出任何改革和突破的保守派。两类人群分别构成了社会结构中的两种群体。在庄子看来，只有像大鹏一样，敢于摆脱外物的役使和累赘，身随心动，打破窠臼，才能获得精神无羁和意志自由。

庄子在文学创作技巧上既延续了先秦散文严谨细密，富于逻辑，鞭辟入里，大气磅礴的论说风格，同时又独创了寓理入微，寓情于物的"寓言体"风格，可谓"亦庄亦谐"，于幽默中抛出箴言，于诙谐中掷出冷峻思索，于细微处昭示天地道理。他宛如一位独具慧眼高瞻远瞩的智者，将战国时代纷纷攘攘、战乱频仍的社会中的种种丑恶现象，借用浅显易懂，形象生动，而又极富哲理的故事娓娓道来。听众倾耳细听，初始懵懂混沌，而后恍然大悟。这种独特的创作技巧可谓开中国文学史上寓言散文之先河。

在语言方面，"赋体诗"一般的语言，在庄子手里运作熟稔，如"小知不及大知，小年不及大年""朝菌不知晦朔，蟪蛄不知春秋""知效一官，行比一乡，德合一君"，韵律整饬铿锵，语势从弱至强，真真如大鱼顺水游弋，轻划鳍尾，便如净水湖心起涟漪，令人读来如痴如醉，如沐春风，用钟嵘的"初发芙蓉，错彩镂金"来形容再合适不过。

在修辞方面，暗喻、拟人、类比、夸张等手法比比皆是。庄子真不愧是文学大师，他拿捏文字的力度和巧劲令人叹服。《逍遥游》即是其诸种写作技巧驾轻就熟，融通圆润的精彩呈现。"鲲""鹏""蜩（知了）""学鸠（斑鸠）""斥鷃（小雀）"等虫鸟均被赋予了"人"的属性，前两者喻指心怀远大目标高瞻的一类人，而后两者则喻指见识浅陋故步自封的一类人，两类人群的形象反差，在庄子笔下，仅以寥寥数语便跃然纸上。之后，"水"与"舟"，"适百里"与"千里者"，是比喻和象征手法的联合运用，将该篇的主旨推向了高潮：要实现真正的"逍遥游"，只有抛弃一切束缚个性，桎梏思想的外在之物，方有可能。

而《逍遥游》为何会被编排在全书之首，这个问题也许无人可以给出最为精当的答案。但从全书的宏观主旨立意来判断，"逍遥"这一主题正是庄子最为核心的哲学思想之一："今子有大树，患其无用，何不树之于无何有之乡，广莫之野，彷徨乎无为其侧，逍遥乎寝卧其下。不夭斤斧，物无害者，无所可用，安所困苦哉！""无所用"而"逍遥乎"是庄子反复倡导的处世态度，以实现其"天地与我并生，万物与我同一"这种物我两忘的"大道"之境。其中，大鲲、鹏、野马、尘埃、冥灵、大椿、许由、姑射神人等物或仙人，都是庄子"逍遥无羁"的内在意识和精神的外化和延伸。而蜩（知了）、学鸠（斑鸠）、斥鷃（小雀）、狸（野猫）、狌（黄鼠狼）之辈皆为被外物和自我紧紧束缚的世俗之物，是庄子意欲人们彻底摆脱的

第二章 《庄子》经典篇章英译选读

"非逍遥"状态的具象化和实体化。

有研究者评论《逍遥游》说:"本篇的题旨虽在于宣扬庄子的哲学思想,但它所体现的艺术成就却是高超的,它想象丰富奇特,构思巧妙宏大。所描之场景,所叙之寓言,都有极强的感染力。它的语言细致而生动,雄壮中有幽默,深邃里见形象。"的确一语中的。

Free and Easy Wandering (Excerpt)

In the Northern Darkness there is a fish and his name is K'un. The K'un is so huge I don't know how many thousand li he measures. He changes and becomes a bird whose name is P'eng. The back of the P'eng measures I don't know how many thousand li across and, when he rises up and flies off, his wings are like clouds all over the sky. When the sea begins to move, this bird sets off for the southern darkness, which is the Lake of Heaven.

The *Universal Harmony* records various wonders, and it says: "When the P'eng journeys to the southern darkness, the waters are roiled for three thousand li. He beats the whirlwind and rises ninety thousand li, setting off on the sixth month gale." Wavering heat, bits of dust, living things blown about by the wind—the sky looks very blue. Is that its real color, or is it because it is so far away and has no end? When the bird looks down, all he sees is blue too.

If water is not piled up deep enough, it won't have the strength to bear up a big boat. Pour a cup of water into a hollow in the floor and bits of trash will sail on it like boats. But set the cup there and it will stick fast, for the water is too shallow and the boat too large. If wind is not piled up deep enough, it won't have the strength to bear up great wings. Therefore when the P'eng rises ninety thousand li, he must have the wind under him like that. Only then can he mount on the back of the wind, shoulder the blue sky, and nothing can hinder or block him. Only then can he set his eyes to the south. The cicada and the little dove laugh at this, saying, "When we make an effort and fly up, we can get as far as the elm or the sapanwood tree, but sometimes we don't make it and just fall down on the ground. Now how is anyone going to go ninety thousand li to the south!" If you go off to the green woods nearby, you can take along food for three meals and come back with your stomach as full as ever. If you are going a hundred li, you must grind your grain the night before; and if you are going a thousand li, you must start getting the provisions together three months in advance. What do these two creatures understand?

Little understanding cannot come up to great understanding; the short-lived cannot come up to the long-lived. How do I know this is so? The morning mushroom knows nothing of twilight and dawn; the summer cicada knows nothing of spring and autumn. They are the short-lived. South of Ch'u there is a caterpillar which counts five hundred years as one spring and five hundred years as one autumn. Long, long ago there was a great rose of Sharon that counted eight thousand years as one spring and eight thousand years as one autumn. They are the long-lived. Yet P'eng-tsu alone is famous today for having lived a long time, and everybody tries to ape him. Isn't it pitiful!

Among the questions of T'ang to Ch'i we find the same thing. In the bald and barren north, there is a dark sea, the Lake of Heaven. In it is a fish which is several thousand li across, and no one knows how long. His name is K'un. There is also a bird there, named P'eng, with a back like Mount T'ai and wings like clouds filling the sky. He beats the whirlwind, leaps into the air, and rises up ninety thousand li, cutting through the clouds and mist, shouldering the blue sky, and then he turns his eyes south and prepares to journey to the southern darkness. The little quail laughs at him, saying, "Where does he think *he's* going? I give a great leap and fly up, but I never get more than ten or twelve yards before I come down fluttering among the weeds and brambles. And that's the best kind of flying anyway! Where does he think *he's* going?" Such is the difference between big and little.

Therefore a man who has wisdom enough to fill one office effectively, good conduct enough to impress one community, virtue enough to please one ruler, or talent enough to be called into service in one state, has the same kind of self-pride as these little creatures. Sung Jung-tzu would certainly burst out laughing at such a man. The whole world could praise Sung Jung-

第二章 《庄子》经典篇章英译选读

tzu and it wouldn't make him exert himself; the whole world could condemn him and it wouldn't make him mope. He drew a clear line between the internal and the external, and recognized the boundaries of true glory and disgrace. But that was all. As far as the world went, he didn't fret and worry, but there was still ground he left unturned. Lieh Tzu could ride the wind and go soaring around with cool and breezy skill, but after fifteen days he came back to earth. As far as the search for good fortune went, he didn't fret and worry. He escaped the trouble of walking, but he still had to depend on something to get around. If he had only mounted on the truth of Heaven and Earth, ridden the changes of the six breaths, and thus wandered through the boundless, then what would he have had to depend on?

Therefore I say, the Perfect Man has no self; the Holy Man has no merit; the Sage has no fame.

——Burton Watson（伯顿·华兹生）

英译鉴赏简评

汪榕培教授评价华兹生译本"是《庄子》英译本中的佼佼者。"能被称为佼佼者的作品，一定有其他作品所不能及之处，如何界定华兹生《庄子》英译本的佼佼不群之处，也是鉴赏品评的关键所在。

在词语运用上，华兹生的译本用词比较简洁通透、平实易懂，消解或降低了艰涩生硬的哲学化或文学化的术语表达给读者带来的困惑和不解，但又能紧扣原文主旨，准确把握庄子哲学语言含而不露的隐喻效果。如首句之"北冥有鱼，其名为鲲"，"冥"本意为昏暗不明，或指人去世后所去的阴曹地府；引申为深邃幽远，或广漠貌。清人郭庆藩《庄子集释》"逍遥游第一"引唐代成玄英《庄子注疏》："溟，犹海也，取其溟漠无涯，故谓之溟。"又引唐人陆德明《释文》解："北冥，本亦作溟……北海也。"今人陈鼓应《庄子今注今译》："北冥，冥，通溟，训海。"诸位学者均释"冥"为"溟"之通假字，且取意为"海"，此种解读曾引起其他研究者的质疑。"冥"又见于《庄子·在宥》篇："至道之精，窈冥冥。"此处注："冥，了无也。"近于"冥"之本义。

华兹生若沿袭诸位学人对"冥"的释义，"北冥"译为"the northern sea/ocean"似乎更为合适，但他却译为"the northern darkness"，其中"darkness"一词的语义不止于"黑暗无光（absence of light or illumination）"，还有"幽远、深邃、未知"之意。诸种词义均远离"北海"之意，但从内涵上却更加贴近庄子向外界传达的思想：深远旷达之域，既包含了广袤的大海，同时也能容纳天地四宇、无极八荒之地，这正是"鲲"即将展翅翱翔一飞而去的无限之境，也是"逍遥"能够抵达的最远处。所以，"darkness"一词立刻为本篇立下了更加宏观高远的抽象空间，而非实体化的"北海"，从一开始，便将读者带入了文字表象背后的深层哲学语境，它的力量力度非"northern sea/ocean"所能比。

再如，"《齐谐》者，志怪者也"，训诂学释"齐谐"为"先秦时期记载逸事传闻的一部志怪神话书"，故此，音译法往往被用于书名的翻译，译为"*Qi Xie*（或 *The Book of Qixie*）"，但这种译法，实际犹如隔靴搔痒，译又似未译。相较之下，华兹生所采用的意译法"*The Universal Harmony (Records Various Wonders)*"，从语义转换层面，与本篇的主旨高度契合，可谓直达核心；同时，又丝毫不减《齐谐》这本书的志怪属性。

另如，"野马也，尘埃也，生物之以息相吹也"一句，古代汉语文本在传抄传播的过程中，也许带有一定的不稳定性，野马，郭象注："野马者，游气也。"成玄英疏："此言青春之时，阳气发动，遥望薮泽之中，犹如奔马，故谓之野马也。"陆宗达《训诂简论》曰："塺（尘）字假借。"此段文字解释了"野马"一词的语义模糊性，因此，译者如何取舍此类语词，也是考验其翻译水平的一个重要因素。华兹生将此句译为"Wavering heat, bits of dust, living things blowing each other about"，可见其驾驭文字的技巧和机智之妙，完全略去汉语原文意象词"野马"的具象化，而采用模糊化处理"wavering heat（飞旋上升的热势）"。这种译法显然要比直译为"wild horses"更有利于消减源语文本的隔膜或不确定性，将原文大鹏"扶摇而上九万里"的升腾气势成功传达给西方读者。

对于"蜩""学鸠""朝菌""蟪蛄""冥灵""斥鴳"等独特而生僻的汉语文化负载词的处理非常灵活，分别译为读者熟知的 cicada, the little dove, morning mushroom, the summer cicada, caterpillar, little quail，比较成功地保留了原文用词中所蕴含的语内对比义和文化寓意。

在句式方面，庄子好用骈文句式，而华兹生对此深谙于心，尽力采用排比结构以保留原文的句式特点，比如"Only then can he mount on the back of the wind. Only then can he set his eyes to the south.""The morning mushroom knows nothing of twilight and dawn; the summer cicada knows nothing of spring and autumn.""the Perfect Man has no self; the Holy Man has no merit; the Sage has no fame"。

第二章 《庄子》经典篇章英译选读

总体而言,华兹生《庄子》英译本,从形音义三个维度再现了庄子"汪洋恣肆,吊诡奇崛"的语言魅力。

《庄子》经典篇章英译选读之二

内篇·养生主(节选)

吾生也有涯,而知也无涯①。以有涯随无涯,殆②已;已而为知者,殆而已矣。为善无近名③,为恶无近刑④。缘督以为经⑤,可以保身,可以全生,可以养亲⑥,可以尽年⑦。

庖丁为文惠君⑧解牛,手之所触,肩之所倚⑨,足之所履⑩,膝之所踦⑪,砉然响然⑫,奏刀騞然⑬,莫不中音⑭;合于《桑林》之舞,乃中《经首》之会⑮。文惠君曰:"嘻⑯,善哉!技盖⑰至此乎?"

庖丁释刀对曰:"臣之所好者道也,进乎技矣。始臣之解牛之时,所见无非全牛者。三年之后,未尝见全牛也。方今之时,臣以神遇⑱而不以目视,官⑲知止而神欲行。依乎天理,批大郤⑳,导大窾㉑,因其固然。技经肯綮㉒之未尝微碍㉓,而况大軱㉔乎!良庖岁更刀,割也;族庖㉕月更刀,折也。今臣之刀十九年矣,所解数千牛矣,而刀刃若新发于硎㉖。彼节者有间,而刀刃者无厚;以无厚入有间,恢恢㉗乎其于游刃必有余地矣。是以十九年而刀刃若新发于硎。虽然,每至于族㉘,吾见其难为,怵然为戒㉙,视为止,行为迟。动刀甚微,謋然已解㉚,牛不知其死,如土委地㉛。提刀而立,为之四顾,为之踌躇满志㉜,善刀而藏之㉝。"

文惠君曰:"善哉!吾闻庖丁之言,得养生焉。"

【注释】

①〔吾生也有涯,而知也无涯〕人的生命是有限的,但知识是无限的。〔涯(yá)〕

中华典籍英译选读

水边,泛指边际,范围,限度。
② 〔殆(dài)〕危险,困境,困顿。
③ 〔为善无近名〕做善事不求名利。
④ 〔为恶无近刑〕做坏事免受刑戮之苦。
⑤ 〔缘督以为经〕自然之道。〔缘〕因循,顺应。〔督〕人体经络中的督脉,主气。与主血的任脉并称为人体经脉的两大主脉,任督二脉若通,则八脉通;八脉通,则百脉通;百脉通,则身强体健。
⑥ 〔养亲〕休养精神。
⑦ 〔尽年〕颐养天年。
⑧ 〔文惠君〕人名,不知何许人。旧注为战国时期魏国第任国君魏惠王,因魏国国都从安邑(今山西省夏县西北)迁都大梁(今河南省开封市),此后魏亦称为梁,魏惠王又称梁惠王。
⑨ 〔肩之所倚〕肩膀所倚靠的地方。
⑩ 〔履(lǚ)〕名词意为"鞋子";动词意为"踩,踏"。
⑪ 〔踦(qī)〕脚跛,行走不便;读"yǐ",意为"用膝顶住"。
⑫ 〔砉然响然〕发出哗哗的声响。〔砉(huā)〕形容迅速动作的声音。
⑬ 〔奏刀騞然〕执刀快速解牛发出哗啦声。〔騞(huō)〕用刀解剖东西的声音。
⑭ 〔莫不中音〕没有不合乎音律的。〔中(zhòng)〕合于,符合。
⑮ 〔《桑林》〕古乐曲名,传为殷天子之乐,为殷汤祈雨时所奏之乐。〔《经首》〕传说中尧时的乐曲名。
⑯ 〔嘻(xī)〕表示悲叹或惊叹的语气。
⑰ 〔盍(hé)〕通"何",为何,怎样。
⑱ 〔神遇〕心领神会。
⑲ 〔官〕人的感官。
⑳ 〔却〕通"隙",空隙,裂缝,此指筋骨间隙。
㉑ 〔窾(kuǎn)〕空隙,空洞,此指骨头之间的空隙。
㉒ 〔技经肯綮〕经络相连、筋骨相接处。〔技〕据清人俞樾考证,当是"枝"字之误,指支(枝)脉。〔经〕经脉。〔肯〕骨头上附着的肉。〔綮(qìng)〕筋骨连接处。
㉓ 〔微碍〕小障碍。
㉔ 〔大軱(gū)〕大骨。
㉕ 〔族庖〕族,众多。众庖,指一般的厨师。
㉖ 〔硎(xíng)〕磨刀石。
㉗ 〔恢恢〕宽绰广大貌。

第二章 《庄子》经典篇章英译选读

㉘〔每至于族〕每次遇到筋骨交错处。〔族（zú）〕筋骨交错聚结的地方。
㉙〔怵然为戒〕因担心（筋骨交错不好处理）而变得小心谨慎。〔怵（chù）〕恐惧，害怕。〔戒〕小心警惕。
㉚〔謋然已解〕牛的身体哗啦一下就分解开了。〔謋（huò）〕迅速分裂的声音，骨肉分离的声音。
㉛〔如土委地〕此指牛的身体解剖后像土一样散落一地。〔委〕古书常用字，堆放，存放。
㉜〔踌躇满志〕得意满足貌。
㉝〔善刀而藏之〕擦拭干净牛刀收拾好。〔善〕通"缮"，收拾，修治。

白话释义

人的生命是有限的，而知识是无限的。用有限的生命去追求无限的知识，就会陷入困顿疲惫中；既然如此，如果还要不懈地去追求知识，就更加疲累了。做善事不求名利，做坏事不要触犯刑法。一切顺应自然法则，可以养护身体，保全生命，休养精神，颐养年寿。

庖丁为文惠王杀牛，凡手所触及、肩膀所倚、脚所踩踏之处，皆发出哗啦哗啦的声响，下刀时发出呼啦哗啦的声音，简直与音乐别无二致。与《桑林》的节奏、《经首》的音律完全合拍。文惠王惊叹道："咿，真不错！技法怎能如此娴熟？"

庖丁放下牛刀说："大王，臣下追求的是道，非技法所能及。开始解剖牛的时候，眼里看到的是整个一头牛。三年之后，看到的不再是一头全牛了。现如今，臣下完全靠心领神会，而不用看整头牛，感官不再起作用，只靠心神感应。循着牛的自然纹路，劈开筋骨交错之处，顺入骨节间的空隙，依照牛身体的原本理路。经络交错筋骨相连的地方都不成问题，更不用说大骨结了！好的厨师每年更换一次牛刀，因为用牛刀切割牛肉；一般的厨师每个月都要换一把牛刀，因为用牛刀砍剁牛骨。我的牛刀已用了十九年了，宰杀过千头牛了，但刀刃仍然像刚刚用磨刀石磨过的一样锋利。牛骨之间是有间隙的，而这把刀却薄如发丝，插入牛骨间隙，绰绰有余，易如反掌。因此，这把牛刀用了十九年还锃亮如新。即便如此，但凡碰到骨节交错的地方，我知道不好操作，便会分外注意，眼神专注，动作谨慎。虽然轻轻下刀，牛的身体瞬间剖解开来，牛却感觉不到丝毫痛苦，牛体便像散土洒落一地。之后，我收起刀站起来，环顾四周，心满意足，擦干净牛刀收拾好。"

文惠王听罢说道："厉害啊,听你这么一说,我完全明白了养生之道!"

主题鉴赏

《养生主》在"内篇"7篇中篇幅最短,但信息量并未缩减,反而表现出庄子关于人生更为高远的精神启悟。

晋代郭象注《南华经(16卷)》"南华经总评"引凌季默言:"六经而下,近古而闳丽者,左丘明、庄周、司马迁、班固四巨公,具有成书,其文卓卓乎,擅大家也。《左传》如杨妃舞盘,回旋摇曳,光彩射人;《庄子》如神仙下世,咳吐谑浪,皆成丹砂;子长之文豪,如老将用兵,纵骋不可羁,而自中于律;孟坚之文整,方之武事,其游奇布列不爽尺寸,而部勒雍容可观,殆有儒将之风焉。"

《养生主》篇,即有"神仙下世,咳吐谑浪,皆成丹砂"之妙意。该篇第一节开首句:"吾生也有涯,而知也无涯",言简而意丰,有"丹砂"之效用,真可谓"如露入心,似醍醐灌顶",令读者不由得陷入对人生意义的思考之中。第二节以"庖丁解牛"为喻题,为众生指明一条处理人与自然万物如何相处的至理箴言,以及"养生"之精髓:只有遵循天理,了解事物的本然原理(缘督以为经),方能彻底通悟事物之本质,做到"游刃有余""善刀而藏",不拘役于物,实现"可以保身,可以全生,可以养亲,可以尽年"的"养生"目标。第三节相当于本篇的附言部分。庄子以"十步一啄,百步一饮"自由在野的泽雉为例,进一步升华本篇主题。"不畜乎樊中"的泽雉,虽苦却自由逍遥的生活状态,与"神虽王,不善也"这种拘于藩篱,虽然物质富足而精神拘囿的困境构成了鲜明的对比。只有前者才是人生至求之境;也是对第一篇《逍遥游》的进一步阐发。最后一节以秦失(音"佚")吊唁老聃为例,表明了庄子宽达豁然的"死亡观",即"适来,夫子时也;适去,夫子顺也(该来的时候,老聃应时而生;该离开的时候,老聃应时而死。)"即傅佩荣先生所指出的"培养自己具备透视整体的眼光,再以安时而处顺的心态去面对挑战,就可以安其天年。"本节最后一句"指(通"脂",指油脂)穷于为薪,火传也,不知其尽也",有锦上添花、画龙点睛之用。原本以为庄子的自由逍遥与安时处顺让人难免对人生有些懈怠,但读完这一句,方才明白他老人家的良苦用心:人生苦短,生死有命,但这并不意味着可以"躺平",不去努力追求生命的真谛。相反,众生在遵循天理的前提下,在豁达于自然赋予的生命个体的前提下,更要努力发掘短暂生命中的"光(火)",并让个体生命之火可以续传给他人,为世界之光,为自由之光。

第二章 《庄子》经典篇章英译选读

The Secret of Caring for Life (Excerpt)

Your life has a limit but knowledge has none. If you use what is limited to pursue what has no limit, you will be in danger. If you understand this and still strive for knowledge, you will be in danger for certain! If you do good, stay away from fame. If you do evil, stay away from punishments. Follow the middle; go by what is constant, and you can stay in one piece, keep yourself alive, look after your parents, and live out your years.

Cook Ting was cutting up an ox for Lord Wen-hui. At every touch of his hand, every heave of his shoulder, every move of his feet, every thrust of his knee—zip! zoop! He slithered the knife along with a zing, and all was in perfect rhythm, as though he were performing the dance of the Mulberry Grove or keeping time to the Ching-shou music. "Ah, this is marvelous!" said Lord Wen-hui. "Imagine skill reaching such heights!"

Cook Ting laid down his knife and replied, "What I care about is the Way, which goes beyond skill. When I first began cutting up oxen, all I could see was the ox itself. After three years I no longer saw the whole ox. And now—now I go at it by spirit and don't look with my eyes. Perception and understanding have come to a stop and spirit moves where it wants. I go along with the natural makeup, strike in the big hollows, guide the knife through the big openings, and follow things as they are. So I never touch the smallest ligament or tendon, much less a main joint."

"A good cook changes his knife once a year, because he cuts. A mediocre cook changes his knife once a month, because he hacks. I've had this knife of mine for nineteen years and I've cut up thousands of oxen with it, and yet the blade is as good as though it had just come from the grindstone. There are spaces between the joints, and the blade of the knife has really no thickness. If you insert what has no thickness into such spaces, then there's plenty of room—more than enough for the blade to play about it. That's why after nineteen years the blade of my knife is still as good as when it first came from the grindstone.

"However, whenever I come to a complicated place, I size up the difficulties, tell myself to watch out and be careful, keep my eyes on what I'm doing, work very slowly, and move the knife with the greatest subtlety, until—flop! the whole thing comes apart like a clod of earth crumbling to the ground. I stand there holding the knife and look all around me, completely satisfied and reluctant to move on, and then I wipe off the knife and put it away."

"Excellent!" said Lord Wen-hui. "I have heard the words of Cook Ting and learned how to care for life!"

——Burton Watson（伯顿·华兹生）

英译鉴赏简评

《养生主》为《内篇》第三篇，题名意为"养生之道"，主，即"道"之意。本篇核心要旨在于强调养生之道要"缘督以为经"，意即只有顺乎自然，方能颐养天年。首段以"生而有涯"引题："吾生也有涯，而知也无涯"，表明以有限的生命去追寻无限之物会劳逸身体，殚竭心力，就无法"保身，全生，养亲，尽年"这一鲜明的道家立场。在庄子看来，刻意追求外物，无论是名或利，都是违背"天道"，远离"自然"的做法，因此，为进一步阐明这一主题，庄子巧妙地引入"庖丁解牛"的典故。表面看来，这个故事与本篇主旨似乎关联不大，但典故所反映的核心思想不在庖丁如何解牛，而在于庖丁技法中所蕴含的"遵循天理，施法自然"的道理，"天理"即事物本身的运行规律，"自然"即顺遂事物的发展状态，只有如此做法，方能恬淡怡然，游刃有余，领悟人生真谛之所在。

本节文字最难翻译的部分是对庖丁解牛具体动作的细节性描述。动词如"手之所触，肩之所倚，足之所履，膝之所踦""批大郤""导大窾""割""折"等，以及大量的拟声词如"砉然响然，奏刀騞然""恢恢""謋然"等的连续使用，为读者呈现出一幅庖丁解牛的逼真画面。此类汉语动词和拟声词，语意相近，声效铿锵，一方面表现出庖丁动作的连贯和娴熟，给人一种动态画面的既视感；拟声词穿插于动词之中，又给人以声效感，这些关键文字对于呈现庖丁解牛这一画面非常关键，但也成为翻译的难点，因此，英译本选词的准确性和生动性尤其必要。华兹生先生对于汉语语意和声效的处理可谓游刃有余，他采用词性转化

第二章 《庄子》经典篇章英译选读

法,将原本可能需要采用复杂句式的汉语语句及比较棘手的动词简化为以下几组并置短语:"At every **touch** of his hand, every **heave** of his shoulder, every **move** of his feet, every **thrust** of his knee; **strike** in the big hollows, **guide** the knife through the big openings;"音形意三者皆备,短语化的表达和单音节词语的选用极富语言技巧,读来声音急促,停顿短暂,成功再现庖丁动作的顺畅无阻和娴熟。"zip!""zoop!""zing""flop!",短小同韵拟声词完全吻合汉语同声母拟声词的和谐音效:"砉(huā)然响然,奏刀騞(huō)然""恢恢(huī)""謋(huò)然"。以此两例,或可知华兹生先生英译本选词造句的精妙之处。

《庄子》经典篇章英译选读之三

外篇·秋水(节选)

秋水时至,百川灌河;泾流①之大,两涘渚崖②之间不辨牛马③。于是焉河伯④欣然自喜,以天下之美为尽在己。顺流而东行,至于北海,东面而视,不见水端⑤,于是焉河伯始旋其面目⑥,望洋向若⑦而叹曰:"野语⑧有之曰,'闻道百,以为莫己若者',我之谓也⑨。且夫我尝闻少仲尼之闻⑩而轻伯夷之义⑪者,始吾弗信⑫;今我睹子之难穷也,吾非至于子之门,则殆矣,吾长见笑于大方之家。"

北海若曰:"井蛙不可以语于海者,拘于虚⑬也;夏虫不可以语于冰者,笃于时⑭也;曲士⑮不可以语于道者,束于教⑯也。今尔出于崖涘⑰,观于大海,乃知尔丑⑱,尔将可与语大理矣。天下之水,莫大于海,万川归之,不知何时止而不盈;尾闾⑲泄之,不知何时已而不虚;春秋不变,水旱不知。此其过江河之流,不可为量数。而吾未尝以此自多者,自以比形于天地⑳而受气于阴阳㉑,吾在天地之间,犹小石小木之在大山也,方存乎见少㉒,又奚以自多㉓!计四海之在天地之间也,不似礨空㉔之在大泽乎?计中国之在海内,不似稊米㉕之在大仓乎?号物之数谓之万㉖,人处一焉;人卒九州㉗,谷食之所生㉘,舟车之所通,人处一焉;此其比万物也,不似豪末之在于马体㉙乎?五帝之所连⑩,三王之所争㉛,仁人之所忧,任士之所劳,尽此矣! 伯夷辞之以为名,仲尼语之以为博,此其自多也,不似尔向之自多于水乎㉜?"

河伯曰:"然则吾大天地而小豪末㉝,可乎?"

北海若曰"否,夫物,量无穷,时无止,分无常㉞,终始无故。是故大知观于远近㉟,故小而不寡,大而不多㊱,知量无穷㊲;证向今故㊳,故遥而不闷㊴,掇而不跂㊵,知时无止;察乎盈虚,故得而不喜,失而不忧,知分之无常也;明乎坦涂㊶,故生而不说,死而不祸㊷,知终始之不可故㊸也。计人之所知,不若其所不知;其生之时,不若未生之时;以其至小求穷其至大之域㊹,是故迷乱而不能自得也。由此观之,又何以知毫末之足以定至细之倪㊺! 又何以知天地之足以穷至大之域!"

【注释】

① 〔泾(jīng)流〕直流的水波,此指水流。〔泾〕通"径"。
② 〔涘(sì)〕《说文》:涘,水厓也。〔渚(zhǔ)〕水中小块陆地。〔两涘渚崖〕河水的两岸到河洲的高岸之间。
③ 〔牛马〕暗喻手法,形容物体形体庞大,此指水流的洪大之势。〔不辨牛马〕河水奔流,浩浩荡荡,河岸与河中小洲因而不辨其形。
④ 〔河伯〕古代神话传说中的水神。河伯姓冯,名夷,一名冰夷,一名冯迟,传为华阴潼阳人,因渡河溺亡,天帝封其为黄河水神。
⑤ 〔端〕事物的一头。〔不见水端〕河水一望无际,看不到尽头。
⑥ 〔旋(xuán)〕改变,回转。〔旋其面目〕(河伯)改变先前的自矜态度。另解为(河伯)扭头向四周看了看(或为正解)。
⑦ 〔若〕海神名。〔望洋向若〕望着大海里的若神,喻指向高明者折服,自叹弗如。
⑧ 〔野语〕民间传闻或私人杜撰的俚俗之语。
⑨ 〔我之谓也〕倒装句,即"谓之我也",说的就是我。
⑩ 〔仲尼〕孔子名丘,字仲尼。古人称呼他人时,不直呼其名,而使用对方的字,以示尊重。〔少仲尼之闻〕孔子的见识短浅,知道得太少。
⑪ 〔轻伯夷之义〕此指伯夷忠于故国的义气受人轻视。〔伯夷〕商朝末年孤竹国君的儿子。《史记·伯夷列传》:"武王已平殷乱,天下宗周,而伯夷、叔齐耻之,义不食周粟,隐于首阳山,采薇而食之。"周武王灭商,伯夷与其弟叔齐拒

第二章 《庄子》经典篇章英译选读

食周粟,一同饿死在首阳山(今山西省永济市南)。后人称颂他们忠于故国之志。

⑫〔弗信〕不信。〔弗〕"不"的同源字。

⑬〔拘〕局限,限制。〔虚〕古语指"住所"。〔拘于虚〕受到生活环境的局限。

⑭〔笃〕同"拘",局限,限制。〔笃于时〕受限于时令季节。

⑮〔曲(qū)〕远离城市穷乡僻壤的地方。〔曲士〕乡曲之士,比喻孤陋寡闻的人。

⑯〔教〕教养见识。〔束于教〕受到教养见识的束缚。

⑰〔出于崖涘〕指河神从河岸走出。

⑱〔丑〕陋劣,鄙陋。〔乃知尔丑〕才知道自己见识浅陋。

⑲〔尾闾〕闾(lú),汇聚。古代传说中海水所归之处,今指江河的下游。《文选·嵇康〈养生论〉》注引司马彪云:"尾闾,水之从海水出者也,一名沃燋(wò jiāo,一作沃焦,古代传说中东海南部的大石山)。尾者,在百川之下故称尾;闾者,聚也,水聚族之处,故称闾也。在扶桑之东,有一石方圆四万里,厚四万里,海水注者无不燋尽,故名沃燋。"

⑳〔比形于天地〕从天地那里接受了形体。〔比〕接受,受到。

㉑〔受气于阴阳〕从阴阳中获得元气。

㉒〔方存乎见少〕正存在着自以为小的想法,才觉得自己很渺小。〔方〕才,只。〔存〕存想,持有某种念头。〔见(xiàn)〕出现,显露。

㉓〔奚以自多〕意为哪里会自满呢,怎么会觉得自己知道得多呢。〔奚〕怎么。〔自多〕自诩,自满。

㉔〔礨(lěi)〕古同"礧",小穴。一说,小洞或小土堆。陆德明《释文》:"空音孔。礨孔,……一云蚁冢也。"另解:"礨"应是"畾(léi)"之假借字,为田间之地,用以与"大泽"相对比。

㉕〔稊米〕喻指微小之物。〔稊(tí)〕稗子一类的草,果实像糜子。

㉖〔号物之数谓之万〕号称事物的数量成千上万。〔号〕号称,宣称。〔谓〕可谓,可以说。

㉗〔人卒九州〕人们汇聚于九州各地。〔卒〕意同"萃",聚集,萃集。

㉘〔谷食之所生〕粮食生长的地方。〔谷食〕供食用的谷物,即粮食。

㉙〔豪末之在于马体〕就好比马身体上的毫毛。〔豪〕通"毫"。〔豪末〕毫毛的末端,喻微细之物。

㉚〔五帝之所连〕五帝(黄帝、颛顼、帝喾、尧、舜)所接续的功业。

㉛〔三王之所争〕三王(一说为夏禹、商汤、周文王;一说为夏启、商汤、周武王)为争夺天下而发动的战争。

㉜〔不似尔向之自多于水乎〕难道不像你刚才在河水暴涨时的洋洋得意吗？〔尔〕你。〔向〕先前，原来，从前。

㉝〔大天地而小豪末〕以天地为最大，以毫毛为最小。

㉞〔分无常〕此指人生的得失没有常规。〔分(fèn)〕构成事物的不同的物质或因素。

㉟〔大知观于远近〕有大智慧的人能够看到事物大的方面和小的方面，意为观察细致入微。〔知(zhì)〕同"智"。

㊱〔小而不寡，大而不多〕小的事物近观并不小，大的事物远观并不大。

㊲〔知量无穷〕明白事物的量无穷无尽。

㊳〔证向今故〕求证于过去和现在的事物。〔证〕求证，验证。〔向〕于，朝向。〔今故(jīn gù)〕犹今古，现在和过去。

㊴〔遥而不闷〕对遥远的事物不觉得困惑。〔闷〕纳闷，困惑。

㊵〔掇而不跂〕就近拾取，不必踮起脚后跟期盼远方的。〔掇(duō)〕拾取。〔跂(qǐ)〕古通"企"，踮起脚后跟站着。

㊶〔明乎坦涂〕明白人生有顺境，也有逆境。〔坦涂〕亦作"坦途"，平坦的道路。另解：坦，康庄大道。〔涂〕浸湿，渐洳之径，指积水的小路。《汉书·东方朔传》："涂者，渐洳径也。"颜师古注："渐洳，浸湿也。"

㊷〔生而不说，死而不祸〕生于人世间不觉得是喜悦，离开这个世界也不觉得是悲伤。〔说(yuè)〕通"悦"，快乐，喜悦。〔祸〕悲伤。

㊸〔知终始之不可故〕知道开始与终了并非一成不变。〔故〕通"固"，一成不变，固定。

㊹〔以其至小求穷其至大之域〕用人生极为有限的智慧去探求无穷无尽的境域（宇宙天地）。

㊺〔知毫末之足以定至细之倪〕知道毫毛之末就可以确定事物最为细微的限度。〔倪(ní)〕事物的本末始终，边界，尽头。〔至细〕最为细微。

白话释义

秋雨按照时令，期然而至，千百条河水，汇入黄河之中，河面平阔无涯，洪波汹涌，河岸与河洲，难辨其形。于是河神心旷神怡，自认为天下尽美之物皆归于自己。河神顺河往东而行，到达北海边上，向东遥望，大海一片苍茫，看不到边际，于是河神扭头四顾，面对海神"若"慨叹道："俗话说'听了那么多道理，就觉得再没有人能比得过我'，这就是在说我这样的人啊。而且，我曾听人说孔子的

第二章 《庄子》经典篇章英译选读

见识浅陋、伯夷忠于故国的义气不值等等说法,开始我并不相信;直到我看到您的浩瀚无际,如果不是亲眼所见,还真是会陷入危机。我将会成为明白事理的人终生嗤笑的对象了。"

海神"若"答道:"不要与井里的青蛙谈论大海,因为它们受限于生存环境;不要与夏天的虫子谈论冬天的冰雪,因为它们受限于生活时节;不要与孤陋寡闻的人谈论大道理,因为它们受限于教养与见识。现在你离开了河岸,看到了大海,才发现自己多么孤陋寡闻,这样才能够和你谈谈大道理了。天下的河流,没有比大海更大的,千百河流,汇入大海,永无止息,但大海却从不流溢;海水从尾闾泄出,无止无息,大海却从不见减少;一年四季,水灾旱涝,永远如此。大海的数量远远超过江河,无法用数量具体计算。但我却从不因此而自矜,我知道天地赋予我形体,阴阳给予我元气,我生存于天地之间,就好比小石子、小树枝存在于大山之上,怎么能有自夸自大的念头呢?试想一下,四海与天地相比,就好似蚁穴存在于广袤的海泽之中,怎么能自满呢?想想中国存在于四海之内,就好比一颗米粒存在于粮仓之中。世间事物千千万,人不过是其中一员而已;九州大地,人群汇集,粮食生长于此,舟车往来于此,个体不过是众人之中的一员而已;人与万物比较,不过像是马身上的一根汗毛。五帝创立帝业,三王争夺天下,仁者顾虑挂念,贤者操劳辛苦,不过如此而已。伯夷不食周粟以赢得名声,孔子诲人不倦以证明博学,此两者自夸自耀,正如你在河水暴涨时的自矜自满!"

河神回答说:"那么,我把天地看作最大,把毫毛视为最小,这样可以吗?"

北海神若说:"不可以,世间万物,数量无穷,时间不止,得失无定,事物的始与终不循常规。因此,有大智慧者观察事物细致入微,小的事物不代表少,大的事物不意味着多,他们明白事物的量无穷无尽;求证于古今之事,不困惑于过往,不苛求于近前,因为懂得时间无止无息;能体察事物的盈与亏,得之不喜,失之不悲,明白世间得失并无定数;明白人生有坦途有坎坷,因此生在人世间不会觉得是一件万幸之事,离开这个世界也不会觉得悲恸难抑,因为懂得开始与终了并无固定的规律。试想一下,人生所知道的怎比得上所不知道的;生活在世上的时间远比不上不在世间的时间;因此,用有限的认知和智力去探索无限无极的世界,岂不是自找烦恼一无所获吗?由此,又怎能理解用毫毛之微便可以定夺最细微之境的道理呢?怎能明白天地之宽乃最大的境域这样的道理呢?"

河伯说:"那么我把天地看作是最大,把毫末之末看作是最小,可以吗?"

海神回答:"不可以。万物的量是无穷无尽的,时间是没有终点的,得与失的禀分没有不变的常规,事物的终结和起始也并不固定。所以具有大智的人观察事物从不局限于一隅,因而体积小却不看作就是少,体积大却不看作就是多,这是因为知道事物的量是不可穷尽的;证验并明察古往今来的各种情况,因而寿命久远却不感到厌倦,生命只在近前却不会企求寿延,这是因为知道时间的推移是没有止境的;洞悉事物有盈有虚的规律,因而有所得却不欢欣喜悦,有所失也不悔恨忧愁,这是因为知道得与失的禀分是没有定规的;明了生与死之间犹如一条没有阻隔的平坦大道,因而生于世间不会倍加欢喜,死离人世不觉祸患加身,这是因为知道终了和起始是不会一成不变的。算算人所懂得的知识,远远不如他所不知道的东西多,他生存的时间,也远远不如他不在人世的时间长;用极为有限的智慧去探究没有穷尽的境域,所以内心迷乱而必然不能有所得!由此看来,又怎么知道毫毛的末端就可以判定是最为细小的限度呢?又怎么知道天与地就可以看作是最大的境域呢?"

主题鉴赏

晋代郭象注《南华经(16卷)》"南华经总评"引陈君举言:"六经之后,有四人焉。摭实而有文采者,左氏也;凭虚而有理致者,庄子也;屈原变《国风》《雅》《颂》而为《离骚》;而子长易编年而为纪传,皆前未有比,后可以为法,非豪杰特起之士,其孰能之?"此一评价是对庄子文学才华前所未有实至名归的褒扬与肯定。

毫无疑问,举世公认庄子首先是一位哲学家,但称其为文学家也是言中肯綮的。所以闻一多先生说"庄子是一位哲学家,然而侵入了文学的圣城。"

以历史眼光对老子与庄子的哲学性和文学性做出比较公允评判的话,在哲学思想上,庄子几乎可与老子同台而语,二位先贤对道家思想的建树若说平分秋色也不为过。在文学造诣上,老子似乎稍逊于庄子。因此,有人认为庄子与屈原在文学性方面不让伯仲。故而闻一多先生说"古来谈哲学以老庄并称,谈文学以庄屈并称。"

如果说屈原开创了中国文学史上浪漫主义诗歌的先河,那么,庄子堪称中国文学史上魔幻兼浪漫主义散文的肇始者,有的学者甚至称庄子为中国文学史上的第一位"文辞家"。庄子的文才,并不同于屈原的诗才。前者隐秀于哲学的无形无迹之中,后者展露于诗歌的瑰丽整饬之中;前者于高处望向天地更高处,后者于嘤嘤惙惙中望向个人内心里。庄子写美人以他喻:"藐姑射之山,有神人居焉。肌肤若冰雪,绰约若处子,不食五谷,吸风饮露,乘云气,御飞龙,而游乎四海之外;其神凝,使物不疵疠而年谷熟。吾以是狂而不信也。"(《逍遥游》)屈

第二章 《庄子》经典篇章英译选读

原写美人以自况:"朝吾将济于白水兮,登阆风而绁马;忽反顾以流涕兮,哀高丘之无女。溘吾游此春宫兮,折琼枝以继佩;及荣华之未落兮,相下女之可诒。吾令丰隆乘云兮,求宓妃之所在,解佩纕以结言兮,吾令蹇修以为理。"(《离骚》)

所以说,《庄子》不仅具有极其丰富深远的思想性,同时又具有无与伦比的文学性和艺术性。任犀然说:"庄子在文学上最突出的特点就是非常擅长运用比喻、寓言,他因事比喻,随物赋形,寓中设寓,同时又文情奔放,行文多变,将恣意飞扬的文风和张扬的想象力、深沉的思想完美交融。"

若说庄子文采之张扬,文情之奔放,技巧之奇崛,《秋水》篇即是最佳明证之一,此篇也是《庄子》全书 33 篇中文辞最为瑰丽优美、气势最为恢宏、理趣最为绵密者:"秋水时至,百川灌河;泾流之大,两涘渚崖之间不辨牛马。"开篇一言,读者便被眼前这一幅秋水浸漫百川浩荡的磅礴画面所深深迷醉,所谓绘画的观感体验,原来也可以借由文字得以实现。而支撑这一画面的则是另一幅上升至宇宙层面的精辟哲理:河伯与北海若的传神问答,表面是以比喻手法来表现井蛙与夏虫的浅陋,而深层则在于说明大、小、多、寡、时、分、终、始、贵、贱等关乎生命与生存意义的概念并无绝对的哲学道理,与此同时,又巧妙暗示了世间万物,各在其位,各得其乐的睿智之见。与梁相惠子(惠施)的相位之辩,显示出庄子高超的"挖苦"技艺:"鹓鶵(yuān chú,传说中的凤凰)……非梧桐不止,非练实不食,非醴泉不饮。"志高气洁,庸常之辈如鸱(chī,猫头鹰)岂敢与之争锋?而与惠施的"鱼乐之辩":"子非鱼,安知鱼之乐?……子非我,安知我不知鱼之乐?"好似两位高级"杠精"之间的"智识"博弈(惠子全不懂庄子,而又懂透了庄子)。诸种有着不同的意识层次的"物"的比喻手法印证了庄子在创作中自由驾驭的文学创作技巧。

闻一多先生对庄子的文学才华至为推崇:"他那婴儿哭着要捉月亮似的天真,那神秘的怅惘,圣睿的憧憬,无边无际的企慕,无崖岸的艳羡,便使他成为最真实的诗人。"也许有学者认为,庄子的文学才华掩盖了其文字背后高远而深邃的哲学性,但笔者对此不敢苟同。中肯地说,《庄子》的文学性与哲理性之间,是一种无痕渗透水乳相融的关系,两者相得益彰、互不离分,剥离或削弱任何一面,另一面就会大打折扣。所以说,庄子不仅是一位逍遥于天地间的哲人,同时也是一位驰骋于人世间的文人。

Autumn Floods (Excerpt)

The time of the autumn floods came and the hundred streams poured into the Yellow River. Its racing current swelled to such proportions that, looking from bank to bank or island to island, it was impossible to distinguish a horse from a cow. Then the Lord of the River was beside himself with joy, believing that all the beauty in the world belonged to him alone. Following the current, he journeyed east until at last he reached the North Sea. Looking east, he could see no end to the water.

The Lord of the River began to wag his head and roll his eyes. Peering far off in the direction of Jo, he sighed and said, "The common saying has it, 'He has heard the Way a mere hundred times but he thinks he's better than anyone else.' It applies to me. In the past, I heard men belittling the learning of Confucius and making light of the righteousness of Po Yi, though I never believed them. Now, however, I have seen your unfathomable vastness. If I hadn't come to your gate, I should have been in danger. I should forever have been laughed at by the masters of the Great Method!"

Jo of the North Sea said, "You can't discuss the ocean with a well frog—he's limited by the space he lives in. You can't discuss ice with a summer insect—he's bound to a single season. You can't discuss the Way with a cramped scholar—he's shackled by his doctrines. Now you have come out beyond your banks and borders and have seen the great sea—so you realize your own pettiness. From now on it will be possible to talk to you about the Great Principle.

"Of all the waters of the world, none is as great as the sea. Ten thousand streams flow into it—I have never heard of a time when they stopped—and yet it is never full. The water leaks away at Wei-lü—I have never heard of a time when it didn't—and yet the sea is never empty. Spring or autumn, it never changes. Flood or drought, it takes no notice. It is so much greater than the streams of the Yangtze or the Yellow River that it is

第二章 《庄子》经典篇章英译选读

impossible to measure the difference. But I have never for this reason prided myself on it. I take my place with heaven and earth and receive breath from the yin and yang. I sit here between heaven and earth as a little stone or a little tree sits on a huge mountain. Since I can see my own smallness, what reason would I have to pride myself?

"Compare the area within the four seas with all that is between heaven and earth—is it not like one little anthill in a vast marsh? Compare the Middle Kingdom with the area within the four seas—is it not like one tiny grain in a great storehouse? When we refer to the things of creation, we speak of them as numbering ten thousand—and man is only one of them. We talk of the Nine Provinces where men are most numerous, and yet of the whole area where grain and foods are grown and where boats and carts pass back and forth, man occupies only one fraction. Compared to the ten thousand things, is he not like one little hair on the body of a horse? What the Five Emperors passed along, what the Three Kings fought over, what the benevolent man grieves about, what the responsible man labors over—all is no more than this!

"Po Yi gained a reputation by giving it up; Confucius passed himself off as learned because he talked about it. But in priding themselves in this way, were they not like you a moment ago priding yourself on your flood waters?"

——Burton Watson（伯顿·华兹生）

英译鉴赏简评

《秋水》位列《庄子·外篇》第十，包括两大部分：前一部分为北海若与河伯的谈话，一问一答，妙趣横生，构成本篇的主体；后一部分由六个自成一体且互不关联的寓言故事组成，表面似乎与第一部分毫无关联，但实则统一服务于该篇的主题思想——人如何认识自我与外物，带有朴素的认识论辩证色彩。该篇被视为《庄子》一书中最富有文学特质的篇章，有许多带有骈体文性质而且富含哲思的箴言警句，非常值得玩味，比如"井蛙不可以语于海者，拘于虚也；夏虫不可以语于冰者，笃于时也；曲士不可以语于道者，束于教也""天下之水，莫大于海""吾在天地之间，犹小石小木之在大山也""计四海之在天地之间也，不似礨空之在大泽乎?计中国之在海内,不似稊米之在大仓乎?""伯夷辞之以为名,仲尼语之以为博"等等,表现出先秦散文潇洒恣肆,迤逦古雅的独特文风。

华兹生在英译文句式的把握上,的确胜人一筹,"You can't discuss the ocean with a well frog—he's limited by the space he lives in. You can't discuss ice with a summer insect—he's bound to a single season. You can't discuss the Way with a cramped scholar—he's shackled by his doctrines."排比句式的整饬性,如 You can't discuss/he's limited by//he's bound to//he's shackled by;音韵的协和性,如 limit/live in/insect;space/summer/single/season/scholar/shackle;can't/cramp,等都是意美形胜且非常值得学习和模仿的翻译范例。

本章课后练习

一、段落试译。

庄子与惠子游于濠梁之上。庄子曰:"鲦鱼出游从容,是鱼之乐也。"惠子曰:"子非鱼,安知鱼之乐?"庄子曰:"子非我,安知我不知鱼之乐?"惠子曰:"我非子,固不知子矣;子固非鱼也,子之不知鱼之乐,全矣。"庄子曰:"请循其本。子曰'汝安知鱼乐'云者,既已知吾知之而问我,我知之濠上也。"(《庄子·外篇·秋水》)

二、请解释以下《庄子》中的名句名言并尝试翻译为英文。

1. 人生天地之间,若白驹之过隙,忽然而已。(《庄子·外篇·知北游》)

2. 哀莫大于心死,而人死亦次之。(《庄子·外篇·田子方》)

3. 众人重利,廉士重名,贤人尚志,圣人贵精。(《庄子·外篇·刻意》)

4. 井蛙不可以语于海,夏虫不可以语于冰。(《庄子·内篇·秋水》)

5. 至人无己,神人无功,圣人无名。(《庄子·内篇·逍遥游》)

6. 大知闲闲,小知间间;大言炎炎,小言詹詹。(《庄子·内篇·齐物论》)

第二章 《庄子》经典篇章英译选读

7. 天地与我并生,而万物与我为一。(《庄子·内篇·齐物论》)

8. 吾生也有涯,而知也无涯。以有涯随无涯,殆已。(《庄子·内篇·养生主》)

9. 为善无近名,为恶无近刑。(《庄子·内篇·养生主》)

10. 其嗜欲深者,其天机浅。(《庄子·内篇·大宗师》)

三、请比较下列各句两种英译文本的异同。

1. 小知不及大知,小年不及大年。奚以知其然也?(《内篇·逍遥游》)

   白话译文:小智比不上大智,短命比不上长寿。怎么知道是这样的呢?

   译文1:Little understanding cannot come up to great understanding; the shortlived cannot come up to the long-lived. How do I know this is so? (华兹生 Burton Waston)

   译文2:Small knowledge has not the compass of great knowledge any more than a short year has the length of a long year. How can we tell that this is so? (林语堂)

2. 朝菌不知晦朔,蟪蛄不知春秋,此小年也。(《内篇·逍遥游》)

   白话译文:朝生暮死的菌类不知道什么是一天。夏生秋死的寒蝉,不知道一年的时光,这就是短命。

   译文1:The morning mushroom knows nothing of twilight and dawn; the summer cicada knows nothing of spring and autumn. They are the short-lived. (华兹生 Burton Waston)

   译文2:The fungus plant of a morning knows not the alternation of day and night. The cicada knows not the alternation of spring and autumn. Theirs are short years. (林语堂)

3. 泉涸,鱼相与处于陆,相呴以湿,相濡以沫,不如相忘于江湖。(《内篇·大宗师》《外篇·天运》)

   白话译文:泉水干涸,鱼儿困在陆地相互依偎,以唾沫相互湿润求得生存,(此时此境)还不如我们彼此不相识,各自畅游于江湖。

   译文1:When the springs dry up and the fish are left stranded on the

67

ground, they spew each other with moisture and wet each other down with spit—but it would be much better if they could forget one another in the rivers and lakes. (华兹生 Burton Waston)

译文 2：When the springs dry out, the fish are found stranded on the earth. They keep each other damp with their own moisture, and wet each other with their slime. But it would be better if they could just forget about each other in rivers and lakes. (彭马田 Martin Palmer)

4. 大知闲闲,小知间间;大言炎炎,小言詹詹。(《内篇·齐物论》)

   白话译文：大智慧者看上去显得非常广博,小聪明者却十分琐细；高谈阔论者盛气凌人,与人爱辩者喋喋不休。

   译文 1：Men of great wits are open and broad-minded; men of small wits are mean and meticulous. Men of great eloquence speak with arrogance; men of small eloquence speak without a point. (汪榕培)

   译文 2：True depth of understanding is wide and steady, shallow understanding is lazy and wandering; words of wisdom are precise and clear, foolish words are petty and mean. (彭马田 Martin Palmer)

5. 人生天地之间,若白驹之过隙,忽然而已。(《外篇·知北游》)

   白话译文：人生于天地之间,就像一匹白色的骏马从一道缝隙越过,稍纵即逝。

   译文 1：Man's life between heaven and earth is like the passing of a white colt glimpsed through a crack in the wall—whoosh! —and that's the end. (华兹生 Burton Waston)

   译文 2：Human life between Heaven and Earth is like a white colt glimpsed through a crack in the wall, quickly past. (彭马田 Martin Palmer)

第三章

《论语》经典篇章英译选读

【导读】

《论语》是儒家"五经"之首,是一部以记言为主的语录体散文集,主要以语录和对话文体的形式记录了孔子及其弟子的言行,集中体现了孔子的政治、审美、道德伦理和功利等价值思想。《论语》内容涉及政治、教育、文学、哲学及立身处世的道理等多方面。早在春秋后期孔子设坛讲学时期,其主体内容就已初始创成;待孔子去世以后,其弟子和再传弟子代代传授他的言论,并逐渐将这些口头记诵的语录言行记录下来,因此称为"论";《论语》主要记载孔子及其弟子的言行,因此称为"语"。清代史学家赵翼解释说:"语者,圣人之语言,论者,诸儒之讨论也。"其实,"论"又有"纂"的意思,所谓《论语》,是指将孔子及其弟子的言行记载下来编纂成书。

作为儒家经典的《论语》,其内容博大精深,包罗万象,《论语》的思想主要有三个既各自独立又紧密相依的范畴:伦理道德范畴——仁,社会政治范畴——礼,认识方法论范畴——中庸。仁,首先是人内心深处的一种真实的状态,这种真的极致必然是善的,这种真和善的全体状态就是"仁"。孔子确立了仁的范畴,将礼阐述为适应仁、表达仁的一种合理的社会关系与待人接物的规范,进而明确"中庸"的系统方法论原则。"仁"是《论语》的思想核心。

《论语》的篇名通常取开篇前两个字作为篇名,其篇名与各章节的主要内容并无大的逻辑关系。表 3-1 是《论语》各章节内容简表。

表 3-1 《论语》各章节内容简表

序号	篇目	主要内容
1	《学而篇》	为人之本,初学者入门之道
2	《为政篇》	如何治国,何为孝道
3	《八佾篇》	礼乐之道
4	《里仁篇》	重点阐述"仁"
5	《公冶长篇》	从不同角度来讨论何为"仁德"
6	《雍也篇》	为政、为官、做事之道
7	《述而篇》	教育思想、学习态度及"仁德"的深层阐述
8	《秦伯篇》	孔子、曾子的言论及其对古代君王的评价
9	《子罕篇》	孔子的道德教育思想及其弟子对孔子的评论
10	《乡党篇》	孔子言谈举止、衣食住行和生活习惯
11	《先进篇》	孔子对其弟子的评价,孔子对待鬼神及生死等的态度
12	《颜渊篇》	孔子对仁德、何为君子的阐述
13	《子路篇》	孔子的教育思想、治理国家的政治主张
14	《宪问篇》	孔子与弟子谈论修身、为人的道理
15	《卫灵公篇》	孔子的教育思想和政治思想
16	《季氏篇》	孔子论君子修身及如何用礼法治国
17	《阳货篇》	孔子论述仁德并阐述礼乐治国之道
18	《微子篇》	古代圣贤的事迹、孔子周游列国的言行及周游途中世人对于乱世的看法
19	《子张篇》	孔子和弟子们探讨求学为道的言论,弟子们对于孔子的敬仰和赞颂
20	《尧曰篇》	古代圣贤的言论和孔子对于为政的论述

《论语》是儒家最重要的经典之一,两千多年来,历代学者对它不断地进行注释与研究。据统计,历代研究《论语》的专著不下三千余种。可惜的是,这些古籍亡佚者居多。流传有序且影响较大者有汉郑玄《论语注》、魏何晏《论语集解》、梁皇侃《论语义疏》、宋朱熹《论语集注》、刘宝楠《论语正义》、程树德《论语集释》。注释其实是一种文本再创作的过程,是将作者没有想到的深意帮读者备注出来,那么注解者创造出来的意义也就成为这个文本意义中的一部分,这样整个创作过程才完整。

第三章 《论语》经典篇章英译选读

《论语》在全球的其他国家也产生了广泛的影响,对世界文明做出了贡献。当今亚洲基本都是以儒家文化作为核心思想。《论语》在公元5世纪就传入了日本,公元6世纪时,日本开始系统地学习中国儒家经典及其思想,儒学思想对日本后来整个社会的发展产生了一定的影响,对日本后来的明治维新也有一定的启发作用。《论语》的儒学思想对韩国也有很大的影响,儒家的基本理念已经深深地根植于韩国文化之中。《论语》中的一些思想也与欧洲的启蒙思想不谋而合,为启蒙运动提供了更充分的理论依据,被认为是欧洲启蒙思想的"催化剂",并产生了"确认式影响"。

翻译是一种跨文化交际行为,《论语》的英译至今已经有三百多年的历史。《论语》的外译情况也显示了其宝贵的思想价值和文化意义,表明它确实包含着许多的真知灼见,为其他国家的人民打开了智慧的又一扇大门。至今《论语》的英译本有50多个,不同时代的中外译者都对《论语》的翻译传播做出了重要的贡献,促进了中西文化交流。这些译者的风格不同,不同时期的翻译目的也不相同。根据以往所做的研究,这些译本基本上可以按照两个角度来进行划分:即西方中心主义下的《论语》译本和文化多元主义下的《论语》译本。

西方中心主义不是一种理论,也不是一种研究方法,而是一种视角,一种学术态度。它起源于何时至今没有定论,有人说是16世纪,有人说是18世纪,还有人认为起源于亚里士多德时期。西方中心主义认为西方的文明才是世界向前发展的正确选择,东方文明应该依附西方文明,并企图对东方世界进行改造。当时西方人自高自大,认为西方的文化才是最优秀的。这一思想在翻译《论语》时也体现出来。

明朝时期意大利传教士最早来到中国,其中有一位传教士利玛窦将中国的《四书》翻译成了拉丁文,不过未能见过其真迹,其译稿现也已经失传。《论语》最早的译本出现在1691年,由英国人兰德尔·泰勒(Randal Taylor)从拉丁文转译而来,题目翻译为 *The Morals of Confucius*(《孔子的道德》)。

1809年,英国传教士马歇曼的节译本 *The Works of Confucius*(《孔子集》)出版。大约自1805年起,马歇曼开始学习中文。尽管他一生都没到过中国(他的大半生基本都以传教士的身份在印度度过),但其中文学习进步却很神速。马歇曼陆续将儒家经典《论语》译成英文。该书第一卷于1809年在印度出版,长达742页,由中文原文、译文、文字诠释三部分构成,自《论语》第一章"学而"译至第九章"子罕"。该译本首次比较详实地将孔子学说介绍给西方。此书除《论语》的英译之外,马歇曼还在译本前面刊出了正误表,对五册书的每个章节的基本内容也都做了简要的介绍。为了让读者更好地理解《论语》,马歇曼花了较大篇幅介绍了孔子之前的中国历史，并分三个阶段简要地介绍孔子的生平。马歇曼对孔子的描述是谦虚谨慎、严肃庄重、礼貌谦恭、举止文雅和对事理孜孜以求。他认为确切地向英语读者介绍独特的中国语言文字更为重要。他说直译永不容忽视。从译本不难看出，马歇曼在《论语》翻译过程中有着较强的基督教化倾向。作为一名传教士，马歇曼翻译《论语》也是想从该典籍中寻找到基督教是真理的证据，进而用基督教代替孔教，以耶稣代替孔子。

1861年，英国传教士、汉学家理雅各《论语》英译本第一卷出版，成为《论语》英译的一个里程碑。他被誉为19世纪西方汉学界最重要且最具影响力的儒学学者之一，他的译本也是研究文献最多的版本。张萍认为理雅各的翻译可以总结为"忠、厚、逆、释"四个字：忠是对基督教和儒家文化的忠诚；厚是厚重译法，比如添加前言、绪论、大量脚注及附录索引等；逆是推测把握，主要体现在理雅各提出的"知人论世"和"以意逆志"的翻译原则中；释是翻译诠释之意，在翻译过程中力求严谨忠实准确地传达原文文字的客观内容。作为一名传教士，理雅各翻译《论语》的目的是调和耶儒，以耶补儒的弹性传教策略，帮助传教士理解中国人的圣书，形成对儒学的了解，化解中国人的敌对情绪，引导他们"离开孔子去寻找另一位导师"。无论理雅各翻译《论语》采用什么翻译方法，也不管他翻译《论语》是出于何种目的，理版自问世一百多年来，一直被奉为标准译本，对后来学者翻译《论语》产生了重大影响。

《论语》另一个重要英译本是19世纪60年代的威妥玛版本。威妥玛因发明"威妥玛式拼音法"而闻名于世。他早年曾在剑桥大学三一学院读书，1842年来华，先后担任英军驻华使馆参赞、英国驻华公使等职，在中国生活了四十余年。较之于先前及后来的众多译本，威妥玛《论语》英译本绝大多数章节的译文都附有注释，这正是该译本最突出的特色。据统计，威译本附有注释的译文共有466章，占全部章数(499)的百分之九十以上。该译本的注释包括夹注和脚注两类，前者置于译本正文中间，后者附在每页译文底端。威译本正是通过广泛而灵活地运用两类注释来再现原作所蕴含的丰富思想的。身为语言学者，威妥玛翻译态度严谨，其译本采用附注存真的翻译策略，较好地再现了原作的风貌。在19世纪《论语》英译以传教士为主流的背景下，威妥玛从语言学者视角所译的英译本独树一帜，值得当下人们从不同角度加以关注、思考和借鉴。

到了20世纪，美国最具影响的诗人、批评家、翻译家之一的庞德在进行《论语》翻译时，一改以前的翻译风格与方法。他在翻译《论语》时不再强调对原文一对一的重现，译作以理想化创作为主，即创译。庞德希望通过大量外国文学的翻译为本国文学注入生机与活力，革新本国文学的创作，让本国文学吸收接

第三章 《论语》经典篇章英译选读

纳一些新的文学创作模式。外国文学也在英语文学中逐步实现其经典化的进程。更为重要的是,他希望通过翻译解决时代的症结。庞德翻译《论语》的方法不是语文学的、客观的,而是带有政治性的、主观的,他经常在翻译中加入自己的思想,抒发个人的政治、经济和诗学观点。庞德宣称自己翻译《论语》的一个基本目标是要传达原著凝练的风格及鲜活人物讲话的特色。他在翻译儒经中有鲜明的特色,如用拆字法解析汉字,运用生动活泼的英语,再现原文具体简洁的风格。基于汉字的形象性和语言能量说,庞德主要依赖马修斯的《汉英辞典》和马礼逊的《汉语字典》对《论语》进行创造性解读。字典提供了直观的形象甚至图画,供庞德拆解分析,这就是"拆字法"或"表意文字法"。虽然庞德对汉字的解构有牵强附会之感,他对《论语》的翻译也受到很多汉学家的批评和否定,但自他之后,《论语》的英译慢慢摆脱西方中心主义的阴影,开始步入多元文化主义的新语境。

《论语》的第一位华人译者是辜鸿铭,他国学素养深厚又精通外文,在解释一些概念时也多采取一些西方的典故来进行阐释,能让西方读者接受,他的这种翻译方法被称为"归化法"。辜鸿铭所处的时代是19世纪后期的中国。此时的中国内忧外患,西方的文化和经济压迫使西学归来的辜鸿铭颇受震撼。他坚信儒家文化优于西方思想,故大量英译中国经典,借此向西方人传播儒家文化,以重塑中国文化的身份并改变西方人对中国文化的否定态度。有学者批评,辜鸿铭是在西方的哲学背景下对《论语》进行翻译。不过我们也应该承认,他的翻译对西方读者更好地接受这部作品具有重要意义。

辜鸿铭《论语》译本出版半个多世纪后,出现了另一个引起翻译界重视的华人《论语》译本,即林语堂译本。林语堂对《论语》的翻译不同于其他,因为他对《论语》的翻译不是全译,而是典型的摘译和编译。他只选取了《论语》原文的不到40%,以孔子名言及生活性格描述为主章节,按照主题分成十类,列为他的儒学介绍性著作《孔子的智慧》的第五章,并在章首附林语堂对《论语》的思想、行文风格、阅读方法和其摘译、编译行为的阐释。和辜鸿铭一样,林语堂的译本也是消除中国文化陌生感,使用归化翻译方法的范例。他从小接受的是西方的教育,后来又希望找寻中国文化传统的归属感,他在东西方的文化滋养中以一种包容、开放的心态和辩证的眼光来批判地看待东西方文化。林语堂在翻译时试图实现文化的融合,把中国完整地展现给世界。他眼中的儒家思想都是他在对中西文化进行对比之后在批判基础上的选择,他试图以西方的眼光来审视《论语》,在翻译时对中西方文化进行了对比和整合,努力使译文符合英语读者的阅读习惯和思维习惯,真实地传递了孔子思想的精髓。

随着时间的推移,特别是近些年国学热的蔓延,翻译家们对《论语》的翻译热情也是有增无减。梅仁毅的译本在1992年由和平出版社出版,1993年齐鲁书社出版了潘富恩和温少霞的译本,1994年华语教学出版社出版了赖波和夏玉的译本,2005年高等教育出版社出版了许渊冲的译本,2008年中华书局出版了刘殿爵译本,2012年中国对外翻译出版有限公司出版了丁往道的译本,等等。《论语》的不同译本体现了翻译家不同角度的翻译,以及他们为促进中外文化交流所做出的贡献。

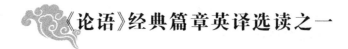《论语》经典篇章英译选读之一

学而篇第一(节选)

子曰①:"学②而时习③之,不亦说④乎?有朋⑤自远方来,不亦乐⑥乎?人不知⑦,而不愠⑧,不亦君子⑨乎?"

有子⑩曰:"其为人也孝弟⑪,而好犯上者⑫,鲜⑬矣;不好犯上,而好作乱者,未之有也。君子务本⑭,本立而道生⑮。孝弟也者,其为仁之本与⑯!"

子曰:"弟子⑰,入⑱则孝,出⑲则悌,谨⑳而信,泛㉑爱众,而亲仁㉒。行有余力㉓,则以学文㉔。"

子夏㉕曰:"贤贤㉖易㉗色;事父母,能竭其力;事君,能致㉘其身;与朋友交,言而有信。虽曰未学,吾必谓之学矣。"

子曰:"父在,观其㉙志;父没,观其行㉚;三年㉛无改于父之道㉜,可谓孝矣。"

子贡㉝曰:"贫而无谄㉞,富而无骄,何如㉟?"子曰:"可也;未若贫而乐㊱,富而好礼者也。"子贡曰:"诗云:'如切如磋,如琢如磨㊲',其斯之谓与?"子曰:"赐㊳也,始可与言诗已矣,告诸㊴往㊵而知来㊶者。"

第三章 《论语》经典篇章英译选读

【注释】

① 〔子〕中国古代对于有地位、有学问的男子的尊称,有时也泛称男子。《论语》书中"子曰"的子,都是指孔子而言。

② 〔学〕孔子在这里所讲的"学",主要是指学习西周的礼、乐、诗、书等传统文化典籍。

③ 〔时习〕在周秦时代,"时"字用作副词,意为"在一定的时候"或者"在适当的时候"。但朱熹在《论语集注》一书中把"时"解释为"时常"。"习",指演习礼、乐,复习诗、书,也含有温习、实习、练习的意思。

④ 〔说(yuè)〕同"悦",愉快、高兴。

⑤ 〔有朋〕一本作"友朋"。旧注说,"同门曰朋",即同在一位老师门下学习的叫朋,也就是志同道合的人。

⑥ 〔乐〕与说有所区别。旧注说,悦在内心,乐则见于外。

⑦ 〔人不知〕一般而言,知是了解的意思。人不知,是说别人不了解自己。

⑧ 〔愠(yùn)〕恼怒,怨恨。

⑨ 〔君子〕《论语》书中的君子,有时指有德者,有时指有位者。此处指孔子理想中具有高尚人格的人。

⑩ 〔有子〕孔子的学生,姓有,名若。在《论语》书中记载的孔子学生,一般都称字,只有曾参和有若称"子"。因此,许多人认为《论语》即由曾参和有若著述。

⑪ 〔孝弟〕弟弟对待兄长的正确态度。〔孝〕奴隶社会时期所认为的子女对待父母的正确态度。〔弟〕同"悌"(音 tì)。

⑫ 〔犯〕冒犯、干犯。〔上〕指在上位的人。

⑬ 〔鲜(xiǎn)〕少的意思。

⑭ 〔务〕专心、致力于。〔本〕根本。

⑮ 〔道〕指孔子提倡的仁道。

⑯ 〔为仁之本〕以孝悌作为仁的根本。仁是孔子哲学思想的最高范畴,又是伦理道德准则。

⑰ 〔弟子〕一指年幼之人,弟系对兄而言,子系对父而言,故曰弟子;二指学生。此处取前义。

⑱ 〔入〕进到父亲住处,或说在家。

⑲ 〔出〕与"入"相对而言,指外出拜师学习。

⑳ 〔谨〕寡言少语。

㉑ 〔泛〕广泛的意思。

㉒ 〔仁〕仁人,即有仁德之人。

㉓〔行有余力〕指有闲暇时间。
㉔〔文〕古代文献,主要有诗、书、礼、乐等文化知识。
㉕〔子夏〕姓卜,名商,字子夏,孔子的学生,生于公元前507年。孔子死后,他在魏国宣传孔子的思想主张。
㉖〔贤贤〕第一个"贤"字作动词用,尊重的意思。贤贤即尊重贤者。
㉗〔易〕改变。
㉘〔致〕献纳,尽力。
㉙〔其〕他的,指儿子,不是指父亲。
㉚〔行(xìng)〕指行为举止等,如品行、操行、德行。《论语·公冶长》:"听其言而观其行。"
㉛〔三年〕表概数,指经过一段较长的时间。
㉜〔道〕原则,操守。
㉝〔子贡〕姓端木名赐,字子贡,卫国人,孔子的学生。
㉞〔谄(chǎn)〕巴结,奉承,谄媚。
㉟〔何如〕怎么样。《论语》书中的"何如"均为此意。
㊱〔贫而乐〕一本作"贫而乐道"。
㊲〔如切如磋,如琢如磨〕此二句见《诗经·卫风·淇澳》。有两种解释:一说切磋琢磨分别指对骨、象牙、玉、石四种不同材料的加工,否则不能成器;一说加工象牙和骨,切了还要磋,加工玉石,琢了还要磨,有精益求精之意。
㊳〔子贡名〕孔子对学生都称其名。
㊴〔诸〕同之。
㊵〔往〕过去的事情。
㊶〔来〕未来的事情。

白话释义

　　孔子说:"学到的东西按时去实践和运用,不也很高兴吗?有朋友从很远的地方来,不也很快乐吗?别人不了解自己,自己却不生气,不也是一位有修养的君子吗?"

　　有子说:"那种孝敬父母、敬爱兄长的人,却喜欢触犯上级,是很少见的;不喜欢触犯上级却喜欢造反的人,更是从来没有的。有德行的人总是力求抓住这个根本。根本建立了便产生了仁道。孝敬父母、敬爱兄长,大概便是仁道的根本吧!"

第三章 《论语》经典篇章英译选读

孔子说:"小孩子在父母跟前要孝顺,出外要敬爱师长,说话要谨慎,言而有信,和所有人都友爱相处,亲近那些具有仁爱之心的人。做到这些以后,如果还有剩余的精力,就用来学习文化知识。"

子夏说:"一个人能够尊重贤者而看轻女色;侍奉父母,能够竭尽全力;服侍君主,能够献出自己的生命;同朋友交往,说话诚实、恪守信用。这样的人,即使他自己说没有学过什么,我也一定要说他已经学习过了。"

孔子说:"当他父亲活着时,要看他本人的志向;他父亲去世以后,就要考察他本人的具体行为了。如果他长期坚持父亲生前那些正确原则,就可以说是尽孝了。"

子贡说:"贫穷却不巴结奉承,富贵却不骄傲自大,怎么样?孔子说:"可以了,但还是不如虽贫穷却乐于道,虽富贵却谦虚好礼。"子贡说:"《诗经》上说:"要像骨、角、象牙、玉石等的加工一样,先开料,再粗锉,细刻,然后磨光,那就是这样的意思吧?"孔子说:"赐呀,现在可以同你讨论《诗经》了。告诉你以往的事,你能因此而知道未来的事。"

英译

The Master said, "Is it not pleasant to learn with a constant perseverance and application? Is it not delightful to have friends coming from distant quarters? Is he not a man of complete virtue, who feels no discomposure though men may take no note of him?"

The philosopher Yu said, "They are few who, being filial and fraternal, are fond of offending against their superiors. There have been none, who, not liking to offend against their superiors, have been fond of stirring up confusion. The superior man bends his attention to what is radical. That being established, all practical courses naturally grow up. Filial piety and fraternal submission—are they not the root of all benevolent actions?"

The Master said, "A youth, when at home, should be filial, and, abroad, respectful to his elders. He should be earnest and truthful. He should overflow in love to all, and cultivate the friendship of the good. When he has time and opportunity, after the performance of these things, he should employ them in polite studies."

Tsze-hsia said, "If a man withdraws his mind from the love of beauty, and applies it as sincerely to the love of the virtuous; if, in serving his parents, he can exert his utmost strength; if, in serving his prince, he can devote his life; if, in his intercourse with his friends, his words are sincere: —although men say that he has not learned, I will certainly say that he has."

The Master said, "While a man's father is alive, look at the bent of his will; when his father is dead, look at his conduct. If for three years he does not alter from the way of his father, he may be called filial."

Tsze-kung said, "What do you pronounce concerning the poor man who yet does not flatter, and the rich man who is not proud?" The Master replied, "They will do; but they are not equal to him, who, though poor, is yet cheerful, and to him, who, though rich, loves the rules of propriety." Tsze-kung replied, "It is said in *The Book of Poetry*, 'As you cut and then file, as you carve and then polish'. The meaning is the same, I apprehend, as that which you have just expressed." The Master said, "With one like Ts'ze, I can begin to talk about the odes. I told him one point, and he knew its proper sequence."

——James Legge（詹姆斯·理雅各）

英译鉴赏简评

这部分节选自《论语》的开首篇《学而篇》，主要内容是为人之本、初学者入门之道。第一章历来被认为是本篇最重要最核心的章节，宋代著名学者朱熹对此章评价极高，说它是"入道之门，积德之基"。第一句"学而时习之，不亦说乎？"通常理解为"学了以后，又时常温习和练习，不也高兴吗？"但也有人解释为"自己的学说，要是被社会采用了，那就太高兴了"。目前多数人认可的释义是"学习知识，并且在合适的时机付诸实践，难道不令人快乐吗？"由此可见，不同的人对此有不同的理解，那出现多种多样的译文也就不足为奇了。

在此，仅举一例，说明不同译文在选词造句方面的差异，孰优孰劣，读者当有己见。我们看对"不亦说乎"中"说"和"不亦乐乎"中"乐"的翻译，理雅各分别翻译为"pleasant"和"delightful"，辜鸿铭分别译为"a pleasure"和"a greater pleasure"。在对比这两种翻译之前，有必要从汉语的角度理解"说"和"乐"的不同："说"同"悦"表示高兴、愉悦，是指内心的喜悦；而"乐"是欢喜、快乐，表示外

第三章 《论语》经典篇章英译选读

在的喜悦。再来分析 pleasant、delightful 和 pleasure 的区别：pleasant 是指使人愉快的事物，delightful 是指强烈而短暂的高兴，而 pleasure 泛指快乐、高兴。通过以上分析我们可以看出，理雅各和辜鸿铭的翻译各有所长，理雅各第二个"乐"用的 delightful，而辜鸿铭第一个"说"用的是 a pleasure，可谓是翻译出了"说"和"乐"的精髓与灵魂，而理雅各对第一个"说"用 pleasant 和辜鸿铭对第二个"乐"也用 pleasure，只是前面加了个比较级 greater，感觉在意思的表达上不是那么到位，所以，在这句的翻译上，他俩打了个平手。这句还有个核心词，那就是对"君子"的理解和翻译，理雅各将君子翻译为 a man of complete virtue，而辜鸿铭翻译为 a wise and good man，个人认为 wise 没什么问题，但是 good 泛指好，把君子翻译为 wise and good man，语义单薄，无法确切地表达或再现儒家思想中"君子"的那种非同一般的美德，理雅各的翻译就略胜一筹了。

《论语》经典篇章英译选读之二

为政篇第二（节选）

子曰："道①之以政，齐②之以刑，民免③而无耻④；道之以德，齐之以礼，有耻且格⑤。"

子曰："吾十有⑥五而志于学，三十而立⑦，四十而不惑⑧，五十而知天命⑨，六十而耳顺⑩，七十而从⑪心所欲，不逾矩。"

孟懿子⑫问孝。子曰："无违⑬。"樊迟⑭御⑮，子告之曰："孟孙⑯问孝于我，我对曰，无违。"樊迟曰："何谓也？"子曰："生，事之以礼；死，葬之以礼，祭之以礼。"

子游⑰问孝。子曰："今之孝者，是谓能养⑱。至于犬马，皆能有养；不敬，何以别乎？"

子夏问孝。子曰："色难⑲。有事，弟子服其劳⑳；有酒食，先生㉑馔㉒，曾是以为孝乎？"

子曰："视其所以㉓，观其所由㉔，察其所安㉕。人焉廋㉖哉？人焉廋哉？"

子曰:"君子周⑦而不比㉘,小人㉙比而不周。"

季康子㉚问:"使民敬、忠以㉛劝㉜,如之何?"子曰:"临㉝之以庄,则敬;孝慈㉞,则忠;举善而教不能,则劝。"

子张问:"十世㉟可知也?"子曰:"殷因㊱于夏礼,所损益㊲,可知也;周因于殷礼,所损益,可知也。其或继周者,虽百世,可知也。"

【注释】

①〔道〕有两种解释:一为通"导","引导,领导";二为"治理"。这里取前者较为贴切。

②〔齐〕整齐,约束。

③〔免〕避免,躲避。

④〔耻〕羞耻之心。

⑤〔格〕有两种解释:一为"至";二为"正"。

⑥〔有〕通"又"。

⑦〔立〕站立的意思,这里是"站得住"。

⑧〔惑〕迷惑。

⑨〔天命〕指不能为人力所支配的事情。

⑩〔耳顺〕一般而言,指对那些于己不利的意见也能正确对待。

⑪〔从〕遵从。

⑫〔孟懿子〕鲁国的大夫,姓仲孙,名何忌,"懿"是谥号。其父临终前要他向孔子学礼。

⑬〔违〕违背。

⑭〔樊迟〕姓樊名须,字子迟,孔子的弟子。

⑮〔御〕驾驭马车。

⑯〔孟孙〕指孟懿子。

⑰〔子游〕姓言名偃,字子游,吴人。

⑱〔养〕晚辈供养长辈,即奉养父母读作"yàng"。宋欧阳修《泷冈阡表》:"祭而丰,不如养之薄也。""皆能有养"的"养"读"yǎng",饲养,抚养。

⑲〔色〕脸色。〔难〕不容易。

⑳〔服〕从事、担负。〔服劳〕服侍。

第三章 《论语》经典篇章英译选读

㉑〔先生〕指长者或父母。
㉒〔馔(zhuàn)〕饮食,吃喝。
㉓〔所以〕所做的事情。
㉔〔所由〕所走过的道路。
㉕〔所安〕所安的心境。
㉖〔廋(sōu)〕隐藏,藏匿。
㉗〔周〕合群,团结。
㉘〔比(bì)〕亲近。《周礼·夏官·形方氏》:"使小国事大国,大国比小国。"汉郑玄注:"比,犹亲也。"此指勾结同党,结党营私,朋比为奸。
㉙〔小人〕没有道德修养的凡人。
㉚〔季康子〕姓季孙名肥,康是他的谥号,鲁哀公时任正卿,是当时政治上最有权势的人。
㉛〔以〕连接词,与"而"同。
㉜〔劝〕勉励。这里是自勉努力的意思。
㉝〔临〕对待。
㉞〔孝慈〕一说当政者自己孝慈;一说当政者引导老百姓孝慈。此处采用后者。
㉟〔世〕古时称三十年为一世。也有的把"世"解释为朝代。
㊱〔因〕因袭,沿用、继承。
㊲〔损益〕减少和增加,即优化、变动之义。

白话释义

孔子说:用政令来治理百姓,用刑罚来制约百姓,百姓可暂时免于罪过,但不会感到不服从统治是可耻的;如果用道德来统治百姓,用礼教来约束百姓,百姓不但有廉耻之心,而且会纠正自己的错误。

孔子说:"我十五岁立志学习,三十岁在人生道路上站稳脚跟,四十岁心中不再迷惘,五十岁知道上天给我安排的命运,六十岁听到别人说话就能分辨是非真假,七十岁能随心所欲地说话做事,又不会超越规矩。"

孟懿子问什么是孝道。孔子说:"不要违背礼节。"不久,樊迟替孔子驾车,孔子告诉他:"孟孙问我什么是孝道,我对他说,不要违背礼节。"樊迟说:"这是什么意思?"孔子说:"父母活着的时候,依规定的礼节侍奉他们;死的时候,依规定的礼节安葬他们,祭祀他们。"

子游请教孝道,孔子说:"现在所说的孝,指的是养活父母便行了。即使狗和马,也都有人饲养。对父母如果不恭敬顺从,那和饲养狗马有什么区别呢?"

子夏问什么是孝道,孔子说:"侍奉父母经常保持和颜悦色最难。遇到事情,由年轻人去做;有好吃好喝的,让老年人享受,难道这样就是孝吗?"

孔子说:"看一个人的所作所为,考察他处事的动机,了解他心安于什么事情。那么,这个人的内心怎能掩盖得了呢?这个人的内心怎能掩盖得了呢?"

孔子说:"德行高尚的人以正道广泛交友但不互相勾结,品格卑下的人互相勾结却不顾道义。"

季康子问:"要使百姓恭敬、忠诚并互相勉励,该怎么做?"孔子说:"如果你用庄重的态度对待他们,他们就会恭敬;如果你能孝顺父母、爱护幼小,他们就会忠诚;如果你能任用贤能之士,教育能力低下的人,他们就会互相勉励。"

子张问:"今后十代的礼制现在可以预知吗?"孔子说:"殷代承袭夏代的礼制,其中废除和增加的内容是可以知道的;周代继承殷代的礼制,其中废除和增加的内容,也是可以知道的。那么以后如果有继承周朝的朝代,就是在一百代以后,也是可以预先知道的。"

英译

The Master said, "If the people be led by laws, and uniformity sought to be given them by punishments, they will try to avoid the punishment, but have no sense of shame. If they be led by virtue, and uniformity sought to be given them by the rules of propriety, they will have the sense of shame, and moreover will become good."

The Master said, "At fifteen, I had my mind bent on learning. At thirty, I stood firm. At forty, I had no doubts. At fifty, I knew the decrees of Heaven. At sixty, my ear was an obedient organ for the reception of truth. At seventy, I could follow what my heart desired, without transgressing what was right."

Mang I asked what filial piety was. The Master said, "It is not being disobedient." Soon after, as Fan Ch'ih was driving him, the Master told him, saying, "Mang-sun asked me what filial piety was, and I answered him, — 'not being disobedient.'" Fan Ch'ih said, "What did you mean?" The Master replied, "That parents, when alive, be served according to propriety; that, when dead, they should be buried according to propriety; and that they should be sacrificed to according to propriety."

Tsze-yu asked what filial piety was. The Master said, "The filial piety of nowadays means the support of one's parents. But dogs and horses likewise are able to do something in the way of support; — without reverence, what is there to distinguish the one support given from the other?"

Tsze-hsia asked what filial piety was. The Master said, "The difficulty is with the countenance. If, when their elders have any troublesome affairs, the young take the toil of them, and if, when the young have wine and food, they set them before their elders, is THIS to be considered filial piety?"

The Master said, "See what a man does. Mark his motives. Examine in what things he rests. How can a man conceal his character? How can a man conceal his character?"

The Master said, "The superior man is catholic and no partisan. The mean man is partisan and not catholic."

Chi K'ang asked how to cause the people to reverence their ruler, to be faithful to him, and to go on to nerve themselves to virtue. The Master said, "Let him preside over them with gravity; — then they will reverence him. Let him be filial and kind to all; — then they will be faithful to him. Let him advance the good and teach the incompetent; — then they will eagerly seek to be virtuous."

Tsze-chang asked whether the affairs of ten ages after could be known. Confucius said, "The Yin dynasty followed the regulations of the Hsia: wherein it took from or added to them may be known. The Chau dynasty has followed the regulations of Yin: wherein it took from or added to them may be known. Some other may follow the Chau, but though it should be at the distance of a hundred ages, its affairs may be known."

——James Legge(詹姆斯·理雅各)

英译鉴赏简评

这部分选自《为政篇》,《为政篇》的主要内容为如何治国和何为孝道。首先看对"五十而知天命"中"天命"的理解与翻译。"天命"通常指不能为人力所支配的事情,但也有研究认为"天命"是在儒君子的生命中逐渐"生成"的,并由儒君子从多重维度不断"证成"的天人双向互动过程,认为孔子自"知天命"起,打开了人、天之隔,开始追求人与天命相合的、超越境界的"天人合一"。也有研究认为"知天命"即认识上天赋予人的使命——"成人",即使之成为真正的、理想的人。个人认为第二种解释更贴近孔子"知天命"的思想。理雅各将"天命"翻译为 the decrees of Heaven,认为"天命"就是顺从上天的旨意,更能表现出冥冥中无所不在的终极真理,更为忠实地再现了原文词汇的文化内涵;而辜鸿铭翻译为 truth in religion,认为"天命"是宗教中的真理,体现出他从儒家的角度对基督教经文的辨读,这也是他的翻译向目的语言归化的体现,译法更为自由。还有两人对"孝"的翻译也不同:理雅各将"孝"翻译为 filial piety,带有浓厚的殖民意味,是殖民企图下的产物;而辜鸿铭将"孝"翻译为 a good son,就是"好儿子"之意,但是中西方对好儿子的标准是不同的,如果考虑读者的身份和文化,显然这种译法还是有不妥之处。个人认为,如果难以找出合适的词,那么将"孝"翻译为"Xiao"可能更为贴切,就如有专家提议将中国的"龙"翻译为 Loong 而不是 dragon 一样,因为东方的"龙"和西方的 dragon,在表层语义上虽指同一物,而深层文化寓意上却差之千里。

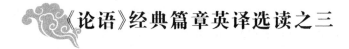《论语》经典篇章英译选读之三

颜渊篇第十二(节选)

颜渊问仁。子曰:"克己复礼①为仁。一日克己复礼,天下归仁焉②。为仁由己,而由人乎哉?"颜渊曰:"请问其目③。"子曰:"非礼勿视,非礼勿听,非礼勿言,非礼勿动。"颜渊曰:"回虽不敏,请事④斯语矣。"

仲弓问仁。子曰:"出门如见大宾,使民如承大祭⑤。己所不欲,

第三章 《论语》经典篇章英译选读

勿施于人。在邦⑥无怨,在家⑦无怨。"仲弓曰:"雍虽不敏,请事斯语矣。"

司马牛问君子。子问:"君子不忧不惧。"曰:"不忧不惧,斯谓之君子已乎?"子曰:"内省不疚⑧,夫何忧何惧?"

司马牛忧曰:"人皆有兄弟,我独亡⑨。"子夏曰:"商闻之矣:死生有命,富贵在天。君子敬而无失,与人恭而有礼,四海之内皆兄弟也。君子何患乎无兄弟也?"

子贡问政。子曰:"足食,足兵,民信之矣。"子贡曰:"必不得已而去,于斯三者何先?"曰:"去兵。"子贡曰:"必不得已而去,于斯二者何先?"曰:"去食。自古皆有死,民无信不立。"

哀公问于有若曰:"年饥,用不足,如之何?"有若对曰:"盍⑩彻⑪乎?"曰:"二⑫,吾犹不足,如之何其彻也?"对曰:"百姓足,君孰与不足?百姓不足,君孰与足?"

【注释】

①〔克己〕克制自己。〔复礼〕使自己的言行符合于礼的要求。
②〔归〕归顺。〔仁〕仁道。
③〔目〕具体的条目。目和纲相对。
④〔事〕从事,照着去做。
⑤〔出门如见大宾,使民如承大祭〕这句话是说,出门办事和役使百姓,都要像迎接贵宾和进行大祭时那样恭敬严肃。
⑥〔邦〕诸侯统治的国家。
⑦〔家〕卿大夫统治的封地。
⑧〔疚(jiù)〕内心痛苦,惭愧。
⑨〔亡(wú)〕通"无",没有的意思。
⑩〔盍〕何,何不,表示反问。《论语•公冶长》:"盍各言尔志?"
⑪〔彻〕西周奴隶主国家的一种田税制度。旧注曰:"什一而税谓之彻。"即抽取十分之一的税。
⑫〔二〕抽取十分之二的税。

白话释义

颜渊问什么是仁。孔子说:"克制自己,使言语和行动都合乎礼,就是仁。一旦做到这些,天下的人都会称许你有仁德。实行仁德要靠自己,难道是靠别人吗?"颜渊说:"请问实行仁德的具体途径。"孔子说:"不合礼的事不看,不合礼的事不听,不合礼的事不言,不合礼的事不做。"颜渊说:"我虽然不聪敏,请让我照这些话去做。"

仲弓问什么是仁。孔子说:"出门好像去见贵宾,役使民众好像去承担重大祀典。自己所不想要的事物,就不要强加给别人。在邦国做事没有抱怨,在卿大夫的封地做事也无抱怨。"仲弓说:"我冉雍虽然不聪敏,请让我照这些话去做。"

司马牛问怎样才是君子。孔子说:"君子不忧愁,不恐惧。"司马牛说:"不忧愁,不恐惧,这就叫君子了吗?"孔子说:"内心反省而不内疚,那还有什么可忧虑和恐惧的呢?"

司马牛忧愁地说:"别人都有兄弟,唯独我没有。"子夏说:"我听说过:'死生由命运决定,富贵在于上天的安排。'君子认真谨慎地做事,不出差错,对人恭敬而有礼貌,四海之内的人,就都是兄弟,君子何必担忧没有兄弟呢?"

子贡问怎样治理政事。孔子说:"粮食充足,军备充足,民众信任朝廷。"子贡说:"如果迫不得已要去掉一些,三项中先去掉哪一项呢?"孔子说:"去掉军备。"子贡说:"如果迫不得已,要在剩下的两项中去掉一项,先去掉哪一项呢?"孔子说:"去掉粮食。自古以来,人都是要死的,如果没有民众的信任,那么国家就站立不住了。"

鲁哀公问有若说:"年成歉收,国家备用不足,怎么办呢?"有若回答说:"何不实行十分抽一的税率呢?"哀公说:"十分抽二,尚且不够用,怎么能去实行十分抽一呢?"有若回答说:"如果百姓用度足,国君怎么会用度不足呢?如果百姓用度不足,国君用度怎么会足呢?"

英译

Yen Yuan asked about perfect virtue. The Master said, "To subdue one's self and return to propriety, is perfect virtue. If a man can for one day subdue himself and return to propriety, all under heaven will ascribe perfect

第三章 《论语》经典篇章英译选读

virtue to him. Is the practice of perfect virtue from a man himself, or is it from others?" Yen Yuan said, "I beg to ask the steps of that process." The Master replied, "Look not at what is contrary to propriety; listen not to what is contrary to propriety; speak not what is contrary to propriety; make no movement which is contrary to propriety." Yen Yuan then said, "Though I am deficient in intelligence and vigor, I will make it my business to practice this lesson."

Chung-kung asked about perfect virtue. The Master said, "It is, when you go abroad, to behave to every one as if you were receiving a great guest; to employ the people as if you were assisting at a great sacrifice; not to do to others as you would not wish done to yourself; to have no murmuring against you in the country, and none in the family." Chung-kung said, "Though I am deficient in intelligence and vigor, I will make it my business to practice this lesson."

Sze-ma Niu asked about the superior man. The Master said, "The superior man has neither anxiety nor fear." "Being without anxiety or fear!" said Nui; "does this constitute what we call the superior man?" The Master said, "When internal examination discovers nothing wrong, what is there to be anxious about, what is there to fear?"

Sze-ma Niu, full of anxiety, said, "Other men all have their brothers, I only have not." Tsze-hsia said to him, "There is the following saying which I have heard: —'Death and life have their determined appointment; riches and honours depend upon Heaven.' Let the superior man never fail reverentially to order his own conduct, and let him be respectful to others and observant of propriety: — then all within the four seas will be his brothers. What has the superior man to do with being distressed because he has no brothers?"

Tsze-kung asked about government. The Master said, "The requisites of government are that there be sufficiency of food, sufficiency of military equipment, and the confidence of the people in their ruler." Tsze-kung said, "If it cannot be helped, and one of these must be dispensed with, which of the three should be foregone first?" "The military equipment." said the Master. Tsze-kung again asked, "If it cannot be helped, and one of the remaining two must be dispensed with, which of them should be foregone?" The Master answered, "Part with the food. From of old, death has been the lot of all men; but if the people have no faith in their rulers, there is no standing for the state."

The Duke Ai inquired of Yu Zo, saying, "The year is one of scarcity, and the returns for expenditure are not sufficient—what is to be done?" Yu Zo replied to him, "Why not simply tithe the people?" "With two tenths," said the duke, "I find it not enough—how could I do with that system of one tenth?" Yu Zo answered, "If the people have plenty, their prince will not be left to want alone. If the people are in want, their prince cannot enjoy plenty alone."

——James Legge（詹姆斯·理雅各）

英译鉴赏简评

这部分节选自《颜渊篇》，《颜渊篇》的主要内容是孔子对仁德和何为君子的阐述。孔子是伟大的思想家，其思想的核心是"仁"。"克己复礼为仁"通常解释为"克制自己，一切都照着礼的要求去做，这就是仁"。"克己"一般理解为克制自己，但也有人认为"克己"不是简单地压抑自己，而是要在现实的利害面前发挥人的精神特性，达到理想的生活状态。也有研究从词性角度去解释"克己复礼为仁"，认为"克"是助动词，而真正的动词是"复"，所以"克己复礼"就是自己复礼，做到自己复礼就是仁。理解了中文解释后，我们来看看理雅各和辜鸿铭对"仁"的翻译：理雅各翻译为 perfect virtue，而辜鸿铭翻译为 a moral life。Perfect 意思是完美的、优秀的，virtue 表示高尚的道德、美德，用 perfect 来修饰 virtue，更好地增强了道德的完美和高尚；moral 意思是道德的、品行端正的，life 表示生命、一生，moral life 就表示有道德的一生。在此分析之上，个人更倾向于采纳理雅各对"仁"的翻译。

本章课后练习

一、请尝试翻译以下句子。

1. 子曰："道千乘之国，敬事而信，节用而爱人，使民以时。"（《论语·学而篇》第五）

第三章 《论语》经典篇章英译选读

白话释义：
英译：

2. 子曰："居上不宽，为礼不敬，临丧不哀，吾何以观之哉？"（《论语·八佾篇》第二十六）
白话释义：
英译：

3. 子曰："君子怀德，小人怀土；君子怀刑，小人怀惠。"（《论语·里仁篇》第十一）
白话释义：
英译：

4. 升车，必正立，执绥。车中，不内顾，不疾言，不亲指。（《论语·乡党篇》第二十六）
白话释义：
英译：

5. 子曰："其身正，不令而行；其身不正，虽令不从。"（《论语·子路篇》第六）
白话释义：
英译：

二、请比较以下名句两种英译文本的异同。

1. 曾子曰："吾日三省吾身：为人谋而不忠乎？与朋友交而不信乎？传不习乎？"（《论语·学而篇》第四）

英译 1：A disciple of Confucius remarked, "I daily examine into my personal conduct on three points：—First, whether in carrying out the duties entrusted to me by others, I have not failed in conscientiousness; Secondly, whether in intercourse with friends, I have not failed in sincerity and trustworthiness; Thirdly, whether I have not failed to practice what I profess in my teaching."（辜鸿铭）

英译 2：The philosopher Tsang said, "I daily examine myself on three points: whether, in transacting business for others, I may have been not faithful; whether, in intercourse with friends, I may have been not sincere; whether I may have not mastered and practiced the instructions of my teacher."(James Legge)

2. 子曰:"学而不思则罔,思而不学则殆。"(《论语·为政篇》第十五)

英译1:Confucius remarked, "Study without thinking is labour lost. Thinking without study is perilous."(辜鸿铭)

英译2:The Master said, "Learning without thought is labor lost; thought without learning is perilous."(James Legge)

3. 子曰:"人而不仁,如礼何?人而不仁,如乐何?"(《论语·八佾篇》第三)

英译1:Confucius remarked, "If a man is without moral character, what good can the use of the fine arts do him? If a man is without moral character, what good can the use of music do him?"(辜鸿铭)

英译2:The Master said, "If a man be without the virtues proper to humanity, what has he to do with the rites of propriety? If a man be without the virtues proper to humanity, what has he to do with music?"(James Legge)

4. 子曰:"见贤思齐焉,见不贤而内自省也。"(《论语·里仁篇》第十七)

英译1:Confucius remarked, "When we meet with men of worth, we should think how we may equal them. When we meet with worthless men, we should turn into ourselves and find out if we do not resemble them."(辜鸿铭)

英译2:The Master said, "When we see men of worth, we should think of equalling them; when we see men of a contrary character, we should turn inwards and examine ourselves."(James Legge)

5. 子贡曰:"我不欲人之加诸我也,吾亦欲无加诸人。"子曰:"赐也,非尔所及也。"(《论语·公冶长篇》第十二)

英译1:A disciple said to Confucius, "What I do not wish that others should not do unto me, I also do not wish that I should do unto them." "My friend," answered Confucius, "You have not yet

第三章 《论语》经典篇章英译选读

attained to that."(辜鸿铭)

英译 2：Tsze-kung said, "What I do not wish men to do to me, I also wish not to do to men." The Master said, "Ts'ze, you have not attained to that."(James Legge)

6. 子曰："贤哉，回也！一箪食，一瓢饮，在陋巷，人不堪其忧，回也不改其乐。贤哉，回也！"（《论语·雍也篇》第十一）

英译 1：Confucius remarked of his disciple, the favourite Yen Hui, saying, "How much heroism is in that man! Living on one single meal a day, with water for his drink, and living in the lowest hovels of the city, —no man could have stood such hardships, yet he —he did not lose his cheerfulness. How much heroism is in that man!"(辜鸿铭)

英译 2：The Master said, "Admirable indeed was the virtue of Hui! With a single bamboo dish of rice, a single gourd dish of drink, and living in his mean narrow lane, while others could not have endured the distress, he did not allow his joy to be affected by it. Admirable indeed was the virtue of Hui!"(James Legge)

7. 子曰："德之不修，学之不讲，闻义不能徙，不善不能改，是吾忧也。"（《论语·述而篇》第三）

英译 1：Lastly, Confucius said, "Neglect of godliness; study without understanding; failure to act up to what I believe to be right; and inability to change bad habits: these are things which cause me constant solicitude."(辜鸿铭)

英译 2：The Master said, "The leaving virtue without proper cultivation; the not thoroughly discussing what is learned; not being able to move towards righteousness of which a knowledge is gained; and not being able to change what is not good: — these are the things which occasion me solicitude."(James Legge)

8. 曾子曰"士不可以不弘毅，任重而道远。仁以为己任，不亦重乎？死而后已，不亦远乎？"（《论语·泰伯篇》第七）

英译1：A disciple of Confucius remarked, "An educated gentleman may not be without strength and resoluteness of character. His responsibility in life is a heavy one, and the way is long. He is responsible to himself for living a moral life; is that not a heavy responsibility? He must continue in it until he dies; is the way then not a long one?"(辜鸿铭)

英译2：The philosopher Tsang said, "The officer may not be without breadth of mind and vigorous endurance. His burden is heavy and his course is long. Perfect virtue is the burden which he considers it is his to sustain;—is it not heavy? Only with death does his course stop;—is it not long?"(James Legge)

9. 孔子曰："益者三友,损者三友。友直,友谅,友多闻,益矣。友便辟,友善柔,友便佞,损矣。"(《论语·季氏篇》第四)

英译1：Confucius remarked, "There are three kinds of friendship which are beneficial and three kinds which are injurious. Friendship with upright men, with faithful men, and with men of much information: such friendships are beneficial. Friendship with plausible men, with men of insinuating manners, and with glib-tongued men: such friendships are injurious."(辜鸿铭)

英译2：Confucius said, "There are three friendships which are advantageous, and three which are injurious. Friendship with the upright; friendship with the sincere; and friendship with the man of much observation:—these are advantageous. Friendship with the man of specious airs; friendship with the insinuatingly soft; and friendship with the glib-tongued:—these are injurious."(James Legge)

10. 子贡曰："君子之过也,如日月之食焉;过也,人皆见之;更也,人皆抑之。"(《论语·子张篇》第二十一)

英译1：The same disciple remarked, "The failings of a great man are eclipses of the sun and moon. When he fails, all men see it; but, when he recovers from his failing, all men look up to him as before."(辜鸿铭)

第三章 《论语》经典篇章英译选读

英译 2：Tsze-kung said, "The faults of the superior man are like the eclipses of the sun and moon. He has his faults, and all men see them; he changes again, and all men look up to him."（James Legge）

三、段落试译。

定公问："一言而可以兴邦，有诸？"孔子对曰："言不可以若是其几也。人之言曰：'为君难，为臣不易。'如知为君之难也，不几乎一言而兴邦乎？"曰："一言而丧邦，有诸？"孔子对曰："言不可以若是其几也。人之言曰：'予无乐乎为君，唯其言而莫予违也。'如其善而莫之违也，不亦善乎？如不善而莫之违也，不几乎一言而丧邦乎？"

（《论语·子路篇》第十五）

子路从而后，遇丈人，以杖荷蓧。子路问曰："子见夫子乎？"丈人曰："四体不勤，五谷不分，孰为夫子？"植其杖而芸。子路拱而立。止子路宿，杀鸡为黍而食之，见其二子焉。明日，子路行以告。子曰："隐者也。"使子路反见之。至，则行矣。子路曰："不仕无义。长幼之节，不可废也；君臣之义，如之何其废之？欲洁其身，而乱大伦。君子之仕也，行其义也。道之不行，已知之矣。"

（《论语·微子篇》第七）

第四章

《大学》经典篇章英译选读

【导读】

　　作为儒家典籍的入门读物,《大学》的地位经历了一个逐渐提升的过程。唐代之前,《大学》只是作为《小戴礼记》的第四十二篇,并没有得到显著的关注;古本的《大学》本身也没有章节之分。

　　两汉之际,佛教传入中国;此后从东晋到隋唐,佛教与道教在学术界占据统治地位。唐代文学家韩愈不满于佛道宣扬的出世无为之说,为了重新确立儒家的道统地位,开始以儒家的修齐治平之说对抗佛教的正心养心说,并在《原道》一文中,特别突出了《大学》的地位。北宋之时,为了给新儒学的义理寻求儒家之道的基础,大儒程颐、程颢二兄弟开始关注《大学》,并对《大学》的文本做了一些调整。程颐认为《大学》是孔氏遗书,是进入儒家的初学入德之门。南宋名儒朱熹继承了尊师程颐的看法,在二程的基础上,对《大学》文本再次改动和调整,并作《大学章句》,将改本《大学》与《论语》《孟子》《中庸》合编为儒家《四书》,《大学》则位列《四书》之首,由此奠定了《大学》一书的经典地位。之后,由宋元开始,《大学》乃作为官方学寮的必读书目和科举考试的重要内容之一,对儒学乃至整个中国文化产生了极大影响。

　　随着《大学》地位的提升,《大学》的结构和内容也经历了一些变化。古本的《大学》只有"三纲领(明明德、亲民、止于至善)、八条目(格物、致知、诚意、正心、修身、齐家、治国、平天下)",以及关于"诚意、正心、修身、齐家、治国、平天下"等六个条目的解释。二程兄弟认为,古本的《大学》文本不完整,其中既没有阐释

第四章 《大学》经典篇章英译选读

"三纲领",又缺少对"格物和致知"两个条目的解释。此外,二程认为,《大学》文本有错简。因此,他们对《大学》文本的顺序做了调整,使《大学》整篇的结构变成了:先提出三纲领,然后是对三纲领的解释;之后是八条目,再是对八条目的解释。朱熹在二程调整的基础上,从宏观上将《大学》进一步分为"经"和"传"两部分:"经"一章和"传"十章;"经"提出主题,"传"是对主题进行具体的解释;其中经一章又分为三纲领和八条目。此外,朱熹的改本还增加了对"格物、致知"两个条目的解释,这是朱熹改本最具特色之处,同时也是最遭人诟病之处。无论如何,朱熹不但进一步规范了《大学》文本的结构层次,还将他的改本编入"四书",整合为《四书章句集注》,即《大学章句》《中庸章句》《论语集注》《孟子集注》,一举奠定了《大学》的经典地位。

依据朱熹的改本,《大学》的主要内容是:"经"一章,讲三纲领八条目;"传"十章,逐条解释三纲领八条目。

具体说来,"经"一章开篇即言"三纲领","大学之道在明明德,在亲民,在止于至善"。三纲领开篇明义,表明儒家大学之道的终极追求是"明明德,亲民,止于至善"。随后提出"八条目":"格物、致知、诚意、正心、修身、齐家、治国、平天下"——"古之欲明明德于天下者,先治其国,欲治其国者,先齐其家,欲齐其家者先修其身,欲修其身者先正其心,欲正其心者先诚其意,欲诚其意者先致其知,致知在格物。"八条目以倒推的形式逐级递增,达于最高境界。每一个步骤,前者都是后者的基础——前者为本、后者为末,所以八条目中,最基本的是"格物"。"其本乱而末治者否也",所以,八条目说明的是儒家追求大学之道的逻辑方法。以上是《大学》"经"一章的核心内容。

"传"是对"经"的分承解释或阐发。其中第一章到第四章是对三纲领的解释,是"统论纲领旨趣",第一章解释"明明德",第二章解释"亲民",第三章解释"止于至善",第四章解释"本末"。第五章之后是对八条目的解释,是"细论条目功夫",第六章解释诚意,第七章解释正心,第八章解释修身、齐家,第九章解释齐家、治国,第十章解释治国平天下。三纲领和八条目非常简括,但是却涉及儒家学说的全部核心思想,因此一直被视作儒家价值系统的纲领。

"大学",自是相对"小学"而言。许慎《说文解字叙》云:"《周礼》八岁入小学,保氏教国子,先以六书。"清代考据学家段玉裁注云:"国子者,公卿大夫之子弟,师氏教之,保氏养之,而世子亦齿焉。六书者,文字声音义理之总汇也。""六书"最早见于《周礼·地官·保氏》,即象形、指事、会意、形声、转注、假借六种汉字的造字之法和用字之法。古代十五岁以前为少年,进入小学,受习"礼、乐、射、御、书、数六艺",包括洒扫、应对、进退之节,礼乐、射御、书数之文,即打扫卫生、应对长辈提问、待人接物之礼及识字等小学学问。十五岁以后为成人,进入大学,学习"穷理、正心、修己、治人"等大学之道。所以,"大学之道",首先是讨论古代大学教育之法、教育之礼、教育之道的意思。

但是,《大学》不仅仅是教育之学。古人对《大学》中的核心问题和核心思想的理解和阐释各有不同,在学术思想史上形成了一个脉络变迁的过程。唐代之前,古人对《大学》的理解以东汉末经学家郑玄的"以其记博学,可以为政"为代表,落脚于为政论,或者说治国论。唐代之后,对《大学》的理解侧重修身论。韩愈《原道》一文引用《大学》之言,并指明"古之所谓正心而诚意者,将以有为也",认为修身的重点是诚意。两宋之际,依照二程和朱熹的理解,《大学》文本对八条目的逻辑论述是以格物致知为根本,因此,修身论的重点变成了格物。明朝王明阳不满于宋朝理学之说和朱熹补作格物致知之举,认为朱熹改本并非古本之原意,转而强调对致知的理解;修身论的重心就此转移到致知、致良知,并在致良知的基础上界定格物。古人对《大学》问题意识和理论重点的变迁说明,《大学》并非仅仅是教育学意义上的教育之道、教育思想,而是与当时的社会问题和最高理想息息相关。用后来的讲法,《大学》不仅仅是修身或内圣,而是儒家内圣外王的政治伦理观的集中体现。从开宗明义的"大学之道",再到"格物、致知、诚意"等修己内明之学,再到"治国平天下"的外用之学,《大学》系统论述了儒家由内圣而至外王的伦理价值体系,蕴含着丰富的政治哲学、道德伦理等思想内涵。

《大学》在中西文化交流史上也占据着重要的地位。早在明末清初、耶稣会士入华传教之际,作为四书之首的《大学》就开始了西译传播之旅。此后的300年时间,到20世纪中后期,至少有12本《大学》英译本问世,译者包括早期的来华传教士及后来的旅美华人学者。这些译本分别以不同的视角和立场,将儒家思想和中国文化价值传播到西方世界。其中最为经典、认可度最高的译本之一是英国汉学家理雅各的译本。

作为儒家学说的经典文本,《大学》可谓是中华传统文化的基础和根源,代表着中华优秀传统文化的主流价值观。即使在利益分化、思想多元化的新世纪,《大学》所蕴含的伦理原则、道德精神仍然具有普世性及不可替代的文化意义。1993年,全世界宗教议会宣言所确认的世界伦理的金律就是《大学》中孔子所说的忠恕之道——"己所不欲,勿施于人"。因此,在21世纪的当代,学习《大学》的文本和思想,不但是对中华传统文化基础的探源,更是对其中有益的思想资源的主动汲取及现代性转化。这对于继承和发展中华优秀传统文化,弘

第四章 《大学》经典篇章英译选读

扬当代社会主义核心价值观,以及加强新时代公民道德建设等,都具有重要的现实意义。

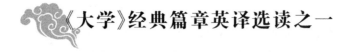

《大学》经典篇章英译选读之一

经一章

大学①之道②,在明明德③,在亲民④,在止⑤于至善⑥。知止⑦而后有定⑧,定而后能静,静而后能安⑨,安而后能虑,虑而后能得。物有本末,事有终始,知所先后,则近道矣。古之欲明明德于天下者,先治其国;欲治其国者,先齐其家⑩;欲齐其家者,先修其身⑪;欲修其身者,先正其心;欲正其心者,先诚其意;欲诚其意者,先致其知⑫。致知在格物⑬。物格而后知至,知至而后意诚,意诚而后心正,心正而后身修,身修而后家齐,家齐而后国治,国治而后天下平。自天子以至于庶人⑭,壹是⑮皆以修身为本。

注:本段选自《大学》第一章,开宗明义,说明大学之道三纲领八条目。三纲八目既是《大学》的纲领旨归,也是儒学"垂世立教"的目标所在。正如朱熹所说,"先学《大学》,以定其规模";定其规模就是明确学习目标、设定学习范围。大学的目标就是三纲领,最终目标是止于至善;学习的范围就是八条目:格物、致知、诚意、正心、修身、齐家、治国、平天下,这也是实现大学目标的具体步骤。可以说,大学的纲领既是人生志向和生命理想的设定,也是儒家垂世立教的目的所在。三纲领和八条目就是从内修到外治的人生进修阶梯。抓住三纲八目,就等于抓住了打开儒家大门的钥匙。要实现大学之道,首先要对大学的宗旨和纲领有深切的认识和体会。

【注释】

① 〔大学〕"大学"一词在古代有两种含义:一是"博学"的意思;二是相对于"小学"而言的。古人八岁入小学,学习"洒扫应对进退、礼乐射御书数"等文化基

础知识和礼节；十五岁入大学，学习"穷理、正心、修己、治人"等政治伦理哲学之大学之道。

②〔道〕本义是指道路，引申为规律、原则等，此处指宗旨、纲领。

③〔明明德〕第一个明是使役动词，表示使彰明、使显发；第二个明是形容词，光明的。明德就是光明正大的品德。

④〔亲民〕二程认为，此处应为"新民"。新民和亲民不同，亲民指亲爱百姓，关心百姓的生活；新民则是指礼乐教化，移风易俗，使百姓弃旧图新、去恶从善，不断提升自己。

⑤〔止〕达成并维持。

⑥〔至善〕最完善圆满的境界。

⑦〔止〕归宿，立场。〔知止〕就是指对目标、归宿等有明确的了解。

⑧〔定〕定向。〔有定〕对目标、归宿了解之后，就能够坚定不移，朝着目标的方向努力。

⑨〔安〕随处而安，安稳。

⑩〔齐其家〕管理好自己的家庭或家族，使家庭或家族和睦兴盛。

⑪〔修其身〕修养自身的品性。

⑫〔致其知〕使自己获得知识。

⑬〔格物〕认识，研究万事万物。

⑭〔庶人〕平民百姓。

⑮〔壹是〕都是，皆是。

白话释义

"大学"的宗旨，就在于发扬光明正大的德行，在于更新民风，在于达到德才完美的最高境界。知道应该达到的境界，然后才能志向坚定；志向坚定，然后才能镇静不躁；镇静不躁，然后才能随处而安；随处而安，然后才能思虑周全；思虑周全，然后才能有所收获。

古代那些想要在全天下发扬光明正大品德的人，先要治理好自己的国家；想要治理好自己的国家，就先要管理好自己的家庭；想要管理好自己的家庭，就先要修养自身的品性；想要修养自身的品性，就先要端正自己的心志；想要端正自己的心志，就先要使自己的意念真诚；想要使自己的意念真诚，就先要使自己获得知识；获得知识的途径在于认识、探究万事万物的原理。探究万事万物的原理后才能获得智慧；获得智慧后意念才能真诚；意念真诚后心思才能端正；心

第四章 《大学》经典篇章英译选读

思端正后才能修养品性;品性修养后才能管理好家庭;管理好家庭后才能治理好国家;治理好国家后天下才能太平。上自国家元首,下至平民百姓,人人都要以修养品性为根本。

英译1

What the great learning teaches, is—to illustrate the illustrious virtues; to renovate the people; and to rest in the highest excellence. The point where to rest being known, the object of pursuit is then determined; and, that being determined, a calm unperturbedness may be attained to. To that calmness there will succeed a tranquil repose. In that repose there may be careful deliberation, and that deliberation will be followed by the attainment *of the desired end*. Things have their root and their branches. Affairs have their end and their beginning. To know what is first and what is last will lead near to what is taught *in the Great Learning*. The ancients who wished to illustrate illustrious virtue throughout the kingdom, first ordered well their own States. Wishing to order well their States, they first regulated their families. Wishing to regulate their families, they first cultivated their persons. Wishing to cultivate their persons, they first rectified their hearts. Wishing to rectify their hearts, they first sought to be sincere in their thoughts. Wishing to be sincere in their thoughts, they first extended to the utmost their knowledge. Such extension of knowledge lay in the investigation of things. Things being investigated, knowledge became complete. Their knowledge being complete, their thoughts were sincere. Their thoughts being sincere, their hearts were then rectified. Their hearts being rectified, their persons were cultivated. Their persons being cultivated, their families were regulated. Their families being regulated, their States were rightly governed. Their States being rightly governed, the whole kingdom was made tranquil and happy. From the Son of Heaven down to the mass of the people, all must consider the cultivation of the person the root of *everything besides*.

——James Legge(詹姆斯·理雅各)

英译2

The object of a Higher Education is to bring out (明) the intelligent(明) moral power (德) of our nature; to make a new and better society (lit. people); and to enable us to abide in the highest excellence. When a man has a standard of excellence before him, and only then, will he have a fixed and definite purpose; with a fixed and definite purpose, and only then, will he be able to have peace and tranquility of mind; with tranquility of mind, and only then, will he be able to have peace and tranquility of soul; with peace and serenity of soul, and only then, can he devote himself to deep, serious thinking and reflection; and it is only by deep, serious thinking and reflection that a man can attain true culture. Men in old times when they wanted to further the cause of enlightenment and civilization in the world began first by securing good government in their country. When they wanted to secure good government in their country, they began first by putting their house in order. When they wanted to put their house in order, they began first by ordering their conversation aright. When they wanted to put their conversation aright, they began first by putting their minds in a proper and well-ordered condition. When they wanted to put their minds in a proper and well-ordered condition, they began first by getting true ideas. When they wanted to have true ideas, they began first by acquiring knowledge and understanding. The acquirement of knowledge and understanding comes from a systematic study of things. After a systematic study of things, and only then, knowledge and understanding will come. When knowledge and understanding have come, and only then, will men have true ideas. When men have true ideas, and only then, will their minds be in a proper and well-ordered condition. When men's minds are in a proper and well-ordered condition, and only then, will their conversation be ordered aright. When men's conversations are ordered aright, and only then, will their houses be kept in order. When men's houses are kept in order, and only then, will there be good government in the country. When there is good government in all countries, and only then, will there be peace and order in the world.

——辜鸿铭

第四章 《大学》经典篇章英译选读

英译3

The way of the great learning is to rid oneself of selfish desires and develop further one's inherent virtues. One should not only develop his own inherent virtues further, but should encourage all persons to do so also. Only then is it possible to reach the acme of perfection. Once the acme of perfection is attained, is a man able to set the orientation of his ambitions. After setting his orientation, he will not waiver in his ambition and will be satisfied with his position. Satisfied with his position, he can ponder well. Being able to ponder well, he will be able to achieve all he wants. All things have their important and unimportant aspects; all events have their start and finish. If one knows the order of priority, he is not far from the way of the great learning. In ancient times, one who intended to carry forward all the inherent virtues in the world and to rid people of material desires had to first rule his state well. To rule his state well, he had to first educate his family. To educate his family, he had first to cultivate himself. To cultivate himself, he had first to set his heart right. To set his heart right, he had first to be sincere and honest. To be sincere and honest, he had first to perfect his knowledge and the perfection of his knowledge depended on his investigation of things. From emperor to the common people, self-cultivation is the base.

——何祚康

英译鉴赏简评

此段是《大学》的开篇之句。开篇即提纲挈领、开宗明义,三个动宾结构简明扼要地点出大学之道的宗旨。因此,对于三纲八目词汇的精准翻译十分重要。首先是题目"大学"的翻译。在古代,"大"有两层意思。一读"太",意思是博学之道;二指大人、成人,在此意义下,"大学"(大人之学)与"小学"(少年之学)相对应。无论是"大学"还是"太学",都隐含以上两种意义。译文"Higher Education"更接近西方现代教育的说法,缩小了"大学"的文化内涵;而译文"the Great Learning"内涵丰富,其抽象语意更加接近"大学"的本义,对原文的还原度较高,也是目前"大学"一词最为通用的译法。

此外,该段中的关键词还包括八条目。三位译者对八条目的翻译对比见表4-1。

表4-1 三位译者对八条目的翻译对比

中文	英译1	英译2	英译3
格物	investigation of things	a systematic study of things	investigation of things
致知	extend to the utmost knowledge	acquiring knowledge and understanding	perfect his knowledge
诚意	to be sincere in their thoughts	have true ideas	to be sincere and honest
正心	rectify their hearts	put their minds in a proper and well-ordered condition	set his heart right
修身	cultivate their persons	put their conversation aright	cultivate himself
齐家	regulate their families	put their house in order	educate his family
治国	order well their States	securing good government in their country	rule his state well
平天下	the whole kingdom was made tranquil and happy	further the cause of enlightenment and civilization in the world	carry forward all the inherent virtues in the world

显而易见,英译2的翻译策略不同于英译1与英译3。前者是意译,后者是直译。意译主要考量目标语读者的接受能力,直译则考量源语文化的传递。两种翻译策略各有侧重。其中,译者对"修身"一词的翻译,差异较为显著。英译2为"put their conversation aright",意思是"正言",与"修身"之意差异较大。英译1为"cultivate their persons",意思是"教育感化人民",英译3为"cultivate himself",意思是"培养自身"。依据朱熹的注释,"修身以上,明明德之事也。齐家以下,新民之事也","修身"应指明己之明德之事,故英译3最为契合。而关于"齐家",英译2"put their house in order"指打扫房屋,英译3"educate their families"指教导家人,与原文相差较远。因古代为宗法社会,采取家族式管理,所以"齐家"是指将家庭或家族事务管理得井井有条,译为

第四章 《大学》经典篇章英译选读

"regulate their families"更为合适。"天下"是一个重要的中华文化负载词,具有"地理、政治、文化"等多层次、多维度内涵,广义上指广袤天地之间的自然界或整个世界,狭义上指中国全境,或仅仅是社会意义上的国家统治权,其指代对象往往依据语境的不同而具有较大的弹性。理雅各将"天下"译为"the whole kingdom",似乎偏差较大,但是,当时周朝是分封制,周天子为天下之共主,各诸侯国都是周天子的臣子,都属于周朝这一政治共同体,因此,这种处理有一定的道理。对于"平",笔者认为理雅各的理解较为透彻,"平"既有"安宁平和"(tranquil)之意,又有"和睦幸福"(happy)之意。相较而言,其他两位译者对"平"字的翻译则与原文差距较大。

理雅各同样采取了直译法来翻译三纲领"明明德、亲民、止于至善",将其处理为对等的英语动宾结构,并对"明德""亲民""止""至善"等核心词做了注释。值得一提的是,理雅各对"明明德"的翻译,同样采取了与汉语原文一致的同词根词汇形式"*illustrate* the *illustrious* virtues",展现出其深厚的语言功底和文化理解力。

作为西学东渐的第一人,辜鸿铭在翻译时采取了异化策略。他将"明德"翻译为"the intelligent moral power of our nature",将"亲民"译为"to make a new and better society",译文更直白、浅明,更多地考虑了西方读者的接受能力,而且兼顾了当时中国社会的大变革背景。英译3何祚康的译文则更像诠释,译文的意思不但包括了原文的内容,而且增补了译者对原文的理解。

到目前为止,《大学》英译本至少有12个。英国汉学家理雅各采取直译策略,译本以中文、译文和注释三行排列,不但附有原文,更从训诂、考证和历代注疏入手,对原文进行多方考证比对,力求呈现原文的本意和作者的原意。因其考据之广博、校勘之严谨,理雅各的译文自面世以来一直被奉为文字学翻译的典范,亦被誉为英语世界的汉学经典。

《大学》经典篇章英译选读之二

传第一、二、三章

《康诰》①曰:"克②明德。"《大甲》③曰:"顾④误⑤天之明命⑥。"《帝典》⑦曰:"克明峻德⑧。"皆自明也。

汤⑨之《盘铭⑩》曰:"苟⑪日新,日日新,又日新。"《康诰》曰:"作⑫新民⑬。"《诗⑭》曰:"周虽旧邦,其命⑮惟新。"是故,君子无所不用其极⑯。

《诗》⑰云:"邦畿⑱千里,惟民所止⑲。"《诗》⑳云:"缗蛮黄鸟,止于丘隅㉑。"子曰:"于止,知其所止,可以人而不如鸟乎!㉒"《诗》云:"穆穆文王,于缉熙敬止㉓!"为人君,止于仁;为人臣,止于敬;为人子,止于孝;为人父,止于慈;与国人交,止于信。

注:以上三段分别是朱熹本《大学》的第二、三、四章,朱子称为传第一、二、三章,分别解释三纲领之"明明德""新民""止于至善"。旧本"明明德"段文字在诚意章"以此没世不忘"句下,二程认为此处有错简,而更考经文,移至《大学》第二章,即传第一章,与"明明德"刚好对应。

【注释】

①〔《康诰》〕《尚书·周书》里面的一篇。
②〔克〕能够。
③〔《大甲》〕即《太甲》,是《尚书·商书》里面的一篇。
④〔顾〕顾念。朱子解释说"谓常目在之也",就是眼睛常常看着的地方。
⑤〔諟(shì)〕通"是",表示"此";另一种解释为审,审查,即省思。
⑥〔明命〕光明的德行。
⑦〔《帝典》〕即《尧典》,是《尚书·虞夏书》里面的一篇。
⑧〔克明峻德〕原句为"克明俊德","峻"与"俊"通,意为大,崇高。
⑨〔汤〕即成汤,商朝的开国君主。
⑩〔盘〕洗澡用具。〔铭〕铭刻的箴言。〔盘铭〕刻在器皿上的、用来警诫自己的箴言。这里是指汤把"苟日新,日日新,又日新"铭刻在自己的洗澡用具上,以便洗澡的时候能够看见这句箴言,提醒自己要及时反省和不断革新。
⑪〔苟〕连词,假设,如果。
⑫〔作〕振作,激励。
⑬〔新民〕即经一章(第一章)里所说的"亲民",新民就是使人弃旧图新,去恶从善。

第四章 《大学》经典篇章英译选读

⑭〔诗〕指《诗经·大雅·文王》。〔周〕周朝。〔旧邦〕旧国。
⑮〔其命〕指周朝所禀受的天命。〔维〕语助词,无意义。
⑯〔是故君子无所不用其极〕所以品德高尚的人无时无处不在追求德性的完善。〔是故〕所以。〔君子〕指品德高尚的人。
⑰〔《诗》〕此处指《诗经·商颂·玄鸟》。
⑱〔邦畿〕王者之都,古代天子都城及周围的郊区。
⑲〔止〕居也,言物各有所当止之处也。《礼记正义》:"此《商颂·玄鸟》之篇,言殷之邦畿方千里,为人所居止。喻良禽择木而居,人君贤则来。
⑳〔《诗》〕此处指《诗经·小雅·绵蛮》。
㉑〔缗蛮〕黄鸟鸣声,一说小鸟貌。〔丘隅〕山丘的一个角落,或曰山岑草木茂密处。
㉒〔于止,知其所止,可以人而不如鸟乎〕此句是孔子说《诗》之辞,云是观于鸟之所止,则人亦知其所止。意思是鸟知道在岑蔚安闲处居止,人也应该选择礼义乐土之处而居。
㉓〔穆穆文王,於缉熙敬止〕圣人之止,无非至善。〔穆穆〕美貌、深远之意。〔於〕叹美词。〔缉〕继续。〔熙〕光明。

白话释义

《康诰》上面说,能够发扬光明的品德。《大甲》上面说:要审视反省上天赋予的光明德性。《帝典》上面说,能够弘扬崇高伟大的品德。这三句话都强调,"明德"是天之所命,是上天赋予的灵明的德性,所以要"自明",即自己开发弘扬自身光明崇高的德性。

商汤王刻在洗澡用具上的箴言说:"如果能够做到一天新,就应保持天天新,新了还要更新。"《尚书·康诰》说:"激励人弃旧图新,焕发新的风貌。"《诗经·大雅·文王》说:"周朝虽然是旧的国家,但是却禀受了新的天命。"所以,品德高尚的人无时无处不在追求完美的道德境界。

《诗经·商颂·玄鸟》上说:"城邦方圆千里的地方,都是百姓聚居的地方。(只要人君贤德,就会有人民来依附他。)"《诗经·小雅·缗蛮》上又说:"缗蛮鸣叫着的微小黄鸟,也懂得寻找一个安全的地方栖息。"孔子说:"连黄鸟都知道在什么地方栖息,难道人还不如鸟儿吗?"《诗经·大雅·文王》上说:"端庄恭敬的文王啊,不断地发挥他的光明品德,做事始终谨慎地使自己处于至善的境地。"所以,做国君的,要以仁爱为最高追求;做臣子的,要以恭敬为最高追求;做子女的,要以孝顺为最高追求;做父母的,要以慈爱为最高追求;与他人交往,要以信实为最高追求。也就是说,各种社会角色都有对应的标准,但是各个社会角色追求的终极目标是一致的,其终极目标都是止于至善。

英译1

In the Announcement to Keang, it is said, "He was able to make his virtue illustrious." In the Tâi Chiâ, it is said, "He contemplated and studied the illustrious decrees of Heaven." In the Canon of the emperor (Yâo), it is said, "He was able to make illustrious his lofty virtue." *These passages* all *show how those sovereigns* made themselves illustrious.

On the bathing-tub of Teang, the following words were engraved:—"If you can one day renovate yourself, do so from day to day. Yea, let there be daily renovation." In the Announcement to Keang, it is said, "To stir up the new people." In *The Book of Poetry*, it is said, "Although Châu was an ancient State, the ordinance which lighted on it was new." Therefore, the superior man in everything uses his utmost endeavours.

In *The Book of Poetry*, it is said, "The royal domain of a thousand li is where the people rest." In *The Book of Poetry*, it is said, "The twittering yellow bird rests on a corner of the mound." The Master said, "When it rests, it knows where to rest. Is it possible that a man should not be equal to this bird?" In *The Book of Poetry*, it is said, "Profound was king Wăn. With how bright and unceasing a feeling of reverence did he regard his resting-places!" As a sovereign, he rested in benevolence. As a minister, he rested in reverence. As a son, he rested in filial piety. As a father, he rested in kindness. In communication to his subjects, he rested in good faith.

——James Legge(詹姆斯·理雅各)

英译2

The *Commission of Investiture to Prince K'ang* says: "He (the Emperor Wen) succeeded in making manifest the power of his moral nature." In the

第四章 《大学》经典篇章英译选读

Address of the Minister I-Yin to the Emperor T'ai Chia, it is said: "He (the great Emperor T'ang) kept constantly before him the clear Ordinance of God." In the *Memorial Record of the Emperor Yao*, it is said: "He succeeded in making manifest the lofty sublimity of his moral nature." Thus all these men made manifest the intelligent moral power of their nature.

The *Inscription on the Emperor T'ang's Bath* says: "Be a new man each day; from day to day be a new man; every day be a new man." The *Commission of Investiture to Prince K'ang* says: "Create a new society." The *Book of Songs* says: "Although the Royal House of Chou was an old State, a new Mission was given to it." Therefore, whatever a gentleman finds for his hands to do, he doeth with all his might.

The *Book of Songs* says: "The Imperial Domain was a thousand li wide; within it all the people found their abode." The *Book of Songs*, again, says: "The twittering yellow bird has found its abode on the side of a little hill." Confucius commenting on this said: "In choosing their abode, even the birds know what to choose. Can it be that man is less intelligent than birds?" The *Book of Songs* says: "Profoundly serious was the Emperor Wen. Ah! how earnestly he strove to realize his ideals." As a ruler, his ideal was to love mankind. As a subject, his ideal was to respect authority. As a son his ideal was to be a dutiful son. As a father, his ideal was to be kind to his children. In intercourse with his fellow men, his ideal was to be faithful and true.

——辜鸿铭

英译3

"Kang Gao" of *The Book of History* said, "One should carry forward one's inherent virtues." "*Tai Jia*" of *The Book of History* said, "One should know his own inherent virtues bestowed by Heaven." "*Di Dian*" of *The Book of History* said, "One should carry forward one's own noble virtues." The idea common to the three excerpts above is to develop one's own inherent virtues.

中华典籍英译选读

The inscription on bath utensils of the Shang Dynasty said, "If a man is to clear the dirt on the bath utensils to make them brighter, he should clean it every day so as to make it brighter and brighter." "*Kang Gao*" of *The Book of History* said, "Everyone should be educated to be a new man." *The Book of Songs* said, "Though Zhou was an ancient country, the government decrees and imperial mandates under King Wen's rule were all new." Therefore no wise and enlightened ruler will not try to do his best.

The Book of Songs said, "The capital covers thousands of miles, all common people would like to settle here." *The Book of Songs* said, "The chirping yellow birds perch at the corner of the mountains." Confucius said, "Yes, yellow birds know where they should perch. How can a person not be of the same wisdom as a bird?" *The Book of Songs* said, "Noble and grave King Wen kept and developed the virtues of ancient emperors, respected his forefathers and was satisfied with his position." As an emperor, a man should be benevolent. As a subordinate official, a man should pay respect to his superior. As a son, a man should be filial to his parents. As a father, a man should be kind to his children. A man should be credible and trustful in his contact with other people.

——何祚康

英译鉴赏简评

此处的翻译首先涉及史书书名,三位译者都采取了"书名加注"或者"书名附诠释"的方法,并无太大差异。重点之一在于对无主句的句子,添加了主语。在儒家的政治伦理体系中,上古圣王的言行举止意义非凡,是儒家道德伦理学说权威性与合法性的来源。因此,翻译中要使英语读者明确此处节选的文字是关于三位上古圣王言行的描述,而非普通人言行的描述。此外,按照理雅各的考据和观点,"大学"并非是普通人学的,而是君主或国家管理者学的知识;同样,依据宋儒理学的观点,能够"明明德"于天下的人,并不是普通人,而是包括士大夫阶层在内的管理层。结合三个引语的语境,前三个无主句的主语应该是君主或帝王,最后一个无主句的主语应该是管理层的人,而非普通人。从这个意义来讲,译文 2 的翻译 He (the Emperor Wen)/He (the great Emperor T'ang)

第四章 《大学》经典篇章英译选读

最明确,译文 1 也比较清晰合理。

此段话中连续出现了五个"新"字。据宋儒程颐的观点,《大学》开篇之句中的"亲民"应为"新民"。因此,"苟日新,日日新,又日新"中的"新"是指"不断反省和革新",英译 3 将其译为字面意"干净明亮",意思与原句有出入。第二句"作新民",(《大学章句集注》中写有,"鼓之舞之之谓作,言振起其自新之民也。"),理雅各将其译为"to stir up the new people",并在注释中补充说明"作新民"也有可能指将殷朝旧民变作周朝新民,对原文意思的把握较为准确。译文 2"create a new society"引申过多。译文 3"be educated to be a new man",遗漏了"作"字,意思有偏差。三位译者对"其命维新"意思的理解一致,英译 1 和 3 采取了直译策略,英译 2 使用了意译策略。关于最末句"君子"的翻译,译者的理解各有不同。理雅各认为,此处的"君子"指有品级的官员,以及道德高尚的人。由于上下文语境无法确认"君子"的明确指代,理雅各将其译为"the superior man",内涵与"君子"基本一致;译文 2 译为"gentleman",表示儒雅之人,过于宽泛;译文 3 译为"wise and enlightened ruler",表示"英明的统治者",词汇内涵有所缩减。儒家文本中"君子"一词的出现频率非常高,但如何准确地进行翻译,的确难度不小。大家普遍认为"men of virtues"或"virtuous men"是不错的译法,这一译法与理雅各的"the superior man"各有千秋。

对"邦畿千里,惟民所止"与"缗蛮黄鸟,止于丘隅"两个《诗经》中诗句的翻译,英译 1 与 3 使用了直译策略,将其译为散文体;译文 2 使用了意译策略,将其译为韵文体。考虑到诗歌语言的句式特点和行文风格,译文 2 更能体现原文诗句语言的形式美和韵律美。此外,"邦畿"乃王者之都,指古代天子都城及周围郊区,因此,译为"The royal domain"或"The Imperial Domain"更为贴切。

"穆穆文王,於缉熙敬止"的翻译较为困难。朱熹认为,"止"就是"必至于是而不迁",即一心朝着"至善"的方向努力,不中途改变。"敬止"就是指文王的诚敬之心从不间断。因此,"止"本身就兼具有比喻义,指"至善"的境界。理雅各将其翻译为"resting-places",语义上有偏差。辜鸿铭译为"realize his ideals",选择了比喻义,语义上更贴切。译文 3"was satisfied with his position",窄化了原始文本的文化内涵,做了过多的诠释,无论在语言形式上,还是在意义上,都与原文差异较大。此外,该句与下句"为人君,止于仁;为人臣,止于敬;"在衔接手法上都具有典型的汉语特点——意合。译文 1 和译文 2 都添加了衔接方法——代词指代,这样既能体现出原文意合的特征,也易于西方读者接受。从最后一句翻译的语言形式来讲,三个译文都采取了与原句相同的反复修辞手

109

法,但是,理雅各的翻译更为简练精悍,不仅具有三言诗的形式特征,语义传递也最为精准。

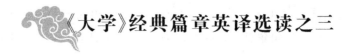《大学》经典篇章英译选读之三

传第四、第五章

子曰①:"听讼②,吾犹人③也,必也使无讼乎!"无情④者不得尽其辞。大畏民志⑤,此谓知本⑥。

〔所谓致知在格物者,言欲致吾之知,在即⑦物而穷⑧其理也。盖人心之灵莫不有知,而天下之物莫不有理,惟于理有未穷,故其知有不尽也。是以《大学》始教,必始学者即凡天下之物,莫不因其已知之理而益穷之,以求至乎其极。至于用力之久,而一旦豁然贯通焉,则众物之表里精粗无不到,而吾心之全体大用无不明矣。此谓物格。〕此谓知之至⑨也。

注:以上两段分别选自《大学》第五、第六章,朱子称为传第四、第五章。《大学》第五章,即朱子称为传第四章,解释"本末"。《大学》第六章,朱子称为传第五章,则是朱熹根据程颐之意所作的补传。

【注释】

①〔子曰〕子:孔子。此段话出自《论语·颜渊》。
②〔听讼〕听诉讼,审案。
③〔犹人〕同别人一样。犹:如同。
④〔情〕实。无情者就是指没有事实,没有道理的人。
⑤〔民志〕民心,人心。
⑥〔知本〕知道根本。
⑦〔即〕接近,接触。
⑧〔穷〕尽,彻底。

第四章 《大学》经典篇章英译选读

⑨〔格物致知〕古人对格物致知的解释各有不同。其中代表性的观点有以下几个。郑玄认为:"格,来也;物,犹事也。其知于善深,则来善物,其知于恶深,则来恶物。言事缘人所好来也"(《礼记正义》)。郑玄的解释是一种道德通感论,意思是每个人会因为个人所好而招来不同的外物。程颐认为:"格,至也,言穷至物理也"(《二程遗书》)。朱熹继承了二程的观点,并强调"即物而穷其理也"(《四书章句集注·大学章句》)。强调"至物"("即物"),即不脱离事物,以区别于佛教的思想。明代王阳明则用正心论解释格物,他说"格者,正也,正其不正以归于正","物者,事也,凡意之所发必有其事,意所在之事谓之物"(《大学问》),"天下之物本无可格者,其格物之功只在身心上做"(《传习录》下)。依照他的解释,正心——纠正意念,就是格物。目前普遍认为,格物致知是指探究事物的原理,从中得到知识(智慧)。

白话释义

孔子说:"判断案件时,我也像一般听讼的人一样,要听两方诉讼的理由,然后再加以宣判,这一点我和别人一样。但是不同之处是,我会通过教化百姓使案件不再发生。让那些隐瞒真实情况、说假话的人不能够申说他那狡辩的言辞,使人心畏服。这就是知道根本。"

我们所说的要获得知识,就要认识、研究万事万物,是指要想获得知识,就必须接触事物,彻底研究它的原理。人类的心都是灵动的,都具有认知能力,而天下万事万物都有一定的道理,只不过因为这些道理还没有被彻底认识,所以使知识显得很有局限。因此,《大学》开始就教导学习者去接触天下的万事万物,用自己已有的知识进一步研究各种事物,以便彻底认识万事万物的原理。求理时间长了,积累多了,一旦豁然贯通,万事万物的里外巨细就都了解了,同时自己的认识能力也会被提升到极致,再也没有蔽塞。这就叫作认识研究事物,也就是知识达到了顶点。

英译1

The Master said, "In hearing litigations, I am like any other body. What is necessary is to cause the people to have no litigation." So, those who are devoid of principle find it impossible to carry out their speeches, and a great awe would be struck into men's minds;—this is called knowing the root.

The meaning of the expression, "The perfecting of knowledge depends on the investigation of things", is this: —If we wish to carry out knowledge to the utmost, we must investigate the principle of all things we come into contact with, for the intelligent mind of man is certainly formed to know, and there is not a single thing in which its principles do not inhere. But so long as all principles are not investigated, man's knowledge is incomplete. On this account, the Learning for Adults, at the outset of its lessons, instructs the learner, in regard to all things in the world, to proceed from what knowledge he has of their principles, and pursue his investigation of them, till he reaches the extreme point. After exerting himself in this way for a long time, he will suddenly find himself possessed of a wide and far-reaching penetration. Then, the qualities of all things, whether external or internal, the subtle or the coarse, will all be apprehended, and the mind, in its entire substance and its relations to things, will be perfectly intelligent. This is called the investigation of things. This is called the perfection of knowledge.

——James Legge(詹姆斯·理雅各)

英译2

Confucius says: "In deciding lawsuits, I am not better than other men. But what I make it a point to do is—I try to make lawsuits impossible. Men who come before me without a just cause have nothing to say for themselves." Watch therefore with fear and trembling over the hearts of the people. That is the root of the matter in knowledge. That is the highest knowledge.

——辜鸿铭

英译3

Confucius says: "In trying cases, I am not different from others. But I try to dissuade people from starting lawsuits." When a person is ashamed of

第四章 《大学》经典篇章英译选读

telling lies and his heart filled with dread, he knows the limit.

The sentence "the perfecting of knowledge depends on the investigation of things" in "*Jing*" *of The Great Learning* means if I intend to perfect my knowledge, I have to study assiduously the ways of things. All minds are so keen that there is not one mind that does not have senses and perceptions inborn, and all things have their way. If one does not study things diligently, his knowledge will be limited and he will not be able to understand things fully and thoroughly. So if we as beginners start education with *The Great Learning*, when in contact with things, we must use the knowledge we have already acquired to study the way of all things until we reach the acme of knowledge. After years of study, I will be enlightened suddenly and know everything thoroughly. In this way, all things, whether their appearance or substance, great or small, can be understood and I can see clearly the substance of and the role played by my heart. This is what is called "the investigation of things" and the acme of knowledge.

——何祚康

英译鉴赏简评

此处引用孔子的话,强调明德的重要性。儒家实现"无讼"结果的逻辑是:"夫无讼,是民德之新,所以使民无讼,是己德之明",即通过树立有德之人的榜样令众人效仿,令品德低下之人自惭形秽,由此推广德行。这与《大学》全文所贯穿的由己及人的类推逻辑是一致的。依照这一内在逻辑审视三种译文可见,理雅各对原文的理解比较到位。至于"无情者不得尽其辞。大畏民志",孔颖达《礼记注疏》:"言无实情虚诞之人,无道理者,不得尽竭其虚伪之辞也"。如此才能"大畏民志",即使人诚其情而有敬畏之心。显而易见,这两句之间是因果关系,译文1和译文2处理得当。"此谓知本",郑玄注:"本,谓'诚其意'也。"人心本来是诚实无妄,皆因沾染物欲而日生伪诈。圣人以其明德而感通天下,使"无情者"去其私欲而复归其善。这是知道了事情(无讼)的根本。因此,"知本"应是动宾短语,译为"knowing the root"(英译1),而不是名词短语"the root of the matter in knowledge"(英译2),知识的根本。

依据朱熹的解释,"致知之道,在乎即事观理,以格夫物。格者,极至之谓",

亦即"即物穷理"。即物,就是接触事物;理,就是"物理",如程颐所说,"如火之所以热,水之所以寒,至于君臣父子间,皆是理"。所以,理,就是事物的道理或原理。依照这个理解,"即物"应译为"come into contact with things";"穷理"应译为"investigate principles of things";而何译将"即物穷理"合为一句,译为"study the way of things",语义上不够精确。此外,汉语是以动词为主的语言,同格物、即物、穷理等短语一样,"致知"也是动宾短语,意思是获取知识,理雅各译为"carry out the knowledge to the utmost",译文在形式虽然对应,在意思上却有偏差。何译"perfect one's knowledge",虽然意义上更契合原文,但是仍然不够精准。原文尾句中的"物格"和"知之至",是由"格物"与"致知"转化过来的同词根名词短语,理雅各使用了同词根的名词,分别译为"investigation of things"和"the perfection of knowledge",相较何译的"the investigation of things"和"the acme of knowledge",理雅各的译文在形式和意义上更符合原文的语言特征。

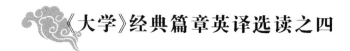《大学》经典篇章英译选读之四

传第六章

所谓诚其意①者:毋自欺也,如恶恶臭②,如好好色③,此之谓自谦④。故君子必慎⑤其独⑥也!小人闲居⑦为不善,无所不至,见君子而后厌然⑧,掩其不善,而著⑨其善。人之视己,如见其肺肝然,则何益矣。此谓诚于中⑩,形于外,故君子必慎其独也。

注:本段选自《大学》第七章,朱子称为传第六章,解释"诚其意"。

【注释】
①〔诚其意〕使自己的意念真实,即忠实于自己的意念。
②〔恶恶臭〕厌恶难闻的气味。
③〔好好色〕喜欢美丽漂亮的女子。
④〔谦〕通"慊"(qiè),满足。〔自谦〕自足,心安理得。

第四章 《大学》经典篇章英译选读

⑤〔慎〕谨慎,慎戒。
⑥〔独〕独处。
⑦〔闲居〕此处指独处。
⑧〔厌然〕掩藏,躲闪的样子。
⑨〔著〕显示。
⑩〔中〕内心。

白话释义

所谓意念真诚,就是不要自欺欺人。就好像讨厌腐臭的气味,喜欢美丽的女子一样,要忠实于自己内心的意念,才能心安理得,所以君子在独处的时候要特别谨慎。那些没有道德修养的人,在独处的时候会为非作歹,什么坏事都做得出来。当他们见到那些有道德修养的人,就躲躲藏藏,企图掩盖他们所做的坏事,设法显示自己的善良与美德。其实大家的眼睛是雪亮的,别人看你就像看透了你的五脏六腑,你掩饰不好的东西,刻意把好的东西给别人看,又有什么益处呢?因为一个人的真实心思必然会在行动或言语上表现出来,所以有道德修养的人即使独处之时,也要谨慎,使自己规行矩步。

英译1

What is meant by "making the thoughts sincere," is the allowing no self-deception, as *when* we hate a bad smell, and as *when* we love what is beautiful. This is called self-enjoyment. Therefore, the superior man must be watchful over himself when he is alone. There is no evil to which the mean man, dwelling retired, will not proceed, but when he sees a superior man, he instantly tries to disguise himself, concealing his evil, and displaying what is good. The other beholds him, as if he saw his heart and reins;—of what use *is his disguise*? This is an instance of the saying—"what truly is within will be manifested without." Therefore, the superior man must be watchful over himself when he is alone.

——James Legge(詹姆斯·理雅各)

英译2

Now what is meant by "to have true ideas" is to have no self-deception, as when one hates a bad smell or loves what is beautiful. That is what is called self-detachment. Therefore a gentleman watches diligently over his secret thought. When he is alone, there is no evil which an immoral man will not do; but when he sees a gentleman, he immediately disguises himself and conceals what is evil and shows off what is good within him. But men see through us as though our hearts and reins lay open to them. What is the use then of concealing? That is what is meant by the saying that what is truly within will surely show without. Therefore a gentleman watches diligently over his secret thought.

——辜鸿铭

英译3

"Be sincere and honest" in "*Jing*" means a man must not deceive himself. He can only be happy and satisfied if he detests evil as he detests a foul smell and does good deeds as he loves beautiful things. So a gentleman is cautious when he is alone. A petty person may do all kinds of evils, but when he is faced with a gentleman, he is evasive, trying to cover up his bad deeds and pretend that he has done good. But others know what he has done as if his body was transparent. What good are all these pretenses to him? Sincerity and honesty will show themselves outwardly. This is why a gentleman will be cautious when he is alone.

——何祚康

英译鉴赏简评

表4-2是不同英译版本对原文核心短语的翻译。

第四章 《大学》经典篇章英译选读

表 4-2 不同英译版本对核心短语的翻译

原文	英译 1	英译 2	英译 3
诚意	making the thoughts sincere	to have true ideas	be sincere and honest
自谦	self-enjoyment	self-detachment	be happy and satisfied
慎独	be watchful over himself when he is alone	watches diligently over his secret thought	is cautious when he is alone
诚于中形于外	what is truly within will surely show without	what is truly within will surely show without	Sincerity and honesty will show themselves outwardly

从以上核心短语的翻译对比可以看出，理雅各的译文明显胜出其他两位译者。因篇幅所限，在此仅以前两个词条为例予以说明。

首先，儒家的"诚其意"，是指外在行为与内在意念的一致。要实现这一目的，关键在于敢于直面自己的恶念并予以纠正。"意"，是心上发动的意念；诚，则是自省的态度和行为。而心之所动、意念之生发，善恶相混。因此，理雅各使用 thoughts 一词不仅能表达出"心"与"意"之间的关系，而且符合原文中"意念"丰富性与模糊性的概念内涵。同时，理雅各使用动＋宾＋补结构"make...sincere"翻译"诚其意"，既还原了原文"诚"的使役用法，又突出了"诚意"所表达的真诚自省的态度。"自谦"，即"心安理得"，是外在行为与内在意念统一之后的闲适自足的状态。辜鸿铭将其译为"self-detachment"，并引用 19 世纪英国诗人马修•阿诺德（Matthew Arnold）的话，解释为"远离物的纠缠"，与原文概念内涵有偏差。

此外，此段文字原文使用了比喻修辞手法。三位译者对"如恶恶臭，如好好色"的翻译大同小异，而对"如见其肺肝然"的处理，相差较大。译文 2 和译文 3 的两位译者都使用了意译手法，译文 2 为"as though our hearts and reins lay open to them"，译文 3 为"as if his body was transparent"，虽然传达了原文的意思，但是"肺腑"的文化内涵丧失殆尽。理雅各使用了直译＋注释的"厚翻译"策略，将其译为"as if he saw his heart and reins"，并在下文注释：中国人认为，肺乃正直之所；肝乃仁爱之所。如此处理，不仅传递了短语的引申义，也说明了其比喻义，彰显了译者精湛的语言能力和深厚的文化功底。

中华典籍英译选读

《大学》经典篇章英译选读之五

传第七章

所谓修身在正其心者,身①有所忿懥②,则不得其正;有所恐惧,则不得其正;有所好乐,则不得其正;有所忧患,则不得其正。心不在焉,视而不见,听而不闻,食而不知其味。此谓修身在正其心。

注:本段选自《大学》第八章,朱子称为传第七章。解释"正心修身"。

【注释】
①〔身〕程颐认为,"身"当作"心"。
②〔忿懥(zhì)〕愤怒。

白话释义

之所以说修身在于端正心念,是因为我们愤怒的时候,心念就不能够端正;有所恐惧的时候,心念就不能够端正;有所喜好、逸乐的时候,心念就不能够端正;有所忧患的时候,心念就不能够端正。如果一个人的心不正,明明在看,却什么也没有看到;明明在听,却什么也没有听见;吃东西也不知道什么滋味。所以说,修养自身的品性在于端正自己的心念。

英译1

What is meant by, "The cultivation of the person depends on rectifying the mind," *may be thus illustrated*:—If a man be under the influence of passion, he will be incorrect in his conduct. He will be the same, if he is under the influence of terror, or under the influence of fond regard, or under that of sorrow and distress. When the mind is not present, we look and do

第四章 《大学》经典篇章英译选读

not see; we hear and do not understand; we eat and do not know the taste of what we eat. This is what is meant by saying that the cultivation of the person depends on the rectifying of the mind.

——James Legge（詹姆斯·理雅各）

英译2

Now what is meant by saying that the ordering of one's conversation aright depends upon putting the state of the mind in a proper and well-ordered condition, is this. When a person is under the influence of passion, his mind is not in a proper and well-ordered condition. When he is under the influence of fear and terror, his mind is not in a proper and well-ordered condition. When he is under the influence of pleasure and amusement, his mind is not in a proper and well-ordered condition. When he is under the influence of sorrow and distress, his mind is not in a proper and well-ordered condition. When the mind is absent, we look, but do not see; we hear, but do not understand; we eat, but do not know the taste of that which we eat. This is what is meant by saying that the ordering of one's conversation aright depends upon putting the state of the mind in a proper and well-ordered condition.

——辜鸿铭

英译3

"A man's self-cultivation depends on setting his heart right" in "*Jing*" means a man's heart can not be set right if he resents, fears, or has favorites and worries. Influenced by these sentiments, he would be absent-minded, look but see not, listen but hear not, eat but taste not. So self-cultivation depends on the setting right of the heart.

——何祚康

英译鉴赏简评

关于"修身",笔者认同译文 1 理雅各的译法。"身"并非"material body, but the individual man, in contact with things, and intercourse with society",因此,译文 1"cultivation of persons"和译文 3"self-cultivation"两种译法比较接近汉语"修身"的文化内涵。"cultivation"的比喻义与"修"相同,二者都表示通过学习提升自我,语义最为贴近。而译文 2"the ordering of one's conversation aright"意为"说话措辞端正",将修身的内涵缩减了许多。

此外,对于"心"的理解,三位译者采用了两种译法,"mind"和"heart"。虽说从语境来讲,"mind"更加准确,因为思虑皆出自脑海。但是,依据程颐的解释,"好乐、忿懥,皆心之用……然一有之而不能察,则欲动情胜,而其用之所行,或不能不失其正矣。"好乐、忿懥、恐惧、忧患,都是人之心志或情感。古人一直认为,心是思维的器官,是思想情感的通称。因此,"正心"译为"rectifying the heart"更为妥帖。

本章课后练习

一、请尝试翻译以下句子。

1. 君子贤其贤而亲其亲,小人乐其乐而利其利,此以没世不忘也。(《大学》第四章)

   白话释义:

   英译:

2. 富润屋,德润身,心广体胖,故君子必诚其意。(《大学》第七章)

   白话释义:

   英译:

3. 一家仁,一国兴仁;一家让,一国兴让;一人贪戾,一国作乱。其机如此。(《大学》第十章)

   白话释义:

   英译:

第四章 《大学》经典篇章英译选读

4. 民之所好好之,民之所恶恶之,此之谓民之父母。(《大学》第十一章)

   白话释义：

   英译：

5. 生财有大道：生之者众,食之者寡,为之者疾,用之者舒,则财恒足矣。(《大学》第十一章)

   白话释义：

   英译：

二、请比较以下名句两种英译文本的异同。

1. 《诗》曰："周虽旧邦,其命惟新。"是故,君子无所不用其极。(《大学》第一章)

   英译 1：In *The Book of Poetry*, it is said, "Although Châu was an ancient State, the ordinance which lighted on it was new." Therefore, the superior man in everything uses his utmost endeavours. (詹姆斯·理雅各)

   英译 2：The *Book of Songs* says: "Although the Royal House of Chou was an old State, a new Mission was given to it." Therefore, whatever a gentleman finds for his hands to do, he doeth with all his might. (辜鸿铭)

2. 所谓致知在格物者,言欲致吾之知,在即物而穷其理也。盖人心之灵莫不有知,而天下之物莫不有理,惟于理有未穷,故其知有不尽也。(《大学》第六章)

   英译 1：The perfecting of knowledge depends on the investigation of things, is this:—If we wish to carry out knowledge to the utmost, we must investigate the principle of all things we come into contact with, for the intelligent mind of man is certainly formed to know, and there is not a single thing in which its principles do not inhere. But so long as all principles are not investigated, man's knowledge is incomplete. (詹姆斯·理雅各)

   英译 2："The perfecting of knowledge depends on the investigation of things" in "*Jing*" of *The Great Learning* means if I intend to perfect my knowledge, I have to study assiduously the ways of things. All minds are so keen that there is not one mind that does not have senses and perceptions inborn, and all things have their way. If one does not study things diligently, his knowledge will be limited and he will not be able to understand things fully and thoroughly.(辜鸿铭)

3. 孝者,所以事君也;弟者,所以事长也;慈者,所以使众也。(《大学》第十章)

英译1:There is fraternal submission:—therewith elders and superiors should be served. There is kindness:—therewith the multitude should be treated.(詹姆斯•理雅各)

英译2:The duties of a good son will teach him how to serve his Sovereign. The duties of subordination in the family will teach him to respect authority. The kindness of a father to his children will teach him how to treat the multitude.(辜鸿铭)

4. 此谓一言偾事,一人定国。(《大学》第十章)

英译1:This verifies the saying, "Affairs may be ruined by a single sentence; a kingdom may be settled by its One man."(詹姆斯•理雅各)

英译2:Hence the saying:"One word can ruin everything; one man can save a nation."(辜鸿铭)

5. 《诗》云:"桃之夭夭,其叶蓁蓁。之子于归,宜其家人。"宜其家人,而后可以教国人。(《大学》第十章)

英译1:In *The Book of Poetry*, it is said, "That peach tree, so delicate and elegant! How luxuriant is its foliage! This girl is going to her husband's house. She will rightly order her household." Let the household be rightly ordered, and then the people of the State may be taught.(詹姆斯•理雅各)

英译2:*The Book of Songs* says:
The peach tree is tender and fair,
With its leaves all in bloom;
The girl is going to her new home,
She will rightly order her household.

第四章 《大学》经典篇章英译选读

Only when there is order in the household, is it possible to teach the people of the nation to be good.(辜鸿铭)

三、段落试译。

《诗》云:"瞻彼淇澳,绿竹猗猗。有斐君子,如切如磋,如琢如磨。瑟兮僩兮,赫兮喧兮。有斐君子,终不可谖兮!"如切如磋者,道学也;如琢如磨者,自修也;瑟兮僩兮者,恂栗也;赫兮喧兮者,威仪也;有斐君子,终不可谖兮者,道盛德至善,民之不能忘也。

(《大学》第四章)

见贤而不能举,举而不能先,命也。见不善而不能退,退而不能远,过也。好人之所恶,恶人之所好,是谓拂人之性,灾必逮夫身。是故君子有大道,必忠信以得之,骄泰以失之。

(《大学》第十一章)

第五章

《诗经》经典篇章英译选读

【导读】

中国堪称"诗之国度"。最早持此论断的是中国文学史上的重量级人物,学衡派创始人梅光迪先生。他主要强调的是文言文是诗歌最好的载体。他说"中国是诗的国家,只要有中国诗存在,中国的文言就不能被白话取代。"华裔学者刘若愚先生对汉诗(尤其是古诗)更是推崇备至,他说:"汉诗乃中华文化之卓越成就之一,亦是中华智慧的集大成者之一,此言并非夸饰之辞。"

两位学者的观点,与闻一多先生所说的"旧文学中最好的是诗"似有相通之处。这一论断出现于1944年闻一多先生在西南联大文艺晚会上发表的有关"文学复古"的演讲中,其本意是批评作新诗的人被旧诗给蒙蔽了,要提倡新思想。但实际上,闻一多先生并未否定传统古典诗歌经久不衰的文学价值和艺术魅力。

中华历史上下五千年,诞生了无数脍炙人口感人肺腑的优美诗篇。"立我臣民,莫匪尔极,不识不知,顺帝之则"(《康衢谣》)。这是一首歌颂尧帝功德的歌谣,意思是说"老百姓衣食无忧,这都是尧帝您的英明之为;老百姓诚恳善良,顺乎自然法则。"尧看到民间殷实无虞,乃"召舜,禅以天下"。"日出而作,日落而息。凿井而饮,耕田而食。帝力于我何有哉!"(《击壤歌》)。这是一首描绘远古先民日出而作日落而息的生活场景的歌谣。朴素平实的语言、恬淡安然的语气、生动和谐的田园生活场景,让人吟罢动容。因此,清人沈德潜说"康衢击壤,肇开声诗"。中华民族五千年之诗歌盛流似乎有了源头可寻。

第五章 《诗经》经典篇章英译选读

降至周秦两汉,风雅赓续前代,诗韵东西两京,遂诞生了中华民族第一部诗歌锦集《诗经》。《诗经》开篇云:"关关雎鸠,在河之洲。窈窕淑女,君子好逑"(《关雎》)。《毛诗序》说:"《关雎》,后妃之德也,风之始也,所以风天下而正夫妇也。"即所谓"诗有美有刺"。故而,孔子曰:"小子何莫学夫诗?诗可以兴,可以观,可以群,可以怨。迩之事父,远之事君,多识于鸟兽草木之名"(《论语·阳货》)。得益于孔子的大力提倡和亲自删削[①],《诗三百》名正言顺地变成了儒家五经之一,登上了中华诗典这一"诗国圣坛",成为传世至今的文学精华。

《毛诗序》有言:"故正得失,动天地,感鬼神,莫近于诗。先王以是经夫妇,成孝敬,厚人伦,美教化,移风俗"(《毛诗·关雎序》)。从内容主题来看,《诗经》之所以被称为儒家典籍之"经",若以传统文学视域来解读,即在于其承载着古圣先贤的哲理和睿思,承托着"微言大义,昭示后人"的教化意图,意即庄子所说的《诗》以道志。因此,《诗经》不仅仅是一部"纯文学"诗集,更是一部承载并发挥儒家治国者政治说教和道德感化功能的"政教诗文集"。这种解读并不会过分美誉儒家经典的"神圣性"。美国汉学家宇文所安先生同样肯定了《诗经》的"政治教化"功能,他说"从政治层面,(诗经中的)诗篇赋予了君权合规性,保证了政体的合法性和延续性。"这也许是《诗经》作为儒家经典得以传于后世的核心价值所在:"先王以是经夫妇,成孝敬,厚人伦,美教化,移风俗"。

实际上,诗歌从来都不纯粹是用来表现个人肝肠喷怨或者群体喜怒哀乐的文学体裁。唐代诗人白居易说:"歌诗合为事而作",这里的"事",有"时事"之意。闻一多先生亦曾撰文讨论诗歌的政教作用,他认为古希腊哲学家柏拉图不喜欢诗人,所以将他们逐出了《理想国》,"因此我们完全有理由拒绝让诗人进入治理良好的城邦。因为他的作用在于激励、培育和加强心灵的低贱部分,毁坏理性部分。"但真实情况并非如此。柏拉图在《理想国》里说:"至于我们的城邦中,我们只需要一种诗人与故事的作者,他的作品必须对我们有好处,必须只模仿好人的语言,且遵守我们原来替保卫者们设计教育时定的规范。"由此可见,柏拉图强调的是诗歌作为一种艺术形式所发挥的教育功能,他特别强调诗歌对青年人的政治感化作用:"诗歌不仅是令人愉快的,而且是对有秩序的管理和人们的全部生活有益的。"无论古圣孔子,还是唐代大诗人白居易,现代诗人闻一多,似乎都认同柏拉图关于诗歌政教功能的这一主张。叶维廉先生曾说,文学始终是一个使者,一个高贵的奴隶——文学总要"载"些什么。

---

① 西汉的孔安国、东汉的王充、郑玄等儒家学者秉持孔子删诗说;唐代孔颖达、清人魏源、今人杨伯峻等学者认为孔子删诗说是对孔子和儒学的过分抬高,但孔子修正《诗经》中的"杂糅"或"重复"内容,补全残句异文的说法或为可信。

强调《诗经》的政治宣教或道德感化功能,并不意味着非要恪守传统儒学经学家们的诠释而不敢越雷池半步作"食古不化"式的解读,这样就会陷入教条主义。孟子有言:"故说诗者,不以文害辞,不以辞害志,以意逆志,是为得之。"西汉大儒董仲舒说:"诗无达诂"(《春秋繁露·精华》),意思是说对诗经的解读要因人而异,因时而变,与时俱进,不可拘泥于古人残守之见。时至今日,我们更应从新时代的文化需求出发,发掘并重温《诗经》中有益于青年一代健康成长的营养成分。

从音乐性来看,《诗经》堪称中国第一部可歌可咏的"乐章集"。清人马瑞辰说:"诗三百篇,未有不可入乐者。"所谓入乐,实际上类似于闻一多先生所说的"诗不能没有节奏。"通俗地讲,西周时期的《诗经》,近似于今日的流行歌曲,记录了当时不同的社会阶层和群体对于功名利禄、田间劳作、爱情婚姻、生老病死、人情往来等的理解和体验。《诗经》长短恒定的诗行结构,一唱三叹的音律规则,音效整饬回环的艺术技巧等,均能体现其浓郁的音律性和传唱性,这也是《诗经》得以传承千年的艺术魅力所在。

到了近现代,《诗经》的传承和流布已打破国家和地域的限制。西方世界对《诗经》的关注和传播,可追溯到17世纪初期。据学者考证,法国传教士尼古拉·特里戈(Nicolas Trigault 中文名金尼阁)是译介《诗经》的首位西方学者。1610年,他用拉丁语翻译了儒家的"五经",其中就包括《诗经》的部分诗篇。第二位将《诗经》传入西方的学者为法国传教士马若瑟(Joseph Henri Marie Premare)。他于1698年将《诗经》中的八首诗翻译为法文,1741年又由法国神甫让·巴普蒂斯特·杜赫德(Jean Baptiste du Halde)转译为英文。而第一部《诗经》全译本是由法国耶稣会的神父孙璋(Alexander de la Charme),大致于1733年至1752年完成的拉丁散体译文,但其手稿未能出版便与世长辞。1830年,东方学家尤利乌斯·冯·莫尔(M. Julius von Mohl)对孙璋的手稿予以整理编辑,交由斯图加特和图宾根的科塔出版社出版,题名为 *Confucci Chi-king, sive liber carminum, ex latina P. Lacharme interpretatione*。总之,《诗经》在西方世界的译介,经历了从拉丁语到法语,再逐渐转向英语这一漫长而曲折的过程,历时约130余年。从《诗经》被多次转译这一事实可以看出,西方汉学家对其重视程度非同一般。

将《诗经》英译推向高潮的是英国翻译家、语言学家威廉·琼斯爵士(Sir William Jones)。他曾选译了《诗经》中的部分爱情诗,并将其编入《东方情诗辑存》出版。英国传教士、汉学家詹姆斯·理雅各(James Legge)分别于1871和1876年发表了两个英文全译本《诗经》(后一版本为前一版本的改进版)。1891

第五章 《诗经》经典篇章英译选读

年,英国传教士、汉学家威廉姆·詹宁斯(M. A. William Jennings)和英国驻江南领事阿连璧(C. F. Allen)分别出版了《诗经》英译本。

1913年海伦·华德尔(Helen Waddell)以理雅各《诗经》英译本及注释为基础,出版了英译本 Lyrics from the Chinese(《中国抒情歌》)。

英国外交官赫伯特·翟里斯(Herbert A. Giles)曾编译出版《中国文学瑰宝·诗歌卷》,其中包括《诗经》诗篇。1916年,亚瑟·韦利委托伦敦劳埃兄弟出版社出版了他的《中国诗选》(Chinese Poems),其中包括《诗经》中三首颂诗的英译。1936年,《亚细亚杂志》发表韦利的"中国早期诗歌中的求爱与婚姻"一文,《诗经》16首以爱情为主题的诗篇被译为英文。1937年乔治·艾伦与昂温公司(George Allen & Unwin Ltd.)出版亚瑟·韦利的《诗经》英文全译本 The Book of Songs。

继亚瑟·韦利之后,美国现代主义诗人艾兹拉·庞德(Ezra Loomis Pound)再次将诗经英译推向新高潮。庞德于1915年出版了代表"意象派"诗学主张的扛鼎之作 Cathay(译作《华夏集》或《神州集》),《诗经·小雅·采薇》被收入其中。

由此得见,在过去的几个世纪,西方世界对《诗经》的热度有增无减。《诗经》回环往复、一唱三叹的音乐性,和寓意深远的意象性、隐喻性等,是从内容到形式,从措辞到句法,从音视觉到影视像等不同层面诗学元素的高度凝合,这或许正是西方汉学家和翻译家关注并研习传播《诗经》的动因之一。

本章选录《诗经》经典诗篇三首,第一首是《载驰》,被称为"诗三百"中第一首表达"爱国情怀"的诗歌;第二首《蓼莪》,为"恩孝"主题,被称为中华千古第一"孝"诗;第三首《蒹葭》,为"爱情(心系怀人)"主题。

《诗经》经典篇章英译选读之一

国风·鄘风·载驰

载驰载驱①,归唁卫侯②。
驱马悠悠③,言至于漕④。
大夫跋涉⑤,我心则忧。

既不我嘉⑥，不能旋反⑦。
视尔不臧⑧，我思不远⑨。

既不我嘉，不能旋济⑩？
视尔不臧，我思不閟⑪。

陟彼阿丘⑫，言采其蝱⑬。
女子善怀⑭，亦各有行⑮。
许人尤之⑯，众稚且狂⑰。

我行其野，芃芃其麦⑱。
控⑲于大邦，谁因谁极⑳？
大夫君子，无我有尤㉑。
百尔所思㉒，不如我所之㉓。

【注释】

① 〔载（zài）〕语助词。高亨注："载，犹乃也，发语词。"〔驰、驱〕车马疾行。孔疏："走马谓之驰，策马谓之驱。"
② 〔唁（yàn）〕吊唁。一说为许穆公夫人归宗国吊唁其去世的父亲卫懿公；一说为许穆夫人悼宗国危亡之意。韩诗："吊生曰唁，吊失国亦曰唁。"
③ 〔悠悠〕路途遥远。
④ 〔漕〕地名，毛传："漕，卫东邑。"
⑤ 〔大夫〕指许国赶来阻止许穆夫人去卫国吊唁的大臣们。〔跋涉〕草行曰跋，水行曰涉，合而用之，意为事急不问水之浅深，直前济渡，视水行如陆行。
⑥ 〔嘉〕同意，赞许。《释诂》："嘉，美也。"
⑦ 〔旋反〕同"还返"，还归，返回。
⑧ 〔视〕表示比较（双方的观点）。〔臧〕好，善。一说许穆夫人追念旧事，之所以请嫁于齐国，为日后宗国有事，可得齐国之援救，因此自己的想法乃是"嘉美也"。果然，宗国今日"不臧（被狄人入侵）"，也无法旋济（不能旋反）。

第五章 《诗经》经典篇章英译选读

⑨〔思〕忧思。〔远〕摆脱。
⑩〔济(jì)〕渡河,有益,另释为"止"。
⑪〔閟(bì)〕同"闭",闭塞不通。一说"閟与祕同,密也。"
⑫〔陟(zhì)〕登山。〔阿丘〕一侧高一侧矮的山丘。
⑬〔言〕语助词。〔虻〕贝母草,产于高山苔原地带。《毛诗传》:"偏高曰阿丘……升至偏高之丘,采其虻者,将以疗疾。"古人采虻以治病,此喻指许穆夫人设法挽救宗国。
⑭〔善怀〕女子多思念其父母之国。〔善〕多。〔怀〕思考。
⑮〔行〕指做事的准则,另释为"道路"。
⑯〔许人〕许国大夫。〔尤〕古同"訧",过失,指责,怪罪。
⑰〔众〕一说同"终";一说"众人"。〔稚〕幼稚,幼小貌,引申为愚妄,不能见事理之大。《说文》:"稚,幼禾也。"〔狂〕《韩非子·解老篇》:"心不能审得失之也,则谓之狂。"
⑱〔芃芃其麦〕此指卫国丧乱已久,救援无人。〔芃(péng)〕草盛貌。《郑笺》:"麦芃芃者,言未收刈,民将困也。"
⑲〔控〕往告,赴告。
⑳〔因〕亲也,依靠。〔极〕至,指来援者的到达。
㉑〔无我有尤〕无过我者,对我不要怪罪。
㉒〔百尔所思〕(虽然)你们有百种想法。〔尔〕女(汝),此指许国的大夫们。
㉓〔之〕前往,指许穆夫人祈求大国以救邦危。

白话释义

驾车急急去赶路,回家吊唁我卫侯。
路途遥远马快跑,终于到达漕城下。
许国大臣挡前路,令我心急如火焚。
即使反对我想法,怎能就此驱马还。
各人想法均不同,我的想法行得通。

登上高高的山丘,采些母贝把病治。
女人善于细思量,想法有理又有据。
许国大夫不明白,想法幼稚欠思虑。

穿过卫国的田野,麦苗葳蕤还未割。
祈求大国能出手,解救卫国于危亡。
各位大夫听清楚,不要对我硬阻挠。
思前想后多犹豫,不如让我去行动。

创作背景

鲁说曰:许穆夫人者,卫懿公之女、许穆公之夫人也。初,许求之,齐亦求之。懿公将与许,女因其傅母而言曰:'古者诸侯之又女也,所以苞苴玩弄,系援于大国也。今者许小而远,齐大而近。若今之世,强者为雄,如使边境有寇戎之事,惟是四方之故,赴告大国,妾在,不犹愈乎?今舍近而就远,离大而附小,一旦有车驰之难,孰可与虑社稷?'卫侯不听,而嫁之于许。其后翟人攻卫,大破之,而许不能救,卫侯遂奔走涉河,而南至楚丘。齐桓往而存之,遂城楚丘以居,卫侯于是悔不用其言。当败之时,许夫人驱驰而吊唁卫侯,因疾之而作诗。"

《诗正义》引《乐稽耀嘉》曰:"狄人与卫战,桓公不救,于其败也,然后救之。……盖齐桓不救者,怀失妇之私嫌,败然后救者,存霸主之公义。"

此诗当作于卫文公元年(公元前659年)。据《左传·闵公二年(公元前660年)》记载:"冬十二月,狄人伐卫,卫懿公好鹤,鹤有乘轩者,将战,国人受甲者,皆曰'使鹤'。……及狄人战于荥泽,卫师败绩。"当卫国被狄人占领以后,许穆夫人心急如焚,星夜兼程赶到曹邑,吊唁祖国的危亡,写下了这首《载驰》。

据前人考证,许穆夫人生于公元前690年(周庄王七年、卫惠公十年)左右,卒于公元前656年(周惠王二十一年、卫文公四年),大约活了三十四岁。年方及笄,当许穆公与齐桓公慕名向她求婚时,她便以祖国为念。汉刘向《列女传·仁智篇》云:"初,许求之,齐亦求之。懿公将与许,女因其傅母而言曰:'……今者许小而远,齐大而近。若今之世,强者为雄。如使边境有寇戎之事,惟是四方之故,赴告大国,妾在,不犹愈乎?'……卫侯不听,而嫁之于许。"由此可见,她在择偶问题上曾考虑将来如何报效祖国。她嫁给许穆公十年左右,卫国果然被狄人所灭。不久,她的姐夫宋桓公迎接卫国的难民渡过黄河,计男女七百三十人,加上共、滕两个别邑的人民共五千人,立戴公于曹邑。戴公即位一月而死,夫人"闵卫之亡,驰驱而归,将以唁卫侯于漕邑,未至,而许之大夫有奔走跋涉而来者,夫人知其必将以不可归之义来告,……乃作此诗以自言其意"(《诗集传》)。据"我行其野,芃芃其麦"二句,诗当作于公元前659年(卫文公元年)春暮。

许穆夫人是中国文学史上第一位女诗人,也是世界文学史上第一位女诗

第五章 《诗经》经典篇章英译选读

人。据清魏源《诗古微》考证,除此篇外尚有《泉水》《竹竿》二诗也为其所作,其中尤以《载驰》思想性最强,它在强烈的矛盾冲突中表现了深厚的爱国主义思想。全诗分为四章,不像《桃夭》《相鼠》等篇每章句数、字数甚至连意思也基本相似,而是每多变化,思想感情也复杂得多。之所以如此,是因为作者的叙事抒情是从现实生活出发,从现实所引起的内心矛盾出发。故诗歌的形式随着内容的发展而发展,形成不同的语言和不同的节奏。

诗歌呈现了一位颇有主张,充满救国之志、爱国之心,忠贞不渝的女性形象。三千年来,许穆夫人的"绵绵爱国情,悠悠报国心"至今令人感怀不已,赞不绝口。

主题鉴赏

许子东先生说,"诗人的个人情感,一旦进入文学,便会具有社会意义。"《载驰》是一篇以个人情感为微观视角的洋溢着爱国情怀的伟大诗篇,体现了文学作品教化民众、针砭时事的社会功能。

身为卫国之女,但嫁与许国的许穆夫人,在获悉父母之邦卫国被狄(翟)人所灭之时,力排众议、冲破重阻、跋山涉水,毅然决然地返回宗国,亲自吊唁兄长戴公,并向当时的大国齐国求救,希望能够拯救宗国于危亡之际。

此诗是她到达漕邑城楼之下,被后面赶来的许国大夫所阻时写下的。个人的情绪,一旦投放到宏大的历史背景下,便产生了非常深远的社会意义。身为一弱小女子,许穆夫人却能大胆地冲破传统礼教和道德的束缚,号召卫国民众团结一心,共御国辱,保全家国。而许国那些固守封建礼教的大夫们,却在家国存亡之际,仍坚守着限制女子抛头露面的传统礼教,对她百般阻挠,不让她亲自去祈请大国之助。一边是心系宗国,敢于冲破礼教束缚的女子,一边是冥顽不化、胆小羸弱的许国大夫,两股力量的矛盾冲突随章节逐层升级,为读者烘托出一位有胆有识的豪情女子的高大形象,让人不禁肃然起敬。

诗歌以第一人称叙事角度切入,截取重大历史事件的瞬间记忆,读者无须深究诗歌背后具体的历史事件,只需将关注点放在许穆夫人这一人物身上,便能被其胆识和勇气所折服。

文学的作用不仅在于娱情,更在于对人的精神和意志的唤起和激活。有学者评论道:"《载驰》是许穆夫人悯其宗国颠覆,归唁卫侯的纪事之作……耿耿爱国之心,可质天日。因此,我们不仅称许穆夫人是公元前 7 世纪中国的爱国女诗人,也是世界史上最早的爱国女诗人。"关注家国命运,支持国家统一,倡导各族人民团结一致,构建休戚与共和谐统一的大中华格局应成为《诗经》的核心教旨之一。作为大学生,我们在阅读如《载驰》这样的传统诗篇时,应唤起自己心怀祖国、热爱人民、与国家和人民同呼吸共命运的家国意识,永远秉持一颗爱国、爱家、爱人民的赤子之心。

Patriotic Baroness Mu of Xu

I gallop while I go
To share my brother's woe.
I ride down a long road
To my bother's abode.
The deputies will thwart
My plan and fret my heart.

"Although you say me nay,
I won't go back the other way.
Conservative are you
While farsight'd is my view?

"Although you say me nay,
I won't stop on my way.
Conservative are you
I can't accept your view."

I climb the sloping mound
To pick toad-lilies round.
Of woman don't make light!
My heart knows what is right.
My countrymen put blame
On me and feel no shame.

第五章 《诗经》经典篇章英译选读

I go across the plains;
Thick and green grow the grains.
I'll plead to mighty land,
Who'd hold out helping hand.
"Deputies, don't you see
The fault lies not with me?
Whatever may think you,
It's not so good as my view."

——许渊冲

2

Tsae ch'e

1

I would have galloped my horses and whipt them,
Returning to condole with the marquis of Wei.
I would have urged them all the long way,
Till I arrived at Ts'aou.
A great officer has gone, over the hills and through the rivers;
But my heart is full of sorrow.

2

You disapproved of my [proposal],
And I cannot return [to Wei];
But I regard you as in the wrong,
And cannot forget my purpose.
You disapproved of my purpose,
And I cannot return across the streams;
But I regard you as in the wrong,
And cannot shut out my thoughts.

3

I will ascend that mound with the steep side,

And gather the mother-of-pearl lilies.

I might, as a woman, have many thoughts,

But every one of them was practicable.

The people of Heu blame me,

But they are all childish and hasty [in their conclusions].

4

I would have gone through the country,

Amidst the wheat so luxuriant.

I would have carried the case before the great State.

On whom should I have relied? Who would come [to the help of Wei]?

Ye great officers and gentlemen,

Do not condemn me.

The hundred plans you think of

Are not equal to the course I was going to take.

——James Legge(詹姆斯·理雅各)

THWARTED

O forth would I gallop and homeward fly

To cheer in his trouble my lord of Wei;

And urging my steeds the livelong day

Ts'o's city would reach without delay.

But an officer hies o'er stream and plain,

And I, to my sorrow, must needs remain.

My pleasure, it seems, is not your own;

My hopes of return ye have overthrown.

Yet, though it is plain ye disapprove,

第五章 《诗经》经典篇章英译选读

The thoughts of my heart no power can move.
My pleasure is not your own, it seems,
And now can I not recross the streams.
Yet, though ye approve not, as 'tis plain,
The thoughts of my heart can none restrain.
I'd climb to the top of yonder hill,
And gather the lily that care can kill.
We women are full of wants (ye say),
And every want must have its way.
But wrong are ye there, ye men of Hiu;
And childish and headstrong all are you!
I'd travel across the wide, wide plain,
Now clad in its rich long waving grain,
And make my appeal to the sovereign State;
For whose is the cause—the need so great?
Ye officers, ye of high degree,
Say not that the error lay with me;
For the counsels of all of you combined
Fall short of the course I had in mind.

——William Jennings(威廉姆·詹宁斯)

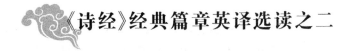

《诗经》经典篇章英译选读之二

谷风之什·蓼莪

蓼蓼者莪①,匪莪伊蒿②。

哀哀③父母,生我劬劳④。

蓼蓼者莪,匪莪伊蔚⑤。

哀哀父母,生我劳瘁⑥。

瓶之罄矣⁷，维罍之耻⁸。
鲜民之生⁹，不如死之久矣⑩。

无父何怙⑪？无母何恃⑫？
出则衔恤⑬，入则靡至⑭。

父兮生我⑮，母兮鞠我⑯。
拊我畜我⑰，长我育我⑱，
顾我复我⑲，出入腹我⑳。
欲报之德㉑。昊天罔极㉒！

南山烈烈㉓，飘风发发㉔。
民莫不穀㉕，我独何害㉖！
南山律律㉗，飘风弗弗㉘。
民莫不穀，我独不卒㉙！

【注释】

① 〔蓼(lù)〕高大貌。〔莪(é)〕莪蒿。李时珍《本草纲目》："莪抱根丛生，俗谓之抱娘蒿。"莪抱根丛生状，就像孩童粘着父母的情状，常以此喻指父母抚育儿女之恩。

② 〔匪莪伊蒿〕不是莪蒿而是（普通的）青蒿。〔匪〕同"非"。〔伊〕是，语助词。〔蒿〕青蒿，菊科黄花蒿地表的干燥部分，别称苦蒿，味苦，性寒。

③ 〔哀哀(āi)〕可怜，悲痛。

④ 〔生我劬劳〕父母生我受尽辛劳。〔劬(qú)〕劳累。

⑤ 〔蔚(wèi)〕本义为茂盛，盛大，富有文采。此指牡蒿，中草药，主清热凉血、解毒之效。

⑥ 〔生我劳瘁〕生育我辛苦憔悴。〔瘁(cuì)〕辛劳憔悴。

第五章 《诗经》经典篇章英译选读

⑦〔瓶〕汲水器具。〔罄(qìng)〕倾尽。
⑧〔维〕语助词。〔罍(léi)〕盛水器具。
⑨〔鲜(xiǎn)〕寡,孤。〔民〕别人。
⑩〔久〕早早地。〔不如死之久〕还不如早点死去。
⑪〔无父何怙〕失去了父亲的依靠。〔怙(hù)〕依靠。
⑫〔无母何恃〕失去了母亲的依靠。〔恃(shì)〕依靠。
⑬〔出则衔恤〕出门在外,心里忧伤难抑。〔衔恤(xián xù)〕内心忧伤。
⑭〔入则靡至〕回家没有父母在,心里空落落。〔靡(mí)〕消失,没有。
⑮〔父兮生我〕父亲生育了我。〔兮〕语助词。
⑯〔母兮鞠我〕母亲养育了我。〔鞠(jū)〕鞠养,抚养,抚育。
⑰〔拊(fǔ)〕通"抚",抚养,抚爱,安慰。〔畜〕通"慉(xù)",喜爱,喜悦。
⑱〔长我育我〕抚育我长大成人。
⑲〔顾我复我〕牵念我,舍不得我。〔顾〕牵挂。〔复〕不舍,离不开。
⑳〔出入腹我〕出门在外或是在家,时时护佑着我。〔腹〕怀抱,护佑。
㉑〔欲报之德〕想要报答父母的生养之情。〔之〕代指父母。
㉒〔昊天罔极〕像广袤的天一样无边无际。〔昊(hào)〕广袤。〔罔〕无。〔极〕准则,边界。
㉓〔烈〕高大伟岸貌。
㉔〔飘风发发〕风大发出拨拨声。〔飘风〕同"飙(biāo)风",暴风,疾风。〔发发〕古通"拨拨",拟声词。
㉕〔民莫不谷〕没有人不赡养父母。〔谷(gǔ)〕谷类作物的总称,此指赡养,孝敬老人。
㉖〔我独何害〕为什么只有我受此殃害(即失去双亲)。〔害〕倒霉,遭殃。
㉗〔南山律律〕南山高大巍峨。〔律〕高峻貌。
㉘〔飘风弗弗〕犹"飘风发发",即风大貌,发出呼呼的声响。
㉙〔卒(zú)〕寿终,去世。

白话释义

看似高大的莪蒿,却是无用的青蒿。
可怜我的父母啊,生我养我真辛劳。

看似茂盛的莪蒿,却是无用的蔚蒿。

哀怜我的父母啊,生我养我费尽心。

酒瓶没酒真遗憾,空空酒瓶真丢脸。
孤寂一人在世上,不如早早死掉好。
失去父爱真可怜,没有母亲谁牵念。
出门在外无人管,回家进门空落落。

父亲给予我生命,母亲把我拉扯大。
疼我护我费尽心,养我育我把力出。
每时每刻挂念我,出门回家把我亲。
好想报答双亲恩,可惜老天心真狠。

南山高峻又伟岸,山风刮起狂又冽。
别人都能养父母,唯我孝心无处敬。
南山峻拔又雄伟,山风呼呼吹不停。
别人孝心敬父母,唯我双亲已不在。

主题鉴赏

《蓼莪》一诗的主题历来争议颇多。《毛诗序》说此诗"刺幽王也,民人劳苦,孝子不得终养尔"。"孝子不得终养"确是中的之言,但至于"刺幽王,民人劳苦"云云,正如欧阳修所说"非诗人本意"(《诗本义》)。清人方玉润称"此诗为千古孝思绝作,尽人能识。"诗篇副标题注"孝子痛不得终养也"。方氏批评了儒家穿凿附会式的"刺幽王说",言其"意涉牵强,情亦不真。盖父母深恩与天无极,孰不当报?唯欲报之,而或不能终其身以奉养,则不觉抱恨终天,凄怆之情不能自已耳。若谓人民劳苦,不得终养,始思父母,则遇劳苦乃念所生,不遇劳苦即将不念所生乎?……中间两章,一写无亲之苦,一写育子之艰,备极沉痛,几于一字一泪,可抵一部《孝经》。"

"诗言志,歌咏言"(《诗大序》)一直被视为贯穿"诗三百"的诗学理念。"志"指"心愿情志",亦带有道德教化的目的。《蓼莪》一诗的主题,谕旨为人儿女在双亲去世后因无法敬奉而生的遗憾悲恸之情。

著名文学史家陈子展先生认为:"《蓼莪》是一首劳苦服役,不得终养父母,因而自伤哀悼之诗。诗人深感父母养育之恩,思有以图报;然而"入则衔恤,出

第五章 《诗经》经典篇章英译选读

则靡至",竟抱终天之恨。特别第四章,情词迫切,字字血泪,足见其哀痛之深。"

因此,笔者认为,此诗乃子女悼念亡故父母的祭歌。诗歌用词质朴无华却入情至深,读来不觉泣涕难抑。全诗由六章组成,前四章每章四句,后两章每章八句,逐层递升。首两章"双譬作起",以比入手,诗人错把"青蒿"与"牡蒿(蔚)"看成了有喻指意义的"莪蒿",以此引出父母生养"我"之不易。而诗人以"莪蒿"与"青蒿""牡蒿"作比的原因在于莪蒿的文化隐喻性:"莪抱根丛生状,就像孩童粘着父母的情状",故此又称为抱娘蒿;且味甘,可食用,喻人成材而且孝顺父母,而"青蒿""牡蒿(蔚)"均味苦性涩,故以青、蔚喻不成材且不能尽孝。前两章最后两行采用叠语句,"哀哀父母,生我劬劳""哀哀父母,生我劳瘁",诗人直抒胸臆,点明"题意",直言父母生养自己费尽辛劳,吃尽苦头。诗人以无限自责的语气将自己未能为双亲恪尽终养奉行恩孝的悔恨推至顶点,痛悔之音环绕天地之间,令人读来泪水潸然。

但诗人仍感觉悔意难尽,至此过渡到中间两章,以更为形象直观的比喻描写失怙失恃的儿子无法言喻的痛楚和懊悔,以直击心灵的言辞回顾了父母在世时给予自己无微不至的关怀和爱护的暖心场景。第三章首行采用两个非常具象的实物类比父母与儿子的关系:酒瓶喻指父母,罍(酒坛)喻指儿子,酒瓶中的酒干了,这是罍的耻辱。诗人以形象的比喻,将失祜无怙的孤单情貌,从抽象转为具象,让读者直观感受到父母去世而子女却未能恪尽恩孝的悲痛之情。明清学者顾炎武《与李湘北书》曰:"一旦祷北辰而不验,回西景以无期,则瓶罍奚偿,风木之悲何及?"成语"瓶罄罍耻""风木之悲"即和此诗有关。

最后两章是诗歌情感的爆发点。第五章连用了九个动词,生、鞠、拊、畜、长、育、顾、复、腹,形异而意近(同),音声铿锵,直击人心;九个第一人称的"我"字,嘭嘭作响,叩击心灵。清人姚际恒云:"勾人眼泪全在此无数'我'字。"

大儒朱熹评论说:"晋王哀以父死罪,每读《诗》至'哀哀父母,生我劬劳',未尝不三复流涕。受业者为废此篇,诗之感人至深。"子女赡养父母、孝敬父母是中华民族的传统美德之一,也应该是人类社会的基本道德义务。此诗是以充沛情感表现这一美德的最早的文学作品之一,对后世影响极大。《诗经》对民族心理、民族精神形成所产生的影响,由此可见一斑。

诗歌是人类对生命有了最真实的体验后,发出的呐喊和呼号,有的欢快,有的悲戚,有的绝望,有的遗憾。这首诗传达的悲恸心境,并不是外向的,而是比较内敛和含蓄的,是欲言又止的。正如叶维廉先生所说:"中国人感情的流露与外国人大不相同,中国人是蕴藏的,外国人大多趋向爆炸性。"本诗所描述的那种哭天天不应,喊地地不灵的悲恸,在那些有过失去双亲的苦痛体验的人身上,或许最能得到共鸣。古语云:"树欲静而风不止,子欲养而亲不待也。往而不可追者,年也;去而不可得见者,亲也。(《孔子家语·卷二·致思第八》)"不要在双亲离开人世之后,才想起他们抚育我们长大成人的如山恩情,那时就只剩下这首诗描述的凄苦情境了。

The Parents' Death

Long and large grows sweet grass,
Not wild weed of no worth.
My parents died, alas!
With toil they gave me birth.

Long and large grows sweet grass,
Not shorter weed on earth,
My parents died, alas!
With pain they gave me birth.

When the pitcher is void,
Empty will be the jar.
Our parents' life destroyed,
How sad we orphans are!

On whom can I rely,
Now fatherless and motherless?
Outdoors, with grief I sigh;
Indoors, I seem homeless.

My father gave me birth;
By mother I was fed.
They cherished me with mirth,

第五章 《诗经》经典篇章英译选读

And by them I was bred.
They looked after me
And bore me out and in.
Boundless as sky should be
The kindness of our kin.

The southern mountain's high;
The wind soughs without cheer.
Happy are those near by;
Alone I'm sad and drear.

The southern mountain's cold;
The wind blows a strong blast.
Happy are young and old;
My grief fore'er will last.

——许渊冲

THE ORPHAN

How tall and strong the southernwood has grown!
Ah no! —the tansy rather.
O mother mine! O father!
And for my life what travail ye have known!
Yea, tall and strong the southernwood I see;
Nay, wormwood—somewhat other.
O father mine! O mother!
And for my life what toil and pain had ye!
Ah, when no more the flagon is supplied,
Disgrace befals the jar.

O better lot by far

Than orphaned life, to long ago have died!

The fatherless—in whom shall he confide?

The motherless find rest?

Abroad, with grief suppressed

He goes; returns,—none hastens to his side

O father, thou didst give my life to me!

O mother, thou didst nourish

And comfort me, and cherish

And rear and train me from my infancy,

And watch and tend and to thy bosom press

At parting or return!

To requite such love I burn,

But, like Great Heaven itself, 'tis measureless.

Around South Hill's bleak eminences moan

The battling, wheeling winds!

Ah, while none other finds

Life robb'd of joy, why suffer I alone?

Yea, round South Hill's acclivities and bluffs

The circling storm-wind beats.

Round me is none but meets

With joy in life: I only meet rebuffs.

——William Jennings(威廉姆·詹宁斯)

Luh ngo

1

Long and large grows the *ngo*;—

It is not the *ngo* but the *haou*.

Alas! alas! my parents,

第五章 《诗经》经典篇章英译选读

With what toil ye gave me birth!

2

Long and large grows the *ngo*;—

It is not the *ngo*, but the *wei*.

Alas! alas! my parents,

With what toil and suffering ye gave me birth!

3

When the pitcher is exhausted,

It is the shame of the jar.

Than to live an orphan,

It would be better to have been long dead.

Fatherless, who is there to rely on?

Motherless, who is there to depend on?

When I go abroad, I carry my grief with me;

When I come home, I have no one to go to.

4

O my father, who begat me!

O my mother, who nourished me!

Ye indulged me, ye fed me,

Ye held me up, ye supported me,

Ye looked after me, ye never left me,

Out and in ye bore me in your arms.

If I would return your kindness,

It is like great Heaven, illimitable.

5

Cold and bleak is the Southern hill;

The rushing wind is very fierce

People all are happy;—

Why am I alone thus miserable?

6

The Southern hill is very steep;

The rushing wind is blustering.

People all are happy;—

143

I alone have been unable to finish [my duty].

——James Legge(詹姆斯·理雅各)

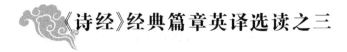《诗经》经典篇章英译选读之三

国风·秦风·蒹葭①

蒹葭苍苍②,白露为霜③。
所谓伊人④,在水一方⑤。
溯洄从之⑥,道阻且长⑦。
溯游⑧从之,宛⑨在水中央。

蒹葭萋萋⑩,白露未晞⑪。
所谓伊人,在水之湄⑫。
溯洄从之,道阻且跻⑬。
溯游从之,宛在水中坻⑭。

蒹葭采采⑮,白露未已⑯。
所谓伊人,在水之涘⑰。
溯洄从之,道阻且右⑱。
溯游从之,宛在水中沚⑲。

【注释】

①〔蒹〕薕。〔葭〕芦苇。郭璞曰:"蒹似萑而细,高数尺。芦,苇也。"
②〔苍苍〕草木茂盛的样子。芦苇入秋茂密,其色深青苍然的样子(陈子展)。
③〔白露为霜〕白露凝结为霜。笺云:蒹葭在众草之中苍苍然强盛,至白露凝而为霜则成而黄。

第五章 《诗经》经典篇章英译选读

④〔伊人〕笺云:伊当作繄,繄犹是也,即那人,指所爱的人。
⑤〔在水一方〕远在大水一边,即隔水而远,言人不可及。
⑥〔溯洄(sù huí)〕逆流而上曰溯洄。〔溯〕向。〔洄〕上水,逆流。〔从〕追寻,寻觅。
⑦〔道阻且长〕道路崎岖险阻。〔阻〕崎岖艰险。
⑧〔溯游〕顺流而下。
⑨〔宛〕好像,仿佛。
⑩〔萋萋〕犹苍苍,草木茂盛的样子。
⑪〔晞(xī)〕干。〔未晞〕未结霜。
⑫〔湄(méi)〕水草交际之处,水之岸。
⑬〔跻(jī)〕升,登高。笺云:"升者,言其难至如升阪",意指道路崎岖难行。
⑭〔坻(chí)〕小渚,即水中高地。《释水》云:"小洲曰渚。小渚曰沚。小沚曰坻。"
⑮〔采采〕犹苍苍,萋萋,茂盛,众多。
⑯〔未已〕未完,未停止。
⑰〔涘(sì)〕韩诗同"沶",大渚曰涘(zhǐ),即水边,水岸之意。
⑱〔右〕弯曲。笺云:"右者,言其迂回也。"马瑞辰云:"周人尚左,故以右为迂回。"
⑲〔沚(zhǐ)〕水中的小块陆地。

白话释义

河畔芦苇秋色浓,芦叶摇曳露凝霜。
心系怀人在何方,水岸那方相遥望。
逆流而上把伊找,崎岖坎坷路途遥。
顺流而下追寻忙,伊人犹在水中央。

河畔芦苇立深秋,芦花依旧白露浓。
心系怀人何所踪,水泽之畔倩影弄。
逆流去寻伊人处,路途劳顿莫要慌。
顺流而下去何处,伊人宛在河渚上。

秋色浓浓染芦苇,芦叶濡湿沾白露。
伊人不知在何处,水岸河畔把身露。

逆流去把伊人找,路途漫漫好难走。
顺流而下去何处,伊人宛在河心驻。

主题鉴赏

《蒹葭》为《诗经·国风·秦风》系列的第四篇,"秦风"主题包括奉时行乐(《车邻》)、游园田猎(《驷驖》)、车马行军(《小戎》《无衣》)、活人殉葬(《黄鸟》)、亲人相送(《渭阳》)、喟叹年老(《权舆》)等政治性内容。《蒹葭》以生于水岸菏泽边的"芦苇"引出诗歌主题,意境缥缈空灵,语言温润如玉,情感惆怅细腻。主题似与"秦风"其他篇什有极不相同之处。《蒹葭》诗旨如何,一直是古今学者争执不下的热点话题。

《毛序》:"(《蒹葭》)刺襄公也。未能用周礼,将无以固其国。"《笺》(《郑笺》)曰:"秦处周之旧土,其人被周之德教日久矣,今襄公新为诸侯,未习周之礼法,故国人未服焉。"魏源云:"襄公初有岐西之地,以戎俗变周民也。豳邠皆公刘太王遗民,久习礼教,一旦为秦所有,不以周道变戎俗,反以戎俗变周民,如苍苍之葭,遇霜而黄。肃杀之政行,忠厚之风尽,盖谓非此无以自强于戎狄。不知自强之道在于求贤,其时故都遗老隐居薮泽,文武之道,未坠在人,特时君尚诈力,则贤人不至,故求治逆而难;尚德怀则贤人来辅,故求治顺而易,溯洄不如溯游也。襄公急霸西戎,不遵礼教,流至春秋,诸侯终以夷狄摈秦,故诗人兴霜露焉。"

有学者认为以上"刺襄公说"或"求贤说",都是依从"释经学"的政教性来阐释《蒹葭》。"政教性"类似于孔子所主张的文学"诗教说","强调文学要为政治教化服务,认为文学是以仁义礼乐教化百姓的最好手段。"

从古至今,持此论断者不在少数,包括东汉经学家郑玄、宋代文学家欧阳修、苏辙、王安石,明清之际的王夫之,清人魏源、姚际恒、方玉润等。可见,以传统"经学"解释《诗经》这一传统赓续时远,持政治教化主张的倾向也是一代甚于一代。

如众所知,汉代已降,"诗教说"颇为流行,《诗经》逐渐被抬升为一部以周朝及之前社会的历史、政治、经济、道德、礼教、战争为主题的儒家"经学"大作,其政教意味似乎远超其文学趣味和艺术价值。当然,诗无达诂,并不是说经学家们的解读都有问题,而是说,在新的时代,阅读《诗经》,如果仍抱守着古代经学家们的"释经学"方法,恐怕有些不合时宜,因此,就需要找到更贴合读者阅读视域和审美趣味的新的诠释角度,让《诗经》旧颜换新装,与时俱进。

那么,《蒹葭》是否可以被解读为一首爱情诗?

在中国封建时代,爱情往往无法成为古代文学的显性主题。因此,古代经

第五章 《诗经》经典篇章英译选读

学家,几乎无人持此观点。而近代及当今一些学者,逐渐放弃以经学释《诗经》这一传统视角,他们开始为"诗三百"寻找更为贴近当今读者趣味的解读路径。一些学者认为《蒹葭》是一首爱情诗,最具代表性的有诗经、楚辞研究专家袁梅先生,其他学者有马持盈、庄穆、孙达、韩峥嵘、葛培岭等。程俊英、蒋见元、余冠英、高亨、屈万里、杨仲义、陈子展等学者都较为审慎。陈子展先生说:"《蒹葭》是一首抒写水上怀人的诗。所谓'在水一方'的'伊人'究竟是指周礼的故都遗老旧臣呢,还是秦国隐于水滨的贤者,是诗人的一个朋友呢,还是诗人所想念的爱人,似乎都属于想象之词,无从臆断。但见秋水迷茫,'伊人'宛在,既寓慕悦诚挚之情,复寄向往追求之意;然而徘徊往复,终不可及。情景潇洒入画,颇有领略不尽的意味。"陈先生的"水上怀人"和"领略不尽的意味",委婉却有些玄虚。朱熹《诗集传》对该诗的主题也是语焉不详,他说:"伊人,犹言彼人……所谓彼人者,乃在水之一方,上下求之而皆不可得。然不知其何所指也。"

笔者以为,将《蒹葭》解读为爱情诗没有什么不可。

古往今来,无论东方还是西方,爱情都是人类恒久的精神追求,也是大多数文学体裁,尤其是诗歌的主题之一。"关关雎鸠,在河之洲。窈窕淑女,君子好逑"(《关雎》)开启了《诗经》君子求佳人,琴瑟相与和的爱情圣境。"蒹葭苍苍,白露为霜。所谓伊人,在水一方。"为我们描绘了一幅伊人水岸,君子遥望的爱情画面。所以,有人说《蒹葭》一诗是除《关雎》外,《诗经》中最能表现真挚而纯美爱情的经典诗作。

王国维先生认为:"《诗·蒹葭》一篇最得风人深致。晏同叔之'昨夜西风凋碧树,独上高楼,望尽天涯路',意颇近之。但一洒落,一悲壮耳。"笔者认为,"风人",意即诗人;"风人深致"表现出诗人至高深远的意境。"洒落"指诗人对"伊人"那种爱而不得的洒脱心境和豁达态度。诗歌以空灵的艺术氛围、奇崛的构思路径、瑰丽的画面维度,呈现给读者一幅清秋河岸,芦苇摇曳,一位谦谦君子万分焦灼地守望着纤纤佳人的画面。"所谓伊人,在水一方",有水的地方是柔软的,柔软的地方总会发生柔软的故事,《蒹葭》就是一首因水而生的温婉而又有些许惆怅的情歌,一个发生在水岸河泽边的爱情故事。诗人以高超的艺术创作手法,独特的文字驾驭技巧和动人的音乐旋律,巧妙地再现出人类对美好爱情无限渴盼的共情心理。

本诗延续《诗经》一贯的"叠咏体",由三章构成,三章迭章复沓,每章诗行基本类似,仅替换个别词语,可谓言简意赅,而又诗意隽永绮丽。诗歌以主人公远眺为广角镜头的抓取点,采用类似蒙太奇的艺术呈现手法,向读者展示了一幅动感极强的从近景到中景,再到远景逐次铺开的秋色芦苇河洲图,从可视的现实逐渐向想象的世界延展。一开始,主人公若有所思地伫立于芦苇摇曳的河洲岸边,望向(或幻想)河岸那方渴盼已久的"伊人"而心悦不已;但可惜,秋色凝重,露水打湿的芦苇那端,"伊人"已渐行渐远。于是,主人公只能逆流而上,去追寻"伊人"远遁于河中小渚上的曼妙身影,无奈路途遥远,艰难而曲折。但主人公毫无退却之心,又顺流而下,终于在河心小洲上看到了"伊人"静立的迷人背影。读者随着诗人也一起进入一种无法言喻的美好意境中。

　　诗以深秋时节,河洲芦苇凝露结霜的自然景色为背景,以高度绮丽的艺术手法,以空间位移的视角,铺陈出主人公对"伊人"无限企慕却遥不可及而怅然若失的复杂心理,揭示了人类精神世界里对美人的期寄和遥望之情,对爱情的憧憬,突出了爱情这一带有共性的最真挚最美好的普适情愫。这种情愫,是游离于诗歌之外的,在"语言的边缘欲言不语",是景外之情的延伸和扩展。这也正是这首诗强大的语言张力所在。

英译1

Where Is She?

Green, green the reed,
Frost and dew gleam
Where's she I need?
Beyond the stream.
Upstream I go;
The way's so long.
And downstream, lo!
She's thereamong.

White, white the reed,
Dew not yet dried.
Where's she I need?
On the other side.
Upstream I go;
Hard is the way.

第五章 《诗经》经典篇章英译选读

And downstream, lo!
She's far away.

Bright, bright the reed,
With frost dews blend.
Where's she I need?
At river's end.
Upstream I go;
The way does wind.
And downstream, lo!
She's far behind.

——许渊冲

英译2

Këen këa

The reeds and rushes are deeply green,
And the white dew is turned into hoarfrost.
The man of whom I think
Is somewhere about the water.
I go up the stream in quest of him,
But the way is difficult and long.
I go down the stream in quest of him,
And lo! he is right in the midst of the water.

The reeds and rushes are luxuriant,
And the white dew is not yet dry.
The man of whom I think
Is on the margin of the water.
I go up the stream in quest of him,

But the way is difficult and steep.
I go down the stream in quest of him,
And lo! he is on the islet in the midst of the water.

The reeds and rushes are abundant,
And the white dew is not yet ceased.
The man of whom I think
Is on the bank of the river.
I go up the stream in quest of him,
But the way is difficult and turns to the right.
I go down the stream in quest of him,
And lo! he is on the island in the midst of the water.

——James Legge（詹姆斯·理雅各）

CHASING THE PHANTOM

When reed and rush grew green, grew green,
And dews to hoar-frost changed,
One whom they speak of as "that man"
Somewhere the river ranged.
Upstream they went in quest of him,
A long and toilsome way;
Downstream they went in quest of him;—
In *mid*-stream there he lay!
When reed and rush grew tall, grew tall,
And dews lay yet undried,
He whom they speak of as "that man"
Was by the riverside.
Upstream they searched for him, along
The toilsome, deep defile;

第五章 《诗经》经典篇章英译选读

  Downstream again—and there he lay,
    Midway, upon the isle!
  When reed and rush were cut and gone,
    And dews still lingered dank,
  He whom they speak of as "that man"
    Was on the river's bank.
  Upstream they searched for him, along
    The toilsome right-hand road;
  Downstream,—and on the island there,
    In *mid*-stream, he abode!

      ——William Jennings（威廉姆·詹宁斯）

本章课后练习

一、请鉴赏《诗经·关雎》宇文所安译本。

关 雎

Classic of Poetry I "Fishhawk"

  The fishhawks sing *gwan gwan*
    on sandbars of the stream.
  Gentle maiden, pure and fair,
    fit pair for a prince.
  Watercress grows here and there,
    right and left we gather it.
  Gentle maiden, pure and fair,
    wanted waking and asleep.
  Wanting, sought her, had her not,
    waking, sleeping, thought of her,
    on and on he thought of her,
  he tossed from one side to another.
  Watercress grows here and there,
    right and left we pull it.

中华典籍英译选读

> Gentle maiden, pure and fair,
> with harps we bring her company.
> Watercress grows here and there,
> right and left we pick it out.
> Gentle maiden, pure and fair,
> with bells and drums do her delight.

——Stephen Owen（宇文所安）

二、配对练习。

1. 诗三百，一言以蔽之，曰："思无邪"。
2. 不学诗，无以言。
3. 小子，何莫学夫诗？诗可以兴，可以观，可以群，可以怨。
4. 诵诗三百，授之以政，不达；使于四方，不能专对；虽多，亦奚以为？
5. 迩之事父，远之事君，多识于鸟兽草木之名。

A. Young men, why do you not study *Poetry*? It can be used to inspire, to observe, to make you fit for company, to express grievances.

B. Though a man can recite the Three Hundred Poems, if he cannot carry out his duties when entrusted with affairs of state, and cannot answer questions on his own when sent on a mission abroad, what is the use of having studied the poems, no matter how many?

C. If you do not study *Poetry*, you will not be able to speak (properly).

D. Near at hand, (it will teach you how) to serve your father, and, (looking) further, (how) to serve your sovereign; it also enables you to learn the names of many birds, beasts, plants, and trees.

E. The Three Hundred Poems may be summed up in one phrase: "No evil thoughts."

三、名句试译。

1. 昔我往矣，杨柳依依。今我来思，雨雪霏霏。(《小雅·采薇》)

2. 死生契阔，与子成说。执子之手，与子偕老。(《国风·邶风·击鼓》)

第五章 《诗经》经典篇章英译选读

3. 投我以木瓜,报之以琼琚。(《国风·卫风·木瓜》)

4. 他山之石,可以攻玉。(《小雅·鹤鸣》)

5. 有匪君子,如切如磋,如琢如磨。(《国风·卫风·淇奥》)

6. 嘤其鸣矣,求其友声。(《小雅·伐木》)

7. 投我以桃,报之以李。(《大雅·抑》)

8. 今夕何夕,见此良人。(《国风·唐风·绸缪》)

9. 关关雎鸠,在河之洲。窈窕淑女,君子好逑。(《国风·周南·关雎》)

10. 桃之夭夭,灼灼其华。之子于归,宜其室家。(《国风·周南·桃夭》)

11. 巧笑倩兮,美目盼兮。(《国风·卫风·硕人》)

12. 知我者谓我心忧,不知我者谓我何求!(《国风·王风·黍离》)

13. 青青子衿,悠悠我心。(《国风·郑风·子衿》)

14. 呦呦鹿鸣,食野之苹。我有嘉宾,鼓瑟吹笙。(《小雅·鹿鸣》)

15. 风雨如晦,鸡鸣不已。既见君子,云胡不喜。(《国风·郑风·风雨》)

第六章

《楚辞》经典篇章英译选读

【导读】

　　《楚辞》是继《诗经》之后我国古代诗歌发展史上的又一座丰碑,"是战国时期以屈原作品为代表的、具有楚语和楚音特征的、富于地方色彩和楚地民歌传统的一种新兴文学样式"。传统认为,《楚辞》大致成书于公元前26年至公元前6年之间,经历了屈原的作品始创,后人仿作,汉初辑佚,至西汉文学家刘向辑录整理成集等几个历史发展阶段。遗憾的是,刘向所辑录的《楚辞》原书早已亡佚,后人只能通过东汉王逸的《楚辞章句》(原书亦佚)、宋人洪兴祖的《楚辞补注》(《楚辞章句》的补充)等书来追溯揣测其原貌。刘向编订的《楚辞》中收录了屈原、宋玉、淮南小山、贾谊等人的作品,并非仅限于屈原一人。

　　作为一种新兴的诗歌体裁,《楚辞》的诗歌题材源于长江流域沅湘之滨,其主要的生发地为今天的湖南湖北,以及以该区域为中心向四周延伸的地理区域,具体范围应该大于今天的两湖地区。

　　公元前11世纪～公元前3世纪是中华诗歌集生成的重要肇始期:第一部中华汉语诗歌总集《诗经》诞生于中国北方的黄河流域;大约三百年后,在秦岭以南的长江流域,第二部中华汉语诗歌集《楚辞》横空出世。如果说《楚辞》代表的是中国南方的诗歌类型,那么,《诗经》则是中国北方诗歌的典型代表。从两者的语言特质、诗歌主题、韵律特征等方面看,《楚辞》与《诗经》有许多关联甚至相通的内容。有学者认为,"十五国风"里的"二南",即《周南》与《召南》,大致来自于经过加工润色的楚地乐歌。

第六章　《楚辞》经典篇章英译选读

《楚辞》继承并发展了"二南"的优秀传统,吸收了楚地民间歌谣的成分,融合了战国时期南、北文学艺术传统,最终形成了自己独特的风格。《楚辞》中的代表作是屈原的《离骚》。《楚辞》的语言风格可用八个字来概括:"汪洋恣肆,奇崛瑰丽"。有人称"楚辞为有韵之庄子,庄子为无韵之离骚"。

西汉刘向的《楚辞》中除了屈原和宋玉的作品,还收录了刘向、东方朔、王褒、贾谊等人仿效屈原和宋玉的作品,共计十六篇,不过其原本已佚。东汉王逸的《楚辞章句》是现存最早的《楚辞》注本,其中增入王逸自己所作《九思》,成十七篇,分别是《离骚》《九歌》《天问》《九章》《远游》《卜居》《渔父》《九辩》《招魂》《大招》《惜誓》《招隐士》《七谏》《哀时命》《九怀》《九叹》《九思》。这种十七篇的篇目构成也成为后世通行本的篇目构成。南宋洪兴祖以《楚辞章句》为基础作《楚辞补注》,此外,南宋朱熹的《楚辞集注》、清代王夫之的《楚辞通释》和戴震的《屈原赋注》等都是《楚辞》比较著名的注本。

从诗体形式上看,《楚辞》打破了《诗经》以四言为主的句式,使用五言、六言,甚至七言、八言的句子,并大量使用"兮"字。该字多出现在句中或句尾,帮助调节音节和节奏,有时还能起到结构助词的作用。《楚辞》极大地突破了《诗经》短章诗体的局限。中国文学史上最长的一首诗——《离骚》,长达 373 行,总计 2477 个字。《楚辞》开启了赋体之先河,并影响其后历代散文创作。此外,《楚辞》的许多作品想象力丰富,多用神话传说,色彩瑰丽,浪漫奔放,不仅抒发了诗人们强烈的个人情怀,而且抒发了更深层次的家国意识。《楚辞》被视为中国文学史上第一部浪漫主义作品,屈原被誉为第一位浪漫主义诗人。

今人研究《楚辞》,主要研究的是屈原和宋玉的作品,尤其是屈原,因他是《楚辞》的创立者和代表人物,其作品数量丰富、内容广泛、思想深刻,体现了《楚辞》的最高艺术特色。对《楚辞》及其研究史作研究的学科,今天称为"楚辞学",上迄汉代,经魏晋隋唐,至宋代大兴。近现代,《楚辞》更成为中国古典文化殿堂之显学,而《楚辞》早在盛唐时便流入日本等汉字文化圈国家,16 世纪之后,流入欧洲。至 19 世纪,《楚辞》引起欧美各国的广泛关注,各种语言的译文、研究著作大量涌现,在国际汉学界,楚辞亦是学术研究的热点之一。

屈原(约公元前 340—公元前 278 年),芈姓,屈氏,名平,字原,中国古代战国时期楚国人,伟大的浪漫主义诗人、政治家。他生活在列国争雄、战争频繁的时代。当时秦国和楚国实力最强,两国都有统一中国的可能。屈原认为变法图强是楚国唯一的出路。而变法必然会侵害旧贵族、旧势力的利益,因而遭到他们的强烈反对和阻挠。楚怀王听信谗言,开始疏远屈原,罢免他的左使之职,只让他做一个闲散的三闾大夫。此后,在楚国面临极大的军事威胁时,屈原主张联合当时另外一个强国——齐国以抗秦。此项主张又一次遇到了亲秦投降派的强大阻力。以上官大夫靳尚、楚怀王幼子子兰、楚怀王宠姬郑袖为代表的亲秦派不断打击和排挤屈原,对楚怀王施加影响。这场亲秦与抗秦的斗争最后以屈原的失败告终,他先后被流放到汉北、江南,一生的政治理想付诸东流。在此背景下,屈原用诗歌来倾吐自己忧国忧民、缠绵悱恻的情绪。司马迁在《史记·屈原列传》里说:"屈平正道直行,竭忠尽智,以事其君,谗人间之,可谓穷矣。信而见疑,忠而被谤,能无怨乎?屈平之作《离骚》,盖自怨生也。"所以,大多认为屈原创作《离骚》是在他被楚怀王疏远时。《离骚》是屈原"发愤以抒情"而创作的一首政治抒情诗,也是《楚辞》中艺术成就最高的一首作品。刘勰评价《离骚》为"气往轹古,辞来切今,惊采绝艳,难与并能矣"。

宋玉,战国末期辞赋家,生卒年不详,生于屈原之后,一般认为他是屈原的弟子。也有学者认为他"不是屈原的授业弟子","与唐勒(约公元前290年—约公元前223年,战国末期辞赋家)、景差[cuō](公元前290年—公元前223年,战国末期辞赋家)同时,大约生于屈原沉江前后,死于楚亡之际。"《楚辞》中的《九辩》一般认为是宋玉所作,是一首长篇抒情诗,共有二百五十多句。王逸在其《楚辞章句》中说:"《九辩》者,楚大夫宋玉之所作也。"也有部分学者认为此篇为屈原所作,但支持者甚少。关于宋玉创作《九辩》的目的,一说是为屈原代言,如王逸认为宋玉"闵惜其师忠而放逐,故作《九辩》以述其志"。另一说为此诗是宋玉遭遇的自述,他自悯其不幸,同时也揭示了当时楚国政治混乱、奸佞当道的黑暗现实。出身寒门的他怀才不遇、报国无门,最后被黜失职。在文学创作上,宋玉继承并发展了屈原的创作形式和风格,并开启了"悲秋"这一文学主题,对后世的文学创作产生了深远的影响。通行本《楚辞》篇章结构见表6-1。

表6-1 通行本《楚辞》篇章结构一览表

编目/数量	题目	作者
《离骚(1篇)》	离骚	屈原
《九歌(11篇)》	东皇太一、云中君、湘君、湘夫人、大司命、少司命、东君、河伯、山鬼、国殇、礼魂	屈原
《天问(1篇)》	天问	屈原
《九章(9篇)》	惜诵、涉江、哀郢、抽思、怀沙、思美人、惜往日、橘颂、悲回风	屈原
《远游(1篇)》	远游	屈原

第六章 《楚辞》经典篇章英译选读

续表

编目/数量	题目	作者
《卜居(1篇)》	卜居	屈原
《渔父(1篇)》	渔父	屈原
《九辩(1篇)》	九辩	宋玉
《招魂(1篇)》	招魂	宋玉
《大招(1篇)》	大招	屈原,或曰景差
《惜誓(1篇)》	惜誓	或曰贾谊
《招隐士(1篇)》	招隐士	淮南小山
《七谏(7篇)》	初放、沉江、怨世、怨思、自悲、哀命、谬谏	东方朔
《哀时命(1篇)》	哀时命	严忌
《九怀(9篇)》	匡机、通路、危俊、昭世、尊嘉、蓄英、思忠、陶壅、株昭	王褒
《九叹(9篇)》	逢纷、离世、怨思、远逝、惜贤、忧苦、愍命、思古、远游	刘向
《九思(1篇)》	九思	王逸

注:几乎每篇作品归属权都曾有歧说,本表据王逸《楚辞章句》说法而作。

由于《楚辞》主题深奥、语句晦涩、内容博大精深,故其外译难度极大。再者,历代学者对《楚辞》进行了勘校、注疏、释义,他们对其中某些字、句甚至某些诗篇的主旨、意境的理解各有不同,这就又增加了翻译的难度。即便如此,国内外的译者仍不辍努力,大胆进行译介。17世纪时,日本出版了《注解楚辞全集》。19世纪上半叶开始,西方陆续有《楚辞》外译问世。虽然《楚辞》英译起步较晚,但势头强劲。截至2013年,《楚辞》已有约40个英译本(包括39个选译本和1个全译本),涉及国内外不同译者。

1874年,英国近代著名汉学家罗伯特·科罗维·道格思(Robert Kennaway Douglas)在 *The Academy* 杂志上发表《评德理文侯爵的<离骚>》一文。这是一篇评论法国汉学家德理文(Marquis d'Hervey de Saint Denys)《离骚章句》(*Le Li-sao: poème du IIIe siècle avant notre ère*)的文章,其中的《渔父》译文是迄今为止发现的最早的《楚辞》英译作品。英国汉学家庄延龄(Edward Harper Parker)于1879年在香港的《中国评论》第五期上发表的《离别之忧离骚》(*The Sadness of Separation, or Li Sao*),在道格思的《渔父》英译文被广为人知之前一直被认为是第一个楚辞英译本。

英国著名汉学家亚瑟·韦利(Arthur David Waley)对《楚辞》英译及向西

方世界介绍"楚辞"文化做出了积极的贡献。1918年伦敦康斯特布公司(Constable & Company Ltd.)出版了韦利的《汉诗一百七十首》(*A Hundred and Seventy Chinese Poems*),其中包括《国殇》(*Battle*)的英译文。1919年,韦利在其《中国文学译作续编》中翻译了《大招》(*The Great Summons*)。旅日作家李长声对韦利的楚辞英译有如下评论:"屈原的《大招》里列举了好多鸟,这些鸟几乎就是个名字,不会给人以具体的形象,但是与百鸟朝凤、百花齐放之类的笼而统之自是不同,文体也就不一样。多识于鸟兽草木之名的人喜欢,却难为了翻译。庞德赞韦利善于修剪,翟理斯非难韦利译了些什么鸟。韦利反驳:"我不追求鸟或动物名称的自然科学性译语……应该找到符合诗中要求的文体的等价语,有时对应不上原语也无奈。我译的是诗,不是博物志……我的目标就是传达原诗。"……韦利尽情地发挥自己的诗才,不做学者式解释,而且将其译成了无韵诗,给20世纪的英诗带来新的韵律,为诗坛赞许。或许庞德、韦利都将未臻精通之处作为大展想象力的空间,对原诗进行再创作。"1955年澳大利亚艾伦与昂温出版公司出版了韦利的《九歌》研究性英译本(*The Nine Songs: A Study of Shamanism in Ancient China*)。

最值得称道的译本之一是英国著名汉学家和翻译家大卫·霍克斯(David Hawkes)翻译出版的《楚辞》全译本《楚辞——南方的歌》(*The Songs of the South: An Anthology of Ancient Chinese Poems by Qu Yuan and Other Poets*)。霍克斯于1945至1947年间在牛津大学主攻中文,师承亚瑟·韦利,1948年赴北京大学中文系攻读研究生,终其一生从事中国文学作品的外译工作。他翻译的 *The Songs of the South: An Anthology of Ancient Chinese Poems by Qu Yuan and Other Poets* 是西方翻译史上规模最大的《楚辞》翻译,也是迄今为止唯一的《楚辞》全译本,自出版之日起就受到了广大学者的赞誉。1985年,英国企鹅图书出版公司出版了该书的修订版,其中补充了大量注释,比之前的版本更为详尽。许渊冲评说"他的译法介乎直译与意译之间,从微观的角度来看,比前人的译本更准确,但从宏观的角度看来,却只能使人知之,不能使人好之、乐之"。其他西方译者及其译著有杰拉·约翰逊(Jerah Johnson)出版的 *Li Sao: A Poem on Relieving Sorrow* 单行本、美国著名翻译家、汉学家伯顿·沃森(又名华兹生,Burton Watson)出版的英译集《哥伦比亚中国诗歌选》(*The Columbia Book of Chinese Poetry: from the Early Times to the 13th Century*),其中收录了他翻译的《离骚》和《九歌》。《九歌》部分选译了《云中君》《河伯》《山鬼》和《国殇》。1996年,美国著名汉学家宇文所安(Stephen Owen)、华裔学者孙康宜出版英译集《中国文学选》(*An Anthology*

第六章 《楚辞》经典篇章英译选读

of Chinese Literature: Beginnings to 1911),其中收录了宇文所安翻译的《九歌》和《离骚》。维克多·梅维恒（Victor H. Mair）编译的《哥伦比亚传统中国文学选集》(Columbia Anthology of Traditional Chinese Literature)收录了梅维恒翻译的《天问》和海陶纬(James Hightower)英译贾谊的《鹏鸟赋》。

国内也有许多译者致力于《楚辞》的英译。1929 年，厦门大学第二任校长林文庆出版了《离骚》英译本(The Li Sao, An Elegy on Encountering Sorrow, by Chu Yuan)，翟理斯和泰戈尔为其作序。1953 年，著名翻译家杨宪益、戴乃迭夫妇在外文出版社出版了他们选译的《楚辞选》，包含 24 篇《楚辞》篇目。大卫·霍克斯评价说，这是匠心独运的一座丰碑，像蒲伯译荷马史诗一样富有诗感，虽然并不忠实于原文。

至 1975 年，近代著名诗人柳无忌和翻译家罗郁正合编的译文集《葵晔集》(Sunflower Splendor: Three Thousands Years of Chinese Poetry)收录了柳无忌英译的五首《楚辞》诗歌，分别为《橘颂》《湘君》《大司命》《离骚选译》和《哀郢》。

近二、三十年来国内出版的英译本有翻译家许渊冲先生的《楚辞》英译本。2009 年再次出版由许渊冲英译，张华中文译注的汉英对照英译本《楚辞》。杨成虎教授评价说："许渊冲的译文着力表现"骚体"的特征，在选词造句上宁美不信……许译念起来朗朗上口，让人有诗的感觉，只是他过多地省略了原文中词语的文化信息。他又说：许译使用了单行与单行押韵，双行与双行押韵，中间加 oh 的形式，这在英诗中是一种很好的尝试……"。另有诗人、翻译家孙大雨先生的《英译屈原诗选》。吴均陶评价其译著说"文辞优美精当，信而有征"。2006 年，典籍英译学者卓振英出版了《大中华文库·楚辞（汉英对照）》，其中选译了《楚辞》的大量篇幅。

由此可见，《楚辞》英译情况比较复杂，涉猎《楚辞》英译的译者人数众多，且大部分译者选译了《楚辞》中的一篇或几篇诗歌。

《楚辞》以高度的思想性和艺术性影响着后世，并且传播到世界各地，受到许多读者的关注和喜爱。《楚辞》创作者中的佼佼者屈原更是冠绝古今，他不仅开启了一种新的诗体形式，开创了古代诗歌的新天地，而且塑造了一种崇高的精神，表现了他对国家和人民的热爱。每年农历五月初五的端午节，国人都会集体缅怀大诗人屈原。1953 年，世界和平理事会提出纪念世界四位文化名人，其中就有中国的诗人屈原，其千古绝唱"路漫漫其修远兮，吾将上下而求索"将会代代传承，一直激荡在华夏大地上。

《楚辞》经典篇章英译选读之一

离骚①(节选)

屈 原

帝高阳之苗裔兮,朕皇考曰伯庸②。
摄提贞于孟陬兮,惟庚寅吾以降③。
皇览揆余初度兮,肇锡余以嘉名④。
名余曰正则兮,字余曰灵均⑤。
纷吾既有此内美兮,又重之以修能⑥。
扈江离与辟芷兮,纫秋兰以为佩⑦。
汨余若将不及兮,恐年岁之不吾与⑧。
朝搴阰之木兰兮,夕揽洲之宿莽⑨。
日月忽其不淹兮,春与秋其代序⑩。
惟草木之零落兮,恐美人之迟暮⑪。
不抚壮而弃秽兮,何不改此度⑫?
乘骐骥以驰骋兮,来吾道夫先路⑬!
昔三后之纯粹兮,固众芳之所在⑭。
杂申椒与菌桂兮,岂维纫夫蕙茝⑮!
彼尧、舜之耿介兮,既遵道而得路⑯。
何桀纣之猖披兮,夫唯捷径以窘步⑰。
惟夫党人之偷乐兮,路幽昧以险隘⑱。
岂余身之惮殃兮,恐皇舆之败绩⑲。
忽奔走以先后兮,及前王之踵武⑳。
荃不查余之中情兮,反信谗而齌怒㉑。
余固知謇謇之为患兮,忍而不能舍也㉒。

第六章 《楚辞》经典篇章英译选读

指九天以为正兮,夫惟灵修之故也㉓。

曰黄昏以为期兮,羌中道而改路㉔。

初既与余成言兮,后悔遁而有他㉕。

余既不难夫离别兮,伤灵修之数化㉖。

注:"离骚"二字,自古以来有多种解释。《史记·屈原贾生列传》中司马迁云:"'离骚'者,犹离忧也。"《离骚赞序》中班固云:"离,犹遭也;骚,忧也,明己遭忧作辞也。"王逸《楚辞章句》云:"离,别也;骚,愁也";"离骚"即"离别的忧愁"。有学者认为《离骚》是楚国古曲名《牢商》,也有学者认为"离骚"即"牢骚"。比较通用的说法是"离"通"罹",意为遭遇,"骚"意为忧愁,《离骚》是诗人遭遇忧愁而写下的诗作。

【注释】

①〔离〕通"罹(lí)",遭,忧患,苦难。〔骚〕忧也。〔离骚〕遭逢忧患之意。

②〔高阳〕古颛顼(zhuān xū)帝之称号;一说指祝融吴回。〔苗裔(yì)〕喻指子孙后代。〔裔〕子孙后代,衣服的末边,边远地区。〔朕〕《说文》:"朕,我也。"秦以前为个人自称,秦始皇定为皇帝专称。〔皇考〕皇,美好,尊贵。〔考〕先秦时用于对父亲的尊称(在世或去世皆可)。古称远祖曰皇考。《礼记·曲礼下》:"生曰父,曰母,曰妻,死曰考,曰妣,曰嫔。"汉郑玄注:"考,成也,言其德行之成也;妣之言媲也,媲于考也。"〔伯庸〕东汉王逸说:"伯庸,字也。屈原言我父伯庸,体有美德,以忠辅楚,世有令名,以及于己。"(《楚辞章句》)

③〔摄提〕岁星(木星)名。太岁在寅时为摄提格。寅时为旧式计时法的一个时刻,凌晨三点到五点。此指寅年。〔贞〕当。〔孟〕始。〔陬(zōu)〕夏历正月。正月为春季之始,故曰"孟陬"。〔庚寅(gēng yín)〕庚,天干的第七位。现常用来表示顺序的第七。〔寅〕地支的第三位。此指庚寅日。〔降〕降生。据推算,公元前342年正月二十六日是庚寅日,是屈原出生之日。

④〔皇〕一说为"皇考"之简称;一说为母也,在楚由母亲为子命名,大概为母系社会之残痕。〔初度〕指上文所言屈原的出生日期,言生日之不平凡。〔肇(zhào)〕开始。〔锡〕赐。〔嘉名〕初生之乳名。

⑤〔正则〕正,善。正则有以善为法之意。〔灵均〕灵通令,吉善之意。屈原的生年、月、日均为吉善,故又字曰"灵均"。

⑥〔纷〕盛多貌。〔内美〕天然的内在美质。〔重〕加上。〔修能〕当作"修态"。〔修〕美好,指修饰容态,此处指后天对道德的修养。

⑦〔扈(hù)〕被(披)也,楚方言。〔离〕香草名,生水边。〔芷〕白芷,香草名。〔辟〕同"僻",幽僻。此指崖岸隐僻之处。〔纫(rèn)〕索也,此处作动词用,以绳索结束兰花以为佩。此处意为我把江离芷草披在肩上。

⑧〔汩(yù)〕疾若水流也,此处形容时光飞逝。〔不吾与〕"不与吾"的倒装,即不待我。光阴似箭我好像跟不上。

⑨〔搴(qiān)〕拔,摘。〔阰(pí)〕山坡。〔木兰〕香木名。〔揽〕采摘。〔洲〕水中小块陆地。〔宿莽〕经冬天而不死的卷施草。《尔雅·释草》谓此草"拔心不死"。此处指屈原以朝夕采撷草木,喻己勤于修德。

⑩〔忽〕倏忽,疾貌。〔淹〕停留。〔春秋〕代四季。〔代序〕代谢,轮换。

⑪〔零落〕凋落,凋残。〔美人〕屈原自喻。〔迟暮〕晚暮,喻年老。

⑫〔抚壮〕抚,凭。凭用年德盛壮之士。〔弃秽〕废弃谗佞秽恶之人。〔此度〕指国之旧有法度。

⑬〔骐骥(qí jì)〕骐,有青黑色纹理的马;骥,好马,骏马,千里马。此处喻贤能之才或喻君王威势。〔骋〕《说文》马部:"骋,直驰也。"〔来〕助动词。〔道〕《文选》作"导",同"引导"之义。"来吾道夫先路",乃楚辞特殊句式,以通常结构而言,为"吾来道夫先路""来道"连读。此句意为"快快乘坐骏马驰骋吧,我愿为您导引前路。"

⑭〔三后〕指楚庄王、楚康王、楚悼王,均为楚国有革新之功的先王。(一说三王为楚先君开国者熊绎(yì)、楚国第十四任君王楚若敖和楚国拓疆者楚厉王蚡冒(fén mào))。〔纯粹〕纯正无私,指三后之德。〔众芳〕芳,香草,喻贤才。

⑮〔杂〕集。申、椒、菌桂均为香木。〔维〕通"唯",只。〔纫〕以绳结束。〔蕙(huì)〕《玉篇》香草,生下湿地。《尔雅翼》:"一干一花而香有余者兰,一干数花而香不足者蕙。"《南方草木状》:"蕙,一名薰草。"〔茝(chǎi)〕茝,古书上指白芷(zhǐ)。蕙茝合指香草。

⑯〔耿介〕光明正大。〔遵〕循。〔道〕正确的道理。〔路〕比喻治国的正确途径。

⑰〔猖披〕行不正貌,猖狂。〔捷径〕斜出之小道,近道,邪道。〔窘步〕因行走太急而感到困难。此处比喻为了达到某种目的所采用的简便的速成办法,其结果并不理想。

⑱〔党人〕结党之群小,指当时结党营私的腐朽集团。〔偷乐〕贪图享乐,苟且偷安。〔幽昧〕不明。〔险隘〕危险狭阨。

⑲〔惮〕害怕。〔殃(yāng)〕祸患。〔皇舆〕皇,君也。舆,君之所乘,以喻国也。

第六章 《楚辞》经典篇章英译选读

㊆〔败绩〕喻君国之倾覆,引申为君主的政权或国家败绩。此句意为并非我害怕自己遭受灾祸,我是担心楚王的国家被颠覆。

⑳〔忽〕疾貌,犹言"匆忙地"。(汉)王逸《楚辞章句》:"急欲奔走先后,以辅翼君者,冀及先王之德,续其迹而广其基也。"〔以〕而。〔先后〕作动词用,谓辅导于前后也。〔及〕追及。〔前王〕即前所云"三后"。〔踵武〕王逸注:"踵,继也。武,迹也。"踵武比喻能赓续继承父、祖,如楚庄王、楚康王、楚悼王等革新之政绩和事业。

㉑〔荃(quán)〕香草名,俗名石菖蒲,此喻楚怀王。〔察〕细看。〔中情〕内心,忠心。〔齌(jì)怒〕不假思索而迁怒,盛怒,暴怒。

㉒〔謇謇(jiǎn)〕本义为口吃,此处当通"乾乾",意为自强不息,忠贞直言貌,指上文"奔走""先后"辅佐怀王进行改革,但却为群小所忌。〔舍〕放弃,控制。此句意为我原本就知道直言进谏会带来祸端,原想忍耐却又控制不住自己去进谏。

㉓〔九天〕古人谓天有九重,以示其高。〔正〕通"证",验也。〔灵修〕有远见卓识之人。此处为楚人对君王的美称。此句意为请苍天给我作证,这一切都为了君王(楚怀王)的缘故。

㉔有些版本无此二句,疑为《九章·抽思》篇中的相似文句所窜入。〔羌〕楚方言发语词。此句意为为什么中途改变了心意。

㉕〔成言〕定言,约定之言。〔悔〕翻悔。〔遁〕隐,隐遁其情。〔有他〕另外的打算。此句意为悔遁指悔改前言。

㉖〔离别〕指被疏离之后,离开朝廷,告别怀王。〔数(shuò)化〕多变。此句意为我并不难于与你别离啊,只是伤心你多次出尔反尔,反复无常。

白话释义

> 我是古帝高阳颛顼的子孙,
> 我的先父名字叫伯庸。
> 岁星出现在寅年的孟春,
> 庚寅日那天我刚好降生。
> 父亲仔细斟酌我的生辰,
> 赐给我相应的美名:
> 为我起的名曰正则,
> 给我取的字叫作灵均。

上天赐予我良好的品质,
我不断加强自身的修养。
我把江离芷草当作披肩,
把秋兰结成索佩挂在身旁。
光阴似箭时不待我,
岁月不等人令我心慌。
早晨我在大坡上采撷木兰,
傍晚在小洲中摘取宿莽。
时光迅速逝去不能久留,
四季更相代谢变化有常。
想到草木不断地在飘零凋谢,
不禁担忧美人也会日益衰老。
何不利用贤人扬弃秽政,
为何还不改变旧的法度?
乘上千里马纵横驰骋吧,
我愿在前面导引开路!
从前三后公正无私德行完美,
所以群贤都汇聚一堂。
杂聚申椒菌桂似的贤才,
岂止于茝蕙般的良臣。
唐尧虞舜多么光明正直,
他们沿着正道登上坦途。
夏桀殷纣多么狂妄邪恶,
贪图捷径必然走投无路。
结党营私的人苟安享乐,
他们要把国家引入险途。
难道我害怕自己身陷祸端吗?
我是担心国家会因此而覆亡。
前前后后我奔走操劳啊,
希望君王能跟上先王脚步。
你(楚怀王)不深入了解我的忠心,
反而听信谗言对我随意发怒。
我早知道忠言直谏会招致灾祸,

第六章 《楚辞》经典篇章英译选读

原想忍耐却又无法控制。
苍天在上请为我作证,
这一切都是为了君王的缘故。
我们两个曾定好在黄昏有约,
你为何中途变心另有他意?
你既然和我有约在先,
现另有打算又追悔当初。
我并不难于与你别离啊,
只是伤心你的反复无常。

LI SAO "ON ENCOUNTERING TROUBLE"
(Excerpt)

Scion of the high lord Gao Yang,
Bo Yong was my father's name.
When SheTi pointed to the first month of the year,
On the day *geng-yin* I passed from the womb.
My father, seeing the aspect of my nativity,
Took omens to give me an auspicious name.
The name he gave me was True Exemplar;
The title he gave me was Divine Balance.

Having from birth this inward beauty,
I added to it fair outward adornment:
I dressed in selinea and shady angelica,
And twined autumn orchids to make a garland.
Swiftly I sped as in fearful pursuit,
Afraid Time would race on and leave me behind.
In the morning I gathered the angelica on the mountains;
In the evening I plucked the sedges of the islets.

The days and months hurried on, never delaying;
Springs and autumns sped by in endless alternation:
And I thought how the trees and flowers were fading and falling,
And feared that my fairest's beauty would fade too.
Gather the flower of youth and cast out the impure!
Why will you not change the error of your ways?
I have harnessed brave coursers for you to gallop forth with:
Come, let me go before and show you the way!

The three kings of old were most pure and perfect:
Then indeed fragrant flowers had their proper place.
They brought together pepper and cinnamon;
All the most-prized blossoms were woven in their garlands.
Glorious and great were those two, Yao and Shun,
Because they had kept their feet on the right path.
And how great was the folly of Jie and Zhòu,
Who hastened by crooked paths, and so came to grief.

The fools enjoys their careless pleasure,
But their way is dark and leads to danger.
I have no fear for the peril of my own person,
But only lest the chariot of my Lord should be dashed.
I hurried about your chariot in attendance,
Leading you in the tracks of the kings of old.
But the Fragrant One refused to examine my true feelings:
He lent ear instead to slander, and raged against me.

How well I know that loyalty brings disaster;
Yet I will endure: I cannot give it up.
I called on the ninefold heaven to be my witness,
And all for the sake of the Fair One, and no other.
There once was a time when he spoke with me in frankness;

第六章 《楚辞》经典篇章英译选读

But then he repented and was of another mind.
I do not care, on my own count, about this divorcement,
But it grieves me to find the Fair One so inconstant.

——David Hawkes（大卫·霍克斯）

英译鉴赏简评

《离骚》主题深刻广泛，内容博大精深，语言独具特色，故其英译难度极大。加之《楚辞》的创作时代较为久远，虽然历朝历代都有学者对其进行了勘校、注疏、释义，但是深刻理解《楚辞》的主旨绝非易事，学者们对某些字、句的理解也有不同。国内外诸多译者因其参考的注疏版本不同，中文造诣程度不同，以及所秉持的翻译理念不同，译文也呈现出多样化趋势。只有对比各种译法，才能看出不同译本的优劣。

先看看"离骚"二字的译法。霍克斯采用拼音加意译的方法，"on encountering trouble"，"trouble"一词语意丰富，指"problems, worries, or difficulties; an unpleasant, difficult, or dangerous situation for which someone is likely to be blamed, criticized, or punished."除了"麻烦，困境"的意思外，还可以引申为"（政治或政局的）风潮，纷扰"，因此，霍克斯对"离骚"一词的解读为"遭遇（政局）困境"。许渊冲采纳的是王逸之说，将"离骚"理解为"sorrow after departure（离别后的忧伤）"。杨宪益、戴乃迭（后文中会将译者采用简称）将其音译为 Li Sao，而卓振英译为"Tales of Woe(a strong feeling of sadness)"，意为比较悲惨的经历或者故事。笔者认为，霍克斯先生的译文和杨氏夫妇采用的"woe"一词更有文化内涵，语意的深度要大于许先生的"sorrow"。

再比如对"美人"的理解，学术界众说纷纭，大部分学者认为"美人"是实际的人物指代，但是指代的是谁又说法不一。比较普遍的观点有以下几种。一、指君王，大致又可分为两种，其一指楚怀王，王逸最早执此说，其《楚辞章句》云，"美人谓楚怀王也。人君服饰美好，故言美人也。"后世许多学者如朱熹等均支持此说；其二指楚顷襄王，近代学者蒋天枢在其《楚辞校释》中提出此观点。二、屈原自指。唐代玄宗开元年间学者陆善经较早提出此说，现代许多学者如游国恩、汤炳正等都执此说。三、兼指楚怀王和屈原，清朱冀《离骚辩》云："盖句法从《国风》'西方美人'来，则谓之称君也可。若与后文'嫉余之娥眉'对看，即谓大夫自况也亦可",由此看出,后世学者认为"美人"泛指一切贤人,包括明君与贤臣。杨、戴并未直译出"美人"一词,但从其译文来看,此译遵从第二种观点,即"美人"指代屈原自己,故有"my"的译法。霍译、许译、卓译均根据字面意思把"美人"译为"beauty",避免了确切的指代引起语义狭窄,留出充分的语义空间,让读者自己去感受、理解。我们在欣赏不同译者的译文时,应该带着思考,用客观、审慎的眼光来欣赏每一位译者的作品,而不是一味挑剔而忽略了本质的内容。

再对《离骚》第一、二行的三种译文作一简要评析:"帝高阳之苗裔兮,朕皇考曰伯庸。摄提贞于孟陬兮,惟庚寅吾以降。"

霍克斯译文:

Scion of the high lord Gao Yang,
Bo Yong was my honored father's name.
When She Ti pointed to the first month of the year,
On the day *geng-yin* I passed from the womb.

杨宪益、戴乃迭译文:

A prince am I of ancestry renowned,
Illustrious name my royal sire hath found.
When Sirius did in spring its light display,
A child was born, and Tiger marked the day.

许渊冲译文:

Descendant of High Sunny King, oh!
My father's name shed sunny ray.
The Wooden Star appeared in spring, oh!
When I was born on Tiger's Day.

从以上三种译文可以看出,对于诗中的人名,霍克斯多选择音译法,如"Bo Yong was my father's name",音译法无法再现原文中古代中国人名蕴含的文化深意,而且忽略了或消解了原文的音韵美。杨氏夫妇在再现原诗人名的文化内涵方面略高一筹,将屈原父亲的名字"伯庸"译为"illustrious name",再现了"伯庸"所包含的独特文化意义。另如 sire(先父,祖先)/hath(has)/Sirius(天狼星)等词也是充分考量中西文化异同而精挑细选出的独特用词。许渊冲教授采

第六章 《楚辞》经典篇章英译选读

用对原文"再创作＋厚翻译"的方式,将"伯庸"译为"name shed sunny ray",对于西方读者理解原诗颇有助益。在诗韵方面,杨氏夫妇与许渊冲先生均能够充分再现汉语诗歌的音韵特质,采用西方诗歌特有的"英雄双行体"(heroic couplet)、尾韵(aabb: renowned/found//display/day)(abab: oh/ray//oh/day)的形式,用悠缓的元音韵,再现了诗人行吟泽畔失意落寞的诗歌氛围,突出了全诗的哀怨主题。霍克斯译文采取散体诗译法,不用尾韵和协律韵,而以破韵(broken rhyme)为主,个别行内押不完全韵(imperfect rhyme)。

总之,文学翻译尤其是诗歌翻译应在"文学性",即音乐性(musicality)、节拍性(tempo)、诗体性(form)、诗意境(imagery)等方面多加努力,才能再现原诗的"文学美"。文学性是原作的异质性之所在。翻译出这种异质性,才能激发读者的审美愉悦,彰显原作语言和形式所蕴含的诗学功能,重现原作的艺术魅力,最终复制甚至升华原作的"文学性"。

《楚辞》经典篇章英译选读之二

九歌·湘夫人①

屈 原

帝子降兮北渚,目眇眇兮愁予②。
嫋嫋兮秋风,洞庭波兮木叶下③。

登白薠兮骋望,与佳期兮夕张④。
鸟何萃兮蘋中,罾何为兮木上⑤?

沅有茝兮澧有兰,思公子兮未敢言⑥。
荒忽兮远望,观流水兮潺湲⑦。

麋何食兮庭中?蛟何为兮水裔⑧?
朝驰余马兮江皋,夕济兮西澨⑨。

闻佳人兮召予,将腾驾兮偕逝⑩。

筑室兮水中,葺之兮荷盖⑪。
荪壁兮紫坛,播芳椒兮成堂⑫。
桂栋兮兰橑,辛夷楣兮药房⑬。
罔薜荔兮为帷,擗蕙櫋兮既张⑭。
白玉兮为镇,疏石兰兮为芳⑮。
芷葺兮荷屋,缭之兮杜衡⑯。
合百草兮实庭,建芳馨兮庑门⑰。
九嶷缤兮并迎,灵之来兮如云⑱。
捐余袂兮江中,遗余褋兮澧浦⑲。
搴汀洲兮杜若,将以遗兮远者⑳。
时不可兮骤得,聊逍遥兮容与㉑!

注:《湘夫人》是《九歌》中的第四篇,接续第三篇《湘君》,两者是歌咏湘水之神的姊妹篇。前后文本情境是:湘君与湘夫人之前相约于北边小岛(北渚),而湘夫人念君心切,故而驾舟去见湘水上游的湘君,湘君实际也出发到北边小岛去见湘夫人,两人彼此扑空。诗歌以湘君的口吻表达对心仪女神的渴盼和思念。《湘夫人》由男神湘君演唱,《湘君》由女神演唱,两者互为唱和,前后呼应,不可分割,构成湘水之神相约不会的完整故事。大约自秦汉时起,湘水流域就流传着这一传说。湘水是楚国境内的一大河流,湘夫人被认为是湘水女性之神,与湘水男性之神湘君是一对配偶神。又说湘君和湘夫人的原型脱胎自古帝舜和他的两位妻子。舜的两位妻子是尧帝的两个女儿,长女娥皇与次女女英,她们追随丈夫到沅湘流域,舜死后,据说娥皇、女英悲伤痛哭,投湘江自尽。屈原根据这个传说创作了诗歌《湘君》和《湘夫人》。自秦汉时起,湘江之神湘君与湘夫人的爱情神话遂被演变成舜与娥皇、女英的凄美传说,后世合称二女为"湘夫人",以象征忠贞不贰之志。

【注释】

①〔湘夫人〕湘水的女神。通篇写湘君望湘夫人赴约深情,及其未来而思之,已

第六章 《楚辞》经典篇章英译选读

来而乐之的情景,用以表达祭者望湘夫人临飨之诚。

② 〔帝子〕据《山海经》,湘江之神为天帝尧之女,故称帝子。〔子〕古代对男女的美称,不分性别。"帝子"相当于后世的"公主"。〔北渚(zhǔ)〕北面小洲,小岛,此为由湘水入郢(yǐng)必经之路。〔眇眇(miǎo)〕即渺渺,远望不见之貌。〔愁予〕使动句,即使我忧愁。予:我。上句"兮"代"于"字,下句"兮"代"然"字。此句为湘君悬想之词,谓湘夫人或已止息于北渚,此时却仍望而不见,使人忧愁。

③ 〔嫋嫋(niǎo)〕清风徐拂貌。〔波〕动词,兴起水波。〔下〕脱落。上句"兮"代"之"字,下句"兮"代"而"字。

④ 〔登〕《广雅释诂》:"蹬,履也。"蹬即登之后起字。〔白薠(fán)〕古书上说的一种似莎(suō)而比莎大的草,可入药,雁喜食。〔骋望〕纵目眺望。〔与〕去声,古多训"为"。〔佳期〕指与湘夫人的约会。〔夕张〕于黄昏夜间陈设铺张。此句指为了相约而于黄昏夜间陈设铺张以待湘夫人之至。上句"兮"代"以"字,下句"兮"代"而"字。

⑤ 〔萃〕聚集。〔蘋(pín)〕今称"四叶菜""田字草",为多年生浅水草本,叶柄长,顶端集生四片小叶,叶浮水面,夏秋开小白花,可入药。〔罾(zēng)〕古代一种用木棍或竹竿做支架的方形渔网。二"兮"皆代"于"字。此言鸟非其所则不集,罾非所施则不得鱼,喻己不陈设以待,则湘夫人未必来。以上为湘君所歌,言湘君盼湘夫人来临,因湘夫人未至而哀愁。

⑥ 〔沅澧(yuán lǐ)〕皆水名。〔茝(chǎn)〕香草名,即白芷。王逸注:"言沅水之中有盛茂之芷,澧水之内有芬芳之兰,异于众草"。后"沅芷(茝)澧兰"比喻高洁的人或事物。〔公子〕指湘夫人,相当于首句的"帝子"。〔未敢言〕思念之情不敢外露。二"兮"皆代"而"字。

⑦ 〔荒忽〕犹仿佛,不明了,神思恍惚貌。〔潺湲(chán yuán)〕水缓慢流动貌。上句"兮"代"而"字,下句"兮"代"之"字。

⑧ 〔麋(mí)〕鹿类,也叫四不像。〔蛟〕传说中的无角龙。〔裔(yì)〕本义为衣服的边缘,后指边远之地或者子孙后代。水裔,即水边。二句"兮"皆代"于"字。这两句是说麋不会舍弃深山而食于庭中,蛟不会舍弃深渊而处于水边,比喻湘夫人不会待己于荒僻之地,与上文湘君所唱"鸟为何"二句相呼应。

⑨ 〔江皋〕江岸。〔皋(gāo)〕水边的高地,岸。〔济〕渡。〔澨(shì)〕楚地称水涯、水边为"澨"。二句"兮"皆代"于"字。

⑩ 〔佳人〕指湘夫人。〔召〕召唤。〔腾驾〕驰车。〔偕逝〕共同前往,指湘君想与湘夫人相会后共赴祭坛。上句"兮"代"之"字,下句"兮"代"以"字。

⑪〔葺(qì)〕以草遮覆屋顶。〔荷盖〕荷叶。上句"兮"代"之"字,下句"兮"代"以"字。我在水中修筑房屋,用荷叶作为屋顶。

⑫〔荪壁〕荪(sūn),古书上指一种香草,类似于"荃"。以荪草为室壁,取其香。〔紫坛〕紫,草名。坛,楚地方言指"庭院"。以紫草为坛,取其美,一说为紫色的贝壳。上句"兮"代"而"字,下句"兮"代"以"字。我用荪草编织室壁,用紫贝/草铺设庭院。

⑬〔桂栋〕以桂树为屋栋。〔兰橑〕橑:读作"liǎo",意为长木条,此处读作"lǎo",意为屋椽(chuán),椽子。以木兰为屋橑,即屋椽饰以木兰。〔辛夷楣〕辛夷(xīn yí),木兰科植物,初春时,花先叶而开,花瓣六片,大如莲,内白外紫,香味浓郁,花蕾可入药,亦称为"木笔""木莲""新夷"。〔药房〕以辛夷木作为门楣,以芍药装饰房室。〔药〕芍药,楚地方言指"白芷"。〔房〕卧房。

⑭〔罔(wǎng)〕同"网",此作动词,编织。此句意为结薜荔香草作为帷帐。〔擗(pǐ)〕或作"擘",掰开,分析之也。〔櫋(mián)〕屋檐的横板。一说为櫋(màn),即"幔",指幕。在旁曰帷,在上曰幕。〔张〕张设。此句指析蕙草以为帐幕,既已张设就绪。上句"兮"代"以"字,下句"兮"代"而"字。

⑮〔镇〕压座席的器具,一说为"殿"。以白玉为殿堂。〔疏〕摆放,铺设。〔石兰〕一种生于石上或树干上的香草,多年生草本,香气馥郁。

⑯〔葺(qì)〕通"缉",连续缝合。〔屋〕当为帷之借字,小帐。此句意为以芷草为绳缝合荷帷。〔缭(liáo)〕用针线缝缀。此句意为以芷缝之不足,又以杜衡缝缀镶嵌。上句"兮"代"其"字,下句"兮"代"以"字。

⑰〔合〕集合。〔实庭〕充实庭院。〔建〕陈设,分布。〔芳馨〕指花气芬芳。〔庑〕厢房。此句意为建起花气芬芳的庑(wǔ)门(堂下周围的走廊、廊屋)。上句"兮"代"以"字,下句"兮"代之"字。

⑱〔九嶷(yí)〕山名,因九峰相似相连而名,在今湖南省。传为舜安葬之地;又指九嶷山之众神。〔缤〕缤纷,众多貌。〔并迎〕九峰并起似迎接湘夫人。〔灵〕神仙。〔如云〕言其盛多。上句"兮"代"然"字,下句"兮"代"也"字。以上为湘君所歌,言湘君为迎接湘夫人而筑室水中,百草芳馨,湘夫人突然降临。

⑲〔捐〕抛弃。〔袂(mèi)〕衣袖。一说为袟(zhì),为古代妇人穿的短袄。捐袂也可指愿相亲而不相离。〔遗〕遗弃。〔褋(dié)〕一说当为"韘(shè)"之借字,玦也,为古代射箭时戴在手上的扳指。另说为古代妇女的单衣、汗衫。遗褋亦指愿不相离而永相好。二句"兮"皆代"于"字。"袂"与"褋"为女性用物,捐袂遗褋,带有生气口吻,意思是说,把你送我(湘君)的短袄和单衣都抛弃不要了。

⑳〔搴(qiān)〕采撷,拔取。〔汀洲〕洲之平者。汀(tīng),水边平地。〔杜若〕香

第六章 《楚辞》经典篇章英译选读

草名；又名杜衡，杜莲，生武陵川泽之地；可入药。《离骚》云："杂杜衡与芳芷。"〔遗〕赠。〔远者〕指湘君，因久别重逢，故云。上句"兮"代"之"字，下句"兮"代"诸"字。宁可把江渚上的杜若送给陌生人，也不送给绝情的心上人（湘夫人不在约定之地等候湘君）。

㉑〔时〕美好的时光。〔骤（zhòu）得〕多次得到。骤，屡次，多次。〔聊〕姑且。〔逍遥〕自由自在。〔容与〕悠闲自得貌。上句"兮"代"以"字，下句"兮"代"而"字。以上为湘夫人所歌，言湘夫人降临，与湘君相会而逍遥娱乐。

白话释义

公主（湘夫人）降临于北边小岛，我极目远眺内心忧伤彷徨。
秋风凄冷天气渐凉，洞庭扬起波浪啊草木飘摇。
登上白薠土坡我举目四望，与佳人有约啊黄昏开始张罗。
鸟儿啊为何聚集于水草之中？渔网啊为何挂在树上？
沅水生芷草啊澧水结兰香，心恋湘夫人啊却不敢明讲。
忧思难忘啊望眼欲穿，江水啊缓缓悠悠在流淌。
麋鹿啊为何在庭院觅食忙？蛟龙啊为何游弋在江滩上？
清晨我驰马在江畔上，黄昏我渡水到西江旁。
我听说湘夫人啊把我召唤，我将驾着飞车与她同往。
我要把房屋啊筑在水中央，荷叶啊盖在我的屋顶上。
墙壁用荪草来装饰庭院铺上那紫贝壳，四壁撒满香椒来装饰我厅堂。
桂木作屋梁啊木兰用作椽，辛夷装门楣白芷饰卧房。
编织薜荔啊做成帷幕，分开蕙草做幔帐也已安放。
用白玉做成镇席玉器，石兰啊摆满房间一片芬芳。
香芷草覆盖上屋顶，杜衡环绕房子的四方。
庭院里布满各种香草，连门厅里都香气满廊。
九嶷山的仙子夹道欢迎，众神仙相互簇如白云一样。
我把那衣袂投入江中，我把那汗衫丢入澧水。
我在沙洲上采撷杜若，还不如送给陌生的姑娘。
美好的时光啊实在难得，我姑且悠闲地徘徊游荡。

JIU GE "NINE SONGS"

"The Lady of the Xiang" (Xiang fu-ren)

The Child of God, descending the northern bank,
Turns on me her eyes that are dark with longing.
Gently the wind of autumn whispers;
On the waves of the Dong-ting lake the leaves are falling.

Over the white sedge I gaze out wildly;
For a tryst is made to meet my love this evening.
But why should the birds gather in the duckweed?
And what are the nets doing in the tree-tops?

The Yuan has its angelicas, the Li has its orchids:
And I think of my lady, but dare not tell it,
As with trembling heart I gaze on the distance
Over the swiftly moving waters.

What are the deer doing in the courtyard?
Or the water-dragons outside the waters?
In the morning I drive my steeds by the river;
In the evening I cross to the western shore.
I can hear my beloved calling to me:
I will ride aloft and race beside her.
I will build her a house within the water
Roofed all over with lotus leaves;

With walls of iris, of purple shells the chamber;
Perfumed pepper shall make the hall.

第六章 《楚辞》经典篇章英译选读

With beams of cassia, orchid rafters,
Lily-tree lintel, a bower of peonies,
With woven fig-leaves for the hangings
And melilotus to make a screen;
Weights of white jade to hold the mats with,
Stone-orchids strewn to make the floor sweet:
A room of lotus thatched with the white flag
Shall all be bound up with stalks of asarum.
A thousand sweet flowers shall fill the courtyard,
And rarest perfumes shall fill the gates.
In hosts from their home on Doubting Mountain
Like clouds in number the spirits come thronging.

I'll throw my thumb-ring into the river,
Leave my girdle-gem in the bay of the Li.
Sweet pollia I've plucked in the little islet
To send to my far-away Beloved.
Oh, rarely, rarely the time is given!
I wish I could play here a little longer.

——David Hawkes（大卫·霍克斯）

英译鉴赏简评

《九歌》的"九"是泛指，并非实数，实际上包括十一篇。《九歌》原是古乐章名，一般认为屈原的《九歌》是其在楚地民间祭祀乐歌基础上加工而成。也有研究者认为《九歌》作于屈原放逐之前，仅供祭祀之用。

就英译情况，简要评析如下。

关于"帝子"到底指代何人，说法不一，因此，也是翻译的难点之一。杨、戴将"帝子"译为"The Queen"，避开了原文语义的模糊性，而选用了能表示其身份的"queen"来指称诗歌中的女主人公，对象为一人。霍克斯采取直译法："The Child of God"，乃从《山海经》之说，即"天帝之子"。许译为"my lady dear"，也指称一人。只有卓译"Your Highnesses"可能指称为两人——娥皇和女英。一般认为此诗是湘君在等待湘夫人,故用复数形式的"Your Highnesses(王子;殿下;陛下)"似乎不符合诗中人物之间的关系。

再通过其他几位译者对"嫋嫋"一词的翻译来评价一下霍克斯的译文。王逸《楚辞章句》云:"嫋嫋,秋风摇木貌也。"汤炳正《楚辞今注》:"嫋嫋,清风徐拂貌。"故此,嫋嫋的秋风并不是疾风,而是柔和的风。杨、戴的"sighs as it flutters slow"用动词来表现秋风"嫋嫋"之貌,语义准确。霍译为"gently whispers"。许译为"ceaselessly grieves"。三种译文均使用拟人化用词来表现风之轻柔,给风赋予了人的情感。杨戴译文头韵效果优于许译和霍译,在音节的短促有力上,霍译更佳。

实际上,霍克斯译文的音效性也是其译文胜出的原因之一。如众所知,《湘君》和《湘夫人》均为楚地祭祀仪式中歌舞唱和的重要内容,相当于男女对唱性质的歌谣,因此,其音乐性尤其突出,比如叠音词"眇眇""嫋嫋"同尾韵词"渚/予""望/张/上""裔/逝/澨"等等。霍克斯很注意再现原诗的音乐特质,富于技巧地采用了许多头韵词,比如"wind//whispers;white //wildly;made//meet";以及独特的尾韵词,比如"longing//falling//evening";"river//her/water"等等。此类精挑细选的韵词使英译文读起来充满乐感和韵律,非常契合原诗唱诵的特质。

《楚辞》经典篇章英译选读之三

九辩(节选)

宋　玉

悲哉,秋之为气也①!

萧瑟兮,草木摇落而变衰②。

憭栗兮,若在远行③。

登山临水兮,送将归④。

泬寥兮,天高而气清⑤。

寂寥兮,收潦而水清⑥。

憯凄增欷兮,薄寒之中人⑦。

第六章 《楚辞》经典篇章英译选读

怆怳懭悢兮,去故而就新⑧。

坎廪兮,贫士失职,而志不平⑨。

廓落兮,羁旅而无友生⑩。

惆怅兮,而私自怜⑪。

燕翩翩其辞归兮,蝉寂漠而无声⑫。

雁廱廱而南游兮,鹍鸡啁哳而悲鸣⑬。

独申旦而不寐兮,哀蟋蟀之宵征⑭。

时亹亹而过中兮,蹇淹留而无成⑮。

悲忧穷戚兮独处廓⑯。

有美一人兮心不绎⑰。

去乡离家兮徕远客⑱。

超逍遥兮今焉薄⑲。

专思君兮不可化⑳。

君不知兮可奈何㉑!

蓄怨兮积思㉒,

心烦憺兮忘食事㉓。

愿一见兮道余意㉔,

君之心兮与余异㉕。

车既驾兮朅而归㉖,

不得见兮心伤悲㉗。

倚结軨兮长太息㉘,

涕潺湲兮下沾轼㉙。

忼慨绝兮不得㉚,

中瞀乱兮迷惑㉛。

私自怜兮何极㉜?

心怦怦兮谅直㉝。

注：《九辩》为古乐曲名。"辩"或为"变"之借字，凡乐曲换章易调谓"变"。汉王逸《楚辞章句卷八》曰："辩者，变也，谓陈道德以变说君也。"王夫之《楚辞通释》说："辩，犹遍也，一阕谓之一遍。"遍也就是乐曲的组成部分，即阕。由此看来，对"九辩"的英译取决于对"辩"的意义的取舍。《九辩》现传本子中，有分为九章的，也有分为十章的。此篇传为宋玉模仿屈原《离骚》的创作手法而作。

【注释】

① 〔气〕气候，气氛，气象。

② 〔萧瑟〕深秋清寒的感觉。〔衰〕衰败枯槁。

③ 〔憀栗(liáo lì)〕哀怆凄凉貌。

④ 〔将归〕指将要归去的人。以上"在远行"与"送将归"都是比喻说法，故以"若"字领起。本句描写秋气萧瑟、一岁将终时人的心境。

⑤ 〔泬寥(xuè liáo)〕空旷静寂貌。〔气清〕古本"清"作"瀞(jìng)"。《说文·水部》："瀞，无垢秽"。一说为"瀞(jìng)"字的衍误。

⑥ 〔寂寥(liáo)〕即"寂寥"，虚静的样子；水平静貌。〔收潦(lǎo)〕潦：大水，蓄积的雨水。本句指水势收敛，水质清澈。

⑦ 〔憯(cǎn)凄〕内心伤痛貌。〔增〕不断地。〔欷(xī)〕嘘唏，哀叹声。〔薄寒〕指秋日的轻寒。〔中(zhòng)〕侵袭，遭受。中人，即袭人。

⑧ 〔怆怳(chuàng huǎng)、懭悢(kuǎng liàng)〕均为悲伤失意貌。懭：或同"恍(huǎng)"。〔去故就新〕季节更换。

⑨ 〔坎廪(lǐn)〕坎坷不平貌。〔贫士〕宋玉自况。〔失职〕失去官职。〔志〕意志。

⑩ 〔廓落〕空旷寂寞貌。〔羁(jī)旅〕客寓在外。〔友生〕即朋友。

⑪ 〔惆怅〕失意貌。

⑫ 〔辞归〕冬季将至，燕将辞去此地飞回南方。〔寂漠〕寂寞。

⑬ 〔雍雍(yōng)〕和谐的雁鸣声。〔鹍(kūn)鸡〕鸟名，黄白色，外形似鹤。〔啁哳(zhāo zhā)〕细碎急促的鸣叫声。

⑭ 〔申旦〕由黑夜至天明。〔蟋蟀之宵征〕蟋蟀夜行夜鸣。

⑮ 〔亹亹(wěi)〕"昧昧"之音近借字，在此为晚暮之意。〔謇(jiǎn)〕语气词，楚方言。〔淹留〕久滞，久留。以上第一章，写秋气降临，万物肃杀，人亦悲伤至极，更何况政治上的失败与无成。

⑯ 〔穷〕困窘。〔戚〕《文选》作"慼(cù)"，急促。〔廓〕空旷孤独之境。

⑰ 〔有美一人〕指贤士，或诗人自喻。〔绎(yì)〕为"怿(yì)"之借字。不怿，不

第六章 《楚辞》经典篇章英译选读

愉快。
⑱〔倈〕同"来"。来远客,意为来荒远之地为客,指流放。
⑲〔超〕遥远。〔逍遥〕逗留徘徊。〔薄〕停止,至。
⑳〔专〕心意专一。〔化〕变化。此句意为思君之心不可变。
㉑〔君不知〕指君主不知臣下之忠心。
㉒〔蓄怨〕心藏怨愤。〔积思〕堆积忧思。
㉓〔烦憺(dàn)〕心绪烦乱。〔食事〕饮食之事。
㉔〔一见〕指见君主。〔道〕说明。
㉕〔异〕指君臣之心不一。
㉖〔揭(qiè)〕去,离去。〔揭而归〕既驾车去见君,又以不得见君而后归。
㉗〔不得见〕指未能面见君主。
㉘〔结軨〕軨(líng):马车车厢上的横木栏,因其纵横交错,故云"结"。〔太息〕叹息。
㉙〔潺湲(chán yuán)〕流水声,此指涕泪长流貌。〔霑(zhān)〕即"沾",雨水浸润。〔轼(shì)〕古代车厢前的横木,用于凭倚。
㉚〔忼慨(kāng kǎi)〕即慷慨,谓志士因不得志而积愤不平。〔绝〕尽。此句意思是欲与君王断绝关系而不能,愤慨难绝。
㉛〔中〕内心。〔瞀(mào)乱〕心绪紊乱,烦乱。
㉜〔极〕穷尽。
㉝〔怦怦〕内心急切冲动貌。〔谅直〕忠诚正直。

白话释义

悲伤啊这秋天的气候,
大地萧瑟啊草木枯衰凋零。
凄凉啊好像要出门远行,
跋山涉水离别情浓。
天宇空廖啊秋高气爽,
寂寥啊夏雨退去秋水清。
凄凉叹息啊,寒意令人惧。
怅然若失啊,季节更替无人念;
路途坎坷啊,丢了官职志难平。
孤独啊流落在外没友朋,

惆怅啊顾影自怜悯。
燕子翩飞向南归,寒蝉寂寞悄无声。
大雁谐鸣往南飞,鹍鸡啾啾悲戚鸣。
茕茕一人难入睡,独闻蟋蟀彻夜哀。
岁月匆匆人半百,一事无成好悲哀。

悲伤忧愁独一人,
有一位美人啊心伤悲。
背井离乡异地客,
孤苦伶仃何日还?
矢志不渝念君王,
可惜君王浑不知!
愁怨满满思虑重,
心烦意乱食不香。
只盼见君表余心,
君王所思与我异。
驾着马车去见君,
不能见君心愈悲。
独倚车轼长叹息,
泪水涟涟湿栏杆。
心中苦闷难自平,
心迷意乱谁能懂。
自怜自艾何时止?
忠贞不贰永无愧。

JIU BIAN 'NINE CHANGES' (Excerpt)

I

Alas for the breath of autumn!
Wan and drear: flower and leaf fluttering fall and turn to decay;
Sad and lorn: as when on journey far one climbs a hill and looks
down on the water to speed a returning friend;

第六章 《楚辞》经典篇章英译选读

Empty and vast: the skies are high and the air is cold;
Still and deep: the streams have drunk full and the waters are clear.
Heartsick and sighing sore: for the cold draws on and strikes into a man;
Distraught and disappointed: leaving the old and to new places turning;
Afflicted: the poor esquire has lost his office and his heart rebels;
Desolate: on his long journey he rests with never a friend;
Melancholy: he nurses a private sorrow.
The fluttering swallows leave on their homeward journey;
The forlorn cicada makes no sound;
The wild geese call as they travel southwards;
The partridge chatters with a mournful cry.
Alone he waits for the dawn to come, unsleeping,
Mourning with the cricket, the midnight traveler.
His time draws on apace: already half is gone;
Yet still he languishes, nothing accomplished.

II

Sad and in sore straits I dwell alone.
There is a Fair One, from my heart never sundered.
I have left home and country, and gone a traveller to distant places.
Far have I wandered: where will my journeying end?
But my lord would have none of it. What could I do?
Storing my resentment up, husbanding my anguish,
I was so sick at heart that I forgot to eat.
I longed but once to see him and give my thoughts expression,
But the heart of my lord was not the same as mine;
And though my chariot was harnessed, I had to turn back again:
It grieved me bitterly that I could not see him.
I leaned upon the chariot-board and heaved a heavy sigh,
And in a stream the tears ran down and wet the chariot-rail.
My high aspirations are cut off without hope;
I have fallen on dark, troubled times; I am lost and bewildered;
But though my private sorrow may be never-ending,

The heart that beats in me will always be loyal and true.

——David Hawkes（大卫·霍克斯）

英译鉴赏简评

　　《九辩》的主题是悲秋。它把秋季万木黄落、山川萧瑟的自然现象与诗人失意巡游、心绪飘浮的悲怆有机地结合起来，人的感情外射到自然界，作品凝结着一股排遣不去、反复缠绵的悲剧气息，勾起人们对自然变化、人事浮沉的感喟。《九辩》在诗歌形式上承袭屈原，却又带有自己的独特风格和创新，甚至在某些方面青出于蓝而胜于蓝。从文学艺术上看，《九辩》的艺术感染力使得"宋玉悲秋"成为一代经典，并且开启了中国"悲秋"这一传统文学的母题，对后世文人产生了极大影响，进而创作出了许多相关的优秀作品。从语言运用上看，《九辩》句式参差错落，节奏感很强。此外，诗人大量使用双声叠韵，如"憭栗""怆怳懭悢""廓落""惆怅""啴哗"等，以及叠音词，如"翩翩""靡靡""亹亹"等，使得诗歌朗朗上口，增加了诗歌的韵律感。然而这也增加了英译的难度。王逸注："辩者，变也，……九者，阳之数，道之纲纪也"，王夫之《楚辞通释》说："辩，犹遍也，一阕谓之一遍"。对标题的英译，霍译仍采用拼音加意译：JIU BIAN "NINE CHANGES"，当从王逸之说；卓译为"The Nine Cantos"，"canto"意为诗歌中的一个章节，故"The Nine Cantos"即为九个章节，当从王夫之之观点；许译为"Nine Apologies"，此处"apology"意为辩解，辩护。三家各执一词，前两者比许译更符合原文的意思。再看看几位译者对"怆怳懭悢"的翻译。王逸注："中情怅惘，意不得也"，朱熹云："怆怳懭悢，皆失意貌"，汤炳正也说："怆怳懭悢，均为悲伤失意貌"，霍译为"distraught and disappointed"，"distraught"意为"心烦意乱的，心急如焚的"，该词与"disappointed"连用，无论从音节、词形、还是词意和音韵上，都很贴近原诗怆怳懭悢（chuàng huǎng kuǎng liàng）四字的形近、韵同、意通的特点，巧妙地再现了诗人不得见心上人的那种从失望失意到心急如焚的心理变化；相较而言，许译"Heart-broken"和卓译"distress'd"，虽都能表现伤心失意，但语意失于平淡，音节过于单调，均不如霍译深刻而生动，更富文学色彩。

第六章 《楚辞》经典篇章英译选读

本章课后练习

一、请尝试翻译以下句子。

1. 既含睇兮又宜笑,子慕予兮善窈窕。(《楚辞·九歌·山鬼》)

   白话释义:

   英译:

2. 亦余心之所善兮,虽九死其犹未悔。(《楚辞·离骚》)

   白话释义:

   英译:

3. 苟余心其端直兮,虽僻远其何伤?(《楚辞·九章·涉江》)

   白话释义:

   英译:

4. 与其无义而有名兮,宁穷处而守高。(《楚辞·九辩》)

   白话释义:

   英译:

5. 孰无施而有报兮,孰不实而有获?《楚辞·九章·抽思》

   白话释义:

   英译:

二、请比较以下名句两种英译文本的异同。

1. 路漫漫其修远兮,吾将上下而求索。(《楚辞·离骚》)

   英译1:For the road was so far and so distant was my journey,

   And I wanted to go up and down, seeking my heart's desire.

   (David Hawkes)

   英译2:The Way was long, and wrapped in Gloom did seem,

   As I urged on to seek my vanished Dream. (杨宪益、戴乃迭)

中华典籍英译选读

2. 登昆仑兮食玉英,与天地兮同寿,与日月兮齐光。(《楚辞·九章·涉江》)

   英译1: Climbed up Kun-lun and ate the flower of jade,

          And won long life, lasting as heaven and earth;

          And the sun and moon were not more bright than I. (David Hawkes)

   英译2: (In Paradise with ancient Kings I'd roam,)

          Or the World's Roof bestride.

          My life should thus outlast the Universe,

          With Sun and Moon supreme. (杨宪益、戴乃迭)

3. 悲莫悲兮生别离,乐莫乐兮新相知。(《楚辞·九歌·少司命》)

   英译1: No sorrow is greater than the parting of the living;

          No happiness is greater than making new friendships. (David Hawkes)

   英译2: For life to part, no Grief more Pain can move;

          No Joy excels the Rapture of first Love. (杨宪益、戴乃迭)

4. 鸟飞反故乡兮,狐死必首丘。(《楚辞·九章·哀郢》)

   英译1: The birds fly home to their old haunts where they came from;

          And the fox when he dies turns his head towards his earth. (David Hawkes)

   英译2: To their old Nests Birds will fly,

          Foxes face the Hill to die. (杨宪益、戴乃迭)

5. 惟天地之无穷兮,哀人生之长勤。往者余弗及兮,来者吾不闻。(《楚辞·远游》)

   英译1: I thought of the limitless vastness of the universe;

          I wept for the long affliction of man's life.

          Those that had gone before I should never see;

          And those yet to come I should never know of. (David Hawkes)

   英译2: Between the boundless earth and sky, oh!

          Forever man must toil, I sigh.

          Beyond my reach are bygone days, oh!

第六章 《楚辞》经典篇章英译选读

Can I hear what the future says? (许渊冲)

6. 朝饮木兰之坠露兮,夕餐秋菊之落英。(《楚辞·离骚》)

 英译1: In the morning I drank the dew that fell from the magnolia;
 At evening ate the petals that dropped from chrysanthemums. (David Hawkes)

 英译2: Dew from Magnolia Leaves I drank at Dawn,
 At Eve for Food were Aster Petals borne. (杨宪益、戴乃迭)

7. 屈原曰:"举世皆浊我独清,众人皆醉我独醒,是以见放。"(《楚辞·渔父》)

 英译1: "Because all the world is muddy and I alone am clean," said Qu Yuan, "and because all men are drunk and I alone am sober, I have been sent into exile." (David Hawkes)

 英译2: Qu Yuan says,
 "When all the world in mud has sunk,
 Alone I'm clean;
 When all the people are drunk,
 Sober I'm seen.
 How can I not get banished?" (许渊冲)

8. 吾不能变心而从俗兮,固将愁苦而终穷。(《楚辞·九章·涉江》)

 英译1: But I cannot change my heart and follow the vulgar crowd,
 And so I must face bitter sorrow and a helpless end as my lot. (David Hawkes)

 英译2: Never to follow Fashion will I stoop,
 Then must live lonely still. (杨宪益、戴乃迭)

9. 善不由外来兮,名不可以虚作。(《楚辞·九章·抽思》)

 英译1: For goodness is not a thing to be got from outside us,
 And fame not a thing we can fabricate from nothing. (David Hawkes)

 英译2: Virtue is not outside us,
 Fame springs from noble Deeds. (杨宪益、戴乃迭)

10."沧浪之水清兮,可以濯吾缨;沧浪之水浊兮,可以濯吾足。"(《楚辞·渔父》)

英译1:'When the Cang-lang's waters are clear, I can wash my hat-strings in them; When the Cang-lang's waters are muddy, I can wash my feet in them.'(David Hawkes)

英译2:"When the River Water's clear,
I can wash my Tassels here.
Muddied, for such Use unmeet,
Here I still can wash my Feet."(杨宪益、戴乃迭)

三、段落试译。

曰:遂古之初,谁传道之?上下未形,何由考之?冥昭瞢暗,谁能极之?冯翼惟象,何以识之?明明暗暗,惟时何为?阴阳三合,何本何化?圜则九重,孰营度之?惟兹何功,孰初作之?

(《楚辞·天问》)

夫尺有所短,寸有所长;物有所不足,智有所不明;数有所不逮,神有所不通。用君之心,行君之意,龟策诚不能知事。

(《楚辞·卜居》)

乱曰:已矣哉!国无人莫我知兮,又何怀乎故都!既莫足与为美政兮,吾将从彭咸之所居!

(《楚辞·离骚》)

第七章

《文选》经典篇章英译选读

【导读】

《文选》,又称《昭明文选》,由南朝梁武帝萧衍之子萧统组织编选。因萧统谥号"昭明",故称作《昭明文选》。《昭明文选》不仅是中国现存最早、最重要的一部诗文总集,同时也是世界上最古老的诗文总集之一。

萧统(501年—531年),字德施,南兰陵郡兰陵县(今江苏常州西北)人,是梁武帝萧衍的长子。据考证,《昭明文选》编成于建康(现南京),梁武帝普通七年(526年)至中大通三年(531年)之间。梁朝虽然国祚短促,但偏安江左,政局稳定,是继战国之后文学创作和文学批评的高潮时期,写作、编辑、整理等文化活动规模空前。作为武帝之长子兼皇位继承人的萧统,"钻阅六经、泛滥百氏",对文史百家有深入的研究,具有独特的审美体验。他不仅自己是作家,著有《昭明太子集》,同时也是选家,在《文选》编纂之前已经编有《古今诗苑英华》和《文章英华》两部总集,萧统在二十出头便开始为其总集筛选诗文作品。

《文选》共计六十卷,收录自周朝至六朝梁之前七八百年间130多位作者的诗文761篇,全部是文学作品,未收录经、史、子等学术著作。这种自觉对经、史、子与文学作品予以区分的思想,打破了我国自先秦以来文史不分的现象,代表了南朝人对文选特点认识的高度。在文学与非文学划清界限之后,《文选》进一步彰明其所选文章的标准。清代经学家阮元《书昭明太子〈文选序〉后》说:"昭明所选,名之曰文,盖必文而后选也,经也,子也,史也,皆不可专门之为文也。故昭明《文选序》后三段特明其不选之故。必'沉思''翰藻',始名为'文',

187

始以入选也。"由此可见,《文选》收录文章的标准是"事出于沉思,义归乎翰藻",即情义与辞采内外并茂的文章才能入选,偏于一面则不收。也就是说,能够体现"文以载道"的观点、主题深刻、具有自己的思想,并且辞藻华丽、善用典故比喻等写作手法的作品,才合乎《文选》的标准。《文选序》中萧统亦自言"略其芜秽,集其清英",显然是将《文选》定位为一部文萃精华,故书中所录,都是近千年来文学名家的代表作。

在体例编排上,《文选》采取了以类聚区分的方式,即按照文章的体裁分类。《文选》将收录作品分为赋、诗、骚、七、诏、册、令、表、檄、教、策、启、辞、颂、赞、箴、铭、诔、碑等三十九类(亦有学者将"难"归于檄类,认为是三十八类),其中,体裁属性相近的文章被编排在一起,并按照其重要性予以排序。

概而言之,《文选》首先将文章分为韵文与散文两大类,等同于诗、文之分,或当时的文、笔之分。前者主要包括赋、诗、骚、七四种文体;其余都是散文体,但不同于现代文类中的散文,是实用性散文。既然定名为《文选》,韵文当然排名在散文之前,且数量较多,约占全书篇幅的三分之二。韵文文体中,赋和诗又是所选作品数量最大的两个文体,其中前十九卷为赋,二十至三十二卷为诗,此两大类因其情况复杂,依照题材又各分若干细目:赋设置十五类子目,即京都、郊祀、耕藉、畋猎、纪行、游览、宫殿、江海、物色、鸟兽、志、哀伤、论文、音乐、情;诗,又细分为公宴、祖饯、咏史、游览、哀伤、赠答、行旅、乐府、杂诗、杂拟等二十四个小类。

韵文体中,骚源于诗,赋出于骚之后。按理诗应该编排在赋之前,但是《文选》中却以赋为首,而诗屈尊其后。这是因为"古诗之作,今则全取赋名"(《文选序》),即萧统认为,《文选》中的诗并非是《诗经》中的诗,反而是赋继承了《诗》的雅正传统。此外,在萧统看来,"诗者,盖志之所之也,情动于中而形于言",诗主要是写志怡情,而赋却是"体国经野,义尚光大",或"触兴至情,因变取会",其重要性自然较诗为重。骚,即《楚辞》,是指收录在《楚辞章句》中的屈原、宋玉以及其他作者的作品。七体争议较多,因为七与赋同源同体,后人认为七就是赋,故指责萧统的分类标准"淆乱芜秽、不可殚诘"。但是,考虑到当时文学的继承与发展,"七"体都以"七"为题,且有固定的"格套",单独设为一体也有其历史合理性。

"七"体之后,皆为散文。第一类散文体包括诏、册、令、教、文,都是帝王向臣民下达的旨意。"诏"是诏书;"册"是册封之书;"令"是政令、命令;"教"为教化;"文"是帝王主持的策试文。其后,表、上书、启、弹事、笺、奏记等散文体与第一大类散文体相对,是臣民向帝王的书面表达。而后的书、檄,则是同级之间的

第七章 《文选》经典篇章英译选读

对话,二者属同一类。其后的颂、赞、符命属于一类,都是仪式上歌功颂德的公文。之后的史论、史述赞、论属同一类,都是史著名篇的摘录。连珠、箴、铭则大都是训诫之语,且有文字游戏的性质。铭则是刻于器物上的文字。最后的诔、哀、碑文、墓志、行状、吊文、祭都是哀悼之文,可归于一大类。

综上所述,《文选》各文体总结归类如下:

(1) 赋、诗、骚、七:有韵之文;
(2) 诏、册、令、教、策:公文,上对下;
(3) 表、上书、启、弹事、笺、奏记:公文,下呈上;
(4) 书、移、檄:公文或私信,同级之间;
(5) 对问、设论、辞、序:言论、著作摘录;
(6) 颂、赞、符命:公文,仪式化的称颂;
(7) 史论、史述赞、论:史著摘录;
(8) 连珠、箴、铭:日常文字游戏;
(9) 诔、哀、碑文、墓志、行状、吊文、祭文:伤悼文体。

《文选》的这种体例区分具有划时代的意义,书中各种文体之间有清楚的界限,并附有表现各种文体特点的代表性文章,《文选》因此成为我国第一部按体区分的文学总集。这种编排模式下,编者辨析文体、指导写作的目的显而易见。

《文选》编成之后,去梁不远的隋朝、萧统的从侄萧该对《文选》进行了研究,写成《文选音义》一书,开创选学之先河。此后,曹宪、李善、公孙罗、许淹等人相继为《文选》做注,李善、公孙罗、许淹等更以《文选》教授生徒,选学因之大兴。现存的《文选》后世注本主要是唐代的两种注本:一是李善注本;一是五臣(吕延济、刘良、张铣、吕向、李周翰)注本。为《文选》做注的学者中,当属李善影响最大,其所著《文选注》不仅奠定了选学的基础,使文选学成为显学,且历代相传,至今仍在学界具有崇高的地位和重大的影响。

自初唐选学兴起至今,选学虽间有起落,但是研阅《文选》者大有其人。原因就在于唐以来诗赋之学一直被视作选才标准。科考中的试律策文有相当一部分来自《文选》或李善所作《文选注》,北宋时期更有"文选烂,秀才半"的说法。《文选》就此逐步变成了士子们实用速效的诗文典范,一步步上升为儒道释之外的"亚经典",其地位已非一般诗文总集可比。其次,《文选》对此后的文学创作有着深远的影响。章学诚赞《文选》为"辞章之圭臬,集部之准绳"。唐以来的各个文学大家,包括韩愈、李白、杜甫等,无不受到《文选》的影响。此外,《文选》在集部编纂上具有垂范作用,在文体分类、体例编辑上对后世文集编者多有影响,唐宋明清的史艺文志中的《续文选》亦颇为普遍。在新世纪的今天,继续学习

中华典籍英译选读

《文选》不仅可以领略中华传统文章的文学技法,更好地体会欣赏古文之美,还可以窥得《文选》精选文章中所蕴含的丰富文化,在阅读中感受华夏文化的源远流长和博大精深。

《文选》经典篇章英译选读之一

《鵩鸟赋》(节选)

贾 谊

且夫天地为炉兮,造化为工;阴阳为炭兮,万物为铜。合散消息兮①,安有常则?千变万化兮,未始有极。忽然为人兮,何足控抟②?化为异物兮③,又何足患?小智④自私兮,贱彼贵我。达人大观⑤兮,物无不可。贪夫殉财兮,烈士殉名。夸者死权兮⑥,品庶每生⑦。怵迫之徒兮,或趋西东⑧。大人不曲兮,意变齐同。愚士系俗兮,僒若囚拘⑨。至人遗物⑩兮,独与道俱。众人惑惑兮,好恶积亿⑪。真人恬漠⑫兮,独与道息。释智遗形兮,超然自丧。寥廓忽荒⑬兮,与道翱翔。乘流则逝兮,得坻则止⑭。纵躯委命⑮兮,不私与己。其生兮若浮⑯,其死兮若休⑰。澹乎若深泉之静⑱,泛乎若不系之舟⑲。不以生故自宝⑳兮,养空而浮㉑。德人无累㉒,知命不忧㉓。

注:本段文字节选自《鵩鸟赋》。作者贾谊,西汉初期著名的政治家和文学家,洛阳(今河南洛阳)人。贾谊本少年有为,却遭权贵群臣忌恨与中伤,23岁时被贬为长沙王太傅(太子或幼帝的老师),后被召回长安,文帝却无意让他参政,仅为梁怀王太傅。梁怀王坠马而亡之后,贾谊因失职自责,忧伤而亡,年仅33岁。《鵩鸟赋》是贾谊被贬为长沙王太傅时期的作品,赋中作者借与鵩鸟的问答抒发自己怀才不遇的愤懑不平,并以老庄齐生死的思想自我解脱。

【注释】

①〔合散〕聚散。〔消息〕指生和死。

第七章 《文选》经典篇章英译选读

②〔控抟(tuán)〕保持,控制,贵生之意。
③〔化为异物〕指人死后身体腐烂转化为其他东西,即死亡。
④〔小智〕自私狭隘智慧浅陋者。
⑤〔达人〕通达知命的人。〔大观〕看得高远。
⑥〔夸者〕贪求虚名的人。〔死权〕死于权势争夺。
⑦〔品庶〕众人,百姓。〔每生〕贪生。
⑧〔怵迫〕怵(chù):指为利所诱。迫:指为贫贱所迫。〔或趋西东〕为生计东奔西走。
⑨〔僒(jiǒng)〕同"窘",困窘,困迫。〔囚拘〕困窘得如罪人受于拘束。
⑩〔至人〕至德之人,道德修养达到最高境界的人。〔遗物〕遗弃物欲,不受物之累。
⑪〔好恶积亿〕为各种喜好厌恶所累,淤积于思维里。
⑫〔真人〕得道之人。〔恬漠〕恬淡,淡泊名利,清静无为。
⑬〔寥廓〕空远。〔忽荒〕同"恍惚"。
⑭〔乘流则逝兮,得坻则止〕遇到潮流则随水而去,遇到沙洲则自然而止。〔坻(chí)〕水中的小洲。
⑮〔纵躯委命〕放松身心,把它委托给命运自然的状态。
⑯〔其生兮若浮〕他活着的样子犹如浮游毫无挂碍。〔浮〕浮寄,浮游。
⑰〔其死兮若休〕他死亡的样子自然而然。〔休〕休息。
⑱〔澹乎若深泉之静〕恬静的样子好比幽静的深渊。〔澹(dàn)〕恬静安然貌。
⑲〔泛乎若不系之舟〕自由的样子仿佛不系缆绳的扁舟。〔泛〕逍遥游兮。
⑳〔不以生故自宝〕不因为贪生而刻意保全什么。〔自宝〕自我宝贵。
㉑〔养空而浮〕涵养空明的心性而使自己恣意浮游无羁无绊。〔养〕涵养,蓄养。
㉒〔德人〕有德之人。〔累〕牵累。
㉓〔知命不忧〕对生命了然于心而无所忧惧。〔忧〕忧虑,忧惧。

白话释义

天地是冶金的匠炉,自然之力(造化)则是冶金的工匠;阴阳是铸化万物的炭火,万物则是等待被铸化的青铜。世间离合聚散、死生寂灭,怎么会有固定的法则呢?其中的千变万化,未曾有过穷尽。偶然转化为人,有什么值得贪恋珍惜的呢?死去化作他物,又有什么值得忧患的呢?自私狭隘的人,以他物为贱,以自己为贵。通达知命的人目光高远,认为自己和万物可以相互适应,所以没有一物不合适。贪婪之辈为财而死,刚义之士舍身殉名。追求虚名者,死于权势争夺,普通老百姓总是贪求性命。为权力所诱被贫贱所迫的人,东奔西走,趋利避害。道德高尚的人不被物欲所害,对千变万化的事物都等量齐观,一视同仁。愚笨的人为世俗之见所束缚,如被拘囚的罪人般窘迫。而修为至于最高境界的人,却不为物欲所累,只和大道同行。世人皆迷惑于物,所爱所憎总是淤积于心。而得真正的得道之人却淡泊恬静,只与大道同游。(得道者)舍弃智虑,遗弃形体,超脱于万物之外而自忘其身,深远空阔,与道浮游,如水上之浮木,行止随流;把自己的身躯完全托付给命运,而不把它当作自己的私有物。活着如同浮木般随流而安,死去好像休憩长眠。安静得好像深渊潭水般幽然,漂浮得好像没有缆绳的小舟般自由自在。不因为活着而以己为贵,涵养空灵的心性,若浮舟般漂游,有德之人不受万物羁绊,知天委命而无忧无虑。

英译1

Heaven and earth are the furnace,
The workman, the Creator;
His coal is the yin and the yang,
His copper, all things of creation.
Joining, scattering, ebbing and flowing,
Where is there persistence or rule?
A thousand, a myriad mutations,
Lacking an end's beginning.
Suddenly they form a man:
How is this worth taking thought of?
They are transformed again in death:
Should this perplex you?
The witless takes pride in his being,
Scorning others, a lover of self.
The man of wisdom sees vastly
And knows that all things will do.
The covetous run after riches,
The impassioned pursue a fair name;
The proud die struggling for power,

第七章 《文选》经典篇章英译选读

While the people long only to live.
Each drawn and driven onward,
They hurry east and west.
The great man is without bent;
A million changes are as one to him.
The stupid man chained by custom
Suffers like a prisoner bound.
The sage abandons things;
And joins himself to the Tao alone,
While the multitudes in delusion
With desire and hate load their hearts.
Limpid and still, the true man
Finds his peace in the Tao alone.
Discarding wisdom, forgetful of form,
Transcendent, destroying self,
Vast and empty, swift and wild,
He soars on wings of the Tao.
Borne on the flood he sails forth;
He rests on the river islets.
Freeing his body to Fate,
Unpartaking of self,
His life is a floating,
His death a rest.
In stillness like the stillness of deep springs,
Like an unmoored boat drifting aimlessly,
Valuing not the breath of life,
He embraces and drifts with Nothing.
Comprehending Fate and free of sorrow,
The man of virtue heeds no bounds.

——Burton Watson（华兹生）

英译2

  Heaven and earth are a crucible, the Creator is the smith.
  Yin and Yang are the charcoal, living creatures are the bronze;
  Combining, scattering, waning and waxing—where is any pattern?
  A thousand changes, a myriad transformations with never any end.
  If by chance one becomes a man, it is not a state to cling to;
  If one be instead another creature, what cause is that for regret?
  A merely clever man is partial to self, despising others, vaunting ego;
The man of understanding takes the larger view: nothing exists to take exception to.
  The miser will do anything for his hoard, the hero for his repute;
The vainglorious is ready to die for power, the common man clings to life.
  Driven by aversions and lured by desires men dash madly west or east;
  The Great Man is not biased, the million changes are all one to him.
  The stupid man is bound by custom, confined as though in fetters;
  The Perfect Man is above circumstance, Tao is his only friend.
  The mass man vacillates, his mind replete with likes and dislikes.
  The True Man is tranquil, he takes his stand with Tao.
Divest yourself of knowledge and ignore your body, until, transported, you lose self,
  Be detached, remote, and soar with Tao.
  Float with the flowing stream, or rest against the isle,
  Surrender to the workings of fate, unconcerned for self,
  Let your life be like a floating, your death like a rest.
Placid as the peaceful waters of a deep pool, buoyant as an unfastened boat
  Find no cause for complacency in life, but cultivate emptiness and drift.
  The Man of Virtue is unattached; recognizing fate, he does not worry.
  Be not dismayed by petty pricks and checks!

——James Robert Hightower（海陶玮）

第七章 《文选》经典篇章英译选读

英译3

Heaven and Earth are the kiln,
The fashioner of things is the smith.
Yin and yang are the charcoal;
The myriad things are the copper.

Things join and dissolve, wax and wane—
Where is the constant rule?
A thousand changes, a myriad mutations,
Never is there an end.

If perchance one becomes a man,
How is this worth clinging to?
If one be transformed into something other,
How is this worthy of concern?

The man of small vision is egoistic,
Demeaning others, valuing self.
The perspicacious man takes a broad view,
And to him nothing is inadmissable.

The greedy man gives his life for riches;
The heroic man gives his life for fame.
The ambitious man would die for power;
The common man covets life.

Men driven by enticement or repulsion
Madly dash west or east.
The Great Man does not bend;
The million changes are all the same to him.

The foolish man is bound by the profane,
Constrained as if a prisoner bound.
The Perfect Man abandons things,
Consorting alone with the Tao.

The multitudes are muddled and confused;
Desire and hate fill their breasts.
The Realized Man is quiet and still,
Existing alone with the Tao.

Divesting himself of wisdom, abandoning physical form,
Dispcissionate, he loses self.
Feeling vast and empty, detached and distant,
He soars with the Tao.

Riding the current, away he goes;
Meeting an obstacle, he stops.
Yielding his body to fate,
He is not partial to self.

His life is like a floating;
His death is like a rest.
He is tranquil like the stillness of a deep pool;
He drifts like an unfastened boat.
He does not for sake of life value self,
But nurturing emptiness, floats about.
The Virtuous Man has no burdens;
Understanding fate, he does not grieve.
Minor matters, petty woes—
How are they worth concern?

——David R. Knechtges(康达维)

第七章 《文选》经典篇章英译选读

英译鉴赏简评

在西方文学文体分类中,并没有一种确切的与"赋"对应的文体。赋是一种韵文混合的文体。相比许多汉赋,贾谊的《鵩鸟赋》在形式上更为整齐,文章以骈偶句的形式铺陈,语句大都为四四拍,偶句两两押韵,骈句则统一以"兮"字押韵。这种对称美和汉字的特点有关,但是赋的文字布局很难以英文的形式重现。因此,三位译者虽然放弃了原文押韵的特点,却也尽量采用四四拍的诗行,形式上也突出了原诗排比和对仗的语言特征。这说明三位译者在翻译时也考虑到了赋韵文混合的文体特征。

考虑到赋的语言难度较大,三位译者的翻译彰显了一定的汉语语言功底。译文都采取了自由诗的形式,译文 2 和译文 3 进一步对诗行进行分节。但是,从语义层来讲,译文 2 更准确。比如,"未始有极",意思是不曾有过穷尽,译文 1 译为"lacking an end's beginning",纯属字译,意思是"没有结尾的开始",与原文之意相差甚远;译文 2 译为"with never any end",则准确许多。"大人不曲兮,意变齐同"意思是"道德高尚的人不被物欲所害,对千变万化的事物都能一视同仁"。译文 1"The great man is without bent; A million changes are as one to him"和译文 3"The Great Man does not bend; The million changes are all the same to him",均取"不曲"的字面意思,译为"without bent"和"does not bend",意思是不弯腰(屈从),仅停留于字表之意,未能译出深层语义;译文 2"The Great Man is not biased, the million changes are all one to him",采取意译策略,有效传递出原文作者"齐生死、等万物"的道家思想。

从英译句式结构方面来看,译文 3 为《文选》英文全译第一人、美国著名汉学家康达维教授所译,业界认为他的译文忠实而严谨,流畅而典雅,充分再现了中国古典诗文的文藻与韵律之美。骈文最突出的文本特点之一在于其句式的整饬谨严、长短划一,音韵的谐和相衬,以及语词的对仗呼应,例如:"贪夫殉财兮,烈士殉名。夸者死权兮,品庶每生。"英译文要成功再现骈文的以上特质,实属不易。译文 3"The greedy man gives his life for riches;//The heroic man gives his life for fame.//The ambitious man would die for power;//The common man covets life."句式整齐划一,重视头韵、尾韵的韵律效果。译文 1"The covetous run after riches,//The impassioned pursue a fair name;//The proud die struggling for power,//While the people long only to live."和译文 2"The miser will do anything for his hoard, the hero for his repute.//The vainglorious is ready to die for power, the common man clings to life."则显得用词啰嗦、音韵失和、句式长短不一。

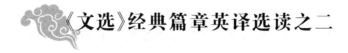《文选》经典篇章英译选读之二

《上林赋》(节选)

司马相如

汩乎混流①,顺阿②而下,赴隘狭③之口。触穹石④,激堆埼⑤,沸乎暴怒,汹涌澎湃。滭弗宓汩⑥,逼侧泌㴢⑦,横流逆折,转腾潎冽⑧,滂濞沆溉⑨。

……

撞千石之钟⑩,立万石之虡⑪;建⑫翠华之旗,树灵鼍⑬之鼓。奏陶唐氏之舞⑭,听葛天氏之歌⑮;千人唱,万人和;山陵为之震动,川谷为之荡波。巴渝宋蔡⑯,淮南干遮⑰,文成颠歌⑱,族居⑲递奏,金鼓⑳迭起,铿鎗闛鞈㉑,洞心骇耳㉒。

注:以上文字节选自司马相如的名作《上林赋》。司马相如,字长卿,西汉蜀郡成都(今属四川)人。一说为四川蓬州(今四川南充市仪陇县)人,迁居至成都,西汉盛世汉武帝时期著名的辞赋家(汉赋四大家之一)、政治家,汉景帝时为武骑常侍,以病免职,后因工于辞赋而受到汉武帝赏识,召为郎,后拜为中郎将,升孝文园令。《上林赋》创作于汉武帝时期,当时朝廷铲除了诸侯王,正处于大一统的全盛时期。司马相如创作此赋,以讽谏汉武帝,作者亦借此大赋而名扬四海,被誉为赋圣、辞宗。其赋辞藻瞻丽、结构宏大、想象丰富。司马相如的代表作除《上林赋》之外,还有其姊妹篇《子虚赋》,以及受托于汉武帝失宠皇后陈阿娇而作的《长门赋》。

【注释】

①〔汩乎混流〕形容水流浩大迅急。〔汩(gǔ)〕水流快。〔混流〕混,同"浑"。

第七章 《文选》经典篇章英译选读

②〔阿(ē)〕高高的丘陵。《说文》:"阿,大陵也。"
③〔隘狭(ài xiá)〕即狭隘,河两岸相近窄小处。
④〔穹(qióng)石〕大石。《尔雅·释诂》:"穹,大也。"
⑤〔堆埼(qí)〕沙石拥堆而形成的曲岸。〔埼〕弯曲的水岸。
⑥〔滭弗(bì fèi)〕水上涌的样子。〔宓(mì)汩〕水流疾速的样子。
⑦〔逼侧〕相逼。〔泌漪(mì zhì)〕泌,泉流轻快的样子。漪,水波冲激貌。
⑧〔滮冽(piē liè)〕水流轻急,快速撞击的样子或声音。
⑨〔滂濞(pāng pì)〕即"彭湃",水浪相击的声音。〔沆溉(hàng gài)〕水流缓慢貌。
⑩〔千石(dàn)之钟〕特别大的编钟。〔石〕古代计量单位,战国时期一石大约为120斤。
⑪〔虡(jù)〕古代悬钟或磬的架子两侧的旁柱。
⑫〔建〕举,立。
⑬〔灵鼍之鼓〕此指用鼍皮做成的鼓。〔鼍(tuó)〕扬子鳄,钝吻鳄科的一种爬行动物,产于长江下游,是中国特产。
⑭〔陶唐氏之舞〕上古唐尧时的舞乐,名"咸池"。尧初封于陶,后封于唐,有天下之后,号称为"陶唐氏"。
⑮〔葛天氏之歌〕上古歌舞。葛天氏,传说中的上古帝王,其治世不言而信,不化而行,是远古社会理想化的政治领袖人物。
⑯〔巴渝〕蜀古地名,后用以借指巴渝舞或巴渝歌。〔宋蔡〕二者都是国名,这里指代宋蔡两地的音乐。
⑰〔淮南〕指淮河以南、长江以北地区。〔干遮(gàn zhē)〕古曲名。
⑱〔文成〕地名,指其地的歌舞乐。〔颠歌(diān gē)〕颠,同"滇",即云南。颠歌指古时西南夷的民歌。
⑲〔族居〕丛居,聚集在一起。〔递奏〕递,顺次交替。此指各种乐曲交替演奏。
⑳〔金鼓〕泛指金属制乐器和鼓。
㉑〔铿鎗(kēng qiāng)〕形容音乐钟鼓及其他金属器声音响亮。〔闛鞈(táng tà)〕象声词,钟鼓声。
㉒〔洞心骇耳〕此句意思是深入人心,令人感到震惊。〔洞〕彻。〔骇(hài)耳〕震耳。

199

白话释义

盛大的水流迅疾而出,沿着高高的丘陵注下,直奔狭隘的山口,迅猛的水流撞击着巨石,冲激着沙岸,怒涛如聚,汹涌澎湃。水盛势疾,相互撞击发出巨响,水流纵横交杂,转折翻腾,激冽作响。

……

撞击千石重的巨大编钟,立起万石重的钟架,高扬着五彩的翠旗,竖起鼍皮蒙就的大鼓,演奏着唐尧时期的陶唐氏之舞,聆听着葛天氏之歌。千人同唱,万人相和,歌声震动山陵,荡漾起河水。巴渝、宋蔡的歌舞,淮南《干遮》,文成和云南的歌舞,齐聚一地,交替演奏。乐鼓之声,此起彼伏,铿锵悦耳,动人心弦。

英译 1

In wild confusion they swirl
Along the bases of the tall hills
And through the mouths of the narrow gorges;
Dashed upon boulders, maddened by winding escarpments,
They writhe in anger,
Leaping and curling upward,
Jostling and eddying in great swells
That surge and batter against each other;
Darting and twisting,
Foaming and tossing,
In a thundering chaos.

...

His courtiers, sounding the massive bells
That swing from the giant bell rack,
Raising the pennants of kingfisher feathers,
And setting up the drum of sacred lizard skin,
Present for his pleasure the dances of Yao
And the songs of the ancient Emperor Ko;
A thousand voices intone,

第七章 《文选》经典篇章英译选读

　　　　Ten thousand join in harmony,
　As the mountains and hills rock with echoes
　And the valley waters quiver to the sound.
　　The dances of Pa-yü, of Sung and Ts'ai,
　　　　The Yü-che song of Huai-nan,
　　　The airs of Tien and Wen-ch'eng,
　　One after another in groups they perform,
　Sounding in succession the gongs and drums
　　　Whose shrill clash and dull booming
　　　Pierce the heart and startle the ear.

　　　　　　　　　　——Burton Watson（华兹生）

英译2

　　　　　Swiftly, wildly flowing,
　　　They descend along the slopes,
　　　Enter mouths of narrow gorges,
　　　Collide with beetling boulders,
　　Smash against winding sand mounds,
　　　Frothing with violent anger.

　Soaring and leaping, surging and swelling,
　Spurting and spouting, rushing and racing,
Pressing and pushing, clashing and colliding,
　　Flowing uncontrolled, bending back,
　Wheeling and rearing, beating and battering,
Swelling and surging, troublous and turbulent.
　　　　　　　...
　　　They beat thousand-catty bells,
　　Erect ten-thousand-catty bell-racks,
　Raise banners adorned with kingfisher tufts,
And plant in place the drum of sacred alligator hide.

> They present the dances of Taotang,
> Perform the songs of Getian.
> A thousand voices sing the lead;
> Ten thousand sing the harmony.
> The mountains and hills thus begin to quake and rock;
> The streams and gorges thus begin to churn and billow.
> The music of Ba-Yu, Song, and Cai,
> The "Ganzhe" of Huainan,
> Songs of Wencheng and Dian,
> Are presented en masse, performed en suite.
> Bells and drums alternately sound,
> Their cling-clang and rat-a-tat-tat
> Pierce the heart and startle the ears.

——David R. Knechtges（康达维）

英译鉴赏简评

以上两段译文分别由美国汉学家华兹生和康达维所译。华兹生将译文的目标读者定位为一般读者，因此译文以通顺畅达为主，没有学术性注释。而康达维则是近年来汉赋研究的专业学者，对汉语古音韵和赋体都颇有研究，也是西方第一位完整翻译并注释《文选》的大家。康达维的译文定位是具有一定专业知识的学者，因此，其译文以学术性和文学性并胜的特点而著称，译文中频繁引用古人注疏，并附有大量的学术性注释。康达维强调译文的准确性，反对为迎合目标读者的阅读习惯而牺牲原文的语言特征。例如，对"逼侧"一词的注释，康查阅了大量的文献，认为"逼"的代表性语素是"偪"，与"迫"字音同且意义相近，而后通过还原"逼侧"二字的古音，康判断"逼侧"是叠韵联绵词，并结合联绵词的特点和文献注疏，推断出"逼侧"的词义是描写波涛相互推挤的状态，从而将"逼侧"一词翻译成"pressing and pushing"，形成英文诗的头韵。对描写水势的精彩文字"汹涌澎湃。潭弗宓汩，逼侧泌㵧，横流逆折，转腾溦洌，滂濞沆溉"的翻译，更加体现出译者对汉语双声叠韵词语的理解深度，展示出其驾驭文字的高超技艺。

> **Soaring** and leaping, **surging** and **swelling**,

第七章 《文选》经典篇章英译选读

Spurting and **spouting**, rushing and racing,
Pressing and pushing, clashing and colliding,
Flowing uncontrolled, bending back,
Wheeling and rearing, beating and battering,
Swelling and **surging**, troublous and turbulent.

大量形近词、同韵词、近韵词的使用,令译文读来铿锵有力,如亲临河岸,水声直击耳膜,视觉直入眼帘,有声且有形,可谓形音义三者有机融于一体。由此可见康达维对于译文"准确性"和"艺术性"的要求之高。

除了在诗行、节奏的设置上和原文一致,康达维的译文在语言、修辞等形式方面也较为契合原文。如"撞千石之钟,立万石之虡,建翠华之旗,树灵鼍之鼓"等句,康达维在句式上采取了和原文一致的动宾结构,将原文中的偏正结构"千石之钟,万石之虡,翠华之旗,灵鼍之鼓"译为英语中相应的名词性短语(中心词+修饰语)。此外,"山陵为之震动,川谷为之荡波"的翻译在形式上也保持了同样的主谓结构。他将末句中的"铿锵"译为"cling-cling and rat-a-tat-tat",保留了拟声词的修饰特点。

《文选》经典篇章英译选读之三

《风赋》(节选)

宋 玉

夫①风生于地,起于青蘋②之末。侵淫③溪谷,盛怒④于土囊⑤之口。缘泰山⑥之阿⑦,舞于松柏之下,飘忽⑧溯涝⑨,激飓⑩熛怒⑪。耾耾⑫雷声,回穴⑬错迕⑭。蹶⑮石伐木,梢杀林莽⑯。至其将衰也,被丽披离⑰,冲孔动楗⑱,眴焕粲烂⑲,离散转移。

注:此段节选自战国末期文学家宋玉创作的《风赋》。宋玉,字子渊,战国后期的楚国文人,善于辞赋。辞作《九辩》以咏秋著称;《风赋》《高唐赋》《神女赋》《登徒子好色赋》《对楚王问》,均被视为宋玉的代表作,在中国文学史上占据重要地位。《风赋》以风为题材,记录了楚襄王与宋玉关于风的一段对话,此节为第三段的前半部分,使用夸张的手法,通过对"大王之雄风"和"庶人之雌风"的描写,

使大王奢靡之风与庶民贫苦之状形成鲜明对比,从而反映社会的不公。此段文字使用铺陈手法,描写风的性质和状态,文笔细腻入微。

【注释】

① 〔夫〕语气助词,无实际意义。
② 〔青蓣(pín)之末〕青蓣的叶尖。〔青蓣〕蕨类植物,多年生浅水草本。可入药。
③ 〔侵淫〕逐渐蔓延侵入。
④ 〔盛怒〕暴怒,此处形容风势猛烈。
⑤ 〔囊(náng)〕洞穴。
⑥ 〔泰山〕大山。〔泰〕通"太"。
⑦ 〔阿(ē)〕高高的丘陵。《说文》:"阿,大陵也。"此处指山脚弯曲凹洼之处。
⑧ 〔飘忽〕往来不定的样子,此处形容风速迅疾。
⑨ 〔浏滂(péng pāng)〕大风吹打物体的声音。唐李善注:"浏滂,风击物声。"
⑩ 〔激飏(yáng)〕疾飞貌,指强风劲吹。《说文·风部》:"飏,风所飞扬也。"
⑪ 〔熛(biāo)怒〕形容风势猛烈迅疾。〔熛〕疾速。
⑫ 〔耾耾(hóng hóng)〕风声,此处指风声很大。
⑬ 〔回穴(xué)〕迂回而变化不定。
⑭ 〔错迕(wǔ)〕迕,交错夹杂。此指风盘旋错杂。
⑮ 〔蹶(jué)〕挖掘,拔出,撼动。
⑯ 〔梢(shāo)杀林莽(mǎng)〕摧毁树林和野草。〔梢杀〕指毁伤草木。〔莽〕草丛。
⑰ 〔被丽(bèi lì)披离〕二者都是联绵词,指四面分散的样子。〔披离〕也作被离,离披,纷披。
⑱ 〔冲孔〕冲进孔穴。〔动楗(jiàn)〕吹动门闩。楗,门闩。
⑲ 〔眴(xuàn)焕、粲烂(càn làn)〕二者都是联绵词,表示色彩鲜明、光华灿烂的样子。

白话释义

风在大地上生成,从蓣的末端兴起,逐渐扩展到山谷,在大山洞口变得迅猛,然后沿着山坳之处,在松柏林里狂舞。疾风往来盘旋,发出撞击物体的声音;风势猛烈迅疾,犹如迸飞的火焰,伴随着轰轰如雷般的风声,风势错综交杂。

第七章 《文选》经典篇章英译选读

飞沙走石,摧树折木,冲击树林和草丛。等风势逐渐平缓,风力衰微,风就开始四面散开,这时候风就只能透进小孔,吹动门闩了。最后风定尘落,各种景物就显得分外灿烂鲜明,微风徐徐,向四面飘散。

英译1

The wind is born in the ground. It rises in the extremities of the green p'ing-flower. It pours into the river-valleys and rages at the mouth of the pass. It follows the rolling flanks of Mount T'ai and dances beneath the pine-trees and cypresses. In gusty bouts it whirls. It rushes in fiery anger. It rumbles low with a noise like thunder, tearing down rocks and trees, smitting forests and grasses. But at last abating, it spreads abroad, seeks empty places and crosses the threshhold of rooms. And so growing gentler and clearer, it changes and is dispersed and dies.

——Arthur Waley(亚瑟·韦利)

英译2

The wind is born from the land
And springs up in the tips of the green duckweed.
It insinuates itself into the valleys
And rages in the canyon mouth,
Skirts the corners of Mount T'ai
And dances beneath the pines and cedars.
Swiftly it flies, whistling and wailing;
Fiercely it splutters its anger.
It crashes with a voice like thunder,
Whirls and tumbles in confusion,
Shaking rocks, striking trees.
Blasting the tangled forest.
Then, when its force is almost spent,

It wavers and disperses,
Thrusting into crevices and rattling door latches.
Clean and clear,
It scatters and rolls away.

——Burton Watson(华兹生)

英译3

The wind is born from the earth,
Rises from the tips of green duckweed,
Gradually advances into glen and vale,
Rages at the mouths of earthen sacks,
Follows the bends of great mountains,
Dances beneath pine and cypress.
Swiftly soaring, blasting and blustering,
Fiercely it flies, swift and angry,
Rumbling and roaring with the sound of thunder.
Tortuously twisting, in chaotic confusion,
It overturns rocks, fells trees,
Strikes down forests and thickets.

Then, when its power is abating,
It scatters and spreads, spreads and scatters,
Charging into crevices, shaking door bolts.
All that it brushes is bright and shiny, dazzling fresh
As it disperses and turns away.

——David R. Knechtges(康达维)

英译鉴赏简评

以上三位译者的译文,译文1的准确性和文学性相对欠缺,这和译者所处

第七章 《文选》经典篇章英译选读

的时代有关。作为西方第一个译介赋的学者,韦利对赋的理解相当有限,也很难获得相关的训诂注疏材料。相较而言,译文 1 并没有紧扣原文,"耾耾雷声"之后漏译了"回穴错迕"。此外,对"青蘋"的翻译未加考证,直接将其音译为"the green p'ing-flower"。句式较为刻板生硬,未能再现赋体文的文学色彩。与译文 1 相比,译文 2 更忠实于原文。首先,在译文形式上散韵分离,散文句译为散文体,韵则以英诗诗行形式翻译;再者,译文没有增删添减,紧扣原文,句句对应。其次,词汇语义更为精准。比如"离散转移",译文 1 译为"disperse and die",意思是"消失,消亡",译文 2 则译为"scatters and rolls away",意思是分散离开,更贴近原文所传递的意义。相较译文 2,译文 3 更为严谨,语义贴近,音韵相和,从形式上划分了诗节,译文语句与原文对应得更为精准。如"被丽披离",两词属同义重复,译文 3 也通过调换位置将其译为同义重复的形式;"晌焕粲烂",译文 1 翻译为"gentler and clearer(柔和清晰)",译文 2 译为"clean and clear(干净清楚)",译文 3 则是"bright and shiny, dazzling fresh(明艳耀眼)",表述最准确。在音韵方面,译文 3 使用大量的头韵、尾韵词来再现赋体文的音效特质。另外,译文 3 的突出优势在于译文后附有详尽的注释和解析。例如:土囊的注释是洞穴;泰山作两解,或专指泰山,或泛指大山;引用相关训诂注疏材料,说明"熛怒"指火焰迸发(李善注)或迅疾(胡绍英)。三位译者的翻译差异表明了赋体译文在英语世界的专业化和学术化进程。

《文选》经典篇章英译选读之四

《洛神赋》(节选)

曹 植

其形也,翩若惊鸿,婉若游龙①。荣曜秋菊,华茂春松②。髣髴兮若轻云之蔽月,飘飖兮若流风之回雪③。远而望之,皎若太阳升朝霞;迫而察之④,灼若芙蕖出渌波⑤。秾纤得衷⑥,修短合度⑦。肩若削成,腰如约素⑧。延颈秀项⑨,皓质呈露⑩。芳泽无加,铅华弗御⑪。云髻峨峨⑫,修眉联娟⑬。丹唇外朗,皓齿内鲜⑭。明眸善睐⑮,靥辅承权⑯。瑰姿艳逸⑰,仪静体闲。柔情绰态⑱,媚于语言。奇服旷世,骨像应图⑲。披罗衣之璀粲兮⑳,珥瑶碧之华琚㉑。戴金翠之首饰,缀明珠以耀躯。践远游之文履㉒,曳雾绡之轻裾㉓。微幽兰之芳蔼㉔兮,步踟蹰于山隅。于是忽焉纵体,以遨以嬉㉕。左倚采旄㉖,右荫桂旗㉗。攘皓腕于神浒兮㉘,采湍濑之玄芝㉙。

……

恨人神之道殊兮,怨盛年之莫当㉚。抗罗袂以掩涕兮,泪流襟之浪浪㉛。悼良会之永绝兮,哀一逝而异乡㉜。无微情以效爱兮㉝,献江南之明珰㉞。虽潜处于太阴㉟,长寄心于君王㊱。

注:以上两段节选自三国曹魏时期建安七子之一曹植所作的《洛神赋》。曹植,字子建,三国魏谯(今安徽亳州)人,曹操第三子。曹植天资聪颖,才思敏捷,却因"任性而行,饮酒不节"而落败于嗣位之争。曹丕即位后,他名为侯王,实为囚徒,受人监管,曾六迁封地,终至陈王,谥号思,因此后人称其为陈思王。他是建安文学成就最高者,现存其诗歌九十余首。《洛神赋》写于黄初三年(公元222年)作者32岁朝觐京都洛阳途经洛水时,有感于战国时期宋玉与楚襄王对答梦遇巫山神女之事而作,梦中与神女的分别象征着作者对人神异途,知音难觅的慨叹,喻指作者破碎的政治梦想和坎坷的人生际遇。该赋手法多变、形式隽永、辞藻华丽,被视作汉代铺排大赋向六朝抒情小赋转化的桥梁。其中对女性美的细致入微的捕捉和描写,被视为摹写美女的"神来之笔",是继《诗经·硕人》和宋玉《神女赋》之后,另一篇刻画女性美的传世佳作,在中国文学史上有着非常广泛而深远的影响。

【注释】

①〔翩〕鸟疾飞貌,此指飘忽摇曳的样子。〔惊鸿〕惊飞的鸿雁。〔婉〕蜿蜒曲折。此句意思是翩然若惊飞的鸿雁,蜿蜒如游动的蛟龙,描写洛神的体态轻盈柔美。

②〔曜〕照耀;明亮。此句意思是容光焕发如秋日下的菊花,体态丰茂如春风中的松树,描写洛神容光艳色、体态丰盈。

③〔髣髴(fǎng fú)〕似乎,好像,近似。〔飘飖(yáo)〕风吹状。〔流风〕流动的风。〔回雪〕形容舞姿曼妙,如雪因风而回翔一般。此句意思是像薄云遮住月亮,

第七章 《文选》经典篇章英译选读

轻盈飘逸,像流风吹动雪花,描写洛神婀娜多姿,举止飘逸。

④〔迫〕靠近。〔察〕细看,观察。

⑤〔灼〕鲜艳。〔芙蕖(qú)〕荷花的别称。〔渌(lù)〕水清貌。此句意思是洛神艳丽迷人如娇艳欲滴的出水芙蓉。

⑥〔秾(nóng)〕花木繁盛貌,此指人的体态丰腴。〔纤(xiān)〕细小,娇小。〔得衷(zhōng)〕正好,合适。〔秾纤得衷〕指洛神体态苗条纤细,胖瘦合宜,恰到好处。

⑦〔修短〕修长和低矮,指洛神的个子高矮。〔合度〕恰到好处。

⑧〔削成〕形容两肩瘦削下垂的样子。〔约素〕一束白绢。〔素〕白细丝织品。这句是写洛神的肩膀和腰肢线条圆美。

⑨〔延、秀〕均指修长。〔颈〕脖子的前部。〔项〕脖子的后部。此句指洛神脖颈秀美修长。

⑩〔皓〕洁白。〔呈露〕显现,外露。此句指修长秀美的颈项露出白皙的皮肤。

⑪〔泽〕润肤的油脂。〔铅华〕粉。〔御〕使用,施用。此句指既不施脂,也不敷粉。

⑫〔云髻〕发髻如云。〔峨峨〕高耸的样子。

⑬〔修眉〕长眉。〔联娟〕也作"连娟"。此句指眉毛微弯、美好的样子。

⑭〔丹唇〕红唇。〔朗〕明润。〔鲜〕光洁。此句指洛神嘴唇鲜润,牙齿洁白。

⑮〔眸(móu)〕眼中瞳仁。〔睐(lài)〕左右顾盼。此句指洛神有一双善于顾盼的明亮的眼睛。

⑯〔靥(yè)〕酒窝。〔辅〕面颊。〔权〕颧骨。此句指颧骨下有两个甜甜的酒窝。

⑰〔瑰〕奇妙。〔艳逸〕瑰丽飘逸。

⑱〔柔情绰态〕舒缓柔美的样子。〔绰(chuò)〕绰约。

⑲〔骨像〕骨骼形貌。〔应图〕如同画中人一般。骨像应图指风骨体貌如同图画中的一样。

⑳〔罗衣〕绮罗衣,丝质的衣服。〔璀粲〕鲜明的样子。

㉑〔珥(ěr)〕用珠子或玉石做的耳环,此处用作动词,意思是佩戴。〔瑶、碧〕均为美玉。〔华琚(jū)〕刻有花纹的精美佩玉。

㉒〔践〕穿着。〔远游〕鞋名。〔文〕动词,用花纹装饰。〔文履(lǚ)〕即饰有花纹图案的鞋子。此句指洛神脚穿饰有花纹的远游鞋。

㉓〔曳(yè)〕拖,拉。〔雾绡(xiāo)〕薄雾似的轻纱,亦指用此种材料做的衣服。〔裾(jū)〕裙边,衣服的大襟。

㉔〔微〕隐隐,隐约。〔芳蔼(ǎi)〕芳香而繁盛,香气。此句指隐隐散发出幽兰的清香。

㉕〔纵体〕身体轻举飘飞貌。〔遨(áo)〕游逛,游戏。此句指忽然身体又飘然轻举,且行且戏。
㉖〔采旄(máo)〕彩旗,采,同"彩"。〔旄〕旗杆上旄牛尾饰物,此处指旗。此句指左面倚靠着彩旗。
㉗〔荫〕庇护,遮蔽。〔桂旗〕以桂木做旗杆的旗,形容旗的华美。此句指右边有桂旗遮蔽。
㉘〔攘(rǎng)〕捋起袖子,挽袖伸出。〔浒(hǔ)〕水边,指离水稍远的岸上平地。〔神浒〕为神所游的水边泽畔。
㉙〔湍濑(tuān lài)〕石上湍急的水流。〔玄芝〕黑色的芝草,相传是一种神草。此句指采撷水流边的黑色芝草。
㉚〔盛年〕少壮之年。〔莫当〕无匹,即两人不能结合。此句指怨恨正当盛年,却因人神殊道而无法结合。
㉛〔抗〕举。〔罗袂(luó mèi)〕丝罗的衣袖,亦指华丽的衣着。〔浪浪〕水流不断貌,此处指泪流不止。
㉜〔良会〕美好的相会。〔逝〕离去。此处指一别两地不再相见。
㉝〔微情〕柔情。〔效爱〕致爱慕之意。此句指无法以细微的柔情来表达爱慕之心。
㉞〔明珰〕以明月珠作的耳珰。〔珰(dāng)〕古代妇女戴在耳垂上的装饰品。
㉟〔潜处〕幽居。〔太阴〕鬼神所居之处。
㊱〔君王〕指曹植的哥哥曹丕。

白话释义

洛神的姿态形影,翩然飘行就像惊飞的鸿雁,婉婉徐步就像游动的蛟龙。容光艳色如同秋日照耀下的菊花,体态丰盈如同春风沐浴中的青松。她时隐时现,就像薄云罩皎月,行动飘忽,就像流风吹白雪。远远望去,明耀得如同朝霞中初升的太阳;趋近观察,艳丽的如同绿波间刚刚绽放的新荷。她体态适中,高矮合宜,窄肩如削,细腰如束,秀美修长的颈项露出白皙的皮肤。不施脂敷粉,如云般的发髻高高耸立,长眉弯曲,红唇鲜润,牙齿洁白,一双明眸善于顾盼,面颊下有两个甜甜的酒窝。她仪态优雅,举止娴静,温柔和顺,言辞得体;奇丽的服饰世所罕见,风骨体貌如同画中人一般。她身着明丽的罗衣,戴着精美的佩玉。头戴金银翡翠首饰,缀以周身闪亮的明珠。她脚穿着饰有花纹图案的远游鞋,拖着轻如薄雾般的裙裾,隐隐散发出幽兰般的清香,在山边徘徊徜徉。忽而

第七章 《文选》经典篇章英译选读

又飘然轻举,且行且戏,左倚彩旗,右面有桂旗庇荫,在神之游玩的泽畔旁轻拢袖口,伸出素手,采撷水流边的黑色芝草。

……

只怨恨人神有别,彼此虽然都处在盛年而无法结合。说着不禁举起罗袖掩面而泣,止不住泪水涟涟沾湿了衣襟,哀念交织欢乐的相会就此永绝,如今一别身处两地,不曾以细微的柔情来表达爱慕之心,只能赠以明珰作为永久的纪念。自己虽然身处太阴,却时时怀念着君王。

英译1

In appearance, she lightly flutters like a startled swan,
Curvets like a roaming dragon.
Her luster is more brilliant than autumn chrysanthemum,
Her resplendence is more luxuriant than spring pine.

She is dimly descried like the moon obscured by light clouds,
She drifts airily like whirling snow in streaming wind.
Gaze at her from afar,
And she glistens like the sun rising over morning mists,
Examine her close up,
And she is dazzling as lotus emerging from limpid ripples.

Between plump and thin, she strikes a mean;
Her height conforms to proper measure.
Her shoulders seem as if sculpted,
Her waist is like bundled silk.
On her long throat and slender neck,
White flesh is clearly revealed.
Fragrant oils she does not apply,
Flower of lead she does not use.

Billowy chignons rise high and tall,
Long eyebrows are delicately curved,

Scarlet lips shine without,

White teeth gleam within.

Bright eyes do well at casting sidelong glances,

Dimples lie on either cheek.

Her wondrous manner is of uncommon beauty;

Her comportment is quiet, her body relaxed.

With tender feeling and graceful bearing,

She enthralls with her lovely words.

Her wondrous attire is unsurpassed in the world;

Her figure and form accord with the paintings.

She drapes herself in the shimmering glitter of a gossamer gown,

Wears in her ears ornate gems of carnelian and jade,

Bedecks her hair with head ornaments of gold and halcyon plumes,

Adorns herself with shining pearls that illumine her body.

She treads in patterned Distant Roaming slippers,

Trails a light skirt of misty gauze.

Obscured by the fragrant lushness of thoroughwort,

She paces hesitantly in a mountain nook.

Then, suddenly she moves light and easy,

Rambling and playing about.

On her left rests a colored streamer,

On her right she is shaded by a cassia-staff banner.

Extending her albescent arms toward the margin of the divine stream,

She plucks dark mushrooms from the raging rapids.

......

She regrets that the ways of humans and spirit are different,

And laments that in her flourishing years she cannot find a fit mate.

She raises a gauze sleeve to wipe her eyes,

And tears fall in streams soaking her lapel.

She grieves that this good tryst must cease forever,

And sorrows that, once departed, we shall go to different realms.

第七章 《文选》经典篇章英译选读

"lacking even the slightest feeling with which to express my love,
I present you a shining pearl earring from Yangtze south.
Although I dwell submerged in the Great Yin,
I shall always lodge my heart with you, my prince."

——David R. Knechtges(康达维)

2

Her form:
swept along lightly like startled swan,
was sinuous as the swimming dragon,
shimmering like sheen on fall's chrysanthemums,
splendid like pines that swell in the spring.
She was a blur as when pale clouds form a film on the moon,
she floated through air as when winds send snow swirling.

When I gazed on her from afar,
she shone like the sun through morning clouds mounting;
when nearer I viewed her.
she glowed like a lotus coming out of clear waves.

She achieved the mean between slender and stout,
between tall and short she met the right measure.
Her shoulders seemed hewn to perfection,
her waist was tight as if bound with white silk.
When she stretched her neck, the throat was fair,
and her radiant flesh was displayed,
unassisted by aromatic lotions
and with no powder lending it aid.
Her hair coiled high in lofty clouds,
and long brows formed delicate arches.
Scarlet lips on the outside luminous,

with shining teeth gleaming within.
Her bright eyes cast wondrous glances,
dimples stood close by her cheekbones.
A rare bearing, alluring, aloof,
her manner was poised, her body calm.
With tender feeling and lovely expression,
her speech was enthralling.

Her singular garb was unique in these times,
her figure well fitted what we find pictured.
She wore a gown of shimmering gauze,
in her ears were gems cut cunningly;
her head was adorned with feathers and jade,
and strung pearls made her body sparkle.
She wore patterned slippers for roaming far,
she trailed light sleeves of misty mesh.
Through a filmy aromatic haze of orchids
she paced, then paused on the fold of the hill.

All at once she broke loose, moving wild and free,
she skipped and cavorted here and there,
she leaned on bright streamers to her left,
to her right she was shadowed by cassia flags.
She bared bright wrists on those sacred shores,
and from seething shallows picked purple asphodel.

...

and regretting how men and gods stood apart,
grieved that no match could be made in my prime.
Then she lifted gauze sleeves and wiped away tears
that flowed in streams on the folds of her gown.
"It is sad that our union is now lost forever,
once gone, we must dwell in realms set apart.

第七章 《文选》经典篇章英译选读

> I have no way to show all the love in my heart,
> but I give you bright earrings from southern lands.
> Though I will dwell concealed in the shadow world,
> my heart will forever be yours, my prince."

——Stephen Owen(宇文所安)

英译鉴赏简评

学者成仿吾曾提出,理想的译诗应具有以下标准。第一,译诗本身应当也是诗;第二,译诗传递了原诗的情绪;第三,译诗传达了原诗的内容;第四,译诗具有原诗的形式。然而,不同语言系统的差异,如英语和汉语在语调、声调、音节上的差异、表音和表意文字的差异,加之诗性语言所特有的非常规化特征,使译文要实现形式和语义的双重对等非常困难。无怪乎著名翻译家许渊冲先生感慨,译诗难,难于上青天!

此处曹植对洛神的描写,极尽妍媚之辞,此后文章无有出其右者。虽然两篇译文总体的意思表述都比较契合原文,但相较而言,译文1更具文采。"翩若惊鸿",译文1译为"flutters like a startled swan",突出了洛神轻盈飘然的体态美。译文2"swept along lightly"是轻轻走过之意,与原文意思有偏差。同时,译文1使用"more brilliant than""more luxuriant than"表示荣耀、华茂之意,比译文3"shimmering"(微微发光)更能表现出耀眼、华丽的意思。最精妙之处则是译文1对"仿佛兮"二句的翻译,译文不但意思表述极为精准,且形式上用四个诗行,两两对应,同时一、三句分别使用头韵和腹韵,最大限度地传递出赋的骈偶、对仗、韵文混合等文学特征。此译文精妙绝伦,实现了许渊冲所说的"音、形、义"三美译文。

节选《洛神赋》的第二段诗行是洛神向作者倾诉自己的一片衷肠。共五行,行内上下句各六字(上句多语助词"兮"),两两对仗,押"ang"韵。显而易见,两位译者都考虑到了原赋的语言特色,译诗都尽量使用英诗的六音步诗行,实现译文和原赋在音节特点上的对等;同时两位译者试图在每个诗行中,使上下句押韵。当然,在语义层面上,康译(译文1)采取了一贯的逐字逐词翻译的方法,原赋中的每个字词几乎都可以在译文中找到对应的英译。例如:良会——good tryst;异乡——different realms;微情——slightest feeling;江南——Yangtze south;潜处——dwell submerged;寄心——lodge my heart 等。相较而言,宇文所安采取了意译的策略,更多时候放弃了词汇短语的对等,使用了更自然更易于西方读者理解的英语表达方式。两位译者都是汉学之集大成者,此段译文意思准确,情绪、内容传递到位,策略上虽有差异,却各有特色,不相伯仲。

《文选》经典篇章英译选读之五

《文赋》(节选)

陆 机

诗缘情而绮靡①,赋体物而浏亮②。碑披文以相质③,诔缠绵④而凄怆。铭博约而温润⑤,箴⑥顿挫而清壮。颂优游以彬蔚⑦,论精微而朗畅。奏平彻以闲雅,说炜晔而谲诳⑧。虽区分之在兹,亦禁邪而制放⑨。要辞达而理举⑩,故无取乎冗长。

其为物也多姿,其为体也屡迁;其会意也尚巧⑪,其遣言⑫也贵妍。暨音声之迭代⑬,若五色之相宣⑭。虽逝止之无常⑮,故崎锜而难便⑯。苟达变而识次⑰,犹开流以纳泉⑱。如失机而后会,恒操末以续颠⑲。谬玄黄之秩叙⑳,故淟涊㉑而不鲜。

注:以上文字节选自《文赋》。作者陆机(261年—303年),字士衡,吴郡吴县(今江苏省苏州市)人,西晋著名的文学家、书法家。陆机为孙吴丞相陆逊之孙,其父陆抗是吴国大司马,吴灭亡后投降西晋。陆机由于博学多才而倾动一时,与其弟陆云合称"二陆"。曾历任平原内史、祭酒、著作郎等职,世称"陆平原"。其诗文多重藻绘排偶,且多拟古之作,在西晋文坛上负有盛名。著述除《文赋》外,还有史学著作《晋纪》《吴书》《洛阳记》《吴章》等,均已亡佚。其《平复帖》是中国古代存世最早的名人书法真迹。《文赋》是陆机所创作的文艺理论作品,也是我国文论史上第一篇系统的创作论。梁代刘勰的《文心雕龙》曾受其影响。

【注释】

①〔缘情〕因情。〔绮靡(qǐ mí)〕华丽,浮艳(多指诗文)。

第七章 《文选》经典篇章英译选读

② 〔体物〕状物,即表现事物。〔浏(liú)亮〕清朗明亮。
③ 〔披〕载。〔相质〕即文与人相称。
④ 〔诔(lěi)〕表哀祭的一种文体。〔缠绵〕(多指病或感情)不能脱解,此指文章的基调哀婉忧伤。
⑤ 〔铭〕刻在青铜、石器上用以记功的文体。〔博约〕文章内容广博,言简意明。〔温润〕温和柔润。
⑥ 〔箴(zhēn)〕古代一种规诫性的文体,以讥刺得失,故顿挫清壮。
⑦ 〔颂〕一种颂扬的文体。〔彬蔚(bīn wèi)〕文质华盛的样子。
⑧ 〔炜晔(wěi yè)〕谓文辞明丽晓畅,亦作"炜烨"。〔谲诳(jué kuáng)〕诡谲,有夸张诡辩之意。
⑨ 〔禁邪〕禁止邪说。〔放〕放纵。〔制放〕制止荒诞。
⑩ 〔辞达〕语言通畅。〔举〕显出。
⑪ 〔会意〕立意。〔尚巧〕崇尚奇巧。
⑫ 〔遣言〕犹遣词,即运用语言。
⑬ 〔暨(jì)〕至,到。〔迭代〕相互替换。音声之迭代指文辞更替。
⑭ 〔五色〕本指青、黄、赤、白、黑五种颜色,后泛指各种颜色。〔相宣〕互相映衬而显现。
⑮ 〔逝止〕去留,指语辞取舍。〔无常〕无穷。
⑯ 〔崎锜(qí yǐ)〕艰险不安,引申为曲解附会。〔难便〕不适合。
⑰ 〔达变〕通达变化之道。〔识次〕认识事物的次序。
⑱ 〔开流〕凿开河流,疏通河道。〔纳泉〕引入泉流。
⑲ 〔末〕末尾。〔颠〕头顶,最高最初的部分。此意为使头尾颠倒,首尾混乱。
⑳ 〔谬〕弄错。〔玄黄〕本义指天地的颜色,玄为天色,黄为地色。此指彩色的丝织物,丝帛。〔秩叙〕犹秩序,次第。
㉑ 〔涊淟(tiǎn niǎn)〕污浊,卑劣;垢浊混沌,不鲜明的样子。

白话释义

诗是用来抒发思想和情感的文体,所以要辞藻华丽、感情细腻;赋是用来描述和表现事物的文体,所以要条理清晰、语言清朗。碑是用来刻记人物功德的文体,所以必须人文相称;诔是用来哀悼死者的文体,所以情调应该缠绵凄怆。铭是用以记载功劳的文体,所以要言简意深、温和顺畅;箴是用以讽谏得失的文体,所以要抑扬顿挫、理清辞壮。颂是用来歌功颂德的文体,所以要从容舒缓、辞藻华美；论是用来评述是非功过的文体，所以要精辟缜密、语言流畅。奏是向君王陈情叙事的文体，所以要言辞平和、说理透彻；说是以论辩说理，所以文意奇诡、辞彩鲜亮。虽然文体的区分大致如此，但是不同文体的共同要求是禁止邪放。要辞义畅达、说理透彻，就要切记不能冗长。

　　文章表现事物的千姿百态，它的格式也变化无常。创作的立意崇尚奇巧，运用文辞贵在华美，音调高低相互交替，就好像五色配合在一起相得益彰。虽然取舍本无定律，文辞搭配很难调适，但如果明白了变化的规律、次序，行文就像凿开河流将水引入清泉般自然。假如错过变化的时机再去凑合，就好像以尾续首，颠倒混乱。如果处理不当，如同不懂颜料及其搭配一样，文章就混浊不清，失去了应有的光彩。

英译1

　　Poems follow from feeling, they are sensuous, fine;
Poetic expositions give forms of things, clear and bright;
　　Stele inscriptions unfurl patterns to match substance;
　　　　Lamentations swell with pent-up sorrow;
　　Inscriptions are broad and concise, warm and gentle;
　　　Admonitions repress, being forceful and sharp;
　　　　Odes move with grand ease, being opulent;
　　　　Essays treat essence, expansive and lucid;
　Statements to the throne are even, incisive, dignified, calm;
　　　Persuasions are flashy, deluding, entrancing.
　　　　Though fine distinctions are made in these,
　　　　They forbid deviation, restrain rash impulse.
　Ask that words attain their ends, that principle come forth;
　　　Have nothing to do with long-winded excess.

　　　　　　In things there are many stances,
　　　　　　In forms there are frequent shiftings.
　　　　When shaping conceptions, value deft craft,
　　　　　　In delivering words, honor allure.
　　　　When it comes to the alternation of sounds,

第七章 《文选》经典篇章英译选读

They are like the five colors, each sets off the other:
Though there is no law in their passing or halting—
A rocky path, one that we cannot make easy—
Still, if one grasps variation and knows succession,
It is like opening channels to draw in a stream.
If you miss your chance, draw together too slowly,
Your beginnings will always be following ends.
Errors in orientation of Earth and of Heaven
Bring mere muddiness and no vividness.

——Stephen Owen（宇文所安）

英译2

Lyric poetry springs from feelings and is exquisitely ornate;
The rhapsody gives form to an object, and is limpid and clear.
The epitaph displays outer form to support substance;
The dirge wrenches the heart and is mournful and sad.
The inscription is broad yet concise, gentle and smooth;
The admonition restrains, and is crisp and bold.
The eulogy is dignified and relaxed, lush and luxuriant;
The treatise is subtle and exact, pellucid and coherent.
The memorial is calm and clear, refined and elegant;
The discourse dazzles and glitters but is deceptive and deceitful.
Although there are distinctions among these forms,
They all repress the wayward, control wild abandon.
Words must convey meaning, and principle must be properly set forth;
Thus, there is no need for prolix verbiage.
It is the nature of things to take on many postures,
And forms are frequently changing.
In putting together the ideas, craft is foremost;
In arranging words, beauty is paramount.
When it comes to the sounds, they should alternate,

Just as the five colors enhance one another.
Although they depart on remain by no fixed rule,
And truly follow a tortuous path hard to make smooth,
If one can understand the variations and know the proper order,
It would be like opening a channel to receive the spring.
But if one loses the moment and misses the opportunity,
He will always place the end following the head.
If one disorders the proper sequence of black and yellow,
Things look muddied and mired, lacking in clarity.

——David R. Knechtges（康达维）

英译鉴赏简评

作为我国文论史上第一篇系统的文学理论文献，《文赋》兼具"批评"之理性与"赋"之艺术性的双重特征。不同于一般的社会、哲学思想典籍，《文赋》包含大量的具有中国特色的文学理论专业术语，翻译难度非一般文体可比。其目标读者群体较为单一，如不具备一定的中国文学理论背景知识，要理解《文赋》就并非易事。因此，以上两位学者均采用了学术翻译的方法——即厚重翻译策略来翻译《文赋》，译文后均附有详细的注释和评论。康译后附有大量对照注释，宇文译本则逐段附有大量解释，两位译者都充分利用了历代积累起来的训诂注疏等成果，最大限度地缩短读者与译文的距离，为西方读者诠释原文中的语言难点（因篇幅所限，此处译文没有提供两位学者所附的注释和解释）。

对于文化负载词和固定术语的翻译，宇文所安和康维达采取了极具特色的两种译法。宇文所安采取意译法，将"诗、赋、碑、箴"等文体分别译为"poems, poetic explications, stele inscriptions, admonitions"等等，用文体概念的内涵来翻译文体概念。在西方文论中，除了"poem"表示诗歌一大文类，"poetic explication, stele inscription, admonition"等都不是西方文体概念。所以，宇文所安的译法在语义上较为准确，但是不易被西方读者理解。相反地，康维达对文体名称的翻译则借用了西方文论中常用的概念名称。例如，将"诗、赋、碑、箴"译为"lyric poetry, rhapsody, epitaph, dirge"等等。"lyric poetry"是抒情诗，"rhapsody"本为古希腊叙事史诗（epic poem）的一种，"epitaph"指"碑文、祭文，（尤指）墓志铭"，"dirge"指"挽歌，哀乐"。这种归化译法虽然弥补了宇文

第七章 《文选》经典篇章英译选读

所安译法的缺点,但是这些对应的中西文体概念在内涵上并不完全吻合,其过强的民族性容易使西方读者忽略中国古典文体的特色。

本章课后练习

一、请尝试翻译以下句子。

1. 东家之子,增之一分则太长,减之一分则太短。著粉则太白,施朱则太赤。眉如翠羽,肌如白雪;腰如束素,齿如含贝;嫣然一笑,惑阳城,迷下蔡。(《登徒子好色赋》宋玉)

    白话释义:
    英译:

2. 自仲秋而在疚兮,逾履霜以践冰。雪霏霏而骤落兮,风冽冽而夙兴。雷泠泠以夜下兮,水溓溓以微凝。(《寡妇赋》潘岳)

    白话释义:
    英译:

3. 惟西域之灵鸟兮,挺自然之奇姿。体金精之妙质兮,合火德之明辉(晖)。性辩慧而能言兮,才聪明以识机。故其嬉游高峻,栖跱幽深。飞不妄集,翔必择林。绀趾丹觜,绿衣翠衿。采采丽容,咬咬好音。虽同族于羽毛,固殊智而异心。(《鹦鹉赋》祢衡)

    白话释义:
    英译:

4. 若乃凉夜自凄,风篁成韵。亲懿莫从,羁孤递进。聆皋禽之夕闻,听朔管之秋引。于是弦桐练响,音容选和。徘徊《房露》,惆怅《阳阿》。(《月赋》谢庄)

    白话释义:
    英译:

5. 前开唐中,弥望广潒。顾临太液,沧池漭沆。渐台立于中央,赫昈昈以弘敞。清渊洋洋,神山峨峨。列瀛洲与方丈,夹蓬莱而骈罗。上林岑以垒嶵,下崭严以岩齖。长风激于别岛,起洪涛而扬波。浸石菌于重涯,濯灵芝以朱柯。(《西京赋》张衡)

白话释义：

英译：

二、请比较以下名段两种英译文本的异同。

1. 万物变化兮,固无休息。斡流而迁兮,或推而还。形气转续兮,变化而嬗。沕穆无穷兮,胡可胜言! 祸兮福所倚,福兮祸所伏。忧喜聚门兮,吉凶同域。彼吴强大兮,夫差以败。越栖会稽兮,勾践霸世。(《鹏鸟赋》贾谊)

英译1：

All things alter and change,
Never a moment of ceasing,
Revolving, whirling, and rolling away,
Driven far off and returning again,
Form and breath passing onward,
Like the mutations of a cicada.
Profound, subtle, and illimitable,
Who can finish describing it?
Good luck must be followed by bad,
Bad in turn bow to good.
Sorrow and joy throng the gate,
Weal and woe in the same land.
Wu was powerful and great;
Under Fu-ch'a it sank in defeat.
Yüeh was crushed at K'uai-chi,
But Kou-chien made it an overlord.

——Burton Watson（华兹生）

英译2：

The myriad things change and transform,
Verily without cease or rest.
Swirling, coursing, shifting,
At times thrusting forward, then turning back.
Matter and spirit follow one upon another,

第七章 《文选》经典篇章英译选读

Changing, transforming, and transmuting.
The process is dark and deep, unending;
How can one express it in words?
Disaster is where good fortune rests;
Good fortune is where disaster lurks.
Grief and joy crowd the gate;
Good luck and bad share the realm.
Wu was powerful and strong,
But Fucha met with defeat.
Yue took refuge on Guiji,
Yet Goujian was acclaimed hegemony over the world.

——David R. Knechtges（康达维）

2. 夫庶人之风，塕然起于穷巷之间，堀堁扬尘，勃郁烦冤，冲孔袭门。动沙堁，吹死灰，骇混浊，扬腐馀，邪薄入瓮牖，至于室庐。(《风赋》宋玉)

英译1：

The wind of the common people
Comes whirling from the lanes and alleys,
Poking in the rubbish, stirring up the dust,
Fretting and worrying its way along.
It creeps into holes and knocks on doors,
Scatters sand, blows ashes about,
Muddles in dirt and tosses up bits of filth.
It sidles through hovel windows
And slips into cottage rooms.

——Burton Watson（华兹生）

英译2：

The wind of the common people
Gustily rises from a remote lane
Scooping out grime, raising dust.

223

  Sullen and sad, fretting and fuming,
  It dashes through holes, invades doors,
    Stirring up sand piles,
    Blowing dead embers,
  Throwing up filth and muck,
   Blowing rotten residue.
 In oblique attack, it enters jar-windows,
   Reaching into cottage rooms.

——David R. Knechtges（康达维）

3. 叹匏瓜之无匹兮,咏牵牛之独处。扬轻袿之猗靡兮,翳修袖以延伫。体迅飞凫,飘忽若神,陵波微步,罗袜生尘。动无常则,若危若安。进止难期,若往若还。转眄流精,光润玉颜。含辞未吐,气若幽兰。华容婀娜,令我忘餐。(《洛神赋》曹植)

英译1：
   Sighs that the Gourd Star has no spouse,
  Laments that the Herdboy must live alone.
   Lifting the rare fabric of her thin jacket,
She makes a shield of her long sleeve, pausing in hesitation,
   Body nimbler than a winging duck,
   Swift, as befits the spirit she is;
   Traversing the waves in tiny steps,
   Her gauze slippers seem to stir a dust.
  Her movements have no constant pattern,
    Now unsteady, now sedate;
  Hard to predict are her starts and hesitations,
    Now advancing, now turning back.
   Her roving glanceflashes fire;
A radiant warmth shines from her jade-like face.
  Her words, held back, remain unvoiced,
Her breath scented as though with hidden orchids;
   Her fair face all loveliness—

第七章 《文选》经典篇章英译选读

She makes me forget my hunger!

——Burton Watson（华兹生）

英译 2：

She sighs that the Gourd Star has no mate,
Laments that the Oxherd must dwell alone.
Her light jacket, so delicate and fine, waves in the wind;
Screening her face with a long sleeve, she stands and waits.
Her body, swifter than a soaring duck,
Suddenly drifts away like a god.
Crossing the billows, she walks with dainty steps,
Her gauze slippers stirring up dust.
Her movements follow no constant pattern,
As if precariously poised, then standing steady.
Her advances and stops are hard to predict;
She seems to depart, then returns again.
Her turning gaze reveals a fiery essence;
Her face is bright and sleek as jade.
The words in her mouth are not yet uttered,
Yet her breath is as sweet as dark boneset.
Her lovely countenance so gentle and fair
Makes me forget to eat.

——David R. Knechtges（康达维）

4. 白杨早落，寒草前衰。棱棱霜气，蔌蔌风威。孤蓬自振，惊沙坐飞。灌莽杳而无际，丛薄纷其相依。通池既已夷，峻隅又以颓。直视千里外，唯见起黄埃。凝思寂听，心伤已摧。若夫藻扃黼帐，歌堂舞阁之基；璇渊碧树，弋林钓渚之馆；吴蔡齐秦之声，鱼龙爵马之玩，皆薰歇烬灭，光沉响绝。东都妙姬，南国佳人，蕙心纨质，玉貌绛唇，莫不埋魂幽石，委骨穷尘。岂忆同辇之愉乐，离宫之苦辛哉！（《芜城赋》鲍照）

中华典籍英译选读

英译1：

White poplars shed their leaves early,
Bleak grasses withered long ago;
Breath of frost, keen and biting;
Soo, soo, the bullying of the wind:
A lone tumbleweed trembles by itself,
Puffs of sand for no reason suddenly start up.
Dense copses murky and unending,
A jungle of weeds and brush leaning on each other;
The circling moat caved in long ago,
Towering battlements—they too have tumbled:
One looks straight out a thousand li or more,
Seeing only the whirls of yellow dust.
Dwell on it, listen in silence—
It wounds the heart, breaking it in two.
And so
The painted doors, the gaily stitched hangings,
Sites where once were halls of song, pavilions of the dance,
Jasper pools, trees of jadeite,
Lodges for those who hunt in woods, who fish the shores,
Music of Wu, Ts'ai, Ch'i, Ch'in,
Vessels in shapes of fish and dragon, sparrow and horse—
All have lost their incense, gone to ash,
Their radiance engulfed, their echoes cut off.
Mysterious princess from the Eastern Capital,
Beautiful lady from a southern land,
With heart of orchids, limbs of white lawn,
Marble features, carmine lip—
None whose soul is not entombed in somber stone,
Whose bones do not lie dwindling in the dust.
Do you recall now what joy it was to share your lord's carriage?
The pain of being banished to a palace apart?

——Burton Watson（华兹生）

第七章 《文选》经典篇章英译选读

英译 2：

White poplars early shed their leaves;
Wall grasses prematurely wither.
Bitter and biting is the frosty air;
Roaring and raging, the wind's might.
A lone tumbleweed bestirs itself;
Startled sand flies without cause.
Brushy scrub darkly stretches without end;
Clustered copses wildly intertwine.
The surrounding moat had already been leveled;
The lofty turrets too have fallen.
Looking straight ahead for a thousand miles and beyond,
One only sees rising yellow dust.
Focus one's thoughts, quietly listen:
The heart is pained and broken.
As for
Carved gates, embroidered curtains,
Sites of singing halls and dance pavilions;
Carnelian pools, prase trees,
Lodges of fowling groves and fishing isles;
The music of Wu, Cai, Qi, and Qin,
Amusements of the dragon-fish, ostrich, and horse:
All have vanished in smoke, have been reduced to ashes,
Their brilliance engulfed, their sounds silenced.
Exquisite consorts from the Eastern Capital,
Beauties from southern states,
With hearts of melilot, complexions of white silk,
Jade features, scarlet lips:
There is none whose soul rests unburied in somber stones,
Whose bones lie unscattered in bleak dust.
Can you recall the joyful pleasures of sharing the carriage,
Or the painful misery of the sequestered palace?

——David R. Knechtges（康达维）

5. 遭纷浊而迁逝兮,漫逾纪以迄今。情眷眷而怀归兮,孰忧思之可任？凭轩槛以遥望兮,向北风而开襟。平原远而极目兮,蔽荆山之高岑。路逶迤而修迥兮,川既漾而济深。悲旧乡之壅隔兮,涕横坠而弗禁。昔尼父之在陈兮,有归欤之叹音。钟仪幽而楚奏兮,庄舄显而越吟。人情同于怀土兮,岂穷达而异心！(《登楼赋》王粲)

英译1:

    Encountering tumult and turmoil, I wandered afar;
     A long decade has passed until now.
With my heart longing and languishing, I cherish a return;
    Who can bear such anxious thoughts?
   Leaning on the grilled railing, afar I gaze,
    Face the north wind and open my collar.
The plain distantly stretches as far as the eyes can see,
  But it is obscured by Jing Mountains' high ridges.
    Roads sinuously snake, distant and far;
     Rivers are long, fords are deep.
I am sad to be blocked and cut off from my homeland;
Tears stream down my face, and I cannot hold them back.
     Of old, when Father Ni was in Chen,
    There was his sad cry "Let us return!"
   When imprisoned, Zhong Yi played a Chu tune;
  Though eminent, Zhuang Xi intoned the songs of Yue.
All men share the emotion of yearning for their lands;
  How can adversity or success alter the heart?

          ——David R. Knechtges（康达维）

英译2:

     Facing troubled times, I set off to wander;
   Twelve years and more have slipped by since then;
  Thoughts forever taken up with memories of home,
    Who can endure such longing and pain?
    Propped on the railing, I gaze into the distance,

第七章 《文选》经典篇章英译选读

Fronting the north wind, collar open wide.
The plain is far-reaching, and though I strain my eyes,
They are blocked by tall peaks of the mountains of Ching.
The road winds back and forth, endless in its turning;
Rivers are wide and deep where one would ford.
I hate to be so cut off from my native land;
Tears keep coming in streams I am helpless to check.
Confucius long ago in Ch'en
Cried out in sorrow, "Let me return!"
Chung Yi, imprisoned, played the music of Ch'u;
Chuang Hsieh, though honored, sang the songs of Yüeh.
All shared this feeling, the yearning for home—
Neither success nor failure can change the heart.

——Burton Watson（华兹生）

三、段落试译。

黯然销魂者，唯别而已矣！况秦吴兮绝国，复燕宋兮千里。或春苔兮始生，乍秋风兮暂起。是以行子肠断，百感凄恻。风萧萧而异响，云漫漫而奇色。舟凝滞于水滨，车逶迟于山侧。棹容与而讵前，马寒鸣而不息。掩金觞而谁御，横玉柱而沾轼。居人愁卧，怳若有亡。日下壁而沉彩，月上轩而飞光。见红兰之受露，望青楸之离霜。巡曾楹而空掩，抚锦幕而虚凉。知离梦之踯躅，意别魂之飞扬。故别虽一绪，事乃万族。

（《别赋》江淹）

（傲）邀坟素之长圃，步先哲之高衢。虽吾颜之云厚，犹内愧于宁蘧。有道吾不仕，无道吾不愚。何巧智之不足，而拙艰之有余也！于是退而闲居，于洛之涘。身齐逸民，名缀下士。陪京溯伊，面郊后市。浮梁黝以径度，灵台杰其高峙。窥天文之秘奥，睹人事之终始。其西则有元戎禁营，玄幕绿徽，溪子巨黍，异 同机，炮石雷骇，激矢虹飞，以先启行，耀我皇威。其东则有明堂辟雍，清穆敞闲，环林萦映，圆海回渊，聿追孝以严父，宗文考以配天。

（《闲居赋》潘岳）

第八章

《文心雕龙》经典篇章英译选读

【导读】

　　《文心雕龙》为南朝齐梁之际的刘勰创作的文学评论作品,堪称中国文学批评史上首屈一指的鸿篇巨制。清代学者章学诚称"《文心》体大而虑周……专门著述,自非学富才优,为之不易。"该部作品对中国古代文学创作,对当代历史文化文学研究等,产生了重大而深远的影响,是中国古典文学,甚至现当代文学的研究者案头必备的阅读书目之一。

　　《文心雕龙》在齐梁时期的文学圈所受的重视度可能不高。有学者认为原因之一在于,刘勰在当时只不过是一位名不见经传的微寒之辈,其社会地位和影响力不足以让该部作品受到大范围的关注。另一方面,可能在于《文心雕龙》带有更多的"僧院之气",无法融入当时的主流文学创作、评论和论争圈子。清代以降,人们对于该部作品的关注度逐渐升温,相关学术研究成果较之前各朝各代均显著增多。根据镇江"文心雕龙资料中心"的数据,1907 年至 2004 年,有关《文心雕龙》的论文近三千篇,出版专著二百一十多种,涉及十多个国家。而当前对该部作品的研究成果更是翻空出奇、新说涌出、蹊径迭筑,学术界的"龙学"流派,可谓前有古人后有来者,赓续不断。美国汉学家宇文所安先生亦曾指出,"清以前的重要文学批评和理论著述很少把《文心雕龙》作为权威著作来引述,该书在清以前的地位与它在今天的地位不可同日而语"。

　　刘勰生卒年及其创作《文心雕龙》的确切时间史料阙载。据范文澜先生考证,刘勰大概生于公元 456 年,卒于公元 520 至公元 521 年间。另据清代学者

第八章 《文心雕龙》经典篇章英译选读

刘毓崧考证,《文》大约完成于公元501至公元502年间。《梁书·列传(第四十四)》载:"勰早孤,笃志好学,家贫不婚娶,依沙门僧祐,与之居处,积十余年,遂博通经论,因区别部类,录而序之。今定林寺经藏,勰所定也。"刘勰在该书《序志》章里首先解释了该书名之来由,同时说明创作该部作品的意图和目的:"夫'文心'者,言为文之用心也。……古来文章,以雕缛成体,岂取驺奭之群言雕龙也。夫宇宙绵邈,黎献纷杂,拔萃出类,智术而已。岁月飘忽,性灵不居,腾声飞实,制作而已。夫人肖貌天地,禀性五才,拟耳目于日月,方声气乎风雷,其超出万物,亦已灵矣。形同草木之脆,名逾金石之坚,是以君子处世,树德建言,岂好辩哉?不得已也!……盖《文心》之作也,本乎道,师乎圣,体乎经,酌乎纬,变乎骚,文之枢纽,亦云极矣。大意是说,作文,为人之心声;文章,要靠雕龙(缛),所谓"言之无文行之不远"。人生在世,犹如草木,易折易逝,因此要师法圣人,以经为体,学习《诗经》,效法《楚辞》,用文章弘传自然之道,所谓"雁过留声,人过留名",如此才可能名传万世,启谕后学。据学者推测,刘勰创作此部著作时,不过"三十而立",却因家贫,不曾婚娶,因此,无家无妻无子的刘勰,宅居于南朝齐都城建康之定林寺,与青灯作伴,以古佛为侣,晓看幽篁抚阑,暮听佛鼓穿堂,数十年如一日,不问世间繁华,心无旁骛地创作出中国文学批评史上这一部被传颂千载的嚆矢之作。

《文心雕龙》一书共五十篇,体例如表8-1所示。

表8-1 《文心雕龙》体例

章节	体例说明
卷一·原道 卷二·征圣 卷三·宗经 卷四·正纬 卷五·辨骚	前五篇为"文之枢纽",阐释文学创作的总体指导原则。五经(《诗》《书》《礼》《易》《春秋》)乃圣人之文,文章之首,是为文之要道,经世之根本。
卷六·明诗 卷七·乐府 卷八·诠赋 卷九·颂赞 卷十·祝盟 卷十一·铭箴 卷十二·诔碑	梳理历朝历代的诗歌、辞赋、论说、书信等各种文学体裁的不同风格、流派、特色、创作文理、美学价值、鉴赏技巧等,指导当时学人的文学创作。

续表

章节	体例说明
卷十三·哀吊 卷十四·杂文 卷十五·谐讔 卷十六·史传 卷十七·诸子 卷十八·论说 卷十九·诏策 卷二十·檄移 卷二十一·封禅 卷二十二·章表 卷二十三·奏启 卷二十四·议对 卷二十五·书记	
卷二十六·神思 卷二十七·体性 卷二十八·风骨 卷二十九·通变 卷三十·定势 卷三十一·情采 卷三十二·熔裁 卷三十三·声律 卷三十四·章句 卷三十五·丽辞 卷三十六·比兴 卷三十七·夸饰 卷三十八·事类 卷三十九·练字 卷四十·隐秀 卷四十一·指瑕 卷四十二·养气 卷四十三·附会 卷四十四·总术	泛论写作风格,阐述写作之道,包括遣词造句、构思布局、修辞之术等较为宏观的理论和原则。

第八章 《文心雕龙》经典篇章英译选读

续表

章节	体例说明
卷四十五·时序 卷四十六·物色 卷四十七·才略 卷四十八·知音 卷四十九·程器	杂论性质,讨论文学与时代、自然景物之关系,历代作家的品德与才能,文学批评应有的态度与方法,创作修养的重要性等。
卷五十·序志	全书总序,阐释创作意图,所谓"形同草木之脆,名逾金石之坚,是以君子处世,树德建言",体现出刘勰积极的入世思想。

实际上,刘勰在创作此书时,其体例编排的意图和思路如何,至今仍无确论。稍加注意,读者就会发现,起提纲挈领作用的《序志》一章,却被编排在书末,这与大多数古代作品章节次序不大相似。多数学者认为《文心雕龙》是一部深度梳理和剖析中国古代文学创作理论的作品,但这部作品实际也是刘勰抒发政治情怀、表达仕途愿望的政治性作品,书中不少篇章字里行间都蕴含着作者浓郁的儒家思想和"入仕情结"。如众所知,中国传统儒家思想本身就包含着修身、齐家、治国、平天下的"入仕"之论。"从《文》全书涉及的内容看,他(刘勰)对于经、史、子、集四部的许多典籍,都相当熟悉。"刘勰比较尊崇佛学,同时又通达儒学,谙熟儒家各类经典,可谓"半儒半佛",这种儒佛交织的思想倾向在全书不同篇章多有体现。虽如此,刘勰并不太过于倡导或执念于任一端,他只是注重从儒家和佛教中吸取有益成分,以助推个体的为文之道,倡导作家的作文之理,挖掘作品的人性光辉,彰显其"文学即人学"的人文主张,因此,龙学专家杨国斌先生称其为"人文主义的批评家"。

由此看来,在《序志》一章,刘勰提到的"形同草木之脆,名逾金石之坚,是以君子处世,树德建言",也许可视为其政治追求的最好总结,放在全书最后一章,与前五章有首尾呼应之用:"长怀《序志》,以驭群篇,下篇以下,毛目显矣。位理定名,彰乎《大易》之数,其为文用,四十九篇而已。"这种"总——分——总"的总体架构,严丝密合、前后贯通,可能也是《文心雕龙》整个体例编排的一种动机。

从文体属性来看,《文心雕龙》当归为文学批评一类,但实际上,它又不单纯是一部批评性作品,其语言词句仍带有非常鲜明的魏晋南北朝时期骈俪文体的诸多特质,突显"齐梁之绮缛"。若撇开文学批评这一视角,以纯文学的眼光去品读它,仍能令人感受到刘勰驾驭骈俪文字游刃有余的能力和高超谑美的艺术手段。譬如,刘勰对思想与语言关系的独到见解,"心生而言立,言立而文明,自然之道也。"(《文心雕龙·原道》)"登山则情满于山,观海则意溢于海"(《文心雕龙·神思》),是自然美景与人类精神世界碰撞后的视觉之美;"昭昭若日月之明,离离如星辰之行"(《文心雕龙·宗经》)是刘勰对君子至高道德境界的歌咏;"权衡损益,斟酌浓淡。芟繁剪秽,弛于负担"(《文心雕龙·熔裁》)是刘勰对创作行为提出的黄金法则;"主佐合德,文采必霸"(《文心雕龙·事类》)强调人的文才应与后天的学习相辅相成,这样才能做到"言之有文行之方远";"吟咏之间,吐纳珠玉之声。眉睫之前,卷舒风云之色。"(《文心雕龙·神思》)描摹了诗赋创作者出神入化的艺术掠影;"谈欢则字与笑并,论戚则声共泣偕。"(《文心雕龙·夸饰》)诠释了文章与作者(读者)情感共鸣的密切关系。欢快的文章,字里行间都是笑容;悲伤的文章,词句无不充满着泪水……

近代民主人士,著名语言学家黄季刚(黄侃)先生对《文心雕龙》的评价最高。他说:"论文之书,鲜有专籍。自桓谭《新论》,王充《论衡》,杂论篇章。继此以降,作者间出,然文或湮阙,有如《流别》《翰林》之类;语或简括,有如《典论》《文赋》之俦。其敷陈详覆,征证丰多,枝叶扶疏,原流粲然者,惟刘氏《文心》一书耳。"美国汉学家李又安(Adele Austin Rickett)称《文心雕龙》是中国文学史上第一部也是唯一的一部文学批评著作。美国著名汉学家宇文所安(Stephen Owen)先生甚至认为《文心雕龙》"开动了5世纪的修辞和分析技术的机器。刘勰的天才表现在他驾驭这一解说机器的高超本领"。可见《文心雕龙》在中国文学批评史上的地位,连同它无与伦比的文学气质和修辞技巧,实非其他著作可比肩。

近一个世纪以来,由于历史、军事、政治、文化等各种综合因素,中西文化之间的沟通频率较前大为增加,渠道呈现多样化多维度特征,因此,中外学者对《文心雕龙》的研究亦呈现多元化。学者打破《文心雕龙》作为一部文学批评理论这样比较单一的认识,从不同层面深度挖掘该部著作其他方面的价值,比如研究其"骈体文"的风格、历史渊源,对齐梁以后各朝各代文学创作具体产生的方法论意义和表征;探讨刘勰的个人生平与其作品之间的衍互意义;从该作品中深挖刘勰潜意识中的"入仕"意图;剖析《文心雕龙》与萧统《文选》之间文学观的关联性;比较不同译本的翻译风格和策略等等,既有对全书作宏观层面的综述和批评,亦有就不同章节的不同英译文本作横向对照比较分析的论文和专著,可谓成果丰硕。

《文心雕龙》具体何时传入西方世界,目前尚无定论。多数学者认为其传入西方的时间大致在19世纪下半叶,以1867年伟烈亚力(Alexander Wylie)撰写的《汉籍解题》(*Notes on Chinese Literature*)一书为标志。该书对《文心雕

第八章　《文心雕龙》经典篇章英译选读

龙》有简短评述:"This is looked upon as a work of considerable merit...",意思是说《文》是一部"体大虑周(of considerable merit)"的著作。虽然这在当时影响并不太大,我们仍可以说这是西方研究中国诗学的一个重要开端。《汉籍解题》因此成为《文》首次出现于西方学者视野之中的开启性标志。

在此之后的一个世纪,由西方汉学家、华裔学者,及中国翻译家等完成的《文心雕龙》英语全译本、节译本及专论著作等陆续问世。美国学者对《文心雕龙》的译介和研究经历了从"译介为主,研究为辅"到"研究为主,译介为辅"这一认知上的转变过程。而且其阅读人群和传播范围已开始摆脱精英化小众路线,从传统大学、研究机构逐步扩展到北美各国的主流社会中,并在大众群体中传播开来。

宇文所安先生认为,《文心雕龙》一书在中国现代逐渐受到关注的原因在于"西方传统对于系统诗学的评价甚高",这种因果关系的错置,显然是对中国文学评论的历史认可度不高导致的,对此,我们可以提出反驳意见。但毋庸置疑,从19世纪末期开始,西方学者对《文心雕龙》的译介,在一定程度上反映出西方世界对《文心雕龙》作为文学评论巨著的认可度和接纳度是非同一般的,而且,对现代中国"龙学"研究产生了极大的推动作用。

第一部全译本为华裔学者施友忠先生(Vincent Yu-chung Shih)翻译的 *The Literary Mind and the Carving of Dragons*。此译本开《文心雕龙》英语翻译之先河,受到西方汉学界的一致好评。

另一部重量级的译本(节译)为宇文所安先生的《中国文论:英译与评论》(*Reading in Chinese Literary Thought*),该书选译(节译)了《文心雕龙》的十八个章节:《原道》《宗经》《神思》《体性》《风骨》《通变》《定势》《情采》《镕裁》《章句》《丽辞》《比兴》《隐秀》《附会》《总术》《物色》《知音》《序志》。宇文所安在该书的"中译本序"中说,要"为未来中国文学思想的研究提出一些方向性建议",也许他选择翻译这18章的动机是出于"方向性建议"的考虑。

香港中文大学黄兆杰(Siu-kit Wong)先生与卢仲衡(Allan Chung-hang Lo)、林光泰(Kwong-tai Lam)两位学者合作出版了《文心雕龙》全译本 *The Book of Literary Design*。译本序言部分有这样的评论:"事实上,它如同——的确是——一座前无古人后无来者的丰碑,气势恢宏,卓然于群,详赡而宏富。(Literally looking before and after it sits majestically like a monument—is a monument—monarch of all it surveys, a complete organized work of noble proportions.)"。研究者对该译本有这样的评价:"黄氏的译文后面有不少注解,多为对词句的简单解释及作者翻译过程中的随感,有较大的随意性。乍一看,语言轻松诙谐,贴近西方文化,对初学者而言,可能有一定的吸引力。但是,仔细翻阅起来,除少数注明出处的注释之外,黄兆杰并没有对书中所涉史实、作品、人物等作严肃解释。……总的来说,观此书之译文,译者意识到原文典多义繁,对英文读者而言是很大的挑战,因此有归化的趋向。"

最值得称道的译本为华裔学者杨国斌先生翻译的 *Dragon-Carving and the Literary Mind*。杨先生从 1988 年动笔到 1999 年完成,可谓"十年磨一剑"。在翻译过程中,他不仅参考了《文》一书所有中外汉语底本及各种注释本,还借鉴了翻译界不同的翻译文本,以期带给读者一部详赡可靠,可读性高的全译本。译者匠心,令吾辈敬仰。岭南大学的欧阳桢教授评论说,此英文翻译"可读、清晰,诗意之处适宜,分析之处恰当,可以适于任何感兴趣、有智识的非专业读者。"

其他节选译本或章节性译文主要包括埃尔文·戈登(Erwin Esiah Gordon)的硕士论文《中国古代文学批评的理想模式》(*Some Early Ideals in Chinese Literary Criticism*)中的《原道》篇译文、俄国的柯立夫(Francis Woodman Cleaves)翻译的俄国学者阿历克谢夫(V. M. Alexeev)引用《原道》阐释"文"的一段话、休斯(E. R. Hughes)的著作《文的艺术:论陆机〈文赋〉》附录中的《原道》篇英译。中国著名翻译家杨宪益与戴乃迭夫妇翻译了五个有关文学创作技巧的章节,分别是《神思》《风骨》《情采》《夸饰》《知音》,发表于 *Chinese Literature*。

西方第一部《文心雕龙》论文集为华裔汉学家蔡宗齐先生编写的《中国文学思想:〈文心雕龙〉中的文化、创意与修辞》(*A Chinese Literary Mind: Culture, Creativity, and Rhetoric in Wenxin Diaolong*)。该书为 1997 年 4 月在伊利诺伊斯大学举行的"文心雕龙"研讨会论文集,收录了宇文所安、孙康宜、蔡宗齐、张少康等十余位中西方重量级专家学者有关《文心雕龙》的研究成果,可谓"龙学"研究之"饕餮大餐"。该书前两部分重点阐释刘勰对中国文学传统的剖析和解读;第三部分从现代批判视角入手,深度挖掘刘勰的文学创作理论;第四部分着重分析刘勰有关修辞学的认识和理念。

2004 年,蔡宗齐先生编辑出版了另一部以"六朝美学"为主题的论文集,共收录了十篇论文,《文心雕龙》成为该论文集被多次引述论及的核心汉典文本。

《文心雕龙》从公元 5 世纪传至今日,已历经一千多年。它长盛不衰的原因非一言两语可以解释清楚。但一言以蔽之,《文》一书为读者提供了有关中国古代文学创作理论不同流派、不同风格详赡丰沛的史料性文本,具有非其他文论类作品能够替代的文献学价值;同时,它作为一部语言优美,文字精妙的古文作

第八章 《文心雕龙》经典篇章英译选读

品,带给了读者不可言喻的文学美感和阅读愉悦感。

《文心雕龙》经典篇章英译选读之一

《序志》第五十(节选)

夫"文心"者,言为文之用心也。昔涓子《琴心》①,王孙《巧心》②,心哉美矣,故用之焉。古来文章,以雕缛成体,岂取驺奭③之群言"雕龙"也?夫宇宙绵邈,黎献纷杂④,拔萃出类,智术而已。岁月飘忽,性灵不居,腾声飞实,制作而已。夫肖貌天地,禀性五才,拟耳目于日月,方声气乎风雷,其超出万物,亦已灵矣。形同草木之脆,名逾金石之坚,是以君子处世,树德建言。岂好辩哉?不得已也!

……

盖《文心》之作也,本乎道,师乎圣,体乎经,酌乎纬⑤,变乎骚:文之枢纽,亦云极矣。若乃论文叙笔,则囿别区分⑥,原始以表末,释名以章义,选文以定篇,敷理以举统,上篇以上,纲领明矣。至于剖情析采,笼圈条贯,摛⑦神性⑧,图风势⑨,苞会通⑩,阅声字⑪,崇替于《时序》,褒贬于《才略》,怊怅于《知音》,耿介于《程器》,长怀《序志》,以驭群篇,下篇以下,毛目显矣。位理定名,彰乎《大易》之数⑫,其为文用,四十九篇而已。

夫铨序⑬一文为易,弥纶⑭群言为难,虽复轻采毛发⑮,深极骨髓,或有曲意密源⑯,似近而远,辞所不载,亦不可胜数矣。及其品列成文,有同乎旧谈者,非雷同也,势自不可异也。有异乎前论者,非苟异也,理自不可同也。同之与异,不屑古今,擘肌分理⑰,唯务折衷。按辔⑱文雅之场,环络⑲藻绘之府⑳,亦几乎备矣。但言不尽意,圣人所难;识在瓶管㉑,何能矩矱㉒?茫茫往代,既沈予闻㉓;眇眇㉔来世,倘尘彼观㉕也。

赞㉖曰：

生也有涯，无涯惟智㉗。逐物㉘实难，凭性良易㉙。

傲岸泉石㉚，咀嚼文义。文果载心㉛，余心有寄㉜。

注：本节文字节选自《文心雕龙》第五十章《序志》篇，虽然该篇被置于全书之末，但实际却是全书的自序。主要内容为作者写作本书的意图、主要思想、体例编排和写作方法等，是全书的统领性篇章。

【注释】

①〔涓子〕名环渊，传为老子的弟子。〔《琴心》〕据《文选卷十八》说为环渊所作。

②〔王孙《巧心》〕《汉书·艺文志》儒家类著录《王孙子》一篇，并注："一曰《巧心》。"

③〔䲹奭(shì)〕战国齐国学者，阴阳家，齐之三邹子之一，人称"雕龙奭"。《史记·孟子荀卿列传》："䲹奭者，齐诸䲹子，亦颇采䲹衍之术以纪文。……故齐人颂曰：'谈天衍，雕龙奭。'"裴骃《集解》引刘向《别录》说："䲹奭修衍之文，饰若雕镂龙文，故曰'雕龙'。"

④〔绵邈(mián miǎo)〕辽远，深远。〔黎献(lí xiàn)〕民众中的贤人，有才之士。此句指宇宙无边无际，人才代代无绝，无穷无尽。

⑤〔酌乎纬〕第五篇《正纬》分析了纬书之谬，此言纬书中绮丽的文采可酌采而用。

⑥〔囿(yòu)〕局限，拘泥，此指文体的分类范围。〔区〕同"囿"。此指文章的文体分门别类。

⑦〔摛(chī)〕舒展，散布，发布。

⑧〔神〕指第二十六章《神思》篇，主要讨论人在创作时的思维活动和文章的构思问题。〔性〕指第二十七章《体性》篇，主要讨论文章的体貌风格和作家性情与个性的关系。

⑨〔风〕第二十八章《风骨》篇，主张文章应取法有明朗刚健文风的经、子、史书等优秀作品，摒弃片面追求辞藻的华而不实的骈文体。〔势〕第三十章《定势》篇，主要讨论不同文体所决定的文章体势，即外在的表现形式。

⑩〔会〕指四十三章《附会》篇，讨论如何把内容、文辞等材料连缀组合，形成完整的篇章。〔通〕指第二十九章《通变》篇，篇名源于《易·系辞下》："穷则变，变

第八章 《文心雕龙》经典篇章英译选读

则通,通则久。"此篇强调作文应紧跟变化,质文兼备,宗法经典,随时通变,方能变化出新。

⑪〔声〕指第三十三章《声律》篇,主要讨论文章的声律。〔字〕指第三十九章《练字》篇,主要论述文字的起源、作用,在作文时,应根据字的形状,从视觉美感上审慎地选择用字,以区别美恶。

⑫〔彰〕显,明。《易传·系辞上》:"大衍之数五十,其用四十有九。"彰乎《大易》之数指《文心雕龙》总篇次的数目与《周易》中的"大衍五十之数"相吻合。

⑬〔铨(quán)〕衡量,选用。〔铨序〕指文章顺序排列的选定。

⑭〔弥纶(mí lún)〕统摄,治理,贯通。

⑮〔毛发〕喻指写作中的细枝末节。

⑯〔曲意密源〕曲折的意旨,隐秘的根源。

⑰〔擘(bò)〕剖开,分开。〔理〕肌肉的纹理。擘肌分理指深入细致地加以分析。

⑱〔辔(pèi)〕驾驭牲口的缰绳和嚼子。〔按辔〕紧扣马缰绳,令马缓行或止步。

⑲〔环络〕牵引马辔头环行,此指全面考察创作文章的不同领域。

⑳〔藻绘之府〕府,场所,此指文章创作园地。

㉑〔瓶管〕以瓶汲水,以管窥天,意指偏狭之见。

㉒〔矩矱(jǔ yuē)〕规矩,法度,标准。

㉓〔既沈予闻〕此指作者沉浸于前人的见闻或著述之中。〔沈〕通"沉"。

㉔〔眇眇(miǎo miǎo)〕杳远,渺茫。

㉕〔倘〕也许。〔尘〕刘勰自谦语,指污染了读者的眼睛。〔彼〕后世读者。倘尘彼观的意思是自己的这本著作如果传至后世,会弄脏了后世读者的双眼。

㉖〔赞〕全书每一章最后一段的结语词,用来总结每章的内容。

㉗〔生也有涯,无涯惟智〕语出《庄子·内篇·养生主第三节》:"吾生也有涯,而知也无涯。以有涯随无涯,殆已!"人的生命是有限的,追求知识是无限的。

㉘〔逐物〕追求身外之物。

㉙〔凭性良易〕跟随自己的内心会比较容易。

㉚〔傲岸泉石〕高傲地隐居于大自然中。

㉛〔载心〕文章是内心世界的外化和表现。

㉜〔寄〕寄托。

白话释义

这部作品之所以被称为"文心",在于其是阐明写作时所用之心。从前涓子曾写过一部《琴心》,王孙子也曾写过一部《巧心》,"心"这个词的确精妙,所以用它作这部书的书名。古往今来的文章,均以繁丽的文采写成;现在用"雕龙"二字来命名此书,难道不是取法于前人曾用以称赞驺奭(雕龙奭)富有文采的缘故吗?宇宙无穷无尽,人才则代代不绝;他们所以能超出别人,也无非由于其具有过人的才智罢了。但是时光稍纵即逝,人的智慧却无法永存;如果要让声名和业绩流传下去,就只有借助于写作了。人类的形貌取象于大地,又从五行里获得自己的禀性;耳目如同日月,声气如同风雷。他们能超过一切生物,可算是灵异至极了。但是人的形体同草木一样脆弱,而流传久远的声名却比金石还要坚固,所以一个有理想的人活在世上,定要树立功德,撰述写作,立德立言。我并非喜欢空发议论,只是情非得已啊!

......

创作这部《文心雕龙》的缘由,是从自然之道出发,取法于圣人,根据经典,参鉴纬书,并且探究《楚辞》以来的变化创新,如此方能对于文章的核心通透彻悟。至于各种文章的体裁,有属于"文(韵文)"的,有属于"笔(无韵文)"的,作者都对此分门别类。对于每种文体,都追溯其起源,叙述其演变,阐明体裁名称的意义,并举几篇代表作品加以评论,通过阐述写作原理总结各种文体的基本特点。本书的上篇已经把文章的主要类别都说清楚了。下面再从分析作品的内容和形式方面,概括出理论的体系,陈述"神思"和"体性"问题,说明"风骨"和"定势"问题,包括"附会"以上、"通变"以下的一系列问题,还考察了从"声律"到"练字"等具体问题。此外,又以《时序》篇论述了不同时代文章的盛衰兴废,以《才略》篇指出历代作家文学才华的高低,在《知音》篇十分感慨地说明正确的文学评论之不易,在《程器》篇提出道德品质和政治修养对作家的重要性。最后,用《序志》篇叙述自己的志趣和抱负,并将其作为对全书的总结。本书下篇各篇目大致讲到了文学创作和评论的种种具体问题。安排篇目内容,确定各篇篇名,一共写了五十篇,恰好符合《周易》"大衍五十"这个数目,其中讨论文章本身的,不过四十九篇而已。

评论一篇作品,那是比较容易的,但要综合系统地评论许多作品,就比较困难了。虽然这本书中对文章的表面细节讲得很少,而对重要的问题进行了深入探讨,但仍有某些曲折细微之处,看似浅近,实则深奥异常,因而论述中未能明表,这种情形也为数甚多。至于已经写到书中的意见,有些和前人的说法差不多,并不是有意随声附和,而是事理本身不可能有别的说法;有些和前人的说法不同,这也不是随便提出异说,因为按照道理无法赞同旧说。所以,无论与前人相同或不同,并不在于这些说法是古人的还是今人的,主要是通过具体分析,力

第八章 《文心雕龙》经典篇章英译选读

求找出不偏不倚的正确主张来。作者驰骋在文坛之上,挥洒于艺苑之中,有关问题这里差不多都谈到了。不过语言不易把意思完全表达出来,即使是圣人也感到困难。何况我的见识如此浅陋,怎能立起什么创作的法度呢?从历代的浩瀚著作中,我已深受教益。对于未来未知的读者,这部书也许能供他们作参考。

总之,人生有限,学问却无边无际。要理解事物的真相,的确是有困难的,凭着自然的天性去客观地接触事物,那就比较容易了。因此,要如无拘无束的隐居者那样,傲然于泉石之间,心无旁骛,方能细品文章之意。如果这部书能够表达自己的心意,那我的思想也就有所寄托了。

Preface (*Hsü-chih*) (Excerpt)

The literary mind is that mind which strives after literary forms. In a similar sense, Chüan-tzu long ago wrote *Ch'in-hsin* (The mind of the lute), and Wang-sun wrote *Ch'iao-hsin* (The artistic mind). What an excellent term indeed is "mind!" And because it is, I have used it too. [True], since from time immemorial literary writings have always adopted an ornate style, and yet I am not implicating myself in the type of "dragon carving" practiced by Tsou Shih and his group.

...

In writing the *Wen-hsin tiao-lung* I attempt [in Chapter I] to show how literature has its source in the *Tao*, [in Chapter II] how it takes its model from the Sage, [in Chapter III] how it adopts the pattern of the Classics, [in Chapter IV] how it consults the apocryphal writings, and [in Chapter V] how it experiences some changes in the *Sao*. I have dealt with the crucial factors of literature exhaustively here. In discussing *wen*, or writings which are rhymed, in Chapters V to XIII, and *pi*, unrhymed writings, in Chapters XVI to XXV, I have classified them into separate genres and traced each genre back to its source in order to make clear its development, and I have defined a number of literary terms in order to clarify their meaning. I have selected several literary works for treatment under each specific topic, and have advanced arguments to demonstrate their unity. Thus in the first part of the book a clear general outline is presented. In the analysis of emotions and their literary expressions, I have sought in Chapter XXXI to determine their scope systematically. I have elaborated on the theme of creative thinking in Chapter XXVI, and dealt with the relation between style and nature in Chapter XXVII. I have discussed the unity of content and form (or *feng-ku*) in Chapter XXVIII, and explained how to choose the proper style in Chapter XXX. I have developed the principle of organization in Chapter XLIII, and flexible adaptability to changing requirements in Chapter XXIX, and looked into the use of musical patterns in Chapter XXXIII and the choice of words in Chapter XXXIX. The theme of literary development is treated in Chapter XLV, entitled "Shih-hsü," or "Literary Development and Time," and my own evaluation of several literary talents is presented in Chapter 47 entitled "Ts'ai-lüeh," or "Literary Talents." In Chapter XLVIII, entitled "Chih-yin," or "An Understanding Critic," I express my sad disappointment; and in Chapter XLIX, entitled "Ch'eng-ch'i," or "Capacity of a Vessel," I set forth my impartial verdict on the characters of several literary writers. In this "Hsü-chih," or "Preface," are contained the ideas which sum up all the succeeding chapters. Thus in the second part, from Chapter XXVI onwards, the sub-topics are made clear in all their details. The postulation of principles and definition of terms are shown in the number of the Great Change; but only forty-nine chapters are employed for the elucidation of literature.

  It is easy to evaluate and discuss a specific work of literature, but rather difficult to deal comprehensively and critically with all literary works. Some of them may have forms as light as fur and hair, but yet have content deeper than bone and marrow. There are also works without number whose ideas are implicit rather than explicit and whose source is hidden, neither ideas nor sources being directly expressed in words. In appearance they may look commonplace, but they are in fact very profound. As for my evaluation and ranking of the existing literary works, some of my conclusions are the same as those of former writers. It is not that I copied them, but that it is impossible to differ from them. And if some of my judgments differ from previous ones, it is not that I seek difference for its own sake, but that there are certain reasons why I must differ. But whether identical to or different from previous

第八章 《文心雕龙》经典篇章英译选读

judgments, mine have not been influenced by either the modern or the ancient critics. My sole purpose has been to dissect the muscles and trace the veins of literature and endeavour to discover the proper standard. As for my achievement in coursing through the hunting grounds of literature and looping reins in the palace of rhetoric, I think my work is as exhaustive as can be expected. However, words do not completely express ideas; it is difficult even for the Sage to find it otherwise. If one's knowledge is by nature limited to the capacity of a jar or a tube, how can he be expected to offer all the general principles? As I am deeply imbued in my critical experience with the immense heritage of the past, would the unseen generations after me look upon this heritage as dust?

The Tsan:

Life is limited;

Wisdom alone is without bound.

The pursuit of external things is difficult,

But one will easily succeed if he works in accord with his own nature.

Resolute, like a boulder in a creek I stand

Absorbed in the contemplation of literature.

If literature is truly a vehicle for the mind,

My mind has found a place to rest.

——Vincent Yu-Chung Shih（施友忠）

英译鉴赏简评

《序志》为《文心雕龙》最末一章。为什么序言性章节却放在书末？周振甫先生认为，中国唐代以前的著作，序言位置大多置于书末，但其作用却在于说明该书的创作动机，作者的写作方法，各章节的内容概要，全书的结构布局等。美国汉学家宇文所安先生认为，刘勰在《序志》篇里提到自己原本打算做一个经学家，但感觉自己能力不济，所以最终放弃经学而转向文学研究，因此《序志》篇是刘勰的创作动机和人生志向的一个交代。

华裔学者施友忠先生在其译本 *The Literary Mind and the Carving of Dragons* 中，将《序志》译为"Preface"（英语意为"序言"），并将其从原书最末页调整为英译本的第一页,这种做法符合英语书籍的排版规则,适合西方读者的阅读习惯。词缀"pre-"在英文中本来有"……之前"之意,这样一种安排,看起来只是一种位置的改变,实际上却反映出中西习惯上的不同、作者与译者理解上的不同,以及中英文思维方式的不同。其他如对《文心雕龙》关键词的翻译和理解、英语世界对《文心雕龙》理论体系的误读、《文心雕龙》在英语世界汉学研究者中的影响等,都是非常有意义的话题。这些问题,恰恰可以从英语世界《文心雕龙》的研究状况中得到解答。

海陶玮(James R. Hightower)认为施译的前言部分存在不少问题。虽然施友忠对《文心雕龙》以前的文学传统做了简单的梳理,但他有关诗的道德说教意义的论点却是值得商榷的。此外,施友忠将刘勰称为"经(古)典主义者",并在介绍中运用了"现实主义"、"古典主义"等西方文艺理论术语,却没有作明确的解释。海陶玮认为这种做法可能误导普通读者,同时也会遭到专家质疑,实在欠佳。其实,以西方术语来解释中国文论,施友忠也是实出无奈。当时海外汉学研究仅限于寥寥几个专家,中国文学研究还缺少必要的话语环境,常需借助西方强势话语的核心词汇。当然,这种做法也必然使翻译的质量大打折扣。但是,施友忠之后的不少学者纷纷采用"经典主义"一词来阐释刘勰对文学创作的态度,有的完全利用其传统意义,有的则配合中国文学传统自抒新意。这说明施友忠的观点对后来学者有很大的影响。公正地说,这种影响并非完全消极。

在文学术语的翻译技巧上,施友忠先生竭尽全力让西方读者能够理解对他们而言比较晦涩抽象的中国文论术语,采取"音译+意译"翻译策略,比如将"时序"译为"Shih-hsü, or Literary Development and Time",将"才略"译为"Ts'ai-lüeh, or Literary Talents",将"知音"译为"Chih-yin, or An Understanding Critic"等等。这种翻译策略有助于西方读者理解独特的中华文论术语。此外施译的句式和音韵非常吻合《文心雕龙》的骈文特质,这也是施译的亮点。例如"本乎道,师乎圣,体乎经,酌乎纬,变乎骚"的英译"how literature has its source in the Tao//how it takes its model from the Sage//how it adopts the pattern of the Classics//how it consults the apocryphal writings//how it experiences some changes in the Sao",句式齐整严饬、紧凑和谐,语义与视觉融合一体,可谓上乘之译文。

第八章 《文心雕龙》经典篇章英译选读

《文心雕龙》经典篇章英译选读之二

《神思》第二十六(节选)

　　古人云:"形在江海之上,心存魏阙之下。"①神思之谓也。文之思也,其神远矣。故寂然凝虑,思接千载;悄焉动容,视通万里。吟咏之间,吐纳珠玉之声②;眉睫之前③,卷舒风云之色:其思理之致乎!故思理为妙,神与物游④。神居胸臆⑤,而志气统其关键;物沿耳目,而辞令管其枢机⑥。枢机方通,则物无隐貌;关键将塞,则神有遁心。是以陶钧⑦文思,贵在虚静,疏瀹五藏⑧,澡雪精神⑨。积学以储宝⑩,酌理以富才⑪,研阅以穷照⑫,驯致以绎辞⑬。然后使玄解之宰⑭,寻声律而定墨⑮;独照之匠⑯,窥意象而运斤⑰。此盖驭文之首术,谋篇之大端。

　　夫神思方运,万涂竞萌⑱。规矩虚位⑲,刻镂无形⑳。登山则情满于山㉑,观海则意溢于海㉒,我才之多少,将与风云而并驱矣。方其搦翰㉓,气倍辞前㉔,暨乎篇成㉕,半折心始,何则?意翻空而易奇㉗,言征实而难巧也㉘。是以意授于思,言授于意。密则无际㉙,疏则千里㉚。或理在方寸,而求之域表㉛;或义在咫尺,而思隔山河㉜。是以秉心养术㉝,无务苦虑㉞;含章司契㉟,不必劳情也。

……

　　若夫骏发之士㊱,心总要术,敏在虑前㊲,应机立断;覃思之人㊳,情饶歧路㊴,鉴在疑后,研虑方定㊵。机敏故造次而成功㊶,虑疑故愈久而致绩㊷。难易虽殊,并资博练㊸。若学浅而空迟㊹,才疏而徒速㊺,以斯成器,未之前闻。是以临篇缀虑㊻,必有二患:理郁者苦贫㊼,辞溺者伤乱㊽,然则博见为馈贫之粮㊾,贯一为拯乱之药㊿,博而能一,亦有助乎心力矣。

注:本节文字选自于《文心雕龙》第二十六章《神思》,主要讨论创作者的思维活动与为文之道,集中论述了作者如何打破时空限制,运用美妙的词句再现自然界中鲜活的形象;同时强调创作者在谋篇布局之前的构思,以及如何突破构思的局限。刘勰认为,只有多闻广识、储积知识、勤加练习,才能写出好的文章,这些建议,在今天看来仍然很有教益。本篇中有大量优美隽秀的骈体文句,如"形在江海之上,心存魏阙之下""吟咏之间,吐纳珠玉之声;眉睫之前,卷舒风云之色""登山则情满于山,观海则意溢于海"等。

【注释】

① 〔江海〕代指民间。〔魏阙(què)〕高大的宫殿,代指官府或朝廷。全句意为人在江湖民间,心里却牵挂着功名利禄。
② 〔吐纳珠玉之声〕吟咏自然之美,似乎发出珠玉般清朗的声音。
③ 〔眉睫之前〕眼眉之前。
④ 〔神与物游〕精神随万物自由驰骋。
⑤ 〔神居胸臆〕精神存在于心灵深处。〔臆(yì)〕内心深处。
⑥ 〔枢机〕枢纽。
⑦ 〔陶钧〕制作陶器的轮盘,引申为构思酝酿。
⑧ 〔疏瀹五藏〕疏通心里的障碍。〔瀹(yuè)〕疏导(河道)。〔五藏〕五脏。
⑨ 〔澡雪精神〕洗涤纯净思想。
⑩ 〔积学以储宝〕积累学识,就如同储藏宝藏一样。
⑪ 〔酌理以富才〕斟酌事理,才可以丰富一个人的才情。
⑫ 〔研阅以穷照〕博览研究群书方能参透事理。
⑬ 〔驯致以怿辞〕研读他人的作品以寻找文章的辞理和思路。〔怿(yì)〕厘清事物的头绪。
⑭ 〔玄解之宰〕深得妙理的主宰,即心灵。
⑮ 〔寻声律而定墨〕按照文章之法来审定创作的准绳。
⑯ 〔独照之匠〕有独到见解的匠心。
⑰ 〔运斤〕用斧子,此指娴熟地运用写作技巧。全句意为脑海中的意象通过熟练地运用写作方法呈现于文章之中。
⑱ 〔万涂竞萌〕各种想法竞相涌现。〔涂〕通"途",头绪。〔萌〕呈现。
⑲ 〔规矩〕写作手法。〔虚位〕不确定。
⑳ 〔刻镂无形〕刻画的对象尚未成形。

第八章 《文心雕龙》经典篇章英译选读

㉑〔登山则情满于山〕一想到登山,心里便形成对山的美好风光的描画。
㉒〔观海则意溢于海〕一想到观海,心里便有了大海波澜壮阔的景象。
㉓〔搦(nuò)〕拿,捏;挑动,引起。〔翰[hàn]〕长而硬的羽毛,古人用来写字,后指书信、文章等。〔搦翰〕提笔写作。
㉔〔气倍辞前〕创作的才气在提笔开始写作时充沛而高涨。
㉕〔暨乎篇成〕等到文章创作完成。〔暨(jì)〕至,到。
㉖〔半折心始〕写完的文章只能到达开始创作时心气的一半。〔半折〕打对折。
㉗〔意翻空而易奇〕意念仅存在于脑海中时,比较新奇。
㉘〔言征实而难巧也〕语言是实实在在的,就很难做到新奇无比了。
㉙〔密则无际〕构思缜密,文章就会天衣无缝。
㉚〔疏则千里〕构思粗疏,就会千里之别。
㉛〔求之域表〕去遥远的地方寻求(构思)。〔域表〕遥远的地方。
㉜〔思隔山河〕思路(实际在眼前)却遥隔山河。
㉝〔秉心养术〕控制精神意念,蓄养方法技巧。
㉞〔务〕从事,致力于。〔无务苦虑〕没有必要绞尽脑汁,苦思冥想。
㉟〔含章〕借由写作表现美好的事物。〔司契〕掌握规则方法。
㊱〔骏发之士〕才思敏捷之人。
㊲〔敏在虑前〕反应灵敏,无须反复思虑。
㊳〔覃思之人〕构思迟缓之人。〔覃(tán)〕深,延迟。
㊴〔情饶歧路〕思路纷繁多歧。
㊵〔研虑方定〕深思熟虑后才作出决定。
㊶〔机敏故造次而成功〕机敏决断之人可以在短时间内完成作品。
㊷〔虑疑故愈久而致绩〕犹疑不决的人,需要更久的时间才可完成创作。
㊸〔难易虽殊,并资博练〕写作有难有易,都需要勤学苦练。
㊹〔学浅而空迟〕学问浅陋,只是写得慢。
㊺〔才疏而徒速〕才疏学浅却写得匆促。
㊻〔临篇缀虑〕临到写作才开始构思。
㊼〔理郁者苦贫〕思路郁结者缺乏灵动的思想。
㊽〔辞溺者伤乱〕滥用辞藻者文章杂乱。
㊾〔博见为馈贫之粮〕博识广闻是解决思路贫乏者的食粮。
㊿〔贯一为拯乱之药〕主旨连贯统一是解决文章杂乱的良药。

白话释义

古人曾说："有的人身在江湖，心神却系念着朝廷。"这里说的就是精神上的活动（神思）。作家写作构思时，他的精神活动也是无边无际的。所以当作家静静地思考时，他可以联想到千年之前；而在他的容颜隐隐地有所变化时，其视野已到达万里之外了。作家在吟哦推敲之中，就像听到了珠玉般悦耳动听的声音；当他注目凝思之时，眼前就出现了风云般变幻的景色。这就是构思的效果啊！由此可见，构思的妙处，是在使作家的精神与物象融会贯通。精神蕴藏在内心，却为人的情志和气质所支配；外物接触到作者的耳目，主要靠优美的语言来表达。如果语言运用得当，那么事物的形貌就可完全刻画出来；若是支配精神的关键有了阻塞，那么精神就无法集中了。因此，在进行构思时，必须做到沉寂宁静，思考专一，使内心通畅，精神净化。为了做好构思工作，首先要认真学习以积累自己的知识，其次要辨明事理来丰富自己的才华，再次要参考自己的生活经验来获得对事物的彻底理解，最后要训练自己的情致来恰切地运用文辞。这样才能使深得奥理的心灵探索并寻找写作的规则来审定创作的标准。正如一个有独到见解的工匠，根据想象中的样子来运用工具进行创作一样。这是写作的主要手法，也是考虑全篇布局时必须注意的要点。在作家开始构思时，无数的意念都会涌上心头，作家要对这些抽象的意念给以具体的形态，把尚未定型的事物都精雕细刻起来。作家一想到登山，脑海中便充满山的秀色；一想到观海，心里便洋溢着海的奇观。不管作者才华的多寡，他的构思都可以随着流风浮云而任意驰骋。在他提笔之时，旺盛的气势远超文辞本身；等到文章写就之时，却不及开始预想的一半。为何会如此呢？因为文意出于想象，所以容易获得奇思；但语言重在务实，所以难以见巧。由此可见，文章的内容来自作者的构思，而语言又受制于文思。如果三者结合得密切，就天衣无缝，否则就会远隔千里。有时某些道理就在自己心里，却反而到千里之外去求索；有时某些意思本来就在跟前，却又像远隔山河，无法企及。所以要驾驭好自己的心灵，锻炼好写作的方法，无须苦苦萦索；应掌握好写作的规则，表现美好的事物，不必过分劳累自己的情思。

……

那些文思敏捷之人，对写作的主要方法了然于心，他们机智敏锐，无须苦思冥想就能当机立断。而构思缓沓之人，心中思路歧乱，几经思虑方能看清，细细推究才能决定。有些人因为文思敏捷，所以很快就能为文成书；有些人因为疑

第八章 《文心雕龙》经典篇章英译选读

虑难解,所以历时较久才能完成创作。两种人写作虽难易不同,但同样依靠博学精练。假如学问浅薄而只是写得慢,才能疏陋而只是写得快,这样的人要想在写作上有所成就,是前所未闻的。所以在创作构思时,必然出现两种毛病:思理不畅的人写出来的文章内容空乏;辞采繁滥的人又常常伤于杂乱。因此,见多识广可以补救内容的贫乏;主旨突出则可以纠正文辞的杂乱。如果见识广博而又能主旨贯一,这对于创作构思就很有助益了。

Spiritual Thought or Imagination (*Shen-ssu*) (Excerpt)

An Ancient said, "One may be on the rivers and sea in body, but his mind remains at the palace gate." This is what I mean by *shen-ssu*, or spiritual thought or imagination. One who is engaged in literary thought travels far in spirit. Quietly absorbed in contemplation, his thinking reaches back one thousand years; and with only the slightest movement of his countenance, his vision penetrates ten thousand li; he creates the music of pearls and jade between his poetic lines, and he witnesses the rolling of wind and clouds right before his brows and lashes. These things are possible because of the work of the imagination. Through the mystic subtlety of the imagination, the spirit and the things in the outside world are one in their excursion. The spirit resides in the mind, and the key to its secret is controlled by feeling and vital force. Physical things reach our mind through our ears and eyes, and the mechanism bringing about their apprehension is rhetoric. When the key works smoothly, there is nothing which will not appear in its true form; but when its operation is obstructed, the spirit loses its rationale. For this reason, vacancy and tranquility are important in the development of literary thinking: the achievement of this state of vacancy and tranquility entails the cleansing of the five viscera and the purification of the spirit. One has also to acquire learning in order to maintain a store of precious information, and to contemplate the nature of reason so as to enrich his talents; he must search deeply and experience widely in order that he may exhaustively evoke the source of light; he must draw upon literary traditions in order to make his expressions felicitous and smooth. It is only then that he commissions the "mysterious butcher" [who dwells within him] to write in accord with musical patterns; and it is then that he sets the incomparably brilliant "master wheelwright" [who dwells within him] to wield the ax in harmony with his intuitive insight. This, in short, is the first step in the art of writing, and the main principle employed in the planning of a literary piece.

When *shen-ssu* [or spiritual thought] is in operation, all possible vistas open up before it. Rules and principles become mere formalities and there is not the least trace of carving or engraving. When one ascends mountains [in such an inspired state], the whole mountain will be tinged with the coloring of his own feelings; and when his eyes rove over the seas, the seas will be saturated with his ideas. He can roam as companion of the wind and the clouds according to the measure of his talents. At the moment when a writer first picks up his pen, and before anything has yet been written, he feels as if his creative vigor were doubled; but at the completion of the piece, he usually has succeeded in conveying only half of what he had at first contemplated. Why is this so? Because one's ideas may easily be extraordinary when he is free to work in the realm of fancy, but it is very difficult for one to give beauty to his language when he is tied down to the factual details. Therefore, although the idea takes shape from spiritual thinking, and the language receives its form from the idea, idea, thought, and language may be so closely related that they are experienced as one, or they may differ as strikingly as if they were a thousand li apart. A writer may go beyond the world in search of patterns which are there in the square inch of his heart, and sometimes his thought strays over mountain and river for ideas which are only a few inches or feet away. So be vigilant over your heart and cultivate the intuitive method; there is little need of onerous mental effort, for one who is endowed with natural excellence balanced as a harmonious whole has no need to strain himself.

...

A spirited scholar, with the essentials of the art of writing in his mind, is quick to meet situations with an instantaneous response even before he has

第八章 《文心雕龙》经典篇章英译选读

time for consideration; while a man of profound thought, whose emotional reactions are complicated and who is ever aware of all possible alternatives, achieves light and maps plans only after prolonged questioning and inquiring. A man whose mechanism of response is quick does his work in a hurry; but it takes a long time for a man of deliberation to show his accomplishments. Though these two groups of people differ in their ways of writing, one group writing with ease and the other with great labor, both types must be men of comprehensive learning and broad experience. The mind which is only laborious without the support of learning resembles the empty quick-witted mind devoid of talent in that neither has ever been known to accomplish anything. There are two dangers besetting the man who organizes his thought while writing: if he is not clear about principles, his work will seem diffuse and insubstantial; but if he is prolix, his work will suffer from confusion. Comprehensive learning and broad experience are the only foods that will nourish writing afflicted with poverty of substance, and coherence and unity are the only medicines which will cure confusion. To be coherent and unified as well as comprehensive is also one way to reduce mental effort.

——Vincent Yu-Chung Shih(施友忠)

英译鉴赏简评

《神思》为《文心雕龙》写作理论和技巧部分的第一章,由此可见刘勰对本章的重视程度非同寻常。在刘勰看来,只有沿袭中国古老的写作传统,意即创作者只有"神游万物",进入"前创作状态",让精神与自然物相互碰撞,才能在文字世界里纵横捭阖、思接千载、视通万里,激荡出美好的文学作品。该篇首句"形在江海之上,心存魏阙之下",描述了人的思想突破物理空间局限,从江河湖海飞跃到官府庙堂。但实际上,有学者认为此句蕴含着巨大的隐喻性,"江海"指人的肉身,"魏阙"指人的精神世界。另一种解读认为,刘勰的"神思"源于陆机的"神游",但刘勰似乎要尽力摆脱与后者的瓜葛。刘勰本人一直生活在长江流域,而他在本章中含蓄影射的陆机,是从长江流域北上,来到晋的都城洛阳(魏国之旧都),活跃于都城的文学圈子。但刘勰似乎不如陆机走运,他无法融入梁朝的文人圈,无法获得如陆机一样的学术影响力,这种解读似乎迎合了《神思》

的写作基调。如果此种解读合理的话,那么刘勰对陆机含沙射影般的暗讽,就应引起英译者的关注。施友忠先生在文本深度的挖掘上未投入太多精力,采取直译策略,仅保留字面语义,将其译为"One may be on the rivers and sea in body, but his mind remains at the palace gate"。相较之下,宇文所安先生的译文明确指出了该句的暗含语义:"the physical form's being by the rivers and lakes, but the mind's remaining at the foot of the palace towers of Wei"。他有意突出"the palace towers of Wei",可能是为了与该书不同章节中刘勰对陆机的严辞批评保持同一基调。"神思"一词乃中国哲学经典常用术语,施友忠先生对此词关照备至,既保留汉语拼音,又双重加注,将其译为"shen-ssu, or spiritual thought or imagination",宇文所安先生仅将其译为"spiritual thought",前者明显有利于西方读者对"神思"一词的理解。

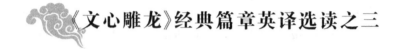《文心雕龙》经典篇章英译选读之三

《知音》第四十八(节选)

知音①其难哉! 音实难知,知实难逢,逢其知音,千载其一乎! 夫古来知音,多贱同而思古,所谓"日进前而不御,遥闻声而相思"也。

昔《储说》②始出,《子虚》③初成,秦皇、汉武,恨不同时;既同时矣,则韩囚而马轻④,岂不明鉴同时之贱哉! 至于班固、傅毅,文在伯仲,而固嗤毅云:"下笔不能自休"。及陈思论才,亦深排孔璋,敬礼请润色⑤,叹以为美谈,季绪好诋诃⑥,方之于田巴⑦,意亦见矣。故魏文称"文人相轻",非虚谈也。至如君卿唇舌,而谬欲论文⑧,乃称"史迁著书,谘东方朔",于是桓谭之徒,相顾嗤笑。彼实博徒⑨,轻言负诮⑩,况乎文士,可妄谈哉! 故鉴照洞明⑪,而贵古贱今者,二主是也;才实鸿懿⑫,而崇己抑人者,班、曹是也;学不逮文⑬,而信伪迷真者,楼护是也。酱瓿之议⑭,岂多叹哉!

……

夫缀文者情动而辞发,观文者披文以入情,沿波讨源⑮,虽幽必

第八章 《文心雕龙》经典篇章英译选读

显。世远莫见其面,觇文⑯辄见其心。岂成篇之足深,患识照之自浅耳。夫志在山水,琴表其情,况形之笔端,理将焉匿⑰?故心之照理,譬目之照形,目瞭则形无不分,心敏则理无不达。然而俗鉴⑱之迷者,深废浅售⑲,此庄周所以笑《折扬》⑳,宋玉所以伤《白雪》㉑也。昔屈平有言:"文质疏内㉒,众不知余之异采。"见异唯知音耳㉓。扬雄自称:"心好沉博绝丽之文㉔",其不事浮浅,亦可知矣。夫唯深识鉴奥㉕,必欢然内怿㉖,譬春台之熙众人㉗,乐饵之止过客㉘。盖闻兰为国香,服媚弥芬㉙;书亦国华㉚,玩绎方美㉛。知音君子,其垂意㉜焉。

赞曰:

洪钟㉝万钧,夔、旷㉞所定。良书盈箧㉟,妙鉴㊱乃订。

流郑淫人㊲,无或失听㊳。独有此律㊴,不谬蹊径㊵。

注:本段文字节选自《文心雕龙》第四十八章《知音》。"知音"一词原指对音乐艺术有独特的认识和见解的人,之后用来指有共同的理念、志趣,对事物有相同认知的人,本篇指对文章创作有深入的认识和理解的人。刘勰在本篇指出,文章种类繁多,内容风格各有差异,读者志趣爱好品味各不相同,因此,要形成合理端正的品鉴和认知,摒弃偏见,避免偏好,形成客观全面的认知和理念。一千多年前刘勰提出的观点,时至今日仍然值得我们借鉴和学习。

【注释】

① 〔知音〕原指对音乐的理解和鉴赏,后引申为对事物具有相似的认知。
② 〔《储说》〕战国末期著名思想家韩非子著有《外储说》和《内褚说》,此为统称。
③ 〔《子虚》〕西汉著名作家司马相如著有《子虚赋》。
④ 〔韩囚而马轻〕秦王久闻韩非大名,但待其入秦后却并未重用,反而轻信丞相李斯谗言将韩非投入大牢。西汉司马相如久负文才,深受汉武帝刘彻的赏识,但汉武帝召其进京后却并未予以重用。此句暗指空有旷世之才,却知音难遇。
⑤ 〔敬礼请润色〕丁廙(yì),字敬礼,三国时期魏国沛郡(今安徽濉溪)人,博学有才,曾请曹植修改文章,因与曹植亲善,被魏文帝曹丕处死。
⑥ 〔季绪好诋诃(dǐ hē)〕刘修,字季绪,喜好批评他人的文章。

⑦〔方之于田巴〕曹植把刘修比作口若悬河的田巴。〔田巴〕战国时齐国的辩士,一生喜好与人辩论,口若悬河。

⑧《汉书·游侠传·楼护》:"楼护,字君卿……为人短小精辩。"此句意为楼护只是善于辩论,却要去妄议批评他人的文章。

⑨〔博徒〕赌徒。此处指楼护之类不过是赌徒低俗之辈。

⑩〔负诮(qiào)〕随便说话遭人讥笑。

⑪〔鉴照洞明〕审查对照透彻明晰。

⑫〔才实鸿懿(yì)〕文才的确鸿大而美好。〔懿〕美好。

⑬〔学不逮文〕学识不及文才。〔逮〕〈古〉到,及。

⑭〔瓿(bù)〕古代采用青铜或陶制作的小瓮,用以盛酒或水,亦用于盛酱。此句意为刘歆担心杨雄的作品会被后人用来盖酱坛。

⑮〔波〕作品的形貌。〔源〕作品的内里。〔沿波讨源〕从作品的形貌风格出发去探究其内在的思想感情。

⑯〔觇文〕仔细观察阅读作品。〔觇(chān)〕暗中察看。

⑰〔理将焉匿〕其中的情理如何藏匿。

⑱〔俗鉴〕世俗的鉴赏者。

⑲〔深废浅售〕深刻的作品被人废弃,浅薄的作品受人赞赏。

⑳〔庄周所以笑《折扬》〕《折扬》,古代的一种俗曲。庄周讥笑浅薄的《折扬》受人吹捧。

㉑〔宋玉所以伤《白雪》〕《白雪》一种高雅的曲调。宋玉哀叹高雅的《白雪》无人问津。

㉒〔文质疏内〕语出屈原《九章·怀沙》:"文质疏内兮,众不知余之异采",意指文章质朴疏阔却不善于表达自我。〔内(nè)〕木讷。

㉓〔见异唯知音耳〕只有知音,才可以看出与众不同之处。

㉔〔心好沉博绝丽之文〕语出杨雄《答刘歆书》,意指我喜欢深沉博达文辞优美的文章。

㉕〔深识鉴奥〕认识深刻,品鉴精奥。

㉖〔内怿(yì)〕内心欢悦。

㉗〔譬春台之熙众人〕语出《老子》:"众人熙熙,如享太牢,如登春台。"此句意指就好比春天登台令人快乐。〔熙〕快乐。

㉘〔乐饵之止过客〕语出《老子》:"乐与饵,过客止。",意为音乐与美食令人愉悦。〔乐〕音乐。〔饵〕美食。

㉙〔兰为国香,服媚弥芬〕语出《左转》:"以兰有国香,人服媚之如是。"兰花是国内最香的花,喜爱的人佩戴上之后满身馨香。

㉚〔书亦国华〕文章是国内最优美的。

第八章 《文心雕龙》经典篇章英译选读

㉛〔玩绎方美〕只有仔细玩味才可感受到其中的美好。〔玩绎〕细细品味。

㉜〔垂意〕留意。

㉝〔洪钟〕大钟。

㉞〔夔(kuí)〕舜帝时的乐官。〔旷〕字子野,平阳(今山东省新泰市南师店)人,春秋时晋国著名乐师。

㉟〔箧(qiè)〕小箱子,藏物之具。大者曰箱,小者曰箧。〔良书盈箧〕好书装满箧子。

㊱〔妙鉴〕高妙的鉴赏。

㊲〔流郑淫人〕郑声淫靡,令人缭乱。

㊳〔失听〕错听,理解失常。

㊴〔独有此律〕音乐遵循的规则。

㊵〔不谬蹊径〕不走错道路。〔谬(miù)〕极端错误,非常不合情理。〔蹊〕《广雅》:蹊(xī),道也。

白话释义

正确的评论多么困难!评论固然难于正确,好的评论家也不易遇见;要碰上好的评论家,一千年也不过一两人吧!(知音难遇啊!深入理解音乐实非易事,要遇到通晓音乐者何其困难,恐怕千年只有一次吧!)自古以来的评论家(知音),常常轻视同代人而仰慕前人,正如《鬼谷子》所说:"天天在眼前的并不任用,老远听到声名却不胜思慕。"

从前韩非子的《储说》刚一传出,司马相如的《子虚赋》刚一写成,秦始皇和汉武帝便深恨不能和他们同代,但是后来相见了,结果却是韩非下狱,司马相如被冷落。这显然就是对同代人的轻视。至于班固和傅毅,作品成就本来相差无几,但班固却讥笑傅毅说:"傅毅写起文章来就没完没了。"曹植评论作家时,也极力贬低陈琳;丁廙请他修改文章,他就称赞丁廙文章得体;刘修喜欢批评别人文章的优劣,他就把刘修比作古代胡乱说话的田巴。那么,曹植的偏见就很明显了。所以曹丕说"文人互相轻视",这不是一句空话。还有楼护只因口才好,居然要评论他人文章,说什么"司马迁著书,曾请教于东方朔",于是桓谭等人都来嘲笑楼护。楼护本来没有什么地位,信口乱说就被人讥笑。作为一个文人学者,怎么能随便乱发议论呢?由此看来,有见识高超而不免崇古非今的人,那就是秦始皇和汉武帝;有才华卓越而抬高自己、压低别人的人,那就是班固和曹植;有毫无文才而误信传说、不明真相的人,那就楼护。刘歆担心扬雄的著作会被后人用来做酱坛盖子,这难道是多余的慨叹吗?

......

文学创作是作家情有所动,后发而为文;文学批评却是先看作品的文辞,然后再深入作家的内心。从末流追溯到根源,即使是隐微的思想也可以变得显豁。对年代久远的作者,固然不能与其见面,但深入阅读他的作品,便可以看到作者的内心。难道担心作品太深奥吗?只恐怕自己的见解太浅薄罢了。弹琴的人如果内心想到山和水,尚可在琴声中表达自己的心情,何况文章是用笔写出来的,其中的道理怎能隐藏得了?所以读者内心对作品中道理的理解,就像眼睛能看清事物的外形一样,看得清楚的话,就没有什么形态不能辨别;内心聪慧的话,就没有什么道理不能明白。然而世俗上认识不清楚的人,常抛弃深刻的作品,浅薄的作品反而受人追捧。因此,庄周就讥笑浅薄者只爱听庸俗的《折杨》,而宋玉也慨叹高雅的《白雪》无人欣赏。从前屈原说过:"我为文质朴,却不善表达于外,所以人们都不知道我的才华出众。"能认识出众的才能的,只有正确的评论家(只有遇到知音)。扬雄曾说他自己:"内心喜欢深刻的、广博的、绝顶华丽的文章",那么他不喜欢浅薄的作品,也就由此可知了。只要是见解深刻,能看到作品深意的人,就必能在欣赏杰作时获得内心的享受,好像春天登台所见的美景可以使众人心情舒畅,音乐与美味可以让过客止步一样。据说兰花是全国最香的花,人们喜爱而佩在身上,就可发出更多的芬芳;文章著作也是国中的香花,要细细体味才知其美妙。希望愿意正确评论作品的知音君子,特别注意这些问题。

总之,万斤重的大钟,只有古时的乐师夔和师旷才能制定。满箱子的好书,就依靠卓越的评论家来判断。郑国的靡靡之音会使人心生迷乱,千万不要被它迷惑听觉。唯有遵守评论的规则,才不会走入歧途。

An Understanding Critic (*Chih_yin*) (Excerpt)

It is indeed difficult to find an understanding critic of personal thought. It is true that personal thought is intrinsically difficult to understand; but what is still more difficult is to find someone who possesses real understanding. Hardly once in a thousand years do we happen upon an understanding critic. The [so-called] understanding critics have since time of old despised their contemporaries and devoted themselves to those who have

第八章 《文心雕龙》经典篇章英译选读

passed into antiquity, just as it is said, "One disdains to harness the horses which are presented to him every day, but dreams of using those whose neighing he hears from a distance."

When [Han Fei's] "Ch'u-shuo" first appeared, the first emperor of the Ch'in expressed great regret for not being Han's contemporary; and Emperor Wu of the Han felt the same way about [Ssu-ma Hsiang-ju] when he first read Hsiang-ju's "Tzu-hsü fu." But once it was known that they were contemporaries, Han [Fei] was thrown into prison and Ssu-ma Hsiang-ju lightly regarded. Are these not clear examples of the contempt in which contemporaries are usually held? Then there were Pan Ku and Fu I, whose achievements in literary writing are about equal, and yet Pan Ku ridiculed Fu I and said, "Once he starts, he does not know how to stop." And Ch'en-ssu [or Ts'ao Chih], in his discussion of talent, also severely criticized K'ung-chang [or Ch'en Lin]. But to the request of Ching-li [or Ting I] that Ts'ao Chih polish his writing, Ts'ao responded with a word of praise for him. Then there was [Liu] Chi-hsü, not a great writer himself, who loved to criticize, and was compared to T'ien Pa by Ts'ao Chih. In these instances we have a glimpse of Ts'ao Chih's opinion. When Wei-wen [or Tsao P'ei] said, "Literary men despise each other," his statement was certainly not groundless. Chün-ch'ing [or Lou Hu], a man of great eloquence, mistakenly estimated his own ability when he dabbled in literary discussion. He once made the statement, "The historian [Ssu-ma] Ch'ien, in the writing of his work, sought advice from Tung-fang So." Huan T'an and his group noted this with sneering laughter. Now if [Lou Hu], who was only a gambler, was censured for passing judgment lightly, can one who considers himself a man of letters afford to make groundless remarks? There are men of high intelligence and keen penetration who value the ancient and despise the modern, like the two rulers mentioned above. There are others, men of talent, who have a tendency to esteem themselves and look down upon others, like Pan Ku and Ts'ao Chih. There are still others who, although they are men of letters, lack scholarship, and are blind to truth and credulous of falsehood, like Lou Hu. [Liu Hsin's] expressed apprehension that [work of profundity] may be fated to cover pickle jars cannot be dismissed as a case of over sensitivity.

...

The writer's first experience is his inner feeling, which he then seeks to express in words. But the reader, on the other hand, experiences the words first, and then works himself into the feeling of the author. If he can trace the waves back to their source, there will be nothing, however dark and hidden, that will not be revealed to him. Although the life of an age may have passed beyond our view, we may often, through reading its literature, succeed in grasping the heart of it. We ought never to blame a work for being too profound, for our failure to understand it is often due to our own lack of experience and knowledge. If it is possible for a man's impressions of mountains and rivers to find expression in his lute playing, how much easier it must be to depict physically tangible forms with a brush, from which no inner feeling or idea can be successfully hidden. Our mind reflects reason just as our eyes perceive physical forms; as long as our eyes are keen, there are no physical forms which cannot be distinguished, and as long as our mind is alert, there are no feelings or ideas which cannot be conveyed. However, because the popular taste is confused, profound writings have come to be discarded, and the superficial types have gained popularity. This is why Chuang Chou ridiculed "Che-yang" music, and Sung Yü was struck with melancholy at the [forlorn] fate of "Pai-hsüeh." Long ago Ch'ü P'ing [or Ch'ü Yüan] said, "There is in my inner nature both form and substance, but the people do not know their wonderful patterns." Indeed, an understanding critic alone is capable of seeing what is [inwardly] wonderful. Yang Hsiung once called himself a lover of literary works which are both profoundly erudite and beautiful. From this statement it is apparent that Yang did not indulge in the superficial and shallow.

Only those with deep knowledge and profound insight will [give the author an] experience of inner joy, which experience may be compared to the warmth people feel while ascending a terrace in the spring, or to the feeling of a wayfarer halting his step for music and viands. For it is said that the orchid, which is the most fragrant thing in the country, will give forth its full scent only when worn; and similarly, literary works, which too are national

第八章 《文心雕龙》经典篇章英译选读

treasures, must be appreciated to display their beauty. May those who consider themselves understanding critics consider these words well.

The Tsan:
>   Grand bells of ten thousand weights
>   Need K'uei and K'uang to determine their tones.
>   Books in the box may be of excellent quality,
>   But they depend on expert knowledge for an appraisal of their value.
>   The popular vulgar music drowns one's soul;
>   So do not let your hearing be misled by it.
>   Only the principles propounded here
>   Mark out the paths which are free from mistakes.

——Vincent Yu-Chung Shih（施友忠）

英译鉴赏简评

《知音》篇包含许多中国历史上的文化名人和传统文论术语,要让西方读者理解这些人名在语篇中的关系并理解文论术语在上下语义中的作用,的确是英译难点之一。施友忠先生也是极尽翻译之能事,力图让这些文化术语恰如其分地再现中国文论背后的历史渊源和文化关联。虽然他在术语的处理上收到多方批评,但他的译本"标志着西方汉学界研究和翻译中国文论的突破性进展"。"知音"一词在中国文化中具有丰富的隐喻性,多次出现于不同的典籍文本中。要解决该篇中这个关键性术语,施友忠先生采取意译+音译法将其译为"An Understanding Critic (Chih-yin)",并在篇章注释部分采用浅显易懂的阐释性语句进一步解释:"Literally, 'Chih-yin' means one who understands music, that is, one who has a sympathetic ear. By extension, it comes to mean an understanding friend."。如此处理,对于读者理解该篇所讨论的内容大有裨益。对于历史典故的翻译,施先生同样费尽心思,增补了大量的注释性内容,比如"韩囚(韩非子被囚禁)"这一典故,字面实难翻译,施先生做了详细的注释:"This was before the emperor knew that Han Fei was actually his contemporary. But when he found that out and succeeded in getting him to his court, he promptly threw him into prison on the advice of the jealous Li Ssu. By the time the emperor realized his mistake, Han Fei had already been poisoned by order of Li Ssu."。因此,英国汉学家霍克斯先生说"施友忠雄心勃勃地尝试将《文心雕龙》介绍给西方读者"。施友忠等华裔学者虽然身处异乡,却心系祖国,情怀家园,他们孜孜不倦地将中华文化向西方引介和推广的探索精神值得我们学习和敬仰。

本章课后练习

一、请尝试翻译以下句子。

1. 情动而言形,理发而文见。(《文心雕龙·体性》)
   白话释义:
   英译:

2. 物色之动,心亦摇焉。(《文心雕龙·五色》)
   白话释义:
   英译:

3. 逍遥以针劳,谈笑以药倦。(《文心雕龙·养气》)
   白话释义:
   英译:

4. 繁采寡情,味之必厌。(《文心雕龙·情采》)
   白话释义:
   英译:

5. 操千曲而后晓声,观千剑而后识器。(《文心雕龙·知音》)
   白话释义:
   英译:

二、请比较以下名句两种英译文本的异同。

1. 吟咏之间,吐纳珠玉之声;眉睫之前,卷舒风云之色。(《文心雕龙·神思》第二十六)

   英译1:He produces pearl-like sounds in recitation and conjures up whirling winds and rolling clouds before his eyes. (杨国斌)

第八章 《文心雕龙》经典篇章英译选读

英译 2: He creates the music of pearls and jade between his poetic lines, and he witnesses the rolling of wind and clouds right before his brows and lashes. (施友忠 Vincent Yu-Chung Shih)

2. 积学以储宝,酌理以富才。(《文心雕龙·神思》第二十六)

英译 1: Use diligence to accumulate knowledge, judgement to enrich talent. (杨国斌)

英译 2: One has also to acquire learning in order to maintain a store of precious information, and to contemplate the nature of reason so as to enrich his talents. (施友忠 Vincent Yu-Chung Shih)

3. 登山则情满于山,观海则意溢于海。(《文心雕龙·神思》第二十六)

英译 1: If at this moment the writer ascends a mountain, his feeling will permeate the mountain. If he surveys the sea, his emotion will overflow the sea. (杨国斌)

英译 2: When one ascends mountains [in such an inspired state], the whole mountain will be tinged with the coloring of his own feelings; and when his eyes rove over the seas, the seas will be saturated with his ideas. (施友忠 Vincent Yu-Chung Shih)

4. 物虽胡越,合则肝胆。(《文心雕龙·比兴》第三十六)

英译 1: Though things were as far apart as Hu [in the north] and Yue [in the south], when put together, they were as liver and gall. (宇文所安 Stephen Owen)

英译 2: Things which are as far apart as *Hu* [in the north] and *Yüeh* [in the south] may through their similarities be as close as the liver and the gall. (施友忠 Vincent Yu-Chung Shih)

5. 乘一总万,举要治繁。思无定契,理有恒存。(《文心雕龙·总术》第四十四)

英译 1: By going with one thing you comprehend all; getting the essentials controls elaborations. Thought has no predetermined patterns, but natural principle is permanent. (宇文所安 Stephen Owen)

英译 2: By the control of the first principle one controls the ten thousand,

and by harnessing the essential element one harnesses all the details. Thinking may not have a fixed form, but the reason is absolutely constant. (施友忠 Vincent Yu-Chung Shih)

6. 岁有其物,物有其容;情以物迁,辞以情发。(《文心雕龙·物色》第四十六)

英译1：The year has its physical things, and these things have their appearances; by these things our affections are shifted, and from out affections language comes. (宇文所安 Stephen Owen)

英译2：Many different things appear in the course of the year, and each has a number of phases. One responds with varying emotions to these varying phases, and the form of language used depends on the emotion. (施友忠 Vincent Yu-Chung Shih)

7. 心生文辞,运裁百虑,高下相须,自然成对。(《文心雕龙·丽辞》第三十五)

英译1：When mind generated literary language, giving thought to all manner of concepts and cutting them to pattern, by Nature parallelism was formed, just as [the concepts of] high and low are necessary to one another. (宇文所安 Stephen Owen)

英译2：The mind creates literary language, and in doing this it organizes and shapes one hundred different thoughts, making what is high supplement what is low, and spontaneously producing linguistic parallelism. (施友忠 Vincent Yu-Chung Shih)

8. 论如析薪,贵能破理。(《文心雕龙·论说》第十八)

英译1：Writing a treatise is like splitting wood: The secret is to follow the grain. (杨国斌)

英译2：In a *lun*, it is as if one were splitting wood; the main thing is to split it according to its grain. (施友忠 Vincent Yu-Chung Shih)

9. 文律运周,日新其业。变则堪久,通则不乏。(《文心雕龙·通变》第二十九)

英译1：The rule of literature is to move in full cycle. Its accomplishment is found in daily renewal: By mutation it can last long; By continuity nothing is wanting. (宇文所安 Stephen Owen)

第八章 《文心雕龙》经典篇章英译选读

英译 2：It is the law of literature both to move along and to come to full circle; the merit of literature renews itself from day to day. If it changes, it will endure; If it adapts itself to the changing tide, it will lack nothing. （施友忠 Vincent Yu-Chung Shih）

10. 权衡损益，斟酌浓淡。芟繁剪秽，弛于负担。（《文心雕龙·熔裁》第三十二）

英译 1：Weigh additions and excisions on the balance; Deliberate whether it's too dense or too thin. Pare away lushness, cut down the weeds to lighten the burden you carry. （宇文所安 Stephen Owen）

英译 2：Weighing what to cut and what to add, considering what to enrich and what to thin, cutting short the lengthy and shearing away the weedy, this is the way to avoid tedious burden. （施友忠 Vincent Yu-Chung Shih）

三、段落试译。

夫桃李不言而成蹊，有实存也；男子树兰而不芳，无其情也。夫以草木之微，依情待实，况乎文章，述志为本，言与志反，文岂足征？是以联辞结采，将欲明理。采滥辞诡，则心理愈翳。固知翠纶桂饵，反所以失鱼。"言隐荣华"，殆谓此也。是以"衣锦褧衣"，恶文太章；《贲》象穷白，贵乎反本。夫能设模以位理，拟地以置心，心定而后结音，理正而后摛藻；使文不灭质，博不溺心，正采耀乎朱蓝，间色屏于红紫，乃可谓雕琢其章，彬彬君子矣。

（《情采》第三十一）

盖人禀五材，修短殊用；自非上哲，难以求备。然将相以位隆特达，文士以职卑多诮；此江河所以腾涌，涓流所以寸折者也。名之抑扬，既其然矣；位之通塞，亦有以焉。盖士之登庸，以成务为用。鲁之敬姜，妇人之聪明耳；然推其机综，以方治国。安有丈夫学文，而不达于政事哉？彼扬、马之徒，有文无质，所以终乎下位也。昔庾元规才华清英，勋庸有声，故文艺不称；若非台岳，则正以文才也。文武之术，左右惟宜。郤縠敦书，故举为元帅，岂以好文而不练武哉？孙武《兵经》，辞如珠玉，岂以习武而不晓文也！

（《程器》第四十九）

唐代诗文经典篇章英译选读

【导读】

　　唐代是中国历史上最灿烂辉煌的朝代之一。唐朝的早期与中期,政治清明、经济发达、国家富强、繁荣昌盛,百姓安居乐业。唐朝晚期,政治衰败、社会混乱。唐代的文学,也实时地反映着当时的社会变迁和民众生活。因此,唐代文学在中国文学史上占据着非常重要的地位。如果说文学是反映社会现实的一面镜子,那么诗歌,尤其是唐诗,作为一种独特的文学体裁,就是反映唐代社会现实的万花筒。

【唐诗】

　　经过汉乐府、建安诗歌、南北朝诗歌的传袭,诗歌在唐朝焕发出新的光彩。可以说,唐代是中国诗歌的黄金时代,名家辈出、杰作如流。据估计,唐诗总量有5万多首,后世辑有各种版本,收录唐诗最全的版本为清代康熙四十四年(1705年),翰林侍讲彭定求奉敕,作为总督责,组织沈三曾、杨中讷、汪士鋐、汪绎、俞梅、徐树本、车鼎晋、潘从律、查嗣瑮等人集体辑录编校的《全唐诗》。《全唐诗》共有九百多卷,收录唐诗48900余首,载录唐代诗人2200余人。唐代诗歌的题材也多种多样,从游子客旅到深宫闺怨,从边塞行军到山水田园,从政论咏史到思乡感怀,都在唐代诗歌中得到了淋漓尽致的表达。

　　唐代诗歌一般被划分为四个时期:初唐、盛唐、中唐与晚唐。初唐时期的诗歌仍未完全褪去南朝以来的绮丽风气,但是已渐渐呈现出新的气象,诗歌从宫

第九章 唐代诗文经典篇章英译选读

廷的奢靡华丽转向更为现实的题材。初唐时期的代表诗人有王勃、卢照邻、骆宾王、杨炯、陈子昂、沈佺期、宋之问等。盛唐时期是中国诗歌史上最为辉煌繁荣的时期,涌现出李白与杜甫这样伟大的诗人。作为浪漫主义诗歌的代表,李白的诗歌想象丰富、气势宏大、诗境轩昂。而杜甫的诗歌沉郁顿挫、铿锵有力,满怀对国家与社会的忧思和对普通民众的同情与悯怀。盛唐时期的田园派诗歌和边塞诗歌同样占据半壁山河,伯仲难分,著名的田园派诗人有孟浩然与王维,边塞诗人有高适与岑参。中唐时期的诗歌,经过白居易与元稹的诗歌改革之后,呈现出鲜明的特点。白居易明确提出"歌诗合为事而作",主张诗歌要反映现实,诗人要关切社会,要对改造社会、促进社会进步担当一份责任。他的诗歌通俗易懂,用词朴实无华,老妪童稚能解,达官贵人可读。晚唐时期,随着李唐帝国的逐渐没落,政治腐败、社会动荡、民不聊生。晚唐的诗人不复有初唐的开阔气象,也没有了盛唐的辉煌气势,诗人的咏怀变得更加个人化、情绪化。晚唐的代表诗人有著名的"小李杜"——李商隐与杜牧。

唐代诗人层出不穷,诗歌种类繁多,要选出"最佳"诗篇实属不易。本章选择伟大的现实主义诗人杜甫的作品《登高》进行研读。杜甫,字子美,自号少陵野老,生于河南巩义市,祖籍湖北襄阳。作为我国文学史上最具代表性的现实主义诗人,杜甫所处的时代是大唐帝国由盛而衰的时代。杜甫一生颠沛流离、辛苦遭逢,因此,他的诗歌具有浓郁的时代特点,蕴含着诗人强烈的爱国主义情怀,具有其他诗歌无法替代的社会意义。

杜甫年轻时过着读书与壮游的生活。他在二十岁的时候南下吴越游览,二十四岁回到洛阳科考,不第,之后他继续前往齐赵之地,与李白、高适相识同游。多年的游历生涯增长了杜甫的见识,丰富了他的写作题材,开阔了他的视野与心胸。这一时期,《望岳》可以作为他的代表作。诗人登上东岳泰山,遥望齐鲁大地,不禁思绪万千,最后一句"会当凌绝顶,一览众山小",遣词造句非同寻常,思想境界非同一般,表现出诗人的博大胸怀和凌云壮志。大概在三十五岁的时候,杜甫移居长安。天宝五年(746年),杜甫参加科举落榜。之后的大约十年里,杜甫一直非常窘迫,为了生活,他追随权贵,仍旧朝不保夕,经常忍饥挨饿,自身的痛苦使杜甫把眼光投向广大的劳苦大众。在这一时期,他写下了著名的《兵车行》《丽人行》及《赴奉先咏怀》等诗歌。此际适逢"安史之乱"爆发,这是一个标志性的历史大事件,标志着大唐王朝由盛及衰的开始。"安史之乱"初期,他与老百姓一起逃离兵乱,颠沛流离,先是被叛军俘虏,当他听到肃宗继位的消息之后,历尽艰险投奔肃宗,被授予左拾遗一职,后因营救房琯而得罪肃宗,因此屡遭贬斥。在辗转各地迁徙逃乱的途中,他看尽世间百态,尝尽人间辛酸,对劳苦大众产生了强烈的同情心,他的爱国情怀也一直没有改变。乾元二年(759年),杜甫在四十八岁的时候,辞官入蜀,暮年穷困潦倒,贫无立锥,在四川漂泊了八九年,又在湖北、湖南漂泊了两三年。大历五年(770年),杜甫卒于潭州赴岳州的舟上。

郝稷在《英语世界中杜甫及其诗歌的接受与传播——兼论杜诗学的世界性》中提到,英语世界对杜甫的介绍大致分为三个阶段。

第一个阶段是 19 世纪,只有简短的生平介绍和少量的诗歌翻译。1870年,英国汉学家德庇时(戴维斯爵士,Sir John Francis Davis)在新扩充版的《汉文诗解》(The Poetry of the Chinese)中对唐诗作了简要评价,并翻译了杜甫的《春夜喜雨》。1874 年英国驻中国外交官、汉学家梅辉立(William Frederick Mayers)出版了《中文读者手册》(Chinese Reader's Manual),里面有数行内容提及杜甫。1884 年,英国汉学家翟理斯(Herbert A. Giles)在《中国文学选珍》(Gems of Chinese Literature)中翻译了杜甫的《佳人》。1898 年翟理斯出版的《古今诗选》(Chinese Poetry in English Verse)翻译了 10 首杜甫的诗歌。1899年,玛丽·埃尔文(Mary Elwin)女士发表了《诗人杜甫的生平》一文,对杜甫的生平进行了较为详细的介绍,而且提供了 3 首译诗来说明杜诗风格。

第二个阶段是 20 世纪 20 年代至 70 年代末。这段时期对杜甫的介绍和对杜诗的翻译都明显增多。1929 年,艾斯柯出版了《杜甫:一个中国诗人的自传》(Tu Fu, The Autobiography of a Chinese Poet),主要描述杜甫童年到中年的生活。这是英语世界的第一部杜甫传记。1934 年推出下册《一个中国诗人之旅:杜甫,江湖客》(Travels of a Chinese Poet: Tu Fu, Guest of Rivers and Lakes),本册重点介绍杜甫晚年的生活和诗歌。这是"英语世界中第一部较为详细的关于杜甫生命历程和诗歌的系统性介绍专著。"第二部则是华裔汉学家洪业(William Hung)在 1952 年交付哈佛大学出版社出版的《杜甫:中国最伟大的诗人》(Tu Fu: China's Greatest Poet)。这套书包括上下两册,上册是正文,选译了 374 首诗来描述杜甫的生平和时代,向一般读者呈现杜甫详细的生平经历及其诗歌风格和意义等;下册则包含了大量的注释、翻译文本的比较,考辨舛误和来源,供汉学家们参考。可以说,这是第一部由中国人用英语向西方介绍和推广杜甫的嚆矢之作,在西方的影响非凡。第三部是澳大利亚学者戴维斯在1971 年出版的《杜甫》。1967 年英国汉学家大卫·霍克思(David Hawkes)翻译了杜甫诗歌,出版《杜诗初阶》。

第三个阶段是 20 世纪 80 年代至今的深化发展期。这一时期研究角度和研究方法趋向多元化。新时期也出现了很多的杜诗译本。宇文所安(Stephen

第九章 唐代诗文经典篇章英译选读

Owen)在1981年出版的《盛唐诗》(*The Great Age of Chinese Poetry：The High T'ang*)中专门有章节提及杜甫。1985年的《传统中国诗歌及诗学》(*Traditional Chinese Poetry and Poetics*),也提及杜甫。大卫·麦克劳(David R. McCraw,中文名麦大伟)1992年出版杜甫研究专著《杜甫来自南方之哀悼》(*Du Fu's Laments from the South*),又译作《杜甫的南方悲歌》),主要介绍、研究、翻译杜甫流离南方时所作的诗歌。大卫·麦克劳在书中说:"现在是杜甫在世界最伟大抒情诗人中占据其应有地位的时候了"。周珊(Eva Shan Chou,又名周杉)1995年出版的《杜甫之再审视:文学的伟大与文化的背景》(*Reconsidering Du Fu：Literary Greatness and Cultural Context*,又译作《再思杜甫:文学成就和文化语境》)也是研究杜甫的专著,由美国著名汉学家海陶玮(James R. Hightower)作序,该书集中讨论并英译了杜甫160多首诗歌(多为短诗和长诗的节译)。在此期间,英语世界的杜诗翻译也取得了一定成就,重要的专门译著有美国诗人汉米尔(Sam Hamill)1988年出版的杜诗专译本《对雪:杜甫之想象》(*Facing the Snow：Visions of Du Fu*,又译作《对雪:杜甫的视域》),书中选有101首杜甫诗歌。1994年,汉米尔编译出版了《午夜之笛:中国爱情与思念诗歌》(*Midnight Flute：Chinese Poems of Love and Longing*),选译了《游龙门奉先寺》等12首杜诗。2004年,汉米尔与美国当代翻译家、北卡罗来纳大学中国与亚洲研究中心荣誉教授西顿(J. P. Seaton)合作出版了《禅诗》(*The Poetry of Zen*),其中选译了5首杜诗。美国诗人、新一代汉诗英译的代表人物大卫·亨顿(David Hinton)在1989年出版的《杜诗选译》(*The Selected Poems of Du Fu*)收录了180多首杜甫诗歌,此书对杜甫不同时期的诗歌进行了详细的分类,并对每一首诗歌的背景、渊源等予以深度剖析,是西方读者了解杜甫生平和诗歌创作的重量级作品。另外,大卫·亨顿分别于2002年出版《山居:中国古代自然诗》(*Mountain Home：The Wilderness Poetry of Ancient China*),2008年出版《中国古诗选》(*Classical Chinese Poetry：An Anthology*)。这两部中国诗歌专著亦收录《杜诗选译》中的不少精彩诗篇。再者,穆思(W. R. Moses)1997年出版的《杜甫诗歌》也是这个阶段杜甫诗歌研究的重要作品之一。

进入21世纪,杜诗的翻译仍旧在持续。翻译家华兹生(Burton Watson)2003年出版了《杜诗选译》(*Selected Poems of Du Fu*)。研究者认为"华兹生翻译的《杜甫诗选》在杜诗英译史上具有重要地位与典范意义……基本再现了诗人及其名下诗文的面貌,丰富了杜诗在美国的译介谱系与维度"。美国诗人翻译家杨大伟(David Young)在2009年出版了《杜甫:诗中的生命》(*Du Fu：*

Life in Poetry),深受读者好评。2015年,美国汉学家宇文所安完成六卷本《杜甫诗集》(*The Poetry of Du Fu*)的翻译,书中囊括杜甫将近一千四百首诗作,是杜甫诗歌第一次最完整的翻译。借用评论者对杜甫的评价,"杜甫:书写永久、秩序与文明的中国诗人"来评价宇文所安先生对杜诗译介所作的贡献:"宇文所安:翻译和传播'书写永久、秩序与文明的中国诗人'的美国诗人"。

唐代除了诗歌这一颗闪耀着璀璨光芒传扬千载的"艺术瑰宝"之外,其他文学体裁,如初唐文赋、唐代散文、唐代传奇等亦应受到后人的关注。非如此,我们便无法睹见享国近乎三百年,声名远播海内外这一"盛世盛国"的文化全貌。

【唐代散文】

散文最早发端于先秦两汉时期,以春秋诸子百家为其集大成者。随着两汉时期辞赋的赓续发展,散文的风格亦愈来愈骈俪化,形成所谓汉魏六朝赋(骈文)。

在某种程度上,骈文体裁源出于先秦两汉的散文,但在形式美上,却比散文更进一步。骈文强调声律音韵,辞藻考究华丽,注重修辞,重于用典,句式讲求对偶,以四句或六句为主,故又称为"俳赋""四六文"或"骈四俪六文"。发展至六朝时期,因士族文人的大力推崇,骈文逐渐成为主流的文章创作形式。但骈文过度重视辞藻,讲究形式,而忽略文章内容的昳丽绮靡风格,表现出脱离社会现实的突出弊端。魏晋以降,至于隋唐,骈文的颓靡之风逐渐降温。此一时期,骈文虽然不再是一种主流的文学活动,但也有不少诗人和文学家并未放弃创作骈文。

初唐时期,最值得称道的骈文是"初唐四杰"之首王勃所创作的《滕王阁序》。而在王勃之前,享誉中国文学史的骈文并不少见,影响深远的有汉代"四大家"——司马相如的《上林赋》《子虚赋》,扬雄的《河东赋》《羽猎赋》《甘泉赋》,班固的《两都赋》,张衡《西京赋》《东京赋》《南都赋》等等。王勃的《滕王阁序》,从文章主题、句式、修辞、意境和艺术魅力等各方面,都远超前代任何骈文作品,因此《滕王阁序》一问世,便受当世万人追捧,被后世称为"千古第一骈文"。时至今日,许多名句依然回响在人们的耳畔:"落霞与孤鹜齐飞,秋水共长天一色""关山难越,谁悲失路之人?萍水相逢,尽是他乡之客""时运不齐,命途多舛。冯唐易老,李广难封""老当益壮,宁移白首之心?穷且益坚,不坠青云之志。"这些掷地有声的千古名句,不是空洞乏力的辞藻卖弄,而是寄托着王勃,甚至千万个如王勃一样的年轻人,心怀梦想、情寄家国、志远意高的人生追求。

唐初另一位大诗人,初唐诗文革新派代表人物陈子昂,率先提倡诗歌要改变六朝以来萎靡绮丽的风格。他的主张对改变当时的绮靡骈俪文风产生了一

第九章　唐代诗文经典篇章英译选读

定的影响,在此之后,骈文的绮丽风格在一定程度上有所削弱,代之以更加贴近社会现实,反映民众生活,抨击官场黑暗,鞭挞政治腐败的散文创作。天宝年间,萧颖士、李华、元结等人研习经典,发扬儒家思想,助推复古思潮一再高涨。元结在创作中大量实践散文书写,力图摆脱六朝骈文的弊端,同时期还有很多文人主张以儒道作为文学创作的主流思想。这些人的主张并没有得到完全的实现,也并没有完全改变骈文写作绮靡浮艳的沉疴旧疾。

随着唐代社会的进一步发展,作为主流文体的骈体文开始被分解,从事散文写作的人数逐渐增多,文风由骈而散的趋势已不可阻挡。与诗歌不同,唐代散文的发展与社会发展有直接密切的关联。安史之乱导致藩镇割据,宦官专权,腐败堕落,民不聊生。此时佛道二教甚嚣尘上,大量的僧尼道士不耕而食、不织而衣,逃避赋税徭役,中兴的表面无法掩盖整个社会动荡不安的状态。一代文宗韩愈的复古主义思想,在贞元时期发展成为一种广泛的社会思想运动。韩愈要宣扬自己的政治主张与儒家思想,而六朝以来的骈文形式已经严重阻碍思想的表达,因此他反对骈文,主张古文。这里的古文,主要指汉以前的散文体。文章句子长短不一、形式自由,便于表达思想。韩愈明确提出"文以载道"的思想,将文风的改革带入社会政治实践之中。文章要去除无用的繁华辞藻,经世致用的文章才值得提倡。比如,在他的《谏迎佛骨表》中,韩愈使用散文的形式,明确地表达出他的政治主张。

同一时期,引领诗坛风骚的白居易亦遥而和之,提出"文章合为时而著,歌诗合为事而作。"(《与元九书》),并大力推动新乐府运动,认为文人要关切社会现实,担负起改造社会、推动社会进步的责任和使命。白居易的主张无疑是对骈文废止所发出的呼号,也是唐代文学走向现实主义道路的开荒之刃。

古文运动的忠实拥趸不应忘记与韩愈并称"韩柳"却比韩愈年长的元老人物,"唐宋八大家"之首的柳宗元。柳宗元,字子厚,唐代中期士大夫、文学家与思想家,又因是河东人氏,人称柳河东。柳宗元年轻时仕途顺利。唐顺宗永贞元年(805年),以王叔文为首的进步士人,为改革社会弊端,发起了一场旨在打击宦官的政治革新运动,史称"永贞革新",柳宗元和刘禹锡也是革新运动的中坚人物。这场革新非常短暂,很快就在多种政治力量的联合打击下失败了。柳宗元获罪贬谪永州,被长期流放。十年后改授柳州刺史,后来死于任上。

柳宗元一生笔耕不辍,作品丰赡,在政论文、寓言、杂文、传记及游记等各类文体中都有建树,其诗文总数达600余篇,散文有近百篇。总体而言,柳宗元的文章论说缜密、风格雅健、思想深邃,有独特的个人风格和时代风貌。

柳氏认为,文章不仅应该形式好,更应该注重内容;文章应该具有褒贬和讽喻的功能。因此,他的散文论说性强、笔锋犀利、讽刺辛辣、针砭时弊、充满力量、积极用世。以韩、柳为代表人物的所发起的古文运动,主张文章的形式和内容要统一,文章要贯穿儒道的精神,文体也要革新,不能因循守旧,要有自己的创新,文章要发挥经世致用的社会功能。他们的这些主张,都和当时的社会时代情况有很大的关系。

本章节选柳宗元的散文进行研读。柳宗元的诗文,在西方世界的传播情况,国内研究者不多。2009年,王丽娜与吴聪聪对柳宗元的诗文在国外的传播状况做了梳理。2016年,林志坚也对柳宗元的诗文在英语世界的翻译和传播做了总结。他们的研究都限于20世纪50年代之前。大致的研究结果如下。

19世纪末期,西方开始柳宗元诗文的翻译。1884年,翟理斯的译文集《中国文学选珍》(Gems of Chinese Literature)选译了柳宗元的六篇文章。

进入20世纪上半叶,柳宗元的诗歌被多次翻译成英文。但是规模相对来说都比较小。美国来华传教士丁韪良(W. A. P. Martin)、英国学者查尔斯·巴德(Charles Budd,中文名布茂林)、英国外交官弗莱彻(W. J. B. Fletcher)、美国翻译家威特·宾纳(Witter Bynner,中文名陶友白)都曾翻译过柳宗元的诗文,但都是一两篇而已。1929年,威特·宾纳与中国学者江亢虎(Kiang Kang-hu)合作完成《唐诗三百首》英译本 *The Jade Mountain*: *A Chinese Anthology*, *Being Three Hundred Poems of the T'ang Dynasty*(又译为《群玉山头》)。此译本是第一个《唐诗三百首》英文全译本,在中美文化交流史上具有极其重要的地位,该书共收录了柳宗元的五首诗作。中国现代著名学者吴经熊(John Ching Hsiung Wu)的《唐诗四季》(*The Four Seasons of T'ang Poetry*)收录了部分柳宗元的诗歌翻译,该书原是用英文撰写,从1938年至1939年,分六批刊登于英文月刊《天下》,后由徐诚斌译成中文,1940年在《宇宙风》杂志上连载,1980年由台湾洪范书店出版发行。1938年,英国汉学家叶女士(Edwards Evangeline Dora,又名爱德华兹)编写《龙书》(*The Dragon Book*),该书收有柳宗元的4篇文章,分别是《蝜蝂传》《三戒序》《黔之驴》及《临江之麋》。1940年,索姆·杰宁斯(Roger Soame Jenyns)完成《唐诗三百首》英文选译本(*Selections from the Three Hundred Poems of the T'ang Dynasty*,一般译为《唐诗三百首选读》),书中收录了柳宗元的两首诗作,分别为《渔翁》和《溪居》。1944年,索姆·杰宁斯的第二个《唐诗三百首》英文选译本(*A Further Selection from the Three Hundred Poems of the T'ang Dynasty*,一般译为《唐诗三百首选读续集》)又收录了柳宗元的三首诗作,《晨诣超师院读禅经》《登柳州城楼寄漳汀封连四州刺史》《江雪》。1949年,英国诗人、翻译家罗伯特·

第九章 唐代诗文经典篇章英译选读

白英(Robert Payne)出版的《白驹集》(*The White Pony: An Anthology of Chinese Poetry*, London: Theodore Brun Limited)收录了部分柳宗元的诗文英译。

20世纪下半叶,西方世界对柳宗元的研究也一直在持续升温。1973年美国著名汉学家、中国古典文学翻译家倪豪士(William H. Nienhauser, Jr.)等人编写的《柳宗元》(*Liu Tsung-yüan*),是一部关于柳宗元的传记。不仅西方人研究柳宗元,中国人也逐渐用英语介绍柳宗元。其中有代表性的作品有1979年中国学者张锡厚的 *Prose Writings of Liu Zongyuan*(《柳宗元散文集》)。1977年,英国华裔学者张心沧(H. C. Chang)在《中国文学 2:自然诗歌》(*Chinese Literature II: Nature Poetry*)中翻译了若干柳宗元的诗歌。1979年,刘师舜(Liu Shih Shun)翻译了《中国古典散文:唐宋八大家》(*Chinese Classical Prose: The Eight Masters of the T'ang-Sung Period*),其中收录了柳宗元的部分作品。1992年,陈若水(Chen Jo-shui)撰写的《柳宗元与唐代思想变迁》(*Liu Tsung-yüan and Intellectual Change in T'ang China*)是第一部用英文全面介绍柳宗元的著作,内容涉及柳宗元生活的各个方面及他的主要作品。

进入21世纪,柳宗元诗文的翻译与研究依然在持续进行。2019年,美国汉学家、当代翻译家比尔·波特(Bill Potter,笔名赤松,Red Pine)翻译出版了柳宗元的诗歌集《写在流放途中:柳宗元诗歌》(*Written in Exile: The Poetry of Liu Tsung-yuan*)。比尔·波特译介柳宗元的诗歌,不仅是因为柳宗元在唐宋八大家中享有至高文学声誉和地位,还缘于他的作品承载着大量的中国哲学思想和智慧。比尔·波特成功地在目的语文化中,重现了这一位古代政治家的探索历程,同时将中国传统古典诗歌译介到美国,在忠实和通顺之间找到了良好的平衡点,实现了诗歌翻译的忠实性、可读性和创造性,是中国典籍英译的一个典范。

本章节所选的散文为柳宗元的代表作之一《捕蛇者说》。

【唐代传奇】

小说在中国有着漫长的历史,在司马迁的《史记》中,很多篇章都带有短篇小说的特质。东汉时期,志怪小说开始形成,至魏晋时期,得到了进一步的发展。

传奇始创于初唐,其产生的原因在于唐代的社会生产力较之前代,得到了极大的发展,社会经济繁荣,文化昌盛,诸种因素为传奇小说创作提供了丰富的主题和素材。唐代传奇中的很多人物都可以找到历史原型，部分传奇的主题则借鉴于志怪小说与民间传说，有的传奇来源于域外神话或传说。文人在创作小说的时候，也会有意识地采用虚构手法，用小说表达自己的理想和抱负，传奇小说因此成为唐代文学中极富时代特色的文体。传奇中人物性格饱满，情节曲折离奇，文风辞藻都显示出浓郁的时代风格。传奇兴盛于中唐，至晚唐趋于静寂，到宋代始告终结。

唐代传奇在 19 世纪后期才得到西方学者的关注，出现了不少英译版本。从 20 世纪初到 20 世纪 50 年代末，唐传奇在英美汉学界的传播和接受处于不成熟时期，主要以译介为主，侧重部分单篇传奇文的翻译，尤以《莺莺传》最受关注，共有 5 个译本，其中 3 名译者为非华裔、2 名译者为华裔。"国内对唐代小说译介的历史梳理和信息整理严重不足；相应地，英语世界的唐代小说译介研究也相当匮乏"。根据刘文静《英语世界的唐代小说译介：翻译历史与研究现状》的研究，最早被翻译成英文的唐代传奇是 1877 年发表在《中国评论》上的由唐代文学家李公佐创作的"南柯太守传"。1911 年，翟理斯在《中国神话故事》中翻译了唐代文学家沈既济创作的《枕中记》。荷兰莱顿大学汉学教授高延 (Jan Jakob Maria Groot) 在 20 世纪早期出版的《中国宗教体系》(*The Religious System of China*, 1892) 一书，收录并翻译了一些唐代小说。1919 年英国汉学家阿瑟·韦利出版了《古文选珍（续）》，其中收录了《莺莺传》和《李娃传》两篇小说的译本。1922 年德国汉学家、传教士卫礼贤 (Richard Wilhelm) 编纂、胡德 (Frederick H. Martens) 翻译的《中国神话故事集》(*The Chinese Fairy Book*) 出版，其中选译了《杜子春》等十多个唐代传奇小说篇目，部分篇目成为迄今为止唯一的英译本。

明确将唐传奇纳入小说范畴的西方译者是英国汉学家叶女士，她在 1937 年出版的《中国唐代散文文学》(*Chinese Prose Literature of the T'ang Period*, 又名《〈唐代丛书〉选译》) 是这一时期最重要的唐传奇译著。该书收录的 79 个故事中，唐传奇的重要作品均列其中，这也是迄今为止最全面的唐传奇译本。该书由上下两卷组成，上卷介绍和翻译了唐代的一般散文，下卷介绍和翻译了唐代传奇作品；两卷共选译唐代小说近四百个篇目，包括了唐代小说的主要篇目，绝大多数篇目此后再未有其他版本出现。这本书在英语世界影响比较大，多次再版重印。叶女士对唐代小说的研究首开西方汉学界研究中国文言小说之先河，对汉学研究领域的拓展具有一定的意义。半个世纪后，英国华裔学者张心沧出版《中国文学 3：神怪小说》，其中包括七篇唐传奇，分别是《任氏传》《离魂记》《庐江冯媪传》以及《续玄怪录》中的《薛伟》《李卫公靖》《张逢》和

第九章 唐代诗文经典篇章英译选读

《张老》,每一篇译作前都有一篇分析该作品的小论文,可以说这是一部翻译和研究并重的专著。

最新出版的由西方学者完成的包含唐代传奇英译内容的代表性作品有两部。

第一部为2000年英国汉学家闵福德(John Minford)和刘绍铭(Joseph S. M. Lau)编选的《中国古典文学英译选集(第一卷)》(*Classical Chinese Literature I*,又译为《含英咀华集》)。该书选入不同译者的9篇唐传奇故事,分别是《枕中记》《任氏传》《离魂记》《柳毅传》《莺莺传》《虬髯客传》《订婚店》《杜子春》《河间传》。编者考虑到原本中的文化韵味在翻译中会不可避免地流失,所以在书中增加了根据题目和故事内容而来的书法、绘画、传统的木刻插图、印章和拓印等。这也体现了该书的与众不同,散发着浓郁的中国传统文化风味。该部恢宏大作是两千多年中国古代文学作品的海外英译总括,参考或选用了93部译作,收录了国外最著名的汉学家的作品,如亚瑟·韦利(Arthur Waley)、大卫·霍克斯(David Hawkes)、詹姆斯·理雅各(James Legge)、埃兹拉·庞德(Ezra Pound)、伯顿·华兹生(Burton Watson)、宇文所安(Stephen Owen)、白芝(Cyril Birch)、葛瑞汉(Angus Charles Graham)、肯尼斯·雷克斯罗斯(Kenneth Rexroth,中文名王红公)等,代表了海外中古典文学研究和翻译的最高成就。该选集是"中国古典文学的现代版,是过去300多年来海外译家作品的集成"。

第二部为2010年美国著名汉学家、中国古典文学翻译家倪豪士(William H. Nienhauser, Jr.)翻译的《唐代传奇故事阅读指南》(*Tang Dynasty Tales: A Guided Reader*),其中翻译了6部唐传奇作品,包括《红线》《杜子春》《枕中记》《南柯太守传》《虬髯客传》《霍小玉传》。这些译本都是极为详尽的注释本,目的是便于读者对唐传奇有更为深入的了解。

20世纪40年代开始,旅英和旅美华裔学者也加入唐代传奇的翻译行列。旅美学者王际真1943年编写的《中国古代小说选》包括14篇唐代小说。旅美翻译家和学者林语堂1952年出版《英译重编传奇小说》(*Famous Chinese Short Stories*),翻译了20篇唐宋传奇小说。其余唐代小说的翻译散见于西方汉学家与旅英旅美的华裔作家的各类著作中,此不赘述。

目前唐代小说已有上百个篇目被翻译成英语,有的篇目还被多次翻译,而且不断有唐代小说集和单个文本的专门译著(本)出现。本章选取的唐代传奇为陈玄祐的《离魂记》。

中华典籍英译选读

唐代诗文经典篇章英译选读之一

登 高①

杜 甫

风急天高猿啸哀②,渚③清沙白鸟飞回。

无边落木萧萧④下,不尽长江滚滚来。

万里悲秋常作客,百年多病独登台。

艰难苦恨繁⑤霜鬓,潦倒新停浊酒⑥杯。

注:杜甫《登高》一诗作为唐代诗歌的代表作之一,是诗人于大历二年(767年)秋天,在夔州寓所困顿寥落的状态下创作的一首七言律诗,在唐代律诗创作的技巧上、立意上、音律上和诗境上都非常成熟,堪称一首完美之作。当时的诗人已是56岁的垂垂老人,饱经离乱,贫病交加。有一天,在他独自登临夔州城外的一处高台时,抬眼遥望,天地苍茫,河水汤汤,回顾一世零落,慨叹生命无常,不觉痛从心生,感慨异常,于是写下了这首传扬千古的诗坛佳作。诗中"无边落木萧萧下,不尽长江滚滚来。万里悲秋常作客,百年多病独登台"两句,立意高远,诗境无穷,凄怆苍凉,直击人心,可谓千古名句。因此,《登高》被誉为唐代七律之冠。

【注释】

①〔登高〕中国有在农历九月九日登高的习俗。

②〔猿啸哀〕《水经注·江水》引民谣为:"巴东三峡巫峡长,猿鸣三声泪沾裳。"这里指三峡中的猿鸣声。

③〔渚〕水中的小洲。

④〔萧萧〕拟声词,风吹落叶的声音。

⑤〔繁〕作动词,增多。

⑥〔浊酒〕未过滤的酒,泛指酒,此指用以消愁解忧的酒。

第九章 唐代诗文经典篇章英译选读

主题鉴赏

唐大历二年(767年),56岁的杜甫客居夔州(今重庆奉节),适逢重阳佳节,杜甫登上白帝城附近的高台,写下了这首七律《登高》。《登高》的前四句写景,诗人目光远望之处,风急天高,白鸟飞旋;近处的树木落叶纷纷,江岸空旷寂寥,一派萧瑟。诗人的视线由眼前的纷纷落叶又投射到远处滚滚东流的长江,"不尽长江滚滚来",不仅是空间的旷远,更表达了岁月的漫长。诗人登上高台,极目远望,目力所及之处全是萧瑟秋景。病苦日久,潦倒不堪的诗人,可谓贫困交加,无以为寄,只有孤独地面对滚滚东逝的长江,体味无边无尽的瑟瑟秋意,自感时日无多,不觉悲从中来,无限感怀、无限悲戚。诗歌没有一句一词提及诗人所处的时代背景,但是字里行间却透露出风雨飘摇之际的唐王朝面临的困境,也是劳苦大众处于水深火热生存窘境的折射,表达出诗人深藏心底却也无可奈何的悲痛悯时之情。因此,这首诗不单单是诗人自己生逢乱世坎坷遭逢的写照,也是哀哀生民共同遭遇的命途舛运。两年之后,杜甫便病死于羁旅之途。

英译

Climbing the Heights

Du Fu

The wind blows hard, the heavens, high, gibbons howl in lament,
  isles clear, sands white, where birds turn in flight.
Endless trees shed their leaves that descend in the whistling wind,
  unending, the long River comes on churning.
Grieving for fall across ten thousand leagues, always a traveler,
  often sick in this century of life I climb the terrace alone.
In hardship I bitterly resent these tangled, frost-white locks,
  down and out, I recently quit cups of thick ale.

——Stephen Owen(宇文所安)

英译鉴赏简评

享誉全球的美国汉学家宇文所安先生，从 1981 年开始系统性整理和翻译杜甫的所有诗歌。至 2015 年，他终于完成了《杜甫诗集》的全部英译工作，这是目前为止杜甫诗歌英译最全面、最权威的版本。译者充分利用其英语母语的优势，通过细致入微地描述中文古诗中的意境和景色，使用西方读者熟悉的日常意象，让读者在不知不觉中，想象出旷远辽阔的秋景，使读者感受到一千年前的中国诗人面对苍凉的空间与无尽的流逝时光而产生的寥落寂寞之情。

严格来讲，《登高》这首诗是唐代七律诗歌的最高成就，在翻译中要完全呈现其七律特征并非易事，原诗中的平仄与韵脚，要在翻译版本中得到完美体现，译者需要有很高的汉诗音韵、节拍、修辞等方面的翻译技巧。宇文所安先生对汉诗韵律的把握还是比较成功的，他对头韵（alliteration）如 hard, heavens, high, howl//white, where, whistling wind, 和辅音［s］的大量使用，成功再现了本诗忧伤哀叹的音律感、回旋感，读来让人有种悲怆寂寥不绝于耳之感。句式上，汉语格律诗固有的形式被拆解，代之以英文自由体的诗歌形式。总体而言，英译文还是比较成功地再现了原诗的感情基调和意象特征。

以下为其他译者的译文与宇文所安先生的译本逐行对照版，读者可自行感受两种译文的优劣。

    a. Hiking to High Ground

    b. Climbing the Heights

风急天高猿啸哀，

    a. Apes howl mournfully in high wind under clear sky,

    b. The wind blows hard, the heavens, high, gibbons howl in lament,

渚清沙白鸟飞回。

    a. Birds circle above islet and sand amid limpid water.

    b. isles clear, sands white, where birds turn in flight.

无边落木萧萧下，

    a. Leaves whistle down from a boundless stretch of woods,

    b. Endless trees shed their leaves that descend in the whistling wind,

不尽长江滚滚来。

    a. An endless length of river keeps rolling forward.

第九章 唐代诗文经典篇章英译选读

b. unending, the long River comes on churning.

万里悲秋常作客,

a. In autumn, I'm saddened to be a visitor far away from home,

b. Grieving for fall across ten thousand leagues, always a traveler,

百年多病独登台。

a. I, a sick old man, go up a tower alone.

b. often sick in this century of life I climb the terrace alone.

艰难苦恨繁霜鬓,

a. My hair turns gray in hardship, indignation and confusion,

b. In hardship I bitterly resent these tangled, frost-white locks,

潦倒新停浊酒杯。

a. Poverty-stricken, I stop drinking cheap wine lately.

b. down and out, I recently quit cups of thick ale.

唐代诗文经典篇章英译选读之二

捕蛇者说①

柳宗元

永州之野产异蛇,黑质而白章②,触草木尽死,以啮人,无御之者。然得而腊③之以为饵,可以已大风④、挛踠⑤、瘘⑥、疠⑦,去死肌,杀三虫。其始,太医以王命聚之,岁赋其二,募有能捕之者,当其租入,永之人争奔走焉。

有蒋氏者,专其利三世矣。问之,则曰:"吾祖死于是,吾父死于是,今吾嗣⑧为之十二年,几死者数矣。"言之,貌若甚戚者。余悲之,且曰:"若毒之乎?余将告于莅事者,更若役,复若赋,则何如?"

蒋氏大戚,汪然出涕曰:"君将哀而生之乎?则吾斯役之不幸,未若复吾赋不幸之甚也。向吾不为斯役,则久已病矣。自吾氏三世居是乡,积于今六十岁矣,而乡邻之生日蹙⑨。殚⑩其地之出,竭其庐之入,号呼而转徙,饥渴而顿踣⑪,触风雨,犯寒暑,呼嘘毒疠,往往而死者相藉⑫也。曩⑬与吾祖居者,今其室十无一焉;与吾父居者,今其室十无二三焉;与吾居十二年者,今其室十无四五焉,非死而徙尔。而吾以捕蛇独存。悍吏之来吾乡,叫嚣乎东西,隳突⑭乎南北,哗然而骇者,虽鸡狗不得宁焉。吾恂恂⑮而起,视其缶,而吾蛇尚存,则弛然⑯而卧。谨食⑰之,时而献⑱焉。退而甘食其土之有,以尽吾齿⑲。盖一岁之犯死者二焉,其余则熙熙而乐⑳,岂若吾乡邻之旦旦㉑有是哉!今虽死乎此,比吾乡邻之死则已后矣,又安敢毒㉒耶?"

余闻而愈悲。孔子曰:"苛政猛于虎也!"吾尝疑乎是㉓,今以蒋氏观之,犹信。呜呼!孰知赋敛之毒,有甚是蛇者乎!故为之说,以俟㉔夫观人风㉕者得焉。

注:唐顺宗时期(761年—806年),柳宗元参与了以王叔文为首的官僚士大夫发起的永贞革新运动(因在永贞[805年8月—806年]年间进行,故得名)。这场以打击宦官势力、革除政治积弊为主要目的政治改革最终以失败告终,柳宗元因此被贬谪永州。在永州为官期间,他接触到大量的下层人民,亲身体会了劳苦大众的困苦生活,对他们产生了深切的同情。在此期间,他创作了大量忧民恤世的现实主义作品,《捕蛇者说》就是其中的代表作。文章叙述了捕蛇者一家三代的悲惨生活,引申出苛政的毒害。捕蛇者宁愿忍受毒蛇的剧毒,也不敢面对赋税之毒,强烈的对比引发了读者对劳苦大众的悲切同情。这篇现实主义风格的散文犀利地揭示了社会的黑暗和苛政对老百姓的压迫,柳宗元也在这篇散文中表达了自己一贯的文学主张,文章要起到社会作用。他希望文章能被上层看到,希冀统治者去变革以改善劳动人民的生活,改善整个社会的黑暗现状。

【注释】

①选自《柳河东集》卷一六(中华书局1979年版)。
②〔质〕质地,底子,东西的本体,此指蛇的身体。〔章〕花纹,斑纹。
③〔腊(xī)〕干肉。此处用作动词,指把蛇晾干。
④〔大风〕麻风病。

第九章 唐代诗文经典篇章英译选读

⑤〔挛踠(luán wǎn)〕手脚弯曲不能伸展之病。
⑥〔瘘(lòu)〕中医指颈部生疮,久而不愈,常出脓水。
⑦〔疠(lì)〕恶疮。
⑧〔嗣(sì)〕接续,继承。
⑨〔蹙(cù)〕窘迫,穷困。
⑩〔殚〕用尽,竭尽。
⑪〔顿踣(bó)〕跌倒在地上。
⑫〔相藉(xiāng jiè)〕相互挨着,形容死亡者之多。
⑬〔曩(nǎng)〕以往,从前,过去。
⑭〔隳突(huī tū)〕冲撞、破坏、骚扰。
⑮〔恂恂(xún)〕担心忧虑的样子。
⑯〔弛(chí)然〕放松,松懈,解除。
⑰〔谨食(sì)〕小心地喂养。
⑱〔时而献〕到规定的时间就交纳上去(指以蛇交纳赋税)。
⑲〔以尽吾齿〕此指生活下去。〔齿〕指人的年龄。
⑳〔熙熙〕和乐,快乐,心情舒畅。
㉑〔旦旦〕天天。
㉒〔安敢毒〕怎么敢怨恨(捕蛇这件事)。〔毒〕怨恨,不满。
㉓〔尝〕曾经。〔疑〕怀疑。〔乎〕介词,相当于"对"。〔是〕代词,这。"疑乎是",介宾结构后置,正常语序应为"乎是疑",即:对此存有怀疑。〔吾尝疑乎是〕我曾经对此(这里指孔子说的"苛政猛于虎")存有怀疑。
㉔〔俟(sì)〕等待。
㉕〔观〕考察,调查。〔人风〕民风、民情,因避唐代李世民讳而改为"人风"。

白话释义

　　永州的野外出产一种奇特的蛇,它有着黑色的身体白色的花纹。如果这种蛇碰到草木,草木全都干枯而死;如果咬了人,没有能够抵挡蛇毒的方法。然而捉到后晾干把它拿来做药引,可以用来治愈麻风、手脚蜷曲、脖肿、恶疮,去除死肉,杀死人体内的寄生虫。起初,太医用皇帝的命令征集这种蛇,每年征收这种蛇两次,招募能够捕捉这种蛇的人,充抵他的赋税。永州的人都争着去做捕蛇这件事。

　　有个姓蒋的人家,享有这种好处已经三代了。我问他,他却说:"我的祖父死在捕蛇这件差事上,我父亲也死在这件事情上。现在我继承祖业干这差事也已十二年了,好几次也险些丧命。"他说这番话时,脸上露出忧伤的神色。我同情地对他说:"你怨恨捕蛇这件事吗?我打算告诉管理政事的地方官,让他更换你的差事,恢复你的赋税,怎么样?"

蒋氏听了更加悲伤,满眼含泪地说:"你是哀怜我,使我活下去吗?然而我干这差事的不幸,还比不上恢复我缴纳赋税的不幸那么厉害呀。假使我不干这差事,那我就早已困苦不堪了。我家住到这个地方已经六十年了,可乡邻们的生活一天比一天窘迫,把他们土地上生产出来的都拿去,把他们家里的收入也尽数拿去交租税仍然不够,只得号啕痛哭辗转逃亡,又饥又渴倒在地上,一路上顶着狂风暴雨,冒着严寒酷暑,呼吸着带毒的废气,一个接一个地死去,经常是死人压着死人。从前和我祖父同住在这里的乡邻,现在十户当中剩不下一户了;和我父亲住在一起的乡邻,现在十户当中只有不到两三户了;和我一起住了十二年的乡邻,现在十户当中只有不到四五户了。那些乡邻不是死了就是迁走了。我凭借捕蛇这个差事才活了下来。凶暴的官吏来到我们村,到处吵嚷叫嚣,到处骚扰,那种喧闹叫嚷惊扰乡民的气势,不要说人即使鸡狗也不得安宁啊!我就小心翼翼地起来,看看我的瓦罐,还好,我的蛇还在,于是放心地躺下了。我小心地喂养蛇,到规定的日子就把它献上去。回家后有滋有味地吃着田地里出产的东西,度过我的余年。估计一年当中冒死的情况只是两次,其余时间我都可以快快乐乐地过日子。哪像我的乡邻们那样天天都有死亡的威胁呢!现在即使我死在这差事上,与我的乡邻相比,我已经死在他们后面了,又怎么敢怨恨捕蛇这件事呢?"

蒋氏的诉说令我越听越悲伤。孔子说:"苛酷的统治比老虎还要凶暴啊!"我曾经怀疑过这句话,现在根据蒋氏的遭遇来看这句话,还真是可信啊。唉!谁知道苛捐杂税的毒害比这种毒蛇的毒害更厉害呢!所以我写了这篇文章,以期待那些朝廷派来考察民情的人能看到它。

Catching Snakes

In the wilds of Hu-Kuang there is an extraordinary kind of snake, having a black body with white rings. Deadly fatal, even to the grass and trees it may chance to touch; in man, its bite is absolutely incurable. Yet if caught and prepared, when dry, in the form of cakes, the flesh of this snake will soothe excitement, heal leprous sores, remove sloughing flesh, and expel evil spirits. And so it came about that the Court physician, acting under imperial orders, exacted from each family a return of two of these snakes every year; but as few persons were able to comply with the demand, it was subsequently made known that the return of snakes was to be considered in lien of the usual taxes. Thereupon there ensued a general stampede among the people of those parts.

However, there was one man whose family had lived there for three generations; and from him I obtained the following information: "My grandfather lost his life in snake-catching. So did my father. And during the twelve years that I have been engaged in the same way, death has several times come very near to me." He was deeply moved during this recital; but when I asked if I should state his sad case to the authorities and apply for him to be allowed to pay taxes in the regular manner, he burst into tears and said, "Alas! sir, you would take away my means of livelihood altogether. The misery of this state is as nothing when compared with the misery of that. Formerly, under the ordinary conditions of life, we suffered greatly; but for the past three generations we have been settled in this district, now some sixty years since. During that period, my fellow-villagers have become more and more impoverished. Their substance has been devoured, and in beggary they have gone weeping and wailing away. Exposed to the inclemency of wind and rain, enduring heat and cold, they have fled from the cruel scourge, in most cases, to die. Of those families which were here in my grandfather's time, there remains not more than one in ten; of those here in my father's time, not more than two or three; and of those still here in my own time, not more than four or five. They are all either dead or gone elsewhere; while we, the snake-catchers, alone survive. Harsh tyrants sweep down upon us, and throw everybody and everything, even to the brute beasts, into paroxysms of terror and disorder. But I, — I get up in the morning and look into the jar where my snakes are kept; and if they are still there, I lie down at night in peace. At the appointed time, I take care that they are fit to be handed in; and when that is done, I retire to enjoy the produce of my farm and complete the allotted span of my existence. Only twice a year have I to risk my life; the rest is peaceful enough and not to be compared with the daily round of annoyance which falls to the share of my fellow-villagers. And even though I were to die now in this employ, I should still have outlived almost all my contemporaries. Can I then complain?

This story gave me food for much sad reflection. I had always doubted the saying of Confucius that "bad government is worse than a tiger," but now I felt its truth. Alas! who would think that the tax-collector could be more venomous than a snake? I therefore record this for the information of those whom it may concern.

——Herbert Allen Giles(赫伯特·翟理斯)

英译鉴赏简评

赫伯特·翟理斯(Herbert Allen Giles)是英国著名的汉学家。他于1867至1892年间曾担任英国驻华外交官。1897年,翟理斯成为剑桥大学汉语教授,1932年退休。翟理斯翻译过很多中国古典文学作品,是西方汉学界最早翻译和评价柳宗元诗文的汉学家。其专著《中国文学史》(*A History of Chinese Literature*. 1973.)一书,是西方汉学家撰写的第一部中国文学史专著,也是最早向西方读者系统介绍中国文学发展概况的杰作,因此,虽然初版于19世纪末,却具有长久的生命力,在东西方汉学界产生了积极的影响。全书共分八章,第四章唐代专题的第二小节"古典文学和一般文学(Classical and General Literature)"重点评述了韩愈、柳宗元,翻译了柳宗元的《捕蛇者说》《种树郭橐驼传》等散文,并做了深入的分析。翟氏评述文字准确生动,译文流畅可读,受到读者的喜爱。在为数不多的柳宗元散文翻译中,翟理斯翻译的作品显得尤为珍贵,他翻译的几篇柳宗元的散文,被多次收录在不同的书中。

翟理斯通晓中国文化,精通汉语语言。这篇《捕蛇者说》的英译版本,语言简单易懂,行文流畅顺达,是不可多得一篇翻译佳作。兹举几例,以作说明。

"曩与吾祖居者,今其室十无一焉;与吾父居者,今其室十无二三焉",此句带有明显的唐代骈文的特质,而翟理思的译文句式同样简约整饬,工整对仗:

"**Of those families** which were here in my grandfather's time, there remains not more than one in ten; **of those here** in my father's time, not more than two or three; and **of those still here** in my own time, not more than four or five."

另如"则吾斯役之不幸,未若复吾赋不幸之甚也"句,翟译:"The misery of this state is as nothing when compared with the misery of that",句法结构紧凑顺畅,深得汉语文句修辞之美、语义之质。

唐代诗文经典篇章英译选读之三

《滕王阁序》(节选)

王 勃

时维①九月,序②属三秋③。潦水尽④而寒潭清⑤,烟光凝而暮山紫。俨⑥骖䭽⑦于上路⑧,访⑨风景于崇阿⑩;临帝子之长洲,得天人之旧馆⑪。层峦耸翠,上出重霄⑫;飞阁流丹⑬,下临无地⑭。鹤汀凫渚⑮,穷岛屿之萦回⑯;桂殿兰宫,即冈峦之体势⑰。

披绣闼⑱,俯雕甍⑲,山原旷其盈视⑳,川泽纡其骇瞩㉑。闾阎扑地,钟鸣鼎食之家㉒;舸舰迷津,青雀黄龙之舳㉓。云销雨霁,彩彻区明㉔。落霞与孤鹜齐飞,秋水共长天一色。渔舟唱晚,响穷彭蠡之滨㉕;雁阵惊寒,声断衡阳之浦㉖。

遥襟甫畅,逸兴遄飞㉗。爽籁发而清风生,纤歌凝而白云遏㉘。睢园绿竹㉙,气凌彭泽之樽㉚;邺水朱华㉛,光照临川之笔㉜。四美具,二难并㉝。穷睇眄㉞于中天,极娱游于暇日。天高地迥㉟,觉宇宙㊱之无穷;兴尽悲来,识盈虚之有数㊲。望长安于日下,目吴会于云间㊳。地势极而南溟㊴深,天柱高而北辰远㊵。关山㊶难越,谁悲失路之人?萍水相逢㊷,尽是他乡之客。怀帝阍㊸而不见,奉宣室㊹以何年?

嗟乎!时运不齐㊺,命途多舛。冯唐易老,李广难封㊻。屈贾谊于长沙㊼,非无圣主;窜梁鸿于海曲,岂乏明时㊽?所赖君子见机㊾,达人知命。老当益壮,宁移白首之心?穷且益坚,不坠青云之志㊿。酌贪泉而觉爽[51],处涸辙[52]以犹欢。北海虽赊,扶摇可接[53];东隅已逝,桑榆非晚㊽。孟尝㊾高洁,空余报国之情;阮籍猖狂,岂效穷途之哭㊿!

【注释】

① 〔维〕正逢。一说此字为语气词,趁四字之韵。
② 〔序〕春夏秋冬四时之序。
③ 〔三秋〕古人称七、八、九月为孟秋、仲秋、季秋,三秋即季秋,九月。
④ 〔潦(lǎo)水〕雨后的积水。〔尽〕没有。此处指雨后地上的积水消尽。
⑤ 〔寒潭清〕寒凉的潭水清澈见底。
⑥ 〔俨〕通"严",整齐划一的样子。
⑦ 〔骖騑(cān fēi)〕古代驾车的马若是三匹或四匹,就有骖、服之分。中间驾辕的马叫"服",两旁的马叫"骖"。一说"服"左边的马叫"骖","服"右边的马叫"騑"。骖服和骖騑,又泛指拉车的马或车马。
⑧ 〔上路〕高高的山路。
⑨ 〔访〕看,游览。
⑩ 〔崇阿(ē)〕阿,山的凹曲处。此指高大峻峭的山陵。
⑪ 〔临〕得,到达。〔长洲〕滕王阁前赣江中的沙洲。〔旧馆〕指滕王阁。〔帝子、天人〕均指滕王李元婴。有版本为"得仙人之旧馆"。
⑫ 〔层峦〕山峦重叠。〔上〕上达,耸入。
⑬ 〔飞阁〕架空建筑的阁道。〔流〕形容彩画的阁楼色彩鲜丽。〔丹〕丹漆,泛指彩绘。此指飞檐涂饰着色彩鲜艳的漆。有版本为"飞阁翔丹"。
⑭ 〔下临无地〕从滕王阁高处俯视,看不到地面。
⑮ 〔汀〕水边平地。〔凫〕野鸭。〔渚〕水中小洲。〔鹤汀(tīng)凫渚(zhǔ)〕鹤所栖息的水边平地,野鸭聚集的小洲。
⑯ 〔萦回〕曲折迂回。
⑰ 〔桂,兰〕两种名贵的树,形容宫殿的华丽,讲究。〔冈峦之体势〕依着山岗的形势(而高低起伏)。
⑱ 〔披〕开。〔绣闼(tà)〕雕饰华丽精美的大门。
⑲ 〔雕甍(méng)〕雕饰华美的屋脊。
⑳ 〔旷〕辽阔。〔盈视〕极目远望,满眼都是。
㉑ 〔纡〕曲折蜿蜒。〔骇瞩〕惊骇于所看到的景象。
㉒ 〔闾阎〕里门,这里代指房屋。〔扑〕布满。〔钟鸣鼎食〕古代贵族鸣钟列鼎而食,所以用钟鸣鼎食指代名门望族。

第九章 唐代诗文经典篇章英译选读

㉓〔舸〕船《方言》:"南楚江、湘,凡船大者谓之舸。"〔弥〕满。〔青雀黄龙〕船的装饰形状,船头作鸟头型、龙头型。〔舳〕船尾把舵处,这里代指船只。

㉔〔销〕"销"通"消",消散。〔霁〕雨过天晴。〔彩〕日光。〔区〕天空。〔彻〕通贯。

㉕〔响穷〕穷尽,引申为"直到"。〔彭蠡〕古代大泽,即今鄱阳湖。此指歌声传到了鄱阳湖畔。

㉖〔衡阳〕今属湖南省,境内有回雁峰,相传秋雁到此就不再南飞,待春而返。宋范仲淹《渔家傲·秋思》:"塞下秋来风景异,衡阳雁去无留意。"〔断〕止。〔浦〕水边、岸边。

㉗〔遥〕远望。〔襟〕胸襟。〔甫〕顿时。〔兴〕兴致。〔遄〕迅速。〔畅〕舒畅。此指登高望远,胸怀顿觉舒畅,超逸的兴致生起于心胸。

㉘〔爽籁〕清脆的排箫音乐。〔籁〕管子参差不齐的排箫。〔遏〕阻止,引申为"停止"。〔白云遏〕形容音响优美,能驻行云。《列子·汤问》:"薛谭学讴于秦青,未穷青之技,自谓尽之,遂辞归。秦青弗止,饯于郊衢。抚节悲歌,声振林木,响遏行云。"此句意为清风徐徐,清丽的排箫乐音吸引来漂游的白云,在此停驻。

㉙〔睢园〕西汉文帝第二子,汉景帝之弟梁孝王所建的菟园(故址在今河南商丘市梁园区)。梁孝王曾在园中聚集文人饮酒赋诗。《水经注》:"睢水又东南流,历于竹圃……世人言梁王竹园也。"

㉚〔凌〕超过。〔彭泽〕县名,在今江西湖口县东,此代指陶潜。〔陶潜〕陶渊明,曾官彭泽县令,世称陶彭泽。〔樽〕酒器。陶渊明《归去来兮辞》有"有酒盈樽"之句。睢园绿竹,气凌〔彭泽之樽〕今日盛宴好比当年梁园雅集,大家酒量也胜过陶渊明。

㉛〔邺水〕在邺下(今河北省临漳县)。邺下是曹魏兴起的地方,三曹常在此雅集作诗。曹植在此作《公宴诗》。〔朱华〕荷花。曹植《公宴诗》:"秋兰被长坂,朱华冒绿池。"

㉜〔临川〕郡名,治所在今江西省抚州市,代指即谢灵运。谢灵运曾任临川内史,《宋书》本传称他"文章之美,江左莫逮"。

㉝〔四美〕指良辰、美景、赏心、乐事。另一说指:音乐、饮食、文章、言语之美。刘琨《答卢谌诗》:"音以赏奏,味以殊珍,文以明言,言以畅神。之子之往,四美不臻。"〔二难〕指贤主、嘉宾难得。谢灵运《拟魏太子邺中集诗序》:"天下良辰、美景、赏心、乐事,四者难并。"王勃说"二难并"活用谢文,良辰、美景为时地方面的条件,归为一类;赏心、悦目为人事方面的条件,归为一类。

㉞〔睇眄〕看。〔中天〕长天。此指极目远望天空。

㉟〔迥〕大。

㊱〔宇宙〕喻指天地。《淮南子·原道训》高诱注:"四方上下曰'宇',古往今来曰'宙'。"

㊲〔盈虚〕消长,指变化。〔数〕定数,命运。此指知道万事万物的消长兴衰是有定数的。

㊳〔吴会(kuài)〕古代绍兴的别称,绍兴古称吴会、会稽,是三吴之首(吴会、吴郡、吴兴),唐代绍兴是国际大都市,与长安齐名。同时期的诗人宋之问也有意思相近的一首诗:"薄游京都日,遥羡稽山名。"《世说新语·排调》:荀鸣鹤、陆士龙二人未相识,俱会张茂先坐。张令共语。以其并有大才,可勿作常语。陆举手曰:"云间陆士龙。"荀答曰:"日下荀鸣鹤。"《古代汉语》解释:"陆云,字士龙,三国吴丞相陆逊之孙。陆逊封华亭侯,陆氏世居华亭。华亭古称'云间'。荀隐,颍川人。颍川,地近京城。后以'日下'喻'京都'。"此句字面意思是远望长安在夕阳下,遥看吴越在云海间。

㊴〔南溟〕南方的大海。

㊵〔天柱〕传说中昆仑山高耸入天的铜柱。《神异经》:"昆仑之山,有铜柱焉。其高入天,所谓天柱也。"〔北辰〕北极星,比喻国君。《论语·为政》:"为政以德,譬如北辰,居其所而众星共(拱)之。"

㊶〔关山〕关隘和高山。〔悲〕同情,可怜。〔失路〕仕途不遇。

㊷〔萍水相逢〕浮萍随水漂泊,聚散不定。比喻向来不认识的人偶然相遇。

㊸〔帝阍〕天帝的守门人。屈原《离骚》:"吾令帝阍开关兮,倚阊阖而望予。"此处借指皇帝的宫门。

㊹〔奉宣室〕代指入朝做官。贾谊迁谪长沙四年后,汉文帝复召他回长安,于宣室中问鬼神之事。〔宣室〕汉未央宫正殿,皇帝召见大臣议事之处。〔命途〕命运。

㊺〔齐〕通"济",顺利,有益。〔不齐〕不顺,蹉跎坎坷。〔时运不齐(jì)〕命运不佳。

㊻〔冯唐易老〕冯唐在汉文帝、汉景帝时不被重用,汉武帝时被举荐,已是九十多岁。〔李广难封〕李广,汉武帝时名将,多次与匈奴作战,军功卓著,却始终未获封爵。

㊼〔屈贾谊于长沙〕贾谊在汉文帝时被贬为长沙王太傅。〔圣主〕指汉文帝,泛指圣明的君主。

㊽〔梁鸿〕东汉人,作《五噫歌》讽刺朝廷,因此得罪汉章帝,避居齐鲁、吴中。〔明时〕指汉章帝时代,泛指圣明的时代。

㊾〔机〕通"几"，预兆，细微的征兆。《易·系辞下》："君子见几(机)而作。"〔达人知命〕通达事理的人。

(50)〔老当益壮〕年纪虽大，但志气更旺盛，干劲更足。《后汉书·马援传》："丈夫为志，穷当益坚，老当益壮。"〔坠〕坠落，引申为"放弃"。〔青云之志〕《续逸民传》："嵇康早有青云之志。"

(51)〔贪泉〕在广州附近的石门，传说饮此水会贪得无厌，吴隐之喝下此水操守反而更加坚定。据《晋书·吴隐之传》，廉官吴隐之赴广州刺史任，饮贪泉之水，并作诗说："古人云此水，一歃怀千金。试使(伯)夷(叔)齐饮，终当不易心。"

(52)〔处涸辙〕干涸的车辙，比喻困厄的处境。典出《庄子·内篇·大宗师》和《庄子·外篇·天运》鲋鱼处涸辙的故事："泉涸，鱼相与处于陆，相呴以湿，相濡以沫，不如相忘于江湖。"

(53)〔北海虽赊，扶摇可接〕北海虽然遥远，乘风万里亦可抵达。

(54)〔东隅已逝，桑榆非晚〕早年的时光消逝，如果珍惜时光，发愤图强，晚年也并不晚。语出《后汉书·冯异传》："失之东隅，收之桑榆。"〔东隅〕指日出处，表示早晨，引申为"早年"。〔桑榆〕日落处，表示傍晚，引申为"晚年"。

(55)〔孟尝〕据《后汉书·孟尝传》，孟尝字伯周，东汉会稽上虞人，曾任合浦太守，以廉洁奉公著称，后因病隐居。桓帝时，虽有人屡次荐举，终不见用。

(56)〔阮籍〕字嗣宗，晋代名士，不满世事，佯装狂放，常驾车出游，路不通时就痛哭而返。《晋书·阮籍传》：籍"时率意独驾，不由径路。车迹所穷，辄恸哭而反。"〔猖狂〕狷狂，狂放不羁。

白话释义

时值深秋九月，雨后地上的积水消尽，潭水清澈冰冷，天空中云淡雾轻，暮霭中山峦紫光一片。驾着马车走在高高的山路上，在崇山峻岭中访求风景。来到昔日帝子的长洲，找到仙人居住过的宫殿。这里山峦重叠，青翠的山峰耸入云霄。凌空的楼阁，红色的阁道犹如飞翔在天，从阁上看不到地面。仙鹤野鸭栖止的水边平地和水中小洲，极尽岛屿的迂回曲折之势；华丽威严的宫殿，依凭起伏的山峦而建。

推开雕花精美的阁门，俯视彩饰的屋脊，山峰平原尽收眼底，河流蜿蜒得令人惊讶。遍地是里巷宅舍，许多钟鸣鼎食的富贵人家。舸舰塞满了渡口，尽是雕上了青雀黄龙花纹的大船。云消雨停，阳光普照，天空晴朗；落日映射下的彩霞与孤鸟一齐飞翔，秋天的江水和辽阔的天空连成一片，浑然一色。傍晚时分，渔夫在渔船上歌唱,那歌声响彻彭蠡湖滨;深秋时节,雁群感到寒意而发出惊叫,哀鸣声一直持续到衡阳的水滨。

放眼远望,胸襟顿时感到舒畅,超逸的兴致立即兴起。排箫的音响引来徐徐清风,柔缓的歌声吸引住飘动的白云。今日盛宴好比当年梁园雅集,大家酒量也胜过陶渊明。参加宴会的文人学士,就像当年的曹植,写出"朱华冒绿池"一般的美丽诗句,其风流文采映照着谢灵运的诗笔。音乐与饮食、文章和言语这四种美好的事物都已经齐备,贤主、嘉宾这两个难得的条件也凑在一起了。向天空中极目远眺,在假日里尽情欢娱。苍天高远,大地寥廓,令人感到宇宙的无穷无尽。欢乐逝去,悲哀袭来,万事万物的消长兴衰是有定数的。远望长安沉落到夕阳之下,遥看吴郡隐现在云雾之间。地理形势极为偏远,南方大海特别幽深,昆仑山上天柱高耸,缈缈夜空北极远悬。关山重重难以越过,有谁同情我这不得志的人?偶然相逢,满座都是他乡的客人。怀念着君王的宫门,但却不被召见,什么时候才能像贾谊那样到宣室侍奉君王呢?

呵,各人的时机不同,人生的命运多有不顺。冯唐容易衰老,李广立功无数却难得封侯。贾谊这样有才华的人屈居于长沙,并不是因为当时没有圣明的君主,梁鸿逃匿到齐鲁海滨,不是也在政治昌明的时代吗?只不过由于君子能了解时机,通达的人知道自己的命运罢了。年岁虽老而心犹壮,怎能在白头时改变心情?遭遇穷困而意志更加坚定,在任何情况下也不放弃自己的凌云之志。即使喝了贪泉的水,心境依然清爽廉洁;即使身处于干涸的车辙中,胸怀依然开朗愉快。北海虽然遥远,乘着大风仍然可以到达;晨光虽已逝去,珍惜黄昏却为时不晚。孟尝心性高洁,但白白地怀抱着报国的热情,阮籍为人放纵不羁,我们怎能学他那种走到穷途就哭泣的行为呢!

A Tribute to King Teng's Tower (Excerpt)
Wang Bo

It is September, the third month of autumn. The puddles on the ground have dried up, and the water in the pond is cool and translucent. At dusk the rays of the setting sun, condensed in the evening haze, turn the mountains purple. In the stately carriages drawn by the horses we make our way ahead, visiting the attractive scenic spot in the mountains. Soon we arrive at the river

第九章 唐代诗文经典篇章英译选读

bank, where the King Teng's Tower beckons, then we ascend the tower where the fairy once dwelled. Ranges upon ranges of green mountain rise as high as the sky. The red glow in the water is the reflection of the richly painted tower that seems hovering in the air. From its heights no land is visible. Circling around are the wild ducks on the sand-bars. Cassia-wood courts and magnolia-wood halls rise and fall like mountain ranges.

Pushing open the door carved with decorative patterns, I look down upon endless waves of brightly tinted roof tiles, each elaborately engraved with lovely etchings. A panorama of mountains and plains stretches beneath me, and I am mesmerized by the mighty scene of the winding rivers and big lakes. In the city there are houses everywhere. There are families of great affluence, whose meals are served with many cooking tripods of food and to the accompaniment of music. Massive ships and fierce war vessels are densely moored at the ports. On the sterns of many ships are carved designs of blue birds and brown dragons. The rain has just let up and the rainbow has vanished. The sunlight shoots through the rosy clouds, and the autumn water is merged with the boundless sky into one hue. The fishermen can be heard singing the evening songs, their voices drifting as far as the banks of the Poyang Lake. Even the wild geese feel the chill of dusk settling upon them, and they cry all the way while flying southward, disappearing around the south bend of the Heng Mountain.

Looking afar and chanting, and then looking downward and singing, I feel a sudden rush of ecstasy soaring up in me. The music of the panpipe is like a gentle cool breeze. The soft singing lingers on; it is so soothing that even the passing white clouds seem to come to a halt. The gathering here can be compared to the banquet in the bamboo garden hosted by Prince of Xiao of the Liang State, and many a guest is a greater drinker than TaoYuanming. It is also like the feast at River Ye where Cao Zhi composed the poem in praise of the lotus flower. Present are many talented scholars who are as gifted as Xie Lingyun of Linchuan. It is not an easy thing to have four excellent things all at once, that is, good weather, beautiful scenery, full enjoyment and heartfelt happiness, and it is even more difficult to have a generous host and honored guests. I look into the vast expanse of the sky and amuse myself to my heart's content on this festive day. The sky is high and the land is boundless; I cannot but feel the immensity of the universe. Sadness follows happiness. I am aware that success and failure are predestined. I look into the distance, but Chang'an, the capital of the country, is far beyond the setting sun in the west, and Wuhui is unapproachable somewhere amid the clouds. At the farthest end of the south are the depths of the South Sea, and far away in the north is the pillar that upholds the sky, but the Polestar is still farther. Since the mountains and passes are hard to travel over, who would sympathize with the disappointed ones? The people I meet here are all politically frustrated, drifting together like duckweeds. I pine for the Emperor but am not summoned. How long should I wait before I am called to the court again like Jia Yi?

Alas! I am ill fated, and my life is full of frustrations. Feng Tang grew old quickly and Li Guang had difficulty getting promoted. Jia Yi was unjustly exiled to Changsha. Was it because there was no wise emperor on the throne? Liang Hong had to seek refuge at the seaside. Was it because there was no good government in his time? Fortunately what supports one is the belief that a man of noble character always contented with his lot. Old as one is, he gains vigor with age and by no means wavers in his aspiration. Poor as one is, he is all the more determined in adversity and by no means gives up his ambition. One keeps his integrity even if he has drunk the water of the spring of Avarice and is cheerful even as he is confronted with misfortune. Though the North Sea is far away, one can still get there with the help of the strong wind. Though the morning is gone, it is not too late to make up the loss in the evening. Meng Chang was noble and honest, but his devotion to the country was futile. Ruan Ji was unruly and untrammeled, but he burst out crying when in dire straits. How can we learn from him?

——罗经国

英译鉴赏简评

有学者认为,原作与翻译的关系是种子与土壤的关系,种子即使再好,没有

第九章 唐代诗文经典篇章英译选读

适合其生长的土壤,就无法在新的陆地上获得新生。同理,原作要获得异域的认可,必须借助译者的翻译之功,好的译者可以让原作大放异彩,而蹩脚的译者可能让原作被误读误解,甚至无人问津。因此,要翻译好特殊体裁的作品,如骈体文,译者的翻译技巧和悟性应非同平常。王勃的《滕王阁序》有"天下第一骈文"之称,其中许多怡丽优美的句子被传诵至今,如"落霞与孤鹜齐飞,秋水共长天一色""关山难越,谁悲失路之人?萍水相逢,尽是他乡之客""时运不齐,命途多舛。冯唐易老,李广难封""老当益壮,宁移白首之心?穷且益坚,不坠青云之志"。要翻译出才子王勃的"天下第一骈体文"的"味""色""形""音""意",非常不易。而罗经国先生,不愧为资深翻译家,他的译文在以上几个方面皆有亮点可观。兹举几例以作说明。

"老当益壮,宁移白首之心?穷且益坚,不坠青云之志"。罗经国教授的译文句式工整对仗,"**Old as one is**, he gains vigor with age and by no means wavers in his aspiration. **Poor as one is**, he is all the more determined in adversity and by no means gives up his ambition.",选词音韵和谐"vigor/with/waver""as/age/aspiration/all/adversity/ambition";"gain/give"。

"落霞与孤鹜齐飞,秋水共长天一色"。罗经国教授的英译文为:"The sunlight shoots through the rosy clouds, and the autumn water is merged with the boundless sky into one hue."。编者以为,该句的英译,在文学色彩上和骈文的音韵上,不如许渊冲先生的译文精彩,"The rainbow clouds with lonely bird together fly; The autumn water blends with the endless blue sky."。要突出骈文的音效,就要在选词的音和节上下功夫。在参考两位翻译大家精彩译文的基础上,编者尝试对此句做如下拙译,请读者批评,"The sunset glow flows together with a solitary goose; the autumn water infuses with the high sky into siren hues"。

唐代诗文经典篇章英译选读之四

离魂记①

陈玄祐

天授②三年,清河③张镒,因官家于衡州④。

291

性简静，寡知友。无子，有女二人。其长早亡；幼女倩娘，端妍绝伦。镒外甥太原王宙，幼聪悟，美容范。镒常器重，每曰："他时当以倩娘妻之。"

后各长成。宙与倩娘常私感想于寤寐，家人莫知其状。

后有宾寮之选者求之，镒许焉。女闻而郁⑤抑，宙亦深恚⑥恨。托以当调，请赴京，止之不可，遂厚遣之。宙阴恨悲恸，决别上船。

日暮，至山郭数里。夜方半，宙不寐，忽闻岸上有一人，行声甚速，须臾至船。问之，乃倩娘徒行跣足⑦而至。宙惊喜发狂，执手问其从来。泣曰："君厚意如此，寝梦相感。今将夺我此志，又知君深情不易，思将杀身奉报，是以亡命来奔。"宙非意所望，欣跃⑧特甚。遂匿倩娘于船，连夜遁去。

倍道兼行，数月至蜀。凡五年，生两子，与镒绝信。其妻常思父母，涕泣言曰："吾曩日⑨不能相负，弃大义而来奔君。向⑩今五年，恩慈间阻。覆载⑪之下，胡⑫颜独存也？"

宙哀之，曰："将归，无苦。"遂俱归衡州。

既至，宙独身先至镒家，首谢⑬其事。镒曰："倩娘病在闺中数年，何其诡说也！"宙曰："见在舟中！"镒大惊，促使人验之。果见倩娘在船中，颜色怡畅，讯使者曰："大人⑭安否？"家人异之，疾走报镒。

室中女闻，喜而起，饰妆更衣，笑而不语，出与相迎，翕⑮然而合为一体，其衣裳皆重。

其家以事不正，秘之。惟亲戚间有潜知之者。后四十年间，夫妻皆丧。二男并孝廉⑯擢⑰第⑱，至丞⑲、尉⑳。

玄祐少常闻此说，而多异同，或谓其虚。大历㉑末，遇莱芜㉒县令张仲规，因备述其本末。镒则仲规堂叔［祖］㉓，而说极备悉，故记之。

注："离魂题材"在中国古代小说中屡见不鲜，有在世离魂，也有死后重生。魏晋时期已有大量的志怪小说涉及离魂题材，《太平广记》中也有大量的离魂题材小说。《离魂记》作者陈玄祐，其生平事迹不详，大约是唐代大历时人。这是以唐

第九章 唐代诗文经典篇章英译选读

朝宰相张镒(yì)为素材背景的一个故事,情节离奇曲折,反映了年轻人向往美好爱情的心声。这个故事广受欢迎,元代作家郑光祖将这个故事改编为杂剧《倩女离魂》,明代汤显祖的《牡丹亭》也是源于这个故事。

【注释】

① 宋代李昉等编的《太平广记》卷第三百五十八(神魂一〔2831—2832〕)中,题为《王宙》的文章,最早记载了这则故事。鲁迅编辑校订的《唐宋传奇集》收录了此文,题为《离魂记》。鲁迅对《太平广记》中的原文进行过一些校订。例如"倩"被更正为"情","篩"被更改为同义词"饰"。本篇文章源自鲁迅的《唐宋传奇集》的英文译本 Anthology of Tang and Song Tales: The Tang Song Chuanqi Ji of Lu Xun。该英译本中附有汉字原文,即为本篇采用的古文。鲁迅原文在英译本中的文章,被重新分段标点,鲁迅原文中的古文字"槼",在此版中被改为"规"。英文译本附的汉字原文为繁体字,为便于读者阅读而改为简体字,特此说明。

② 〔天授〕唐武则天年号(690年—692年)

③ 〔清河〕今河北清河、枣强和山东清平、高唐、临清等县各一部分地方。

④ 〔衡州〕今湖南衡阳

⑤ 〔郁〕《正字通·邑部》:"郁,愁思也。"

⑥ 〔恚(huì)〕愤怒,怨恨。

⑦ 〔跣(xiǎn)足〕赤脚,不穿鞋袜。

⑧ 〔跃(yuè)〕跳起来。

⑨ 〔曩(nǎng)日〕以往,从前,过去。

⑩ 〔向〕从开始到现在。

⑪ 〔覆载〕《礼记·中庸》:"天之所覆,地之所载"。此处指天地。

⑫ 〔胡〕文言疑问词。〔何〕为什么。

⑬ 〔谢〕认错,道歉。

⑭ 〔大人〕对父母叔伯等长辈的敬称。

⑮ 〔翕(xī)〕闭合,收拢。

⑯ 〔孝廉〕指被推选的士人。〔孝〕孝悌者。〔廉〕清廉之士。

⑰ 〔擢(zhuó)〕提拔,提升。

⑱ 〔第〕科举考试及格的等次,科第。

⑲ 〔丞〕封建时代辅佐主要官员做事的官吏。

⑳〔尉〕古代官名,一般是武官。此篇文章中,"丞、尉"之间有顿号。《太平广记》及《唐宋传奇集》早期版本中,"丞尉"之间无顿号。"丞尉"以词组使用时,一般指县丞,县尉的合称。
㉑〔大历〕唐代宗李豫的年号(766年—779年)。
㉒〔莱芜〕今山东莱芜。
㉓《太平广记》及《唐宋传奇集》早期版本中,无此"祖"字。

白话释义

　　武则天天授三年,河北清河郡有个叫张镒的,因为到衡州(今湖南衡阳市)做官,便在此地安家落户。

　　张镒性情淡泊娴静,很少结交知心朋友。他膝下无子,唯有两个女儿。长女早夭,幼女名唤倩娘,端庄美丽,无人能及。张镒的外甥王宙是太原人士,从小聪颖机敏,仪表堂堂。

　　张镒非常器重这个外甥,每每对他说:"将来定当把倩娘嫁给你做妻子。"渐渐地,倩娘和王宙各自长大了,他们私下里时时彼此爱慕思念,家人却并不知情。

　　后来张镒的幕僚中有优秀者向张家求亲,张镒就同意了。倩娘闻知此事,郁郁寡欢;王宙知道后也深深怨恨,随即托词说要调任他处,于是向张家请辞前往京城。张家劝止不住,于是以厚礼相待送走了外甥。

　　王宙告别舅舅乘船赴任,心中却暗自悲怆。傍晚时分,船行水路穿过重重山峦停在了数里之外。夜半,王宙正辗转难眠,忽然听到岸上有人赶来,步履非常迅速匆忙,片刻之间就到了船边。一问才知道,是倩娘赤着脚徒步追来。王宙欣喜若狂,抓住倩娘的手问她因何而来。倩娘泣声回答道:"你的情谊是如此厚重,即便在睡梦里我都应感谢。如今父亲将我许给别人,强行改变我的意愿,而我又知道你对我情深似海不会轻易改变,我前思后想唯恐你杀身徇情,所以不顾性命,舍弃了家人私自投奔于你。"王宙听完喜出望外,欢欣雀跃。于是就将倩娘隐匿在船中,连夜船行而去。

　　两人马不停蹄,不出数月就到了四川。又过了五年,两人已经育有两个儿子,与张镒更是音信断绝。倩娘思念父母,常常对着王宙哭泣说:"我当年不肯辜负你的情义,背弃了礼仪伦常和你私奔。到如今和双亲隔绝分离,已经足足五年了。可叹我活在天地之下却不能对父母尽孝,还有什么脸面呢?"王宙听了,也为妻子的话伤心难过,说:"我们这就将要回去,再也不必为远离双亲而痛

第九章　唐代诗文经典篇章英译选读

苦。"于是夫妻二人一起回到了衡州。

等到了衡州,王宙独自一个人先到了舅舅张镒家中,为自己带走倩娘的事谢罪叩头。张镒诧异道:"我女儿倩娘明明卧病家中已经好几年了,你怎么这样胡说呢!"王宙说:"你若不信,可以到船上与倩娘相见!"张镒大惊,慌忙差家人一看究竟,果然看见倩娘坐在船中,神情怡然欢畅,见到来验看的家人,还询问说:"我父母可否安泰?"家人惊为异事,急忙返回告知张镒。此时,内室中卧病多年的女儿听闻后也欢喜地起身,梳妆更衣,笑逐颜开却并不言语。这倩娘走出房中与从外归家的倩娘相遇,两人身型叠合融为一体,就连衣服都重为一样。张家觉得此事终究算是离奇不正,于是隐瞒不说。只有亲戚中偶有偷偷知道的。后来又过了四十年,王宙倩娘夫妇过世了。他们的两个儿子因为孝廉而获取了功名,当了县丞县尉。

我(陈玄祐)小时候经常听人讲这个故事,或雷同或相异,或有人说是假的。唐代宗大历年末(779年),我遇见了莱芜县令张仲规,他向我详细讲述了这个故事的本末。因为张镒是他的同门堂叔,而他的叙述也十分细致完备,我因此得以记录此事。

An Account of the Detached Soul

In the third year of the Tianshou period of the Tang Dynasty (692 AD), there was a man from Qinghe[1] named Zhang Yi. For his duties as an official, he was living in Hengzhou.[2]

By nature he lived a simple and quiet life, so he had very few friends. Zhang did not have a son, but he did have two daughters. The elder died at an early age. The younger, called Qianniang, was a reserved and beautiful woman. Zhang Yi also had a nephew, a native in Taiyuan Prefecture,[3] his sister's son, named Wang Zhou. Zhou was a bright and insightful young man and also quite handsome. Zhang Yi looked upon this nephew with great favor and always said to him, "At the appropriate time, I will have you take Qianniang as your wife."

Later, when Zhou and Qianniang were grown and no longer children, they both became obsessed with each other, thinking longingly day and night.

Others in their families did not realize what was going on.

Subsequently, one of Zhang Yi's staff was selected for an official position in the civil ministry and asked to marry Qianniang. Zhang Yi agreed to that. When Qianniang learned of this, she fell into deep depression. When Zhou learned of it, he was angry and resentful, and using the excuse that he had to make some changes for his career, he asked the Zhang family to allow him to leave for the capital. Zhang Yi was powerless to stop him. Zhou was accorded a lavish farewell event, and, swallowing his anger and resentment, he climbed into a boat and was off.

When the curtain of night fell, the boat had made its way through several miles of mountain passages. It was the middle of the night, and Zhou was not asleep, when he suddenly heard someone walking on the embankment where his boat was docked. He could hear how very fast the footsteps were, and in a blink's time, the person was at the boat. As soon as Zhou heard her, he understood of course it was Qianniang, who had come on her own two feet to the boat. Greatly startled and delighted, Zhou took her hand and asked how it was she had come. Through her tears, Qianniang said, "Your feelings were so intensely strong, I could not stop thinking of you day and night. Now my father has offered my hand in marriage to someone else, forcefully redirected my will. And I knew that your feelings would never change, so I feared you might take your life in response. That is why I threw all caution to the wind and didn't consider my own life, just fled here." This was so far beyond anything Zhou had hoped for that his happiness and joy were profound. He hid Qianniang in the boat and proceeded on his journey, traveling night after night.

They hastened along in their journey and in a few months arrived in the Shu region [of modern Sichuan]. Over the course of the next five years, they had two sons. They were no longer in correspondence with Zhang Yi. Qianniang now often thought about her mother and father. She tearfully told Zhou, "On that fateful day, I could not bear to ignore your commitment to me, so I tossed aside all propriety and absconded with you. Now five years have already passed. And though I am still on this earth, I am prevented from filial provision to my parents. What kind of face can I have?"

第九章 唐代诗文经典篇章英译选读

Zhou was deeply moved by her and said, "We will return and we will harbor no bitterness." And so together they returned to Hengzhou.

Upon arrival, Zhou first went to the Yi family home by himself. He began by apologizing for the entire affair, to which Zhang Yi replied, "Qianniang has been lying ill in her boudoir for several years. How come this lie from you?" Zhou said, "She is in the boat right now!" Zhang Yi was overjoyed to hear this and immediately sent someone to the boat to confirm. And indeed he found her in the boat, with her face vibrant and cheerful. She asked the servant, "Are my parents well?" He was of course astonished at this and hastily ran back to report to Yi.

At this point, the "woman" in the boudoir heard what was going on and happily rose from her bed. She groomed herself and changed clothes. She smiled but still said nothing. Then she came out to meet Qianniang, whereupon the two fused together into a single body, as did the clothing they were wearing.

The family thought this was so very abnormal that they kept it secret. Only relatives knew about it. After some forty years, both Zhou and Qianniang passed away. Their two sons, being filial and incorruptible and prevailing in the official examinations, rose to senior military positions.

When I was young, I often heard this story, sometimes exactly the same, sometimes with small variations, and sometimes people said it was all false. At the end of Dali reign period,[4] I encountered the County Magistrate of Laiwu,[5] Zhang Zhonggui. Zhang Yi was his great uncle, and Zhang told me the whole story from beginning to end in great detail. And that is why I record it here.

Notes:

1. Present day Qinghe County, Hebei.
2. A remote and newly established region around modern Hengyang in Hunan.
3. Its seat located in modern Taiyuan City in Shanxi.
4. 766A.D.—779A.D. under Emperor Daizong.
5. Present-day Laiwu city in Shandong.

——Kenneth DeWoskin（肯尼斯·德沃斯金）

英译鉴赏简评

肯尼斯·德沃斯金（Kenneth DeWoskin）是密歇根大学安娜堡分校中国文学系的名誉教授，曾出版过很多关于中国古代早期的小说和文化方面的书籍。这个英文版本非常忠实原作，翻译完整，语言顺畅，深度再现故事离奇曲折的情节，将王宙与倩娘恩爱坚贞的感情刻画得活灵活现。在某些中国文化负载词的翻译上，译者为了使读者更好地理解中国古典文学，除了在译文之后附上了相关的英语注释之外，在译文中也巧妙自然地增补了许多文化信息。比如"二男并孝廉擢第，至丞、尉"句中，"孝廉""擢第""丞尉"，无法找到英文对应语，但肯尼斯的译文完全保留了原文中因两位主人公的恩孝之情而给孩子带来的善果这一重要的文化象征义，"Their two sons, **being filial** and **incorruptible** and **prevailing in the official examinations**, rose to **senior military positions**"。译文没有出现一处信息缺失，远比采取意译法模糊化处理，或改译、删译等破坏性翻译策略要高明许多。

本章课后练习

一、请尝试英译以下句子。

1. 行到水穷处，坐看云起时。（《终南别业》王维）

2. 天长地久有时尽，此恨绵绵无绝期。（《长恨歌》白居易）

3. 夫天地者，万物之逆旅。（《春夜宴从弟桃花园序》李白）

4. 苍然暮色，自远而至，至无所见，而犹不欲归。（《始得西山宴游记》柳宗元）

5. 师者，所以传道授业解惑也。（《师说》韩愈）

二、请比较以下句子的不同英译文本。

1. 春眠不觉晓，处处闻啼鸟。（《春晓》孟浩然）

　　英译1：I awake light-hearted this morning of spring,
　　　　　Everywhere round me the singing of birds.

第九章 唐代诗文经典篇章英译选读

（Witter Bynner、江亢虎，*The Jade Mountain*）

英译2：This morn of spring in bed I'm lying;

Not woke up till I heard birds crying.

（许渊冲，《唐诗三百首（中英文对照）》）

2. 晴川历历汉阳树,芳草萋萋鹦鹉洲。（《黄鹤楼》崔颢）

英译1：Every tree in Han-yang becomes clear in the water,

And Parrot Island is a nest of sweet grasses.

（Witter Bynner、江亢虎，*The Jade Mountain*）

英译2：By sun-lit river trees can be count'd one by one;

On Parrot Islet sweet green grass grows fast and thick.

（许渊冲，《唐诗三百首（中英文对照）》）

3. 天地英雄气,千秋尚凛然。（《蜀先主庙》刘禹锡）

英译1：Even in this world the spirit of a hero

Lives and reigns for thousands of years.

（Witter Bynner、江亢虎，*The Jade Mountain*）

英译2：Your heroism under the sky

From year to year spread far and nigh.

（许渊冲，《唐诗三百首（中英文对照）》）

4. 谁言寸草心,报得三春晖。（《游子吟》孟郊）

英译1：But how much love has the inch-long grass,

For three spring months of the light of the sun?

（Witter Bynner、江亢虎，*The Jade Mountain*）

英译2：Such kindness as young grass receives

From the warm sun can't be repaid.

（许渊冲,《唐诗三百首（中英文对照）》）

5. 少小离家老大回,乡音无改鬓毛衰。（《回乡偶书二首·其一》贺知章）

英译1：I left home young. I return old,

Speaking as then, but with hair grown thin.

（Witter Bynner、江亢虎，*The Jade Mountain*）

299

英译 2：I left home young and not till old do I come back,
　　　　Unchanged my accent, my hair no longer black.
　　　（许渊冲,《唐诗三百首(中英文对照)》）

6. 斯是陋室,惟吾德馨。(《陋室铭》刘禹锡)

　英译 1：My home is humble. But it enjoys the fame of virtue so long as I am living in it.
　　　（罗经国）

　英译 2：And so, too, my hut may be mean; but the fragrance of Virtue is diffused around.
　　　（Herbert Giles, *Classical Chinese Literature Volume 1*）

7. 假如其身至今尚在,奉其国命,来朝京师,陛下容而接之,不过宣政一见,礼宾一设,赐衣一袭,卫而出之于境,不令惑众也。(《谏迎佛骨表》韩愈)

　英译 1：Supposing, indeed, this Buddha had come to our capital in the flesh, under an appointment from his own State, then your Majesty might have received him with a few words of admonition, bestowing on him a banquet and a suit of clothes, previous to sending him out of the country with an escort of soldiers, and thereby have avoided any dangerous influence on the minds of the people.
　　　（Herbert Giles, *Classical Chinese Literature Volume 1*）

　英译 2：In short, let us suppose that this *Fo* were still alive, and that his Prince had deputed him in his Name, to repair to your Court to pay you Homage; how would your Majesty receive it? At most, after a short Audience, you either would treat him hospitably according to the Rites; and make him a Present of a compleat Habit, or else you would order him a Guard which should have an Eye to his Conduct, and which should convey him to your Frontiers, without allowing him an Opportunity of endeavouring to seduce your People.
　　　（R. Brookes, *Classical Chinese Literature Volume 1*）

第九章 唐代诗文经典篇章英译选读

8. 忽有一人,中形,赤髯而虬,乘蹇驴而来。(《虬髯客传》杜光庭)

   英译1:A man of middle weight, with a red, curly beard and whiskers arrived at the inn on a scrawny donkey.

   (Jing Wang, Lin Yutang, *Famous Chinese Short Stories*)

   英译2:Suddenly, a mid-sized man whose red beard was curled like a dragon approached them, riding a lame donkey.

   (Jing Wang, *Anthology of Tang and Song Tales*)

9. 清音宛转,如诉如慕,坐客听之,不觉泪下。(《柳毅传》李朝威)

   英译1:The music had such a deeply haunting sound, it seemed to express the keenest longings and yearnings of the captive princess, and there was hardly a dry eye in the audience.

   (John Minford, *Classical Chinese Literature Volume 1*)

   英译2:The pure notes curved in such sweet cadence, spoke with such yearning, that the seated guests found themselves shedding tears as they listened.

   (Glen Dudbridge, *Anthology of Tang and Song Tales*)

10. 卢生欠伸而悟,见其身方偃于邸舍,吕翁坐其傍,主人蒸黍未熟,触类如故。(《枕中记》沈既济)

    英译1:Whereupon he woke up with a start and found himself lying as before in the roadside inn, with Lü Weng sitting by his side and the millet that his host was cooking still not yet done. Everything was as it had been before he dozed off.

    (Chi-chen Wang, *Classical Chinese Literature Volume 1*)

    英译2:With a yawn Lu stretched and awoke to find himself lying in the inn. He found the oldster was sitting beside him and the millet which the host had been steaming was not yet ready. Everything was as before.

    (William H. Nienhauser Jr., *Anthology of Tang and Song Tales*)

三、段落试译。

离离原上草,一岁一枯荣。
野火烧不尽,春风吹又生。
远芳侵古道,晴翠接荒城。
又送王孙去,萋萋满别情。

(《赋得古原草送别》白居易)

苍苍蒸民,谁无父母?提携捧负,畏其不寿。谁无兄弟?如足如手。谁无夫妇?如宾如友。生也何恩,杀之何咎?其存其没,家莫闻知。人或有言,将信将疑。悁悁心目,寝寐见之。布奠倾觞,哭望天涯。天地为愁,草木凄悲。吊祭不至,精魂何依。必有凶年,人其流离。呜呼噫嘻!时耶命耶?从古如斯!为之奈何?守在四夷。

(节选自《吊古战场文》李华)

方士受辞与信,将行,色有不足。玉妃因征其意,复前跪致词:"乞当时一事,不闻于他人者,验于太上皇。不然,恐钿合金钗,罹新垣平之诈也。"玉妃茫然退立,若有所思,徐而言曰:"昔天宝十年,侍辇避暑于骊山宫。秋七月,牵牛织女相见之夕,秦人风俗,夜张锦绣,陈饮食,树花,燔香于庭,号为乞巧。宫掖间尤尚之。时夜始半,休侍卫于东西厢,独侍上。上凭肩而立,因仰天感牛女事,密相誓心,愿世世为夫妇。言毕,执手各呜咽。此独君王知之耳。"

(节选自《长恨传》陈鸿)

参考文献

爱莲心,2004.向往心灵转化的庄子·内篇分析[M].周炽成,译.南京:江苏人民出版社.

柏拉图,1986.理想国[M].郭斌和,张竹明,译.北京:商务印书馆.

常青,2017.道德经中"道"的翻译嬗变[J].鞍山师范学院学报9(03):37-39+79.

陈鼓应,1984.老子注译及评介[M].北京:中华书局.

陈鼓应,2007.庄子今注今译(修订本)[M].北京:商务印书馆.

陈国华,轩治峰,2002.老子的版本与英译[J].外语教学与研究(06):464-470+480.

陈宏天,赵福海,陈复兴,2007.昭明文选译注(二卷)[M].长春:吉林文史出版社.

陈宏天,赵福海,陈复兴,2007.昭明文选译注(四卷)[M].长春:吉林文史出版社.

陈宏天,赵福海,陈复兴,2007.昭明文选译注(一卷)[M].长春:吉林文史出版社.

陈来,2020.《大学》的作者,文本争论与思想诠释[J].东岳论丛(9).

陈亮,2012.谁将楚辞第一次介绍到英国[N].中国社会科学报(B05).

陈平原,2012.学堂不得废弃中国文辞[N].中华读书报(05)-09.

陈平原,2012.学堂不得废弃中国文辞——关于重建"大一国文"的思考[J].语文建设(17):10-13.

陈延嘉,王大恒,孙浩宇,2018.萧统评传[M].上海:上海古籍出版社.

陈子展,杜月村,2008.诗经导读[M].北京:中国国际广播出版社.

程颢,程颐,2000.二程遗书[M].朱熹,编.潘富恩,导读.上海:上海古籍出版社.

戴文静,2018.北美文心雕龙的译介与研究[D].扬州大学外国语学院博士学位论文.

戴文静,2017.中国文论英译的译者行为批评分——以文心雕龙的翻译为例[J].解放军外国语学院学报40(1):7.

丁魏,2004.老子典籍考二千五百来世界老子文献总目[R].国家社科基金项目成果.

丁巍,2013.由老学典籍考到二千五百来世界老学文献书目数据库[DB].河南省社会科学院图书馆.

方玉润,1986.诗经原始(上下)[M].李先耕,点校.北京:中华书局.

封演,2005.封氏闻见记校注[M].赵贞信,校注.北京:中华书局.

傅云龙,蔡希勤,2006.大学精华版[M].何祚康,译.北京:华语教学出版社.

高明,1996.帛书老子校注[M].北京:中华书局.

郭晨,2021.当代美国华裔汉学家吴光明及其庄学研究[J].国际汉学(1):44-51.

郭庆藩,1985.庄子集释[M].王孝鱼,点校.北京:中华书局.

郭沂,1998.从郭店楚简老子看老子其人其书[J].哲学研究(07):47-55.

郝稷,2011.英语世界中杜甫及其诗歌的接受与传播——兼论杜诗学的世界性[J].中国文学研究(01):119-123.

郝泽华,2016.历代论语注释梳理与研究[J].赤峰学院学报(汉文哲学社会科学版)37(8):124-126.

何文静,2019.英语世界的唐代小说译介:翻译历史与研究现状[J].三峡大学学报(人文社会科学版)41(06).

胡光波,2015.事出于沉思,义归乎翰藻——从昭明文选应用研究说开去[J].湖北师范学院学报(06):152.

胡作友,王文君,2020.关于文心雕龙英译研究的回顾与展望[J].常熟理工学院学报 34(04):78-84.

胡作友,袁俊霞,2018.文心雕龙英译的文化价值[J].福建江夏学院学报 8(06):90-95+103.

黄侃,2000.文心雕龙札记(题词及略例)[M].周勋初,导读.上海:上海古籍出版社.

黄中习,2004.中国古典文学海外英译荟萃——读含英咀华集[J].国外外语教学(01):64-66.

焦艳,刘文娟,2011.道德经英译研究综述[J].郑州航空工业管理学院学报(社会科学版)30(04):148-151.

金景芳,吕绍纲,1997.释"克己复礼为仁"[J].中国哲学史(1):16-20.

金顺敬,2011.儒家思想对韩国文化的影响[D].山东大学文学院硕士学位论文.

孔子,思履,2013.彩图全解四书[M].北京:中国华侨出版社.

李昉,1961.太平广记(全十册)[M].北京:中华书局,李钢,2010. Joshua Marshman 与论语的英译[J].牡丹江大学学报 19(12):116-118.

李钢,李金姝,2012."西方中心主义"观照下的论语英译[J].外语学刊(2):123-125.

李钢,李金姝,2013.庞德论语英译研究[J].湖南社会科学(1):242-244.

李特夫,2012.杜甫诗歌在英语世界的传播——20世纪英语世界主要杜诗英译专集与英语专著解析[J].杜甫研究学刊(03):89-94.

林嘉新,2020.诗性原则与文献意识:美国汉学家华兹生英译杜甫诗歌研究[J].中南大学学报(社会科学版)26(04):180-190.

林志坚,2015.陶友白与江亢虎的合作及群玉山头的译刊[J].青海师范大学学报(哲学社会科学版)37(05):114-118.

林志坚,2016.柳宗元诗文在英语世界的翻译与传播[J].天津中德职业技术学院学报(06):115-121.

刘耕华,2019.欧洲启蒙思想与中国文化有何相干？——就一个学界热点问题回应张西平先生[J].国际比较文学 2(3):428-441.

刘固盛,吴雪萌,2011.西方基督教背景下的老子诠释[J].江汉论坛(04):61-66.

刘家齐,1986."学而时习之"章新解[J].齐鲁学刊(6):54-55.

刘玲娣,2016.陈荣捷与道德经英译[J].华中师范大学学报(人文社会科学版)55(06):136-149.

刘勰,1959.文心雕龙校释[M].刘永济,校释.北京:中华书局.

刘勰,1981.文心雕龙注释[M].周振甫,注.北京:人民文学出版社.

刘勰,2003.大中华文库·文心雕龙英译(汉英对照)[M].杨国斌,英译.周振甫,今译.北京:外语教学与研究出版社.

刘勰,2010.文心雕龙译注[M].王运熙,周锋,译注.上海:上海古籍出版社.

刘学英,银小晋,2020.论语的英译情况研究[J].文学教育(5):52-53.

鲁迅,1972.鲁迅全集(十卷)[M].北京:人民文学出版社.

罗经国,2005.古文观止精选(汉英对照)[M].北京:外语教学与研究出版社.

罗琼,2021.比尔·波特对柳宗元诗歌的译介及其翻译策略——以晨诣超师院读禅经英译为例[J].湖南科技学院学报 42(06):15-18.

马瑞辰,1989.毛诗传笺通释[M].陈金生,点校.北京:中华书局.

马文·哈里斯,1988.文化的起源[M].黄晴,译.北京:华夏出版社.

孟子,2010.孟子·万章上[M].方勇,译注.北京:中华书局.

倪梁,2019.辜鸿铭论语英译本中归化异化策略应用研究.[D].浙江工商大学外国语学院硕士学位论文.

屈原,2016.楚辞选(Selected Elegies of the State of Chu:Chinese-English)(汉英对照)[M].杨宪益,戴乃迭,英译.北京:外文出版社有限公司.

任犀然,2016.老子·庄子(无障碍阅读典藏版)[M].北京:中国华侨出版社.

尚延延,杨萍,2017.译者对翻译生态环境的主动选择——林语堂《论语》英译的译者中心性研究[J].中国海洋大学学报(社会科学版)(5):112-117.

沈德潜,1977.古诗源[M].北京:中华书局.

司马迁,安平秋,2004.二十四史全译:史记·老子韩非列传[M].上海:汉语大词典出版社.

孙大雨,1996.英译屈原诗选(Selected Poems of Chu Yuan)[M].上海:上海外语教育出版社.

孙康宜,宇文所安,2013.剑桥中国文学史[M].刘倩等,译.北京:生活·读书·新知三联书店.

孙蓉蓉,2008.刘勰与文心雕龙考论[M].北京:中华书局.

邰谧侠,2019.老子译本总目[J].国际汉学(S1):7-122+2.

汤炳正,李大明,李诚,熊良智,2012.楚辞今注[M].上海:上海古籍出版社.

田荣昌,2019.文心雕龙中的"入仕"思想探微[J].哈尔滨学院学报40(11):89-94.

汪翠萍,2010.论人文主义者庞德[J].四川师范大学学报37(5):111-115.

汪榕培,1997.比较与翻译[M].上海.上海外语教育出版社.

王国维,1995.人间词话[M].成都:四川大学出版社.

王国轩,2007.大学中庸译注[M].北京:中华书局.

王辉,2004.理雅各,庞德论语译本比较[J].四川外国语大学学报20(5):140-144.

王辉,2005.析字法与庞德的大学译本[J]. 翻译季刊(38):62-82.

王建,2012.权力话语视角下论语英译本的对比解读——以辜鸿铭和理雅各的译本为例[J].山东外语教学33(4):97-103.

王丽娜,吴聪聪,2009.柳宗元诗文在国外[J].河北师范大学学报(哲学社会科学版)32(02):64-67.

王苗苗,2021.孔子天命观研究[J].文华学刊(2):62-65.

王先谦,1987.诗三家义集疏[M].吴格,点校.北京:中华书局.

王逸 2017.楚辞章句[M].黄灵庚,点校.上海:上海古籍出版社.

魏家海,2014.楚辞英译及其研究述评[J].民族翻译(01):89-96.

闻一多,2012.唐诗杂论 诗与批评[M].北京:生活·读书·新知三联书店.

闻一多,2013.古典新义·庄子[M].上海:上海古籍出版社.

闻一多,袁謇正,1993.闻一多全集·庄子[M].武汉:湖北人民出版社.

吴楚材,吴调侯,2012.古文观止(上下)[M].钟基,李先银,王身钢,译注.北京:中华书局.

吴国康.2013.庄子·逍遥游中"冥""溟"释论[J].内蒙古电大学刊(02):18-19+22.

吴慧坚,2015.林语堂介译实践的当代诠释与经验借鉴——以孔子的智慧为例[J].广东第二师范学院学报35(06):60-66.

吴雪萌,2011.英语世界老学研究[D].华中师范大学历史文化学院博士学位论文.

武艳,2019.叶女士的汉学成就初探[D].福建师范大学文学院硕士学位论文.

武志勇,刘子潇,2020.道德经在西方世界传播的历史[J].湖南大学学报(社会科学版)34(05):15-22.

夏歆东,2014.道德经译者理雅各的理解前结构探析[J].外国语文30(02):152-157.

许丙泉,2016.论孔子"克己复礼为仁"的思想[J].青岛职业技术学院学报26(5):55-59.

许渊冲,2006.唐诗三百首(英汉对照)[M].北京:中国对外翻译出版公司.

许渊冲,2008.楚辞(Elegies of the South)(汉英对照)[M].张华,中文译注.北京:中国对外翻译出版公司.

许渊冲,2009.诗经(汉英对照)[M].北京:中国对外翻译出版公司.

许子东,2011.许子东讲稿:张爱玲·郁达夫·香港文学(第2卷)[M].北京:人民文学出版社.

许子东,2018.许子东现代文学课[M].上海:上海三联书店.

杨成虎,2004.典籍的翻译与研究——楚辞几种英译本得失谈[J].宁波大学学报(人文科学版)(04):55-61.

杨平,2009.20世纪论语的英译与诠释[J].北京第二外国语学院学报31(10):21-32.

杨忠,2004.二十四史全译·梁书[M].上海:上海汉语大词典出版社.

姚达兑,2016.译玄:最早英译道德经(1859)译文初探[J].中国文化研究(04):126-136.

姚达兑,2017.道德经最早英译本及其译者初探[J].外语教学与研究49(01):

135—143+161.

叶维廉,2002.叶维廉文集(1卷)[M].合肥:安徽教育出版社.

游国恩,1983.中国文学史(二)[M].北京:人民文学出版社.

宇文所安,2002.中国文论:英译与评论(Readings in Chinese Literary Thought)[M].王柏华,陶庆梅,译.上海:上海社会科学院出版社.

袁梅,1984.屈原赋译注[M].济南:齐鲁书社.

袁晓亮,2015.大学英译研究在中国[J].语文学刊(外语教育教学)(10):43—45+79.

张波,2008.日本入学本土化历程及特色[J].东疆学刊 25(2):16—23.

张淳,刘美玲,2012.中国传统文化经典的英译历史研究[J].理论月刊(06):77—81.

张德福,2016.威妥玛与论语翻译[J].外语研究(01):86—91

张芳彦,1993.儒道释经典译注[M].武汉:湖北教育出版社.

张莉莉,2022.唐传奇的百年域外译介历程[N].中国社会科学报 6—20(007).

张乃芳,2021.论语文本中隐含的"天人合一"思想的三重意蕴[J].河北大学学报(哲学社会科学版)46(02):9—16.

张萍,2018.理雅各翻译思想研究[D].苏州大学外国语学院博士学位论文.

张少康,1999.中国文学理论批评史教程[M].北京:北京大学出版社.

张万民,2017.中国古代文论英译历程的反思[J].暨南学报(哲学社会科学版)39(01):1—11+129.

张娴,2013.楚辞英译研究——基于文化人类学整体论的视角[D].湖南师范大学外国语学院博士学位论文.

张学智,2020.大学简述[J].北京航空航天大学学报(社会科学版)33(06):24—33.

章学诚,1985.文史通义校注[M].叶瑛,校注.北京:中华书局.

章学诚,1990.文史通义·诗话篇(上)[M].严杰,武秀成,译注.贵阳:贵州人民出版社.

郑玄,孔颖达,2008.礼记正义[M].上海:上海古籍出版社.

钟达锋,2016.康达维译文选·赋研究[D].湖南大学外国语学院博士学位论文.

周振甫,1986.文心雕龙今译附词语简释[M].北京:中华书局.

朱熹,1958.诗集传[M].上海编辑所,编辑.北京:中华书局.

朱熹,2002.朱子全书(十四册)[M].上海:上海古籍出版社.

朱熹,2011.四书章句集注·大学章句[M].北京:中华书局.

朱熹,2015.楚辞集注[M].黄灵庚,点校.上海:上海古籍出版社.

庄子,2010.庄子[M].方勇,译注.北京:中华书局.

庄子,思履,2016.庄子·无障碍阅读典藏版[M].北京:中国华侨出版社.

庄子.南华经16卷[M].郭象,注.林希逸,口义.刘辰翁,王世贞,陈仁锡等批.明万历时期凌氏刊五色套印本(21).

ALEXANDER W, 1867. Notes on Chinese Literature with introductory remarks on the progressive advancement of the art; and a list of translations from the Chinese, into various European languages [M]. Shanghae: American Presbyterian Mission Press; London: Trubner & Co. 60, Paternoster Row.

ALEXEI K D, etc., 2017. Tales from Tang Dynasty China [M]. Indianapolis: Hackett Publishing Company, Inc.

ANGUS C G, 1981. Chuang-tzǔ: the seven inner chapters and other writings: from the book chuang-tzǔ[M]. London: George Allen & Unwin.

ARTHUR W, 1939. Three ways of thought in ancient China[M]. London: George Allen & Unwin.

ARTHUR W, 1969. 170 Chinese poems[M]. London: Jonathan Cape Ltd.

ARTHUR W, 2005. Three ways of thought in ancient China[M]. London and New York: Routledge, Taylor & Francis Group.

BILL P, 2019. Written in exile: the poetry of Liu Tsung-yuan[M]. Port Townsend: Copper Canyon Press.

BURTON W, 1964. Chuang Tzu: basic writings[M]. New York: Columbia University Press.

BURTON W, 1971. Chinese rhyme-prose: poems in the Fu form from the Han and Six Dynasties Periods[M]. New York: Columbia University Press.

BURTON W, 1968. The complete works of Chuang Tzu[M]. New York: Columbia University Press.

BYNNER W, 1944. The way of life according to Laotzu[M]. New York: The John Day Company.

CAI Z Q, 2008. How to read Chinese poetry: a guided anthology[M]. New York: Columbia University Press.

CHANG H C, 1977. Chinese literature II: nature poetry[M]. Great Britain: Edingburgh University Press, and New York: Columbia University Press.

CHEN J S, 1992. Liu Tsung-yüan and intellectual change in T'ang China, 773-819[M]. New York: Cambridge University Press.

DAVID R. K, 1982. Wen xuan or selections of refined literature volume one: rhapsodies on metropolises and capitals [M]. New Jersey: Princeton University Press.

DAVID R. K, 1987. Wen xuan or selections of refined literature volume two: rhapsodies on sacrifices, hunting, travel, sightseeing, palaces and halls, rivers and seas[M]. New Jersey: Princeton University Press.

DAVID R. K, 1996. Wen xuan or selections of refined literature volume three: rhapsodies on natural phenomena, birds and animals, aspirations and feelings, sorrowful laments, literature, music, and passions[M]. New Jersey: Princeton University Press.

EDWARDS E D, 1937. Chinese prose literature of the T'ang period, A. D. 618-906[M]. London: Arthur Probsthain.

FENG Y L, 2016. Chuang-Tzu: a new selected translation with an exposition of the philosophy of Kuo Hsiang[M]. Beijing: Foreign Language Teaching and Research Publishing Co., Ltd., and Heidelberg: Springer-Verlag Berlin Heidelberg.

FREDERIC H B, 1881. The divine classic of Nan-Hua: being the works of Chuang Tsze, taoist philosopher[M]. Shanghai & Hongkong: Kelly & Walsh.

HERBERT A G, 1901, 1973. A history of Chinese literature[M]. New York: D. Appleton and Company; First Tuttle Edition, Tokyo: The Charles E. Tuttle Company, Inc.

HERBERT A G, 1922. Gems of Chinese literature[M]. Shanghai & Hong Kong: Kelly & Walsh.

JAMES L J Y, 1962. The art of Chinese poetry[M]. Chicago: The University of Chicago Press.

JAMES L, 1891. The sacred books of China: the text of taoism[M]. Oxford: The Clarendon Press.

JAMES L, 1960. The Chinese classics, the 3rd edition[M]. Hong Kong:

Hong Kong University Press.

JAMES L, 1991. The She King or the book of poetry[M]. Taipei: SMC Publishing INC.

JERAHJ, 1959. Li sao: a poem on relieving sorrow: a prose translation with an introduction and notes[M]. Miami: Olivant Press.

LIN Y T, 1942. The wisdom of China and India[M]. New York: Random House Inc.

LIN Y T, 1948. Translated, edited and with an introduction and notes: the wisdom of Laotse[M]. New York: Random House Inc.

LIN Y T, 1952. Famous Chinese short stories[M]. New York: The John Day Company.

MARTIN P, 1996. The book of Chuang Tzu[M]. Translated, first published by London: Arkana.

MARTIN P, 2006. The book of Chuang Tzu[M]. Second published by London: Penguin Books Ltd.

PAUL C, 1898. Lao-Tzes tao-teh-king: Chinese-English with introduction, transliteration, and notes [M]. Chicago: The Open Court Publishing Company.

RICHARD W, 1922. The Chinese fairy book[M]. Translated by Frederick H. Martens. London: T. Fisher, Unwin, Ltd.

ROBERT P, 1949. The white pony: an anthology of Chinese poetry[M]. London: Theodore Brun Ltd.

STEPHEN O, 1992. Readings in Chinese literary thought[M]. Cambridge: Harvard University Press.

STEPHEN O, 2016. The poetry of Du Fu[M]. Boston/Berlin: Walter de Gruyter Inc.

SUN K Y, STEPHEN O, 1996. An anthology of Chinese literature: beginning to 1911[M]. New York & London: W. W. Norton & Company.

THOMAS C, 1991, 1992. The essential tao: an initiation into the heart of taoism through the authentic Tao Te Ching and the inner teachings of Chuang Tzu[M]. San Francisco: Harper Collins; New York: Harper.

THOMAS M, 1965. The way of Chuang Tzu [M]. New York: New Directions.

VICTOR H M, ed., 1983. Chuang-tzu: composition and interpretation[J]. Journal of Chinese Religions(11).

VICTOR H M, ZHANG Z J, 2020. Anthology of Tang and Song tales, the Tang Song Chuanqi Ji of Lu Xun[M]. World Scientific Publishing Col Pte. Ltd.

VINCENT Y C S, 1959. The literary mind and the carving of dragons[M]. New York:Columbia University Press,

WILLIAM H N Jr., 2010. Tang dynasty tales: a guided reader[M]. Singapore, 5 Toh Tuck Link: World Scientific Publishing Co. Ltd.

WILLIAM H N Jr., 2011. Liu Tsung-Yuan: recent translations, Chinese literature, essays, articles and reviews[M].

WILLIAM J, 1891. Misc (Confucian School), the Shi King, the old "poetry classic" of the Chinese[M]. A Project Of Liberty Fund, Inc.

WITTER B, KIANG K H, 1929. The jade mountain: a Chinese anthology, being three hundred poems of the T'ang dynasty, 618-906[M]. New York: Alfred A. Knopf, Inc.

WONG S K, ALLAN C L, LAM K T, 1999. The book of literary design [M]. Hong Kong: Hong Kong University Press.

WU K M, 2010. "Let Chinese thinking be Chinese, not western": sine qua non to globalization[J]. Dao(9):193-209.

WU K M, 1982. Chuang Tzu: world philosopher at play[M]. New York: The Crossroad Publishing Company & Scholars Press.

参考网址

http://www.moe.gov.cn/srcsite/A13/s7061/201403/t20140328_166543.html

http://www.moe.gov.cn/jyb_xwfb/s5147/202006/t20200608_463695.html

http://www.bopsecrets.org/gateway/passages/tao-te-ching.htm

http://www.wenming.cn/djw/gjgc/201511/t20151103_2946316.shtml

http://blog.sina.com.cn/s/blog_709f49fa0100p5kc.html https://sfl.tongji.edu.cn/3f/82/c9166a81794/page.htm

http://www.360doc.com/content/15/0603/04/363181_475256807.shtml

https://zhidao.baidu.com/question/1795953385726107427.html

https://www.zhihu.com/question/36703441

http://lishisxk.com/lsgs/16766.html

https://baijiahao.baidu.com/s?id=1725560724981399918&wfr=spider&for=pc

https://baike.baidu.com/item/胡子霖/9483700

https://www.duobiji.com/141909.html

http://www.wenming.cn/djw/gjgc/201511/t20151103_2946316.shtml

http://blog.sina.com.cn/s/blog_709f49fa0100p5kc.html https://sfl.tongji.edu.cn/3f/82/c9166a81794/page.htm

https://www.eheart.com/TAO/TTC/TTCbook.html

https://www.zhihu.com/question/36703441

https://zhidao.baidu.com/question/164043060.html

http://www.ywzj08.com/shi/6650.html

http://www.delphiclassics.com

https://www.thepaper.cn/newsDetail_forward_10140091

https://www.zdic.net/hans

https://www.jy135.com/guwen/166754/50_1fanyi.html

https://m.thepaper.cn/newsDetail_forward_7234069

https://zhuanlan.zhihu.com/p/110890393

https://baike.baidu.com/item/离魂记/2489751?fr=aladdin

https://www.zgshige.com/c/2021-07-03/18502525.shtml

https://so.gushiwen.cn/shiwenv_fe678a1136b3.aspx

http://lib.huse.cn/lzy/news_view.asp?newsid=922

https://link.springer.com/article/10.1007/s11712-010-9161-6#citeas

http://chinajapan.org/articles/21/2.